CORNERED

CORNERED

The New Monopoly Capitalism and the Economics of Destruction

Barry C. Lynn

WILEY

John Wiley & Sons, Inc.

Published by John Wiley & Sons, Inc., Hoboken, New Jersey
Published simultaneously in Canada

For general information about our other products and services, please contact our Customer Care Department within the United States at (800) 762-2974, outside the United States at (317) 572-3993 or fax (317) 572-4002.

Wiley also publishes its books in a variety of electronic formats. Some content that appears in print may not be available in electronic books. For more information about Wiley products, visit our web site at www.wiley.com.

Library of Congress Cataloging-in-Publication Data:

Lynn, Barry C.
    Cornered : the new monopoly capitalism and the economics of destruction / Barry Lynn.
        p. cm.
    Includes bibliographical references and index.
    ISBN 978-0-470-18638-1 (cloth)
        1. Monopolies—United States. 2. Capitalism—United States. I. Title.
    HD2757.2.L96 2009
    338.8'2—dc22
                                                            2009020805

Printed in the United States of America
10 9 8 7 6 5 4 3 2 1

Contents

Preface

Of Rule and Ruin

Sometimes, during the long haul of writing a book, reality catches up to what months before seemed mere theory and speculation. So it was when the Meltdown of 2008 cascaded through the U.S. and world economies, knocking over banks and hedge funds and industrial companies, and destroying small businesses and steady jobs and household budgets.

For nearly a decade I had painstakingly gathered stories and spun out analyses to detail the fantastic fragility of many of our vital human systems, and for years I had been warning that these dangers were largely the result of monopolization. Then suddenly I saw a few of my worst fears playing out in real time on CNN and Fox News, as dozens of financial institutions deemed "too big to fail" suddenly came very close to failing. Yet as horrified as I was by the mind-bending events on Wall Street (and the crashing of the automobile industry in Detroit), I soon came to realize that the Meltdown was making my task in this book much easier. These chain reaction crashes and the gargantuan bailouts and nationalizations that followed were educating all Americans, with brutal efficiency, about how things really work in our economy, and how they sometimes don't.

The Meltdown of 2008 even delivered my punch line for me: that American financiers had erected a particular form of socialism that enabled them to dump all the risk in the industrial and banking systems they control onto us, even as they jetted away with all the profit. I had been developing my thinking on this issue for years, and I had planned to lay it out in this book with the utmost care, because as recently as September 14, 2008, the idea that these systems had been socialized in any respect still struck most people as absurd. Then suddenly there was conservative columnist George Will writing that socialism in America is "already here." Moreover, Will made clear that he was fretting not about penny ante redistribution from the rich to the poor but about the "surreptitious socialism of the strong."[1]

The Meltdown of 2008 also delivered the twist I had planned for my punch line, which is that the structural monopolization of so many systems has resulted in a set of political arrangements similar to what we used to call *corporatism*. This means that our political economy is run by a compact elite that is able to fuse the power of our public government with the power of private corporate governments in ways that enable members of the elite not merely to offload their risk onto us but also to determine with almost complete freedom who wins, who loses, and who pays.

Then suddenly there was Secretary of the Treasury Henry Paulson, not long since elevated from Goldman Sachs, using our tax money to fix his bank and the banks of all his friends. And there was Simon Johnson, the former chief economist at the International Monetary Fund, writing about the "quiet coup" that had been staged by America's "financial oligarchy."[2]

I realized that I no longer needed to craft *Cornered* as a sort of murder mystery, in which I patiently reveal and analyze each clue. I was writing a chronicle of a death foretold, and the corpse on the street was the American Republic.

Great disasters often lead to reform and renewal. Unfortunately, our leaders' initial reaction to the Meltdown indicates that they did not learn the key lesson: when something is too big to fail, we must make it smaller. Or perhaps they simply chose to ignore it. Whichever is the case, despite much public awareness of the role that monopolization played in amplifying the Meltdown—one *Financial Times* editorial was titled "The Bigger They Come the Harder We Fall"[3]—the Bush and the Obama administrations and the Democratic-controlled Congress all responded to the collapse of our financial system in most instances by *accelerating* consolidation.

"Our" government used our money to broker and subsidize such whopping mergers as the Wells Fargo takeover of Wachovia, the JPMorgan Chase acquisition of Washington Mutual and Bear Stearns, and Bank of America's absorption of Countrywide Financial and Merrill

Lynch—this despite the fact that in the year up to November 2008, the failure rate for banks with assets of $1 billion or more was *seven times* greater than for banks with less than $1 billion.[4] This was also despite the fact that big banks and financial institutions like Countrywide—which were able to import far greater masses of debt and then dedicate far greater marketing power to selling that debt to us in the form of mortgages—were far more reckless and destructive in their lending than their smaller rivals.

Nor was our "emergency" bailout money used only to subsidize consolidation in our banking system, where at least there was a real crisis. After Congress demanded that our bailed-out banks act swiftly to flush cash into the economy, to get business "moving" again, Citibank and Goldman Sachs and Bank of America jumped to the task. They put $22 billion of our money into the hands of executives at the world's largest drug company, Pfizer, to float a $68 billion takeover of the drug company Wyeth, in a deal that eliminated not only competition at a time of skyrocketing drug prices but also nineteen thousand jobs. Then when the executives at the world's number two drug company, Merck, said they wanted $41.1 billion to merge with Schering-Plough, these same banks ponied up another $9 billion of our money, even though this deal eliminated yet more competition and another sixteen thousand jobs.[5]

We can't blame all of this on greed and opportunism. Simple inertia played a role. So too did plain old confusion.

No matter the cause, however, the effects are clear. Consolidation of power by financiers over the basic institutions of our political economy has resulted in the derangement not merely of our financial systems but also of our industrial systems and political systems. Most terrifying of all is that this consolidation of power—and the political actions taken to achieve it—appears to have impaired our ability to comprehend the dangers we face and to react in an organized and coherent manner.

The Missing Force

The idea that our economy is ruled by monopolists will surprise many of you. The shelves of our stores bulge with goodies. The digital media world has dissolved into a chaotic free-for-all. Yet in the generation since 1981, when we all but stopped enforcing our antimonopoly laws, a very small number of people have consolidated control over just about every activity in the United States, other than making music and launching blogs. Even as we were reassured on a daily, sometimes hourly, basis that America was the greatest "free market" economy in the world, a tiny elite engineered the most phenomenal roll-up of political economic power in our history.

In *Cornered* I aim to help you get to know our monopolies and how they operate. I have structured the book as a sort of tour of monopoly, in all its many guises, in the United States today. We will look at how monopolists rip us off as consumers, raising the prices we must pay for our food, drugs, products, and services, even as they lower variety, quality, and safety. Then we will look at how the monopolists take away our properties and our liberties as entrepreneurs, professionals, workers, and inventors.

The initial task should not be hard. Almost every one of us has had some recent run-in with monopoly, even if we didn't notice at the time. Perhaps you were at the pediatrician's office and learned of yet another shortage of vaccines. Maybe you were at the airport, fuming, bumped from a flight you booked months ago. Perhaps you were at a concert with your child, knowing you had just been scalped not by some scruffy guy on the street but by a national corporation.

Or driving up to your bank, noticing that the new sign on the door advertises the same big bank you left a year ago because service was so lousy. Or hurtling down the highway, marveling at how for thousand-mile stretches at a time in our land of plenty, there seem to be only five chains of restaurants, all serving the same lumps of protein and carbohydrates, albeit blended with different colors and molded into different shapes.

Perhaps you were going through the books in your family's business, wondering how to survive when your biggest suppliers jack up prices even as your biggest customers crank down what they pay. Or standing at the door of your own store, watching a chain backed by billionaires in New Haven or New York set up shop directly across the street.

Maybe you are a doctor, baffled about how to balance your malpractice payments to one dictatorial insurer against your medical insurance reimbursements from another. Or a farmer, wandering through a cold dark dawn to feed pigs that once belonged to you but now, in a way you don't fully understand, belong to a corporation in North Carolina. Or an employee of a large corporation, listening to your boss tell you why he's going to cut your pay, and you know that you have nowhere else to go.

During our tour I will show you entirely new forms of monopoly, and I will show you forms of monopoly that you thought had long since vanished.

I don't expect every reader, here at the beginning, to regard all monopolies as bad or dangerous. As we will see, not all are. What I can promise is to provide every reader with a far better understanding of how the U.S. economy today is structured and really works. In recent years, we have been treated to innumerable books and conferences on globalization and on capital markets. Yet hardly a word has been published on consolidation, despite the fact that a full generation has passed since officials in the Reagan administration stopped enforcing our antimonopoly laws, which over the previous two centuries played a bigger role than any other set of laws in shaping business—and politics—in this country.

Indeed, for anyone who is trying to make sense of what is taking place in our nation and the world today, monopoly is the great missing force. Just as any effort to discuss physics without taking into account the work of Isaac Newton would result in much free-floating nonsense, the same is true of any effort to discuss today's economics without taking into account monopolization. In addition to helping illuminate such recent phenomena as the cascading collapses in our financial system and the near collapse of our automotive industry, monopolization also helps to explain such otherwise mysterious phenomena as the following:

- Why it's so hard to launch a successful small business
- Why so many jobs were moved offshore so quickly
- Why it's so difficult to control medical costs
- Why it's taken so long to blend cleaner technologies into our cars and our homes
- Why the quality of our food, drugs, and toys is declining
- Why the U.S. trade surplus is so huge and persistent
- Why corporate managers outsource so many activities
- Why corporate profits reached such record heights just before the fall[6]
- Why the powerful keep getting more powerful

Not one of these phenomena can be attributed solely to monopolization, yet not one can be understood without taking monopolization into account.

The Next Crash

Once we get our heads around the fact that monopolists rule most of our economy, our next step will be to understand how monopolists ruin our economy. This is especially important in today's complex world, for many of the industrial and financial systems run by monopolists are simply not safe. Today's monopolists, in their attempts to socialize away their risks, often reorganize entire industrial systems in ways that destroy the old structures we relied on to isolate and manage the normal disasters of everyday life. The result is that today we increasingly see everyday failures amplified into big crises that get transmitted around the world in real time. Worse yet, the monopolists often use their immense power precisely in ways that trigger the initial collapse of the very systems they undermined through the process of socializing their risks. That's why another of my main goals in *Cornered* is to convince you that we have no real choice but to reverse the process of monopolization now.

To give you an initial sense of how the systems controlled by monopolists are unsafe, let's take a moment to look at what we have learned about the organization of the North American automotive production system from the bailouts of General Motors and Chrysler. Specifically, let's extract the lessons of a remarkable statement made by Ford CEO Alan Mulally in the late fall of 2008.

During his testimony on Capitol Hill, Mulally asked Congress to provide loans to keep his rivals alive. The automotive industry, Mulally explained, is "uniquely interdependent." This was particularly true, he said, "with respect to our supply base, with more than 90 percent commonality among our suppliers. Should one of the other domestic companies declare bankruptcy, the effect on Ford's production operations would be felt within days—if not hours. . . . Without parts for the just-in-time inventory system, Ford plants would not be able to produce vehicles."[7]

On the surface, the North American automotive industry would seem to epitomize the very idea of robust competition and the freedom to fail. After all, more than ten big companies compete vigorously for our attention and our dollars. Hence, the loss of one or two firms in which managers made big mistakes would hardly seem cause for the government to intervene. Yet Mulally's request, which was soon seconded by Toyota, indicates with great clarity that what we think we see and what actually exists are two very different things. The reason it is often no longer possible to isolate failure and to punish unwise taking of risk is that the operations of these giant firms are no longer as discrete as they were just a few years ago.

We will discuss the emergence of this new industrial structure in more detail in chapter 3. But anyone with even a passing knowledge of the automotive industry will know that this state of affairs is radically different from what existed only a few years ago. Well into the 1990s, the big car companies were still largely "vertically integrated." This meant that each car manufacturer built its own components such as piston rings, windshield wipers, and car seats. Beginning about a decade ago, however, these corporations began to "outsource" most such work and instead buy their parts from outside suppliers. Once these parts manufacturing operations were no longer under the control of the big automakers, financiers took advantage of the opportunity to reorganize many of these activities into monopolies designed to serve *all* automakers at the same time.

The result is that the automotive industry increasingly resembles the Hydra, the many-headed monster from Greek mythology. Toyota, Ford, General Motors, Honda, and the other main automakers are distinct from one another just like the several heads of the Hydra. Yet just as the many heads of the Hydra relied on one body, the automakers increasingly rely on a single *common* body of companies that supply the same components to all of them. From the point of view of the automotive industry, many of these suppliers, although often still quite small in the overall scheme of things, have been rendered for all intents "too big to fail."

Here too, just as with our financial system, failure anywhere can become failure everywhere. Here too, all increasingly stand or fall as one.

This is a big problem. Many intellectuals in our society hold stubbornly to an old myth: that monopolies create a greater sense of "ownership" over the activity that has been monopolized, and hence a greater incentive to care for the machines, skills, and other properties held in the monopoly. But as we will see, unless a monopoly is very carefully regulated, the exact opposite is true. This is especially so of systems that, like the automotive industry, have been structurally monopolized.

The mere knowledge that all stand or fall as one has, if anything, a completely contrary psychological effect. It does not lead individuals to take better care of the system as a whole but instead tends to lead them to conclude that there is little they alone can do to save the system. This, in turn, leads them away from any real sense of responsibility and ownership.

Which, in turn, leads many to take greater risks with their little piece of the common system than they would if the risk were localized in their own hands. In any commonly held system that is not structured to be owned and hence protected by real people, the inevitable competition among real people results in a race to loot and scoot before the whole system fails.

The one entirely new lesson of the Meltdown of 2008 and the bailout of Detroit, then, is not that financiers stole big money from us, although they did. Nor is it that they further undermined our freedoms, although they did. It's that they also stole our safety and security. In the very act of merging our industrial and financial systems into great socialized networks—in order, the financiers told us, to achieve greater "efficiencies"—they stripped out one of our society's most vital forms of wealth: the *resiliency* that systems engineers (and, as we will see, such political "engineers" as James Madison) originally built into the systems we rely on for our food, our drugs, our energy, our machines, our information services, and our money.

The most pressing imperative we face, then, is not to figure out how to create more jobs. Nor is it to structure a regulatory system to ensure that the financial products we buy are safe. Both tasks are immensely important, of course. But our real imperative is to restructure our financial, manufacturing, and service industries so that they always isolate failure. Our goal must be to ensure that no set of traders on any one floor, no earthquake under any distant city, no restless dictator on the far side of the world, and no Homer Simpson who lets loose a wrench or a miswritten code can ever trigger a cascading collapse that threatens an entire system on which we depend.

The solution lies, as I hope to make clear, not in getting the details of regulation right but in getting the politics of ownership and responsibility right.

The Makers of Things

I have organized *Cornered* into three main sections. In the first third of the book, I introduce the reader to some of our monopolies and illustrate some of the destructive economic and political dynamics that are set into motion when concentrated power is not well harnessed. In the middle three chapters, I look at how that power affects individual American citizens who bring property—in the form of ideas, products, and work—to market. In the last third of the book, I look at how concentrated political economic power affects other systems—namely, those we erected to protect peaceful international relations, our knowledge of how to make the products and grow the foods we need, and our political institutions.

I have tried hard to avoid cluttering *Cornered* with lots of numbers or technical jargon. The first task was made easier by the fact that the U.S. government stopped keeping good data on monopolization a generation ago. To achieve the second, I avoided any exhaustive discussion of the arcana of contemporary antimonopoly law. What I did instead was to provide a simple overview of the history of antimonopoly thinking in the United States, to reconnect us to the original political purposes of open markets and industrial corporations. My goal here was, in a sense, to scrape away the many layers of embellishments that usually catch our eyes, in order to reveal the pillar of American democratic republicanism beneath.

I could not, however, find a way around using three terms—*natural monopoly*, *oligopoly*, and *monopoly*. In the case of "natural" monopoly, I generally follow the traditional definition, which holds that there are certain systems—for instance, to deliver water to your house or a car to your driveway—in which the cost of building a secondary and competitive system would clearly waste limited human and material resources. My assumption in such cases is that the public does not need to own such monopolies, but it does have a duty to regulate them very closely to ensure that they are safe and that all members of society are treated fairly.

When I talk about oligopoly, my intent is to describe instances in which there are compelling reasons to concentrate machinery, knowledge, and skill but no compelling reason to allow any one small group of people to dominate more than some portion of the activity. Examples include the manufacture of chemicals, automobiles, and semiconductors. My assumption here is that the American people must use our antimonopoly laws to ensure that these activities remain competitive and open to newcomers, while also avoiding any temptation to break these firms into pieces too small to function well.

As for monopoly itself, in recent years some radical monopolists have tried to define the term as meaning 100 percent control of some activity. Any other condition—like the 90-plus percent shares of market enjoyed by such companies as Intel and Microsoft—is still more than sufficiently competitive, they say. Here also I follow traditional American practice. As the economist Milton Friedman once wrote, a monopoly is any concentration of power by one or a few firms or individuals that allows them "to determine significantly the terms on which" individuals can buy or sell some product or service.[8]

Some of you will fault me for using politically charged language in *Cornered*. Others will find the language refreshing, even liberating. I want to make clear that I use such language neither to provoke nor to incite. My intent here is certainly not to attack the business community. I spent most of my career writing about business, and for many of those years I helped to run a business, in the form of an independent magazine for executives at international companies.

My experiences left me with a great admiration of the entrepreneur and the professional manager. I know how hard the average businessperson works. I also know that the great majority of entrepreneurs and executives are not driven foremost by money. If anything, one of my main goals is to help liberate the entrepreneur and the executive from the monopolist, just as I want to help liberate the engineer, scientist, farmer, professional, and worker from the monopolist.

My intent is also not to attack any one political party today. Ronald Reagan may have been the first to suspend enforcement of our antimonopoly laws, but Bill Clinton promoted monopolization with even greater abandon. My assumption here is that political parties are little more than shells, the content of which changes over time, often swiftly. My hope is that the majority of the American people, regardless of party affiliation, will come to understand the political and economic dangers that these monopolists pose and will stand against them.

A generation ago a highly sophisticated political movement appeared in the United States. This movement was dedicated to taking apart the entire institutional structure that we had put into place, beginning in the mid-1930s, to govern our political economy by distributing power and responsibility among all the people. The goal of this movement was to enable the few, once again, to consolidate power entirely in their own hands.

That's why one of their very first targets was our antimonopoly laws. To justify this action, these revolutionaries preached an alternative philosophy of political economics—sometimes called *free-market fundamentalism*. This philosophy depicted our political economy not as political in nature but as a sort of organic mechanism that worked best if left untouched by human beings. The revolutionaries also promoted an alternative language of economic inquiry—based on the idea that economics is a science. Rather than describe the interaction of people in our economy as a function of law and politics, they preferred the languages of mathematics and mysticism.

I use the language of *political economics* not to make us angry at any person or group but to help us see the *political* lies that have been framed by the free-market fundamentalists and the *economically* deranging effects of those lies. I use the language of political economics—which, by the way, is the language of Franklin Roosevelt, Louis Brandeis, Abraham Lincoln, James Madison, Thomas Jefferson, Adam Smith, and Benjamin Franklin—because it is the only effective practical language through which to understand and affect the institutional structure in which all economic activity takes place. If we wish to stop the rich from ruining, we must speak honestly of how they rule.

President Barack Obama, in his inaugural speech, told us that "it has been the risk takers, the doers, *the makers of things*—some celebrated but more often men and women obscure in their labor—who have carried us up the long, rugged path towards prosperity and freedom" (emphasis added).

So it shall be again—but only once we have taken the actions necessary to protect the craftsman, the entrepreneur, the farmer, the doctor, the engineer, and the rest of us, who actually produce the goods and services on which we all rely, from the brute powers of the monopolists, who are *the breakers of things*.

Acknowledgments

The most important asset of any author is the honesty of his friends. Measured by the number of really smart people who, over the last three years, looked me in the eye and said, "Barry, you're full of it," I can honestly regard myself as truly blessed.

Of all these many mentors, advisers, editors, guides, and bubble poppers, the one whose comments I treasure most is Marcellus Andrews. I would call Marcellus the most gifted economist I know, but from me he'd surely take that as an insult. So let me call him what he is also, which is one of the wisest people in our land, not least because he is a great student of human beings and human history as well as of numbers and theories on a page. I also want to express special gratitude to Michael Lind. One of my great luxuries at New America is to wander fifty feet down the hall to the one-room university where Mike sits and set before him some query about Locke or Croly. Sometimes the result is heat, but mainly it is light, one that illuminates many pages of this book. The third person I want to thank up front is Sherle Schwenninger. In recent years, Sherle has devoted literally weeks of his life to arguing with me. His comments are always smart, often dead-on, and they made *Cornered* a far better work than it should have been.

I began this project after making myself aware, during the writing of my last book, *End of the Line*, of the extent and increasingly extreme effects of monopolization in America. I soon discovered that few people shared my concerns. Even a mere three years ago, the average editor remained squarely convinced that we lived in the most magnificent of self-regulating free-market systems ever conjured into existence anywhere at any time on this earth. Which meant that selling *Cornered* involved finding a series of people with vision sufficient to see this was not true and bravery enough to bet on that fact. The first was Bill Wasik, at *Harper's*, in my experience the best editor in the magazine business, who shaped the article from which *Cornered* would grow. (While on the subject of *Harper's*, I also want to thank John MacArthur, who keeps that best magazine in America in business.) The next person in this chain was my agent, Rafe Sagalyn, who not only can envision a book three or four years before the world is ready for it, but who can also transform a pile of half-processed thoughts and experimental riffs into an outline that actually looks like a book. Last came Eric Nelson, at John Wiley & Sons, my editor and friend, who combines a fine political mind with the ability to edit with grace and subtlety with a lovely lust for battle in the marketplace.

My single greatest debt is to Katherine McFate. Seven years ago I walked into Katherine's office and told her I had discovered a flaw in how corporate managers were organizing the industries on which we rely. Katherine not only believed me, which was rare at the time, but she immediately became my most important partner in my quest to understand how this could be, alternately pushing and leading me to perform deeper and more expansive work than I originally thought myself able to accomplish. Katherine has a vision and energy and courage almost entirely unique in the foundation world. If, God willing, twenty years hence we gaze once again on an American political economy remade entirely to protect and enhance the liberty of the individual American citizen, any honest historian will treat Katherine as one of the prime movers in that restoration. I also am deeply indebted to the friendship and assistance of Janet Shenk. Like Katherine, Janet also saw very early on the potential value in my work, and in many and various ways she has been a steady and stalwart supporter in the years since. More than once in my life I have stood, literally or figuratively, at the barricades. From the first time we spoke, I knew Janet was one of those select few who stand next to you to the end.

Over the last two years I had the unique privilege of working with Steve Coll, Steve Clemons, Leo Hindery, and Ralph Gomory. Sitting in a room with any one of these souls can be a humbling experience, which makes my gratitude for their faith in my work all the greater.

I am deeply grateful to the following people for closely reading part or all of *Cornered*: Chick Perrow, Ha Joon Chang, Mark Schmitt, Pat Choate, Janine Wedel, Phil Longman, Jamie Galbraith, and the

Reverend Roger Verley. This wide range of perspectives, added to those of Marcellus, Mike, and Sherle, helped me immensely in my effort to weave many themes into what I hope is a coherent whole.

I want to thank the many people who have taken time to discuss my work in depth and who offered useful critiques and suggestions. The following list, presented in no particular order, is merely a start, and I apologize to the many I missed in my rush. Thanks to Jody Bernstein, Jacques Gansler, Adrian Costain, Michael Borrus, Rabbi Fred Scherdlinder Dobb, John Zysman, John Cavanaugh, Jorge Castaneda, Michael Greenberger, Alan Riley, Many Hendrickson, Catherine Mann, Michael Osterholm, John Perry Barlow, David Reed, Amb. Thomas Pickering, Amb. Arthur Hartman, Leon Fuerth, Jim Pinkerton, Ellen Seidman, Lou Uchitelle, Richard Parker, Lynn Stout, Margaret Blair, Robert A. G. Monks, Ron Blackwell, Steve Hannaford, Deborah Kops, Dean Baker, Peter Warburton, Theodore Bestor, Christopher Gopal, Peter Gosselin, Adam Bellow, Robert Skidelsky, Christy Hoffman, Takahiro Fujimoto, David Bowers, Jeremy Greenstock, Tom Woodruff, Tadao Yanase, Thea Lee, Steve Abrecht, Jonathan Rowe, Tom Miller, Tam Ormiston, Chuck Hamilton, Toyoo Gyohten, Tsunehiko (Tony) Yamazaki, Stacy Mitchell, Knut Brunjes, Madeline Janis, Gail Pesyna, Tim Sturgeon, Jock Nash, Gary Gerreffi, Damon Silvers, Jim Fallows, Lori Wallach, George Scalise, Andy Grossman, the Rt. Hon. Lord Brittan, Shannon Brownlee, Wim Roelandts, Jennifer Washburn, Harold Meyerson, Patrick Mulloy, Keith Hart, Klaus Zimmermann, Diana Endicott, Gwen Robinson, Liza Tucker, Yoshi Sheffi, and Shashi Tharoor.

Very special thanks to three people whose wisdom infuses every page of this work—Janice Nittoli, Peter Barnes, and Hans Schoepflin.

Many of the most important of these discussions took place within New America itself. I am grateful to Reid Cramer, Ray Boshara, Doug McGray, Jed Purdy, David Gray, Patrick Doherty, Simone Frank, Gregory Rodriguez, Leif Wellington Haase, Steven Hill, Len Nichols, Rachel White, Kate Brown, and Danielle Maxwell. The same is true of the American Antitrust Institute. I could not have written this book without the help of Bert Foer as an individual and of the members of the AAI as a group. Bert is one of the finest gentlemen I know and one of the most patient. Others at AAI who went out of their way to help this project include Diana Moss, Greg Gundlach, Robert Lande, Jack Kirkwood, and John Kwoka. During the summer of 2008, I spent two fascinating months in Japan researching the industrial crash that took place in the automotive industry after a July 2007 earthquake in Niigata. I came home with the story I sought and a renewed affection for Japan and the Japanese people, thanks to the Japan Society and the Foreign Press Center Japan, especially Ruri Kawashima, Betty Borden, Mayuko Fukasawa, Kazuko Koizumi, Shinya Aoki, and the ever brilliant David D'Heilly.

Over the last three years, a number of people at New America helped with various forms of research or similar work. Thanks to Sam Sherraden, Ben Katcher, Sameer Lalwani, Brian Beutler, Jeff Meyer, and Liz Wu for key contributions. And, of course, Katherine Tiedemann, who with remarkable aplomb handled the single most sensitive job in this entire project.

There is an element of madness in writing a book, one that can have a huge affect on any family. Not only does the work often take you out of the house physically, it always takes you away mentally. Luckily my children are of an age when they would have thought me off my rocker no matter what. For Anya, the toll was much greater, not least because she had to serve often as first debater of all the raw rants and ravings out of which I shaped my arguments. My love and gratitude to Anya and Walter and Ezra.

Before I finish, I'd like to raise a glass of bourbon in honor of that great son of Kentucky, Louis Brandeis. More than anyone else, Justice Brandeis is responsible for rekindling the flame of Madisonian and Jeffersonian democracy in America in the early years of the twentieth century. Justice Brandeis is proof that one individual, one teacher, wielding words alone, can make all the difference.

1

The Hidden Monopolies Everywhere

Even with a GPS and a good map, I have a hard time finding Diane Cochrane's home, which is tucked in the crease of a hill a few miles east of Prescott, Arizona. The one-story green frame building sits at the bottom of a steep driveway that drops from a rocky road that cuts off a maze of streets that, as I drive along in my rented Pontiac, seem more like a mad Motocross track than the arteries of a neighborhood.

Yet it is easy to understand why Diane settled here with her husband after they fled the monotony of a Ford assembly line in Ohio. The landscape is a testament to the creativity of both humanity and God. Every one of the hundred or so houses in the community is unique. There are ramblers, chalets, A-frames, ranches, and log cabins. The terrain, meanwhile, seems to change in character almost inch by inch as the roadway drops and twists vertiginously into deep and scrubby ravines, only to crest a moment later to stunning views of a far shimmering horizon.

A few miles down Highway 69, the Wal-Mart Supercenter at the edge of Prescott is a different world. The parking lot alone is the grandest swath of flat space I've seen in the last hour of driving. Then there's the store itself. To fit the big box into the undulating land, the builders had to cut deep into the side of a hill, carving away as much as six or seven stories worth of dirt and rock.

Once I am inside Wal-Mart's door, it takes me nearly two minutes, striding swiftly, to walk from one end of the store to the other. Along the way I pass twenty-seven checkout lines and what seems like a whole town—a savings bank, a McDonald's, a portrait gallery—tucked under this one roof. I almost wish I'd brought along some music to entertain myself, because there isn't much new to look at on my stroll. Other than having a rack of cowboy hats, this Supercenter is filled with the exact same collection of products as every other Wal-Mart Supercenter in the United States, be it in Ohio, California, or Virginia. It also has the same empty feeling. When I arrive, it's early evening and the parking lot is full. Yet the store seems almost vacant, and the few shoppers I do see wander listlessly and almost silently through the aisles.

Diane, who is sixty and has cut her gray hair short, wears a salmon-colored cotton shirt on this ninety-seven-degree April day. She tells me that until recently, she shopped in this Wal-Mart almost every day, often on her way home from her job managing a party store. She doesn't anymore, though, and that's not because filling a basket at the Supercenter can be more exhausting than a trip to the gym. Diane has tried to avoid all Wal-Marts everywhere ever since her two kittens, Bones and Moses, died of kidney failure on the same day in 2007. Diane believes that the food she purchased here—Wal-Mart private label Special Kitty Gourmet Blend foil pouches filled with whitefish and tuna in sauce—is what killed them.

My intent in this chapter is not to blame any one person at Wal-Mart for the deaths of Diane's kittens, nor to blame the rather abstract entity that is Wal-Mart taken as a whole. It is to reinforce the main idea we discussed in the preface: that monopoly exists just about everywhere in America today.

It is also to add two new facts. First, today's monopolies increasingly appear in the shape of giant trading firms like Wal-Mart, which are designed to govern entire production systems, even entire swaths, of our economy. Second, monopoly does not eliminate competition, nor does it automatically result in a rational and efficient governance of the production and service systems under its sway.

On the contrary, monopolization merely shifts competition from a horizontal plane to a vertical plane. That is, rather than having a winner-take-all battle among automobile makers or between Wal-Mart and Target, for example, we have competition between the monopoly and all the people under its power. In the case of Wal-Mart, this includes its workers and its suppliers as well as its customers. The real competition, in other words, is between the billionaires who make and wield monopolies like Wal-Mart and people like you, me, and Diane.

I could have started this chapter with dozens of stories about the deaths of dogs and cats just before and after the great pet food recall of 2007. I chose Diane's story not because we have absolute proof that Wal-Mart cat food killed Bones and Moses—the kittens were cremated days before the first recall was announced. Rather, it was because the circumstantial evidence is so strong. Bones and Moses were healthy kittens. There were two of them, and they died at the same time. During their whole lives Diane fed them only Special Kitty pouches. Diane's veterinarian told Diane that the kittens' blood-urea-nitrogen measurement was the highest she had ever seen. Diane also owned other animals at the time, including a seven-year-old cat named Little Bit and a seven-year-old collie named Sailor, both of whom ate food that was not included in the recall; both of them, she tells me, remain quite healthy.[1]

I chose to focus on the pet food fiasco in general because it was one of those stories that comes along every so often that rips away the veil to reveal how the mechanisms of our economy really work. That's what happened in March 2007, when an Ontario-based company named Menu Foods announced a recall of cans and pouches of wet pet food that had been packed at plants in Kansas and New Jersey.[2] At first, the story seemed simple enough: another case in which poor food-handling techniques resulted in contamination that resulted in sickness and, in a few cases, death, just as we have seen in such other products as spinach and peanut butter.

That's why the initial reports on the recall focused on empty store shelves and terrified pet owners. Within a week, however, the Menu Foods story began to morph into something entirely different: a horror tale about the dangers of food, drugs, toys, and tires made in China. The turning point came on March 23, when three things happened.

First, the Food and Drug Administration (FDA) announced that it suspected that some toxin had been mixed into the wheat gluten that was used to thicken the canned meats.[3] Second, an independent lab reported that it had found rat poison in the recalled cans. Third, Menu Foods pointed a finger at a shipment of wheat gluten that had been purchased from a supplier in China. Although rat poison was later replaced as the main culprit by a chemical named melamine, the story line had now taken shape: cheap and adulterated Chinese products were poisoning Americans, their children, and their pets.

Throughout the coming months, journalists and officials would drag vast piles of horrifying facts into the light. Some Chinese toothpaste makers had used diethylene glycol, a component of brake fluid and antifreeze, as a sweetener. Some Chinese toy makers had coated their products with lead-based paints. Some Chinese farmers had fed unapproved drugs to catfish that were bound for U.S. dinner plates. Some Chinese slaughterhouses had mixed "oversulfated chondroitin sulfate" into the pig intestines that were used as the raw material for the blood thinner heparin.[4]

The details were so nauseating and so terrifying that two of the most important revelations of the Menu Foods meltdown were all but lost. The first was that the corporations we rely on to stock our shelves with food had allowed the production of wheat gluten—which is used to thicken wet foods, bind dry foods, and condition dough—to be captured by a single foreign nation, China. Similarly, these corporations had allowed the production of numerous other vital inputs—like most of the ingredients in our drugs—to be captured by that one nation.

The second overlooked revelation was that almost the entire U.S. pet food industry had come to depend, to various degrees, on a single supplier of canned and pouched pet food. In this case, five of the top six independent brands—including those marketed by Colgate-Palmolive, Mars, and Procter & Gamble—had hired Menu Foods to stuff meat into at least some of the cans and pouches that as of early 2007 bore their labels.[5] So had seventeen of the top twenty food retailers in the United States that sell "private label" wet pet foods under their store brands, including Safeway, Kroger's, and Wal-Mart.[6] In total, the Menu Foods recall covered products that had been retailed under a phenomenal 150 different names.[7]

Perhaps even more disturbing, especially for those pet owners who had been spending their dollars on a premium product, was that the recall revealed that high-end, expensive brands like Iams and Hill's Pet Nutrition Science Diet rolled off the exact same Menu Food packing lines as the cans that were wrapped in labels bearing such names as Supervalu and Price Chopper.[8]

Without access to internal documents from all of these companies, it is almost impossible to know exactly what percentage of wet pet food in the United States came from Menu Foods factories in the months before the recall. The last thing an established brand wants to advertise is how much of its product it buys from outside suppliers. My own figures indicate that Menu Foods accounted for somewhat less than a quarter of the total pet food sold in the United States, by weight.[9]

Even so, Menu Food's octopuslike reach throughout the pet food industry resulted in disruptions that were far greater than would have been the case a decade earlier. Back then, the big pet food brands largely operated their own factories and packed their own cans, and they also actively managed their supply bases to avoid concentration. This means that they would have been able to isolate any supply problem far more swiftly and with far less disruption at the point of sale.

In 2007, the sheer number of brands affected by the Menu Foods recall meant that, as the *Wall Street Journal* noted, it was now much "harder for consumers to find a safe substitute."[10] In some instances, confused store managers pulled all pet food off their store shelves. In other cases, confused consumers did not trust what was still for sale.

For those Americans who believe in what we were taught in civics class and Econ 101, the most disturbing revelation was not even the fragility of our food systems, but that some of our most cherished beliefs about how the U.S. economy works appear no longer to be true. We are told that companies are engaged in a mad scramble to discover exactly what we the U.S. consumers want and to devise perfectly tailored systems to supply those want as efficiently as possible. We are told that our economy is characterized by constantly chaotic yet always constructive competition and that any American with a better product and bit of gumption can bring that product to market and beat the big guys.

Yet the reality, as Menu Foods now taught us, could not be more different—at least not in the pet food aisle in Wal-Mart or Kroger's. Instead of having infinite choice, as we thought, we are really presented with a wall of standard-issue cans and pouches that are distinguished only by the words and colors on their labels. The secret ingredient of U.S. capitalism, at least in this corner of the industrial kitchen, could have been cooked up in the Soviet Union.

More disturbing yet is that such concentration is not the exception in the United States but increasingly the rule. A quick tour of almost any grocery store reveals degrees of concentration that make Menu Foods look like a novice. We will look at this in more detail in the next chapter, but let's take a quick walk around the average U.S. grocery or big-box store.

Over in the health-care aisle we find that Colgate-Palmolive and Procter & Gamble split more than 80 percent of the U.S. market for toothpaste, including such seemingly independent brands as Tom's of Maine.

In the cold case we find that almost every beer is manufactured or distributed by either Anheuser-Busch InBev or MillerCoors, including imports like Corona, Beck's, and Tsingtao; regional beers like Rolling Rock; once independent microbrews like Redhook and Old Dominion; and even "organic" beers like Stone Mill Pale Ale.

Perhaps Americans are comfortable with the fact that Campbell's controls more than 70 percent of the shelf space devoted to canned soups.[11] After all, the firm grew to prominence after its launch in 1869, thanks to its pioneering successes in integrating advanced chemistry, mass manufacturing, and modern advertising.

But what are we to make of the modern snack aisle, where Frito-Lay in recent years has captured half the business of selling salty corn chips and potato chips?[12]

And what about the business of selling tap water in plastic bottles? Here, if anywhere, is an activity that any enterprising young American should be able to master. All you would seem to need to enter the local market for water is a spigot, some bottles, and a cool label. Yet nine of the top ten brands of bottled tap water in the United States are sold by PepsiCo (Aquafina), Coca-Cola (Dasani and Evian), or Nestlé (Poland Spring, Arrowhead, Deer Park, Ozarka, Zephyrhills, and Ice Mountain).

Furthermore, what can we learn from the size of the corporation in whose store we now stand? Until we elected Ronald Reagan president, both Democrats and Republicans made sure that no chain store ever came to dominate more than a small fraction of sales in the United States as a whole, or even in any one region of the country. Between 1917 and 1979, for instance, administrations from both parties repeatedly charged the Great Atlantic and Pacific Tea Company, the chain store behemoth of the mid-twentieth century that is better known as A&P, with violations of antitrust law, even threatening to break the firm into pieces.

Then in 1981 we stopped enforcing that law. Thus, today Wal-Mart is at least *five times* bigger, relative to the overall size of the U.S. economy, than A&P was at the very height of its power.[13] Indeed, Wal-Mart exercises a de facto complete monopoly in many smaller cities, and it sells as much as half of all the groceries in many big metropolitan markets. Wal-Mart delivers at least 30 percent and sometimes more than 50 percent of the entire U.S. consumption of products ranging from soaps and detergents to compact discs and pet food.

For that matter, what can we learn about our twenty-first-century consumer arcadia by looking at how the Supercenter in which we shop was constructed? The price of the steel in the frame reflects the nearly complete roll-up of the world's main sources of iron ore by three firms (two of which recently tried to merge). The price of the store shelves reflects the nearly complete roll-up by these same three firms of the capacity to process bauxite into aluminum. The price of the concrete in the foundation reflects the recent roll-up of the world cement industry by a few immense firms like Mexico's Cemex. The price of the crushed rock in the parking lot reflects the roll-up of control by a few corporations over many of the biggest quarries in the United States.

Big corporations have played a big role in this country for a long time. Companies of men began to build big interstate railroads even before the Civil War, and they began to assemble giant industrial combines soon after. Big companies began to centralize control over the butchery of cattle and hogs, the milling of grains, and the canning of fruit and vegetables and soups in the late nineteenth century.

By the early twentieth century, men had enclosed in the walls of a few corporations the capacity to make automobiles, chemicals, and farm machinery. For much of the last century, however, the American people took steps to disrupt the efforts to completely dominate these businesses, and, as we saw with A&P, we took special pains to restrict the reach of pure trading companies.

That's why we have never before seen such power to govern our industries concentrated in so few hands. That's why we have never before seen such physical concentration of production—be it of vitamin C, wheat gluten, heparin, or aspirin in China, of semiconductors in Taiwan, or of package-sorting capacity in Memphis. That's why we have never before seen such a lack of compartmentalization of our systems and therefore such a socialization of the risk in these systems. That's why we have never before seen such top-down competition and thus the destruction of so many of the real assets, skills, and products enclosed within the fences of these corporations. That's why we have never before faced such a lack of real options.

I know that this last point—that the U.S. consumer faces fewer and fewer options—is, on the face of it, hard to believe. The world we shop in every day appears to be full of choices. Yet in real life, our political economy is filled with hidden monopolies almost everywhere, and these monopolies increasingly control, restrict, and determine what we buy, with little or no regard for any real market forces.

Just ask Diane Cochrane. As much as she wanted to cut Wal-Mart out of her life, she quickly found that she could not. Although Diane was eventually able to find a new—much more expensive—source of pet food for her surviving cat and dog, there are certain items she just can't find in Prescott outside Wal-Mart, which now runs two Supercenters in this community of forty-one thousand people.

"It's getting to where for a lot of things you have to go to Wal-Mart," Diane says. This is true even when she knows that the quality is bad. There is, she tells me, "no other choice."

At the end of this chapter, we will come back to Prescott to complete our look at how the relationship between Wal-Mart and Menu Foods illustrates the way in which a top-down authoritarian power relationship can result in the degradation and destruction of the vital production systems on which we rely. For now, let's continue our tour by introducing ourselves to just a few of the hidden and not-so-hidden monopolies that dominate our economy.

And Then There Was One

In the spring of 2007, the fourth great merger wave of the last twenty-five years was still crashing through the global economy. Almost every day seemed to reveal new deals floating in the surf. Many were take-overs by foreign firms of competitors based in the United States. Thus, we saw the Anglo-Swedish company AstraZeneca pay $15.6 billion for MedImmune of Maryland; the Taiwanese computer giant Acer buy the California PC assembler Gateway; and the Brazilian meatpacker JBS-Friboi acquire the Colorado-based Swift & Company.

Another common deal was for a huge U.S. firm to further consolidate an already tightly controlled domestic industry. Thus we saw Rupert Murdoch's New York–based News Corporation buy the *Wall Street Journal*, and we saw the pharmaceutical giant CVS of Rhode Island pay $26.5 billion to control Caremark Pharmacy Services.

By midyear, more than $1.9 trillion in tie-ups had been booked.[14] This put 2007 on a path to set a record, breaking the one set only the year before, when $3.8 trillion in deals surpassed the previous high-water mark of $3.38 trillion in 2000. Consolidations in 2006 included the purchase of BellSouth for $86 billion by American Telephone and Telegraph (AT&T), Boston Scientific's grab of Guidant, Wachovia's purchase of Golden West Financial, and the Bank of New York's acquisition of Mellon Financial.

The takeovers often unfolded in dizzying sequence. Consider what happened in the metals industry after the *London Times* reported in February 2007 that the world's two biggest mining companies, the Anglo-Australian giants BHP Billiton and Rio Tinto, planned to make separate bids for the U.S. aluminum company Alcoa. A Brazilian paper then reported that the world's third largest mining company, CVRD, also planned to join the fray, even though that firm was still digesting its acquisition of the Canadian nickel miner Inco the year before.

To protect itself, Alcoa dusted off an existing plan to buy its horizontal competitor, the Canadian aluminum maker Alcan, and announced a fresh and hostile $27 billion bid. A New York stock analyst then proposed what is known as the Pac-Man defense for Alcan, in which the Canadian company would respond to Alcoa's bid by trying to take over Alcoa instead. Before that scenario could play out, however, BHP Billiton announced that it might want to make a bid for Rio Tinto. Then CVRD said that it too might want to make a play for Rio Tinto. Rio Tinto responded with a huge defensive bid for Alcan. BHP Billiton and CVRD then floated the idea of jointly taking over Rio Tinto.

In late October, Rio Tinto's deal with Alcan finally closed. Not that Rio Tinto could claim any clear victory, for its $38.1 billion bid was more than 40 percent higher than Alcoa's original, generous offer of only half a year earlier. As it proved, the deal delivered Rio Tinto no protection, for in early November BHP staked a phenomenal $143 billion in a formal play for its "competitor" (I enclose *competitor* in quotation marks because the two firms share so many of the same institutional investors[15]).

Not that this ended the drama. In February 2009, Rio Tinto's management, which had run into trouble paying off its new debt, agreed to accept $19.5 billion from the Aluminum Corporation of China (Chinalco) for an 18 percent stake. As we will see in chapter 7, China has launched a very aggressive effort to ensure long-term access to cheap commodities, and this deal amounted to an attempt by leaders in Beijing to take advantage of the collapse in world asset prices and commodity prices following the economic Meltdown of 2008. Rio Tinto's shareholders promptly objected to the deal, however, and in June, Chinalco dropped its bid. The very next day Rio Tinto and BHP Billiton announced a plan to form a fifty-fifty joint venture that would unify control over their mines in the Pilbara region of Australia, which supply 75 percent of China's iron ore. China responded by threatening to bring an antitrust suit against the two companies and backed this up in more direct fashion by arresting Rio Tinto's top Australian salesman in China and three of his Chinese colleagues.[16]

Sometimes such deals remade an entire industry in the course of a few months. This is what happened with the online advertising business between January and July 2007. After France's Publicis Groupe set off a rush with a $1.3 billion bid for Digitas, Google offered $3.1 billion for DoubleClick in April, and that month Yahoo! offered $640 million for Right Media. Then, on two subsequent days in May, WPP gobbled up Real Media for $649 million and Microsoft plunged in with a $6 billion bid for aQuantive. Finally, in July, AOL settled for Tacoda for $275 million.

At other times the takeovers simply continued a process of consolidating and standardizing an industry that had begun years earlier. In the 1990s, Cisco grew to an immense size by applying an extremely aggressive Standard Oil–style roll-up strategy to Internet hardware and software makers, and IBM relied on its acquisitions to smooth its transformation from being the world's premier manufacturer of computers to the world's biggest supplier of information technology services.

In 2007, both companies were still energetically policing their markets through such deals as Cisco's $820 million purchase of IronPort Systems in January and IBM's $5 billion takeover of Cognos in November. Such strategies were not limited to the high-tech sectors. In the decade up to 2007, the financiers who control Illinois Tool Works built that firm into a $14 billion power by averaging almost fifty acquisitions a year of firms that trade in such products as screws, plastic bags, deli slicers, and plastic rings.[17] The automotive parts maker Collins & Aikman, meanwhile, was used by financiers to roll up a position supplying components like rugs and dashboards to about 90 percent of all cars made in the United States—by Toyota, Honda, and Nissan as well as by GM, Ford, and Chrysler.[18]

Unlike in the past, when American firms had usually been either predator or prey, the most recent mergers and acquisition (M&A) frenzy was much more global in character. In mid-May 2007, I was in London to speak at a *Financial Times* conference on outsourcing. At breakfast one Sunday, I picked up the *Telegraph*, a paper not known foremost for its financial coverage. Yet in this one issue, it seemed that almost the only news was M&A. This included four front-page articles and at least four-teen pieces throughout the paper.

Of top concern was the newly announced plan by the information company Thomson to take over the world's oldest news wire service, Reuters. Other deals reported in that day's paper included one for the pharmacy chain Alliance Boots, one for the company that publishes the *Financial Times*, one for the telecom firm Cable & Wireless, and one for Sainsbury supermarkets. There was also a big update on the dramatic fight to control the Dutch banking conglomerate ABN AMRO, in which a consortium led by the Royal Bank of Scotland had challenged a friendly deal proposed by the London-based giant Barclays.

In a column, the *Telegraph* business editor estimated that a fifth of Britain's top hundred companies had been the subject of M&A speculation just in the previous month. "It won't be long now," he wrote, "before it is easier to keep track of those companies not threatened with takeover."[19]

Every so often came news of a decision that seemed to run counter to this trend, such as Tyco International's plan to spin off its health-care and electronics units. A closer look, however, often revealed that the real goal was still a more effective concentration of power over individual industrial activities, in this instance achieved by selling these units to their direct competitors.[20]

Most deals never even made it close to the pages of a newspaper. Consider the merger of lab equipment giants Thermo Electron and Fisher Scientific in late 2006. Other examples are the mergers of the two main manufacturers of Lasik eye lasers (Advanced Medical Optics and IntraLase) and the two biggest offshore oil exploration and drilling companies (U.S. Transocean and GlobalSantaFe), both in 2007.[21]

Few noticed the merger of two Canadian uranium miners (SXR Uranium One and UrAsia Energy) in February 2007, even after the deal enabled the industry to double the price of a pound of uranium within the next four months.[22] There was barely a flutter in March, when the Dutch chemical firm Akzo Nobel raked in $14.4 billion by selling its drug division, Organon BioSciences, to the drug maker Schering-Plough. The silence was just as complete in August, when the selfsame Akzo Nobel paid $16 billion for the British paint maker ICI in a deal that blended the world's number one paint manufacturer with the world's number five. In June, when the number one U.S.-managed electronics contract manufacturer Flextronics purchased the number two company Solectron, the buyout merited no more than a brief in the *Financial Times*.[23]

Then suddenly the frenzy turned to fear. It is impossible to identify a particular moment as the official conclusion of any particular boom. For many, however, the pinprick that popped this bubble came on June 21, 2007, when the U.S. private equity firm the Blackstone Group raked in $4.13 billion when it offloaded a huge pile of shares onto the public.[24] The sale succeeded despite months of press reports that had wondered whether this sale was, in and of itself, proof that the end had come; one *MarketWatch* headline a week before the Blackstone offering asked, "Is the Smart Money Cashing Out?"

By mid-July, the answer was in. The deal makers were in full retreat—not because there were no other monopolies to forge, but because there was no more money with which to forge them. The U.S. subprime mortgage debacle, still more than a year from melting down Wall Street, had cascaded into international credit markets, many of which now all but froze up.[25]

Then, after the Meltdown of 2008, the M&A mania started right back up again. This time, however, it was powered by the federal government. Despite the proof provided by Lehman Brothers that many U.S. corporations were already "too big to fail," the immediate response of Henry Paulson's Treasury Department to the financial crisis was to engineer as many mergers among the sick banks as possible and to float the deals whenever necessary, both directly with bailout funds and indirectly though the manipulation of the tax code to favor consolidations.

Even when we saw banks split into smaller pieces—such as with Citibank in January 2009—the units that were spun off often ended up in the hands of direct competitors. This is what happened when Citibank spun off its brokerage unit Smith Barney, itself the product of a 1997 merger with Salomon Brothers, to Morgan Stanley.

Nor was the further concentration of power after the Meltdown limited to the financial sector or to industries like pharmaceuticals wherein, as we saw in the preface, managers figured out how to tap indirectly into bailout funds. The Meltdown resulted in the final killings in such consumer categories as electronics and housewares, in which the bankruptcies of Circuit City and Linens 'n Things left Best Buy and Bed Bath & Beyond as the last big chains standing. The Meltdown also gave Wal-Mart a huge boost in its long rivalry with fading number two discounter Target.

Indeed the downturn hurt Target so severely that in late October 2008, right in the midst of a collapse precipitated in no small part by real estate shenanigans, hedge fund runner William Ackman tried to force the once virile company to sell the real estate right out from under its own stores.[26] The Meltdown also accomplished what many long-term predations by big industrial firms against smaller rivals had failed to do. One of the most notable collapses was the October 2008 decision by the semiconductor maker Advanced Micro Devices—which for more than a decade has been fingered for extinction by giant Intel—to offload its manufacturing arm and try to survive as a pure design firm.

The pioneering railroad regulator Charles Francis Adams, in a once-famous 1871 essay about the disasters wreaked on American society by speculators like Jay Gould, wrote that "gravitation is the rule, and centralization the natural consequence, in society no less than physics."[27] A later generation of Americans would prove Adams wrong, by showing how to use law to stop monopolists from capturing complete control over any one activity. Yet in the first year of the Obama administration, given the absence of any strategic effort to use our laws to stop such concentration, it was hard to avoid the feeling that we were being sucked into one wildly warped black hole.

In subsequent chapters, we will examine many of the huge social effects that resulted from this massive reorganization of productive activity and power. For now, let's simply catalog a few of the industries that have been largely or entirely remade by mergers just since the early 1990s.

In mining and energy, iron ore, copper, nickel, lithium, vanadium, uranium, and of course, oil and gas. In heavy industry, semiconductors, appliances, steel, glass, and petrochemicals. In agriculture, the systems that supply our hogs, poultry, corn, soybeans, cotton, even the packing of fresh produce. In information management, this includes the software we use in our computers, in our businesses, and on the Internet, as well as the media companies that dominate the delivery of our news. In retail, the trading companies that provide our groceries, general merchandise, home materials, and even restaurant meals.

Not all of our new private monopolies are the product of consolidation. Through the process we call *deregulation* we've seen the delivery into private hands of turnkey monopolies in electricity, water, roads, and telecommunications. Even in markets that still look highly competitive, like automobiles, the underlying reality is of ever tighter technology alliances and sales alliances among nominal competitors, as well as a growing number of subterranean parts monopolies that are organized into the Hydra structures we touched on in the preface.

One of the more pronounced patterns after this last wave of monopolization was that it was the countries that boasted of having the most "free-market" policies—the United States, Britain, Australia, and Mexico—that ended up with the greatest concentrations of private governance. This was especially true in retail. Just as Wal-Mart has emerged as the superdirector of the U.S. consumer economy, the grocery chain Tesco leaped far into the lead in Britain,[28] and in Australia the grocery business was split by a duopoly of Coles and Woolworths.

Then there is Mexico, one of the more dramatic cases of monopolization of a nation's economy and one of the purest examples of what happens to a nation that follows the Thatcher-Reagan-Clinton approach to economic regulation. Thanks in no small part to the efforts by the last three U.S. presidents to encourage Mexico to adopt gringo-style "free markets" and "free trade," the hundred million or so citizens of Mexico now find themselves crushed under a complex network of monopolies, many of them owned by a single man.

A mere sixteen years after the signing of the North American Free Trade Agreement (NAFTA), a people who expected that following the economic lead of the United States would bring more economic and political liberty and opportunity has discovered instead that a single man, Carlos Slim, whom the *Wall Street Journal* calls "Mexico's Mr. Monopoly," managed to capture control of more than 7 percent of all the business activity in the entire nation.[29] This includes control over 92 percent of Mexico's fixed telephone lines and 73 percent of its cell phone business.

Slim is also a big player in banking, mining, construction, cigarettes, and railways. In all, Slim's empire of more than two hundred companies accounts for a phenomenal one-third of Mexico's top stock market index—and it's spreading north. There is at least one U.S. newspaper in which you are unlikely to read any new exposes of Mr. Slim's power. That's because in early 2009, the struggling *New York Times*, which had once referred to Mr. Slim as a "robber baron," accepted a $250 million "loan" from him.[30]

What matters most for our story is not how maniacally financiers push merger deals at any given moment, or even who wins from any given deal and who loses. Nor is the point whether the ultimate purpose of any one deal is to forge an economic power or merely to rake in a bunch of fast cash by forging what appears to be a power and then offloading it, along with all the debt loaded upon it, onto the public.

What matters is, first, the new physical structures and political powers that these manic bursts of buying and reorganizing leave behind in the real economy. This, of course, is where all the real goods and real services on which we depend are produced and delivered, and it is where most of us earn our real livings. One thing the latest deal delirium did leave behind, even more than the three M&A frenzies it built upon, was a vast number of monopolies and near monopolies.[31] Furthermore, thanks to the debt that was loaded on them to float the deal, an awful lot of these were all but bankrupt at birth.[32]

The second thing that matters is how these deals affect our political landscape. A month before the presidential election of 1912, Woodrow Wilson addressed his supporters in Lincoln, Nebraska.

"Which do you want?" he asked. "Do you want to live in a town patronized by some great combination of capitalists who pick it out as a suitable place to plant their industry and draw you into their employment? Or do you want to see your sons and your brothers and your husbands build up business for themselves under the protection of laws which make it impossible for any giant, however big, to crush them and put them out of business, so that they can match their wits here, in the midst of a free country with any captain of industry or merchant of finance . . . anywhere in the world?"

The United States, Wilson concluded, "is never going to submit to monopoly. America is never going to choose thralldom instead of freedom."[33]

Were Wilson to rise from his grave today, not even a century later, he would have to admit that his worst-case scenario did not come true. That's because in Wilson's vision the monopolists were companies that actually made things. In Wilson's vision, the monopolists were U.S. citizens, who conceivably felt some occasional twitch of patriotism, even if only during a John Philip Sousa march.

Today, by contrast, our monopolists increasingly don't run companies that make anything. Instead they use banks to run trading companies, built to retail products that are manufactured abroad, built to arbitrage among suppliers, communities, and workers. Increasingly, the people who control these banks and trading companies don't become especially misty-eyed when the band plays "Stars and Stripes Forever." On the contrary, they increasingly view themselves as "global citizens." In fact, growing numbers of them don't live anywhere near the United States, and they never have. They are citizens of faraway countries. Some are even officials of faraway countries. Some, like Mr. Slim, half own those countries.

Perhaps worst of all, as we will see throughout the course of *Cornered*, in a growing number of instances, there's actually no real owner of these monopolies at all.

The Unkept Secret

If you happened to turn on your television on the evening of February 15, 2006, you might have heard the following rant: "In late stage capitalism, you get a lot of monopolistic deals that totally shaft most of the population but can make you a lot of money. We are in an age of monopolies. It was one of the earliest theorists who nailed this. The premise is that as capitalism progresses all businesses are going to tend to become monopolies. At least this one bit of Marxism seems to be coming totally true."

Can you remember what show you were watching? Here's a few hints. It was not on PBS or the History Channel or the Spartacist Youth Hour on the local public access station. No, you would have been tuned to one of stock market interlocutor Jim Cramer's nightly tirades on MSNBC.[34]

Is the United States a "free-market" nation? Until the Meltdown and bailout of late 2008, that would have seemed like a trick question—like asking if Old Glory is red, white, and blue. In many a corner office and editorial page of New York and Washington, merely to hint at a flaw in our "free-market" system was to risk being labeled a blasphemer. To suggest that Betsy Ross once shacked up with the Marquis de Sade would have raised fewer eyebrows than to imply that our political economy was perhaps not completely and perfectly open and free.

Yet if you wandered away from the glass towers of Wall Street and the marble corridors of Washington out into the executive suites of Corporate America and the rest of the world, where the actual business of business is conducted, even in 2006 you would have heard a lot less talk about the "free" market and a lot more use of political terms like *control* and *legislation*, of "locking up" markets and "locking" others "out." That's because real businesspeople know that success is less a function of better-quality products at lower prices than of good lawyers, friendly legislators, and, for most of the last twenty-five years, a strategic alliance with financiers who will help you buy off, buy up, or bankrupt the competition.

What is the real secret of success in business in the United States in the twenty-first century? Let's start by reading through some of the polite euphemisms in which that secret has been clothed in recent years. Consider an article by two consultants from McKinsey & Company titled "Strategy in an Era of Global Giants."

The "world's largest corporations are greatly increasing their scale and scope," the consultants wrote. Such "mega-institutions" are able to use "their huge size to develop and exploit intangible assets in novel ways" and thereby generate "disproportionately high profits and market values."[35]

Another group of McKinsey consultants declared that record corporate profits simply reflected that U.S. corporate managers are "getting better at M&A."[36]

Increasingly, however, business experts are willing to drop the doublespeak in favor of straight-up honesty about how to get ahead today in the land of the "free" market. Consider a book called *Monopoly Rules: How to Find, Capture, and Control the Most Lucrative Markets in Any Business*, published in 2006 by a professor of strategy and marketing at the University of Chicago. Among the tidbits of advice you will find in that volume is the following: "In Economics 101, you probably learned that monopolies are unnatural, illegal, and rare. Wrong! Wrong! Wrong! In fact, monopolies are often natural, usually legal, and surprisingly common."

Product development? Marketing? Sales? And all the other staples of gaining that "competitive advantage" that MBAs used to study so assiduously back when Harvard Business School professor Michael Porter was America's chief business guru? These "may be valuable," the author of *Monopoly Rules* writes, "but only as tools for achieving the real objective— monopoly control which *guarantees* a company's profitability." Oh yes, and don't forget that you will have to invest in reshaping the people's law to your needs. "Part of the oligopoly profits you earn," our author advises, "will have to be earmarked to pay for top-flight antitrust attorneys."[37]

The making of monopoly—the imposition of complete or near-complete control over an activity that had been organized in an open or semi-open market—is once again the business of business in America. Increasingly, it seems, everyone knows this except the American people.

Indeed, the most difficult question for many young executives—and the capitalists who back them—is which path to monopoly to take. In addition to the M&A deals described in the section above, and classic price fixing by cartels like that of the European vitamin producers we will meet in chapter 3, the mind of man has devised many options. (Many of these are, for all intents, still illegal. The reason they are not prevented is that beginning with the Reagan administration our government stopped enforcing most of our antitrust laws.) These options include the following:

Home-Base Monopoly. The goal here is to build up a defensible regional monopoly and to use that as a power base to enter other markets. This is one of the core strategies honed by firms like Wal-Mart and Home Depot. Harvard Business School professor Pankaj Ghemawat was one of the first to analyze the secrets of Wal-Mart's success, noting more than two decades ago that the retailer had grown by focusing first on small towns. Given that most of these communities "could not support two discounters," Ghemawat wrote, the result was that Wal-Mart gained a "local monopoly." This provided the company with a "sustainable advantage," he concluded, as it moved into more competitive suburbs and cities.[38]

Pincer Monopoly. One of the oldest techniques for capturing and protecting monopoly positions is to use one's existing power to capture a closely related activity, then use control of that other activity to capture or destroy a troublesome competitor. The Italian eyewear manufacturer Luxottica recently provided an excellent example of how this works when it parlayed a roll-up of eyewear retailers in the United States into a takeover of the sunglasses maker Oakley in June 2007. Another good recent example is the 2006 takeover of Premium Standard Farms of Kansas City by Smithfield Foods. This gave the Virginia hog combine a 31 percent share of the hog-processing capacity in the United States as well as direct control over nearly one-fifth of all live hogs in the country.[39] This control of both processing capacity and raw material gave the company a huge advantage, not merely over independent pig farmers, who must sell into a market in which Smithfield is always able to determine the price but also vis-à-vis other processors who do not have such a fine control over the price of their inputs.

"Railroad" Monopoly. Even before the Civil War, financiers began to use the natural monopoly power of the railroads to capture businesses that depended on the railroads. One classic case was the grain trade in the Midwest, soon after it was concentrated by the Chicago grain elevator operators. In an especially infamous instance, speculators Jay Gould and Jim Fisk, along with political machine operator William "Boss" Tweed, used the Erie Railroad to capture the Pennsylvania Bluestone Company and its highly profitable business selling building materials in New York City.[40] Other capitalists managed to accomplish much the same task without actually owning the railroad but merely by leveraging its power. When John D. Rockefeller was rolling up Standard Oil, one of his more successful tactics was to force the railroads that depended on his business to grant him special rates or to choke off the business of his competitors. The most famous modern version of this tactic was Microsoft's effort to leverage its control of operating systems into control of Internet browsers. An ongoing example of this tactic is the effort by telecommunications and cable companies like AT&T and Comcast to exercise power over the programming and Internet content passing through their networks.

Trading Monopoly. This technique was one of the secrets behind the rise to power of many of the most successful U.S. businesses of the 1990s. One of the best examples is Nike, which owes much of its incredible success to its decision to abandon manufacturing entirely and to rely instead on contract manufacturers in Taiwan and China for almost all of its products. Rather than tie up its capital in machines and skilled laborers, the company invested instead in marketing and strategic alliances with retailers in the United States, a decision that enabled it to capture more than 80 percent of the market for certain types of athletic shoes and then use the dependence this created among all but the biggest retailers to demand the right to "police" the shoes on their shelves.[41]

Middleman Monopoly. Traders have always sought to build positions of power between the producer and the end user. In recent years, Americans have seen a dramatic rise of a new form of middleman, one that is designed to take advantage of the fashion among many firms to outsource basic management functions like purchasing. One of the most powerful examples of such new middlemen is the group purchasing organizations (GPOs) that buy medical supplies for U.S. hospitals. As we will see in chapter 6, the biggest and most powerful GPOs have entered extremely lucrative alliances with monopoly manufacturers like Johnson & Johnson and Becton, Dickinson and Company, with the profit coming out of our pockets.

Privatized Public Monopoly. The simplest and fastest way to build a private monopoly is not to build it at all but merely to buy it or lease it from the government, convince the government to "deregulate" an already existing private monopoly that you control, or persuade a government to "outsource" basic state functions to your private firm. One of the main reasons that the cost of electricity soared in the United States in the decade leading up to September 2008 has nothing to do with the OPEC oil cartel and everything to do with efforts to "unleash competitive forces" in what had been carefully regulated utilities. What was actually unleashed was a pack of financiers who competed among themselves to see who could be the first and fastest to sack these vital systems, such as by selling off or mortgaging crucial assets, confident in their ability to still use these institutions, no matter how degraded, to tax their customers. The fast money to be made through such deals has led to a scramble by U.S. investment banks to broker the sell-off of everything from New Jersey port facilities to Colorado highways to Ohio water plants, nowadays mainly to monopolists overseas.[42]

Leapfrog Monopoly. One of the easiest ways to escape a business environment heavily regulated by government and operate entirely outside the existing framework of law is to repackage an old business in a "new technology." This is especially important in the case of systems that other companies depend on to deliver their products and services to their end customer. This was true of the railroads right after the Civil War, which for a long time managed to avoid the common carriage rules that applied to stagecoaches and steamboats. In recent years we have seen this with cable television providers, which managed to take control of a system that until recently was regulated by our public government. We have also seen this with Internet service providers, search engines, mobile phone services, and Microsoft-style operating-system monopolies.

Futures Monopoly. One of the simplest ways to achieve a monopoly is for a financier to capture power over the supply of futures contracts in the markets for products like wheat and then use that power to, for a short time, set the price. This sort of monopolization was largely kept under control in the early years of the United States by state and local governments and, beginning with the Interstate Commerce Act in 1888, by federal regulatory agencies. The degradation of market regulatory laws since the 1980s has led to a steady increase in such speculation over the last two decades, however, with such activity culminating in a truly spectacular explosion of prices in the four years before July 2008. In the oil industry, for instance, we saw the first supply shock in history achieved not through the physical cutoff of supply at the well, pipeline, border, or refinery but through a cutoff of supply of futures contracts.

The business of business in the United States today is certainly not complete once the monopoly has been forged. Thereafter, the monopoly must be kept and used. Here, too, the mind of man has devised many techniques. The two most simple and important are to:

Respect Others' Monopolies. In exchange, they will respect yours. U.S. health insurers provide a fine example of how this works. A 2006 study revealed that in 166 of the top 294 metropolitan areas, a single insurer controls more than half of the HMO and preferred provider business.[43] We see the same polite retreat from direct conflict with "competitors" in many agricultural activities, like poultry production. Purdue and Tyson, for instance, organize their processing networks so that the farmers who raise birds in certain regions of the country have, for all intents, only one place to sell the products of their labor. Such trading off of markets is also increasingly common among "manufacturing" conglomerates, which every day appear more loath to challenge an entrenched leader. Indeed, through a practice called category management, which we will look at in more detail in chapter 2, big retailers like Wal-Mart often actually force their suppliers to cooperate openly with one another to groom their product lines in ways that suppress or completely eliminate direct, real-time competition.

Perfect Your Own Monopolies. A good example here is the industrial parts manufacturer Parker Hannifin, a $9 billion company that manufactures products ranging from industrial valves to hydraulic fan motors to metal fittings for oil rigs. Beginning in 2001, after years of consolidation within the parts-making industry, the firm realized that it could alter its traditional cost-plus pricing policies. Managers began to actively sift through Parker Hannifin's more than eight hundred thousand parts to identify cases in which the firm enjoyed a monopoly or near monopoly, in order to jack up prices accordingly, often by much more than 50 percent. The strategy has proved so successful that, as the *Wall Street Journal* reported, the company has reorganized its "innovation" process to focus on the development and grooming of new monopoly positions.[44]

The roll-up of control over the U.S. political economy has been so successful and so complete that sometimes even the most vigorous supporters of laissez-faire capitalism admit to having doubts, sometime big ones. Let's flip the channel back to Jim Cramer. After the Justice Department approved Whirlpool's plan to buy Maytag in June 2006 in a deal that gave the people who run that firm control of an astounding 75 percent share of washer and dryer sales in the United States, the MSNBC stock star declared that "Whirlpool and Maytag never should've been allowed to combine. But now that [the deal is] reaping dividends, Cramer likes it."

Then Cramer continued in a more serious vein, saying that if "there was ever any doubt in your mind that we have a government of, by, and for the corporations, if you thought for a second that we weren't right back in the Gilded Age, if you had the least ounce of faith in our regulators to do the right thing, you've gotta believe Cramer now." And in one of the more honest comments we have heard recently about the return of monopoly to America, Cramer concluded, "On TV I play a guy who's just out to make you money, but when you're not trying to get rich, feel free to get mad."[45]

The Feud over Feudalism

How did America, the land of "free-market capitalism," become the land of monopoly? That's a big question, one that requires the full length of this book to answer. Then again, there's no way to structure my argument without offering a provisional answer here at the beginning. Perhaps the best way to do so is to remind ourselves of what monopoly meant to the early Americans, and then reframe the question this way: how did such a well-educated and vigilant people miss such a fantastic political revolution right in their midst?

Most of us are familiar with the grievances that led the colonial-era Americans to renounce British rule and the battles in which we won independence. Most of us, however, are less well versed in the political and economic conflicts that took place in the new republic among different groups of U.S. citizens. In fact, as soon as we declared the United States independent of British rule, we found ourselves faced with the challenge of determining *who among us* would remain independent of *domestic* lords.

Today our recollections of liberty in the early United States tend to be dominated by the fact that the founders accepted, albeit in many cases grudgingly, the perpetuation of racial slavery in the South. Yet the question of which citizens within our new republic would enjoy full liberty within our republic was also of immense importance to the great majority of white Americans, who were mostly descended from English, Scottish, Irish, German, and French immigrants.

In England at that time, the term *independent* was applied mainly to a man who did not have to curry the favor of other, "better" men. This usually meant a man who controlled a significant amount of property, be it land or a trading monopoly. The result was a society characterized by vast class distinctions, in which very few men stood over multitudes of "lesser" men, who both served them and depended from them in what was in essence a feudal relationship.

In the United States, many of the founders planned to perpetuate this same basic social structure within the new republic. This new country would differ from England in that its grand men would be even more free, for they would owe no allegiance to any central sovereign.

Nevertheless, true independence would still be limited to members of a very small class. The great mass of the people would continue to labor for great men and rely upon them both economically and politically.

This way of thinking is often associated with Alexander Hamilton, the first secretary of the treasury. Hamilton was one of the most brilliant of the founders. Few other Americans in those years understood as well as he did that to maintain our independence as a nation we needed to establish a strong economy and a secure industrial base. Fewer still understood how to accomplish this.

Thus, it was Hamilton who established our national financial system, and it was Hamilton who in his *Report on Manufactures* in 1791 drew up the nation's first industrial strategy. The reasoning in that document was quite simple. To defend itself, the United States needed arms.

This required a good infrastructure and large-scale industry. This in turn required concentration of capital and of men.

Which in turn required Americans to decide how to govern such masses of capital and men. And it was at this point that Hamilton made clear that his intent was to use these necessary concentrations not merely to ensure that our new republic was provisioned with, say, modern rifles but also to concentrate political power among a new elite composed of his friends and allies. Hamilton made his intent most clear when he founded the first real political party, the Federalists, to coordinate political work among the men he believed would serve as the ruling class of landlords and industrial masters.

We usually associate opposition to this way of thinking with James Madison and Thomas Jefferson. That's because soon after Hamilton founded the Federalist Party, Madison and Jefferson organized a second party, to oppose Hamilton's vision and to represent the interest of the common citizens of this country. Madison and Jefferson differed from Hamilton most dramatically in their belief that *all* Americans (or at least all white male Americans) could be independent, not merely one out of every hundred or every thousand. These citizens would accomplish great tasks by grouping together more or less voluntarily.

Hamilton and the Federalists in the 1790s swiftly put the new government in Washington to work helping them increase their economic and political power relative to the rest of the American people. They did so in many ways, such as by structuring taxes to favor better capitalized businesses and by distributing grants of monopoly power among the elite over some trade, manufacture, or service. They also dispatched federal agents and, in the case of one antimonopoly rebellion in western Pennsylvania, even an entire army to enforce their claim on these newly minted properties.

Madison and Jefferson, by contrast, believed that the central purpose of government was to protect the individual citizen from falling under the economic power of any such small company of rich men, whether located abroad or at home. In their view, one of the most important roles of government was to break or harness all monopolies. Madison and Jefferson made their political goal clear in the name they chose for their new political organization: the Democratic-Republican Party.

Ever since, the central battle in our political economy has been between those who would use our federal and state governments to establish and protect private monopolies to empower and enrich the few and those who would use our governments to break or harness private monopolies in order to protect the liberties and properties of the many. For most of our history, the American people used the Democratic Party (the eventual heir to the Democratic-Republican Party) as their main tool to fight the monopolists. (The main exception to this came after the Democratic Party fell under the near complete domination of the Southern planters in the 1850s. Many Americans opposed to concentrated political economic power during these years gathered instead under the banners of the Free Soil and newly formed Republican parties.)

This brings us back to our question—how did such a well-educated and vigilant people allow the few among us to reimpose so many monopolies upon us?

The simplest answer is that beginning in the late 1970s, and culminating with the presidential election of Bill Clinton in 1992, the interests that favor monopoly in the United States managed not merely to greatly solidify control over the Republican Party but also, for the first time since Grover Cleveland sat in the White House in the late nineteenth century, to take control of the Democratic Party.

To understand how swiftly this took place, let's look briefly at, first, the bipartisan opposition that met Reagan's plan and then at the rapidity with which the Clinton administration moved to forge monopolies where even Reagan had never dared to tread.

When Reagan's "regulators" made clear that they no longer intended to enforce our antimonopoly laws, the man who took the lead in opposing the putsch was Democratic senator Howard Metzenbaum of Ohio. He made clear that his opposition was based on political rather than economic grounds.

"Vigorous antitrust enforcement is an essential underpinning to the free enterprise private economy," Metzenbaum wrote. Over the course of two hundred years, he said, the American people, acting through Congress, had made repeatedly clear that the main purposes of our antimonopoly laws were "social and political." Higher prices were the least of our worries, he insisted. Monopolists would destroy small businesses and repress U.S. workers. They would retard and pervert innovation, undermine the security of the nation, and corrupt the political system.

Metzenbaum was swiftly joined by a number of moderate liberals and moderate conservatives of both parties, many of whom issued similar apocalyptic warnings. Many of the strongest critics were Republicans, including Senator Arlen Specter of Pennsylvania, Senator Slade Gordon of Washington, and Senator John Danforth of Missouri.[46]

Now let's jump ahead to January 1993, when Bill Clinton took office after twelve years of Republican rule. If anything, the Clinton administration's attitudes toward monopolization were *even more favorable* than those of Reagan or of George H. W. Bush. Almost immediately after Clinton took office, Deputy Secretary of Defense William J. Perry set in motion a process of roll-ups that reduced the number of large defense firms from 107 to 5.

Clinton regulators also cleared the way for massive consolidations in the oil industry, including such megamergers as Exxon with Mobil and BP with Amoco, and in telecommunications, where they allowed financiers to reverse much of the Reagan-era breakup of AT&T. Clinton regulators did nothing to prevent corporations like Tyson and Smithfield from seizing the properties of hundreds of thousands of independent farmers, and they turned their backs to the single greatest period of growth in U.S. history by retailers like Wal-Mart.

Perhaps most disturbing was their decision, after promising to do the opposite, to allow the consolidation of U.S. media companies that had begun under Reagan to continue in a process that cut the number of big firms from more than fifty to six. Clinton did not merely transform the Democratic Party into a mirror of the GOP on this issue of such fundamental importance to the American people. But, if we add in his administration's revolutionary rewriting of our trade laws, our banking laws, and our market regulatory laws, it becomes clear that Clinton set the process of monopolization and concentration of control by the few into overdrive.[47]

The simplest and most obvious reason that we the American people did not notice the political revolution that is monopolization—which resulted in such a vast shift of power away from us and into the hands of a few—is that for a full generation there has been no public debate on the issue. And there has been no public debate because both of our major parties are now under the control of the same monopolist powers.

And Then There Was Less Than One

Some months before I met Diane Cochrane in Arizona, I took a short detour during a trip through the Midwest to drive through Emporia, Kansas. The town is located on the geological divide between the rich and rolling Osage Prairie of eastern Kansas and the choppier Flint Hills, where the thin rocky soils are more suitable to grazing. That's why Emporia is surrounded with immense grain elevators and old cattle corrals and is interlaced with rail lines. It's also why, some years ago, companies that sell pet food began to locate their canning operations here. One of the more recent arrivals was the Canadian-owned firm Menu Foods.

In the late nineteenth century, American writers and illustrators often characterized monopolies as octopuses of immense size, their tentacles entwining farms and markets and state capitol buildings. In retrospect, I suppose that my own trip down Emporia's wide, empty Commercial Street, past the Lariat Lounge and Pupusa Plus, had a certain Ahab-like quality to it.

It was not hard to find the Menu Foods cannery, in an industrial zone southeast of town. Although there was no sign out front, the hard breeze had extended the white flag adorned with the Menu Food's corporate icon, a group of puppies at a pet food bowl. But once I got close to the factory I found it hard to ascribe much evil content to the scene. Perhaps it was the oak leaves glittering in the sun or the workers lounging contentedly at a picnic table outside. Whatever, I knew almost immediately that this was not the great white cetacean that I sought.

So let's return to Arizona, drive back along Highway 69 from Diane Cochrane's home to the nearby Wal-Mart Supercenter, and review the chain of power responsible for setting a foil pouch of Special Kitty filled with melamine on a shelf in Prescott, from where Diane picked it up and dropped it into her shopping cart, in a scene repeated hundreds of millions of times every day all across the United States. Doing so will start us along the path to understanding how the way today's monopolists rule leads so often to ruin, not merely in the pet food industry but throughout our society.

Let's start by reviewing what we know. First, even though the Special Kitty brand is sold only at Wal-Mart, the foil pouches were filled not by Wal-Mart employees but by workers at the Menu Foods plant in Emporia. Many of the other cans and pouches of pet food on Wal-Mart's shelves, which appear to offer "competitive alternatives" to Special Kitty, were also packed in the exact same Menu Foods plant.

Second, Wal-Mart retails *more than half* of all the pet food sold in the United States. This means that although Wal-Mart brand foods like Special Kitty account for only a fraction of the business of Menu Foods, once we add in all of the name-brand cans that are produced here under contract for firms like Procter & Gamble, we see that sales at Wal-Mart, albeit indirectly, account for by far the greatest bulk of this small company's total revenue.

Third, Menu Foods has for years been under huge financial pressure, as indicated by the fact that the company has barely scraped together a profit in years: in 2005, Menu Foods lost $54.6 million, and in 2007, it lost $62 million.[48] Much, if not most, of this pressure comes from Wal-Mart, either directly, as the titanic retailer hammers down day after day what it pays for each Special Kitty pouch, or indirectly, as it also hammers down what it will pay the big food conglomerates like P&G for each can of their "branded" pet food, much of which also comes from Menu Foods.

Fourth, Wal-Mart is also under constant financial pressure from financiers to improve its margins. This pressure comes from mainstream investment funds and banks like JPMorgan Chase and Thrivent. It also comes from shareholder activists like the National Legal and Policy Center, which routinely attacks the firm for even hinting that it might respond to some concern of society—like toxic pet food—by leaving a coin or two on the table.[49]

Fifth, given the natural limits on how swiftly the U.S. economy can grow, the easiest way for Wal-Mart to meet the demands of the financiers is to take business from other retailers, like Target, Safeway, and the now-defunct Circuit City and Linens 'n Things. Given that the surest way for Wal-Mart to take business from these retailers is to offer its customers lower prices than its rivals can offer for the exact same products, Wal-Mart is all but compelled to use its immense power to extract concessions from all those under its sway.

Sixth, on the day I visited Menu Foods in Emporia, everything seemed to be business as usual. Even though it was only half a year or so after the recall, and even though there had been ample speculation that Menu Foods would soon go out of business because of its failings, the front door was still open. So too were the gates to the loading dock out back, where I saw trailers painted with Wal-Mart's name and colors taking on new loads.[50]

Taking all these considerations together, we can reasonably conclude that the purchase by some desperate Menu Foods manager of counterfeit wheat gluten spiked with melamine and the subsequent blending of this toxin into the country's pet food system was an *almost inevitable* result of the particular way that power is exercised through this chain of activity.

Even though Menu Foods is not owned directly by Wal-Mart, it is for all intents *captive* to Wal-Mart. This captivity ensures that Wal-Mart enjoys the ability to exercise its power over the entire pet food canning system in ways that enable the giant trading company to *maximize* the wealth it extracts from that system. But unlike more formal forms of vertical integration, the overall design of the present system ensures that Wal-Mart enjoys the ability to *minimize* any need to consider the well-being of the machines, the livestock, the workers, the managers, or the investors at Menu Foods or at any of the other pet food purveyors that have fallen under its sway. Even when failing to do so results in the degradation of the system and the products that come from it.[51]

In a sense, Menu Foods can be viewed as little more than a mirror image of Wal-Mart, spreading its tentacles though the once diversified system of pet food supply, as it slowly reaches up through this relatively simple industry to meet the touch of the mother monopoly. Menu Foods also helps to illustrate the process of socialization of these activities that Wal-Mart's massive, centralized power sets into motion. In the process of weaving its tentacles through this system, Menu Foods ever so slowly consolidates so many of these once-diversified and compartmentalized activities that it becomes all but impossible to hold any one firm responsible for this crime or to cleanse the overall system of failure.

And sure enough, even though Menu Foods is for all intents both financially and physically bankrupt, and even though the company failed so egregiously to accomplish the prime task it theoretically exists to perform—to deliver safe food to pets—it remains in business today.

It is important that we situate Wal-Mart in the proper position in this newfangled hierarchy. Many of Wal-Mart's boosters like to claim that the company unifies the interests of all U.S. consumers. By merging Diane Cochrane into an army of a hundred million or so other pet owners in America who shop at Wal-Mart, the company can exercise power in ways that will serve Diane's interests, or so these Wal-Mart defenders claim.

Yet as the capture and control of Menu Foods clearly shows, Wal-Mart is not a consumer-friendly agent located *between* the consumer and Menu Foods. On the contrary, the company sits *atop* the entire system, from where it determines—not necessarily consciously—who shall make what and how much they shall earn, and who shall buy what and how much they shall pay.

In 1962, Milton Friedman wrote that "the consumer is protected from coercion by the seller because of the presence of other sellers with whom he can deal."[52] The American consumer today has almost no power over Wal-Mart. As Diane mentioned, the company's stores so dominate our landscape that we have no choice in the matter anymore. Not only must we take whatever can of food they decide to stick into our hands, sometimes we and our pets must also swallow a little poison in the bargain.

Before we go on, let's make sure that we do not blame Wal-Mart per se or any one person in that corporation for this state of affairs. As we have seen with similar poisonings in our systems of supply for spinach, peanut butter, heparin, and flu vaccines, and as we have also seen from the *structural socialization* of industrial activities ranging from electronics to chemicals and to the making of piston rings, superconsolidation is pretty much standard operating procedure for all industries in the United States these days. And one of its standard results is the degradation of these systems.

There is nothing mysterious about any of this. Monopoly is, after all, merely a form of government that one group of human beings imposes on another group of human beings. Its purpose is simple—to enable the first group to transfer wealth and power to themselves. Monopolists use such private governments to organize and disorganize, to grab and smash, to rule and ruin, in ways that serve their interests only. At bottom, monopoly is merely a political tool. Individual monopolies succeed economically usually not because the particular firm in question offers a better product or service but merely because it was better capitalized.

Take Wal-Mart. If founder Sam Walton had never been born, America's financiers, as a class, would simply have erected their government under some other corporate banner.

2

Supply and Command

When it comes to walking around malls, I was trained by a master. I grew up in Miami, and under my mother's tutelage I came to know not merely every store in every shopping complex, from Dadeland to Lincoln Road to Omni to 163rd Street to the Hollywood Fashion Center, but also pretty much every crack in every tile in front of every Orange Julius stand along the way.

Not that we would return home loaded with bags of useless items to stuff into closets or, for that matter, with all that many useful items. We rarely climbed into the LeMans with anything more than a Hallmark bag in our hands and maybe a mustard stain on our lips. The purpose of our excursions was not to buy anything but merely to shop—or, to be honest, to know where to find the things we might want if ever we stumbled across a suitcase of cash washed up on the beach.

The Fashion Place Mall south of Salt Lake City is housed in a tan-colored, white-roofed building that seems intended to evoke the snow-capped wall of the Wasatch Range that looms behind it. It's a late winter's day, and a haze diffuses the sun into a colorless and ubiquitous glow that makes my eyes feel as if I had spent the morning submerged in a motel pool. Yet as the front door of the mall swishes shut behind me, I feel a deep and familiar sense of ease. I am here to do a little comparison shopping for prescription sunglasses—and some on-the-ground research for the book—so my first stop is one of those multicolored illuminated mall maps.

According to the directory, I've come to the right place. There are four retail outlets here: LensCrafters, Knighton Optical, Sears Optical, and Sunglass Hut. Sure enough, as I stroll along the central corridor, I am treated to a series of mall tableaux that, had I not done my research beforehand, would surely have convinced me I was wandering through a well-kept garden of competition. In the optical department at Sears, I spy two customers perusing the eyewear offerings. At Sunglass Hut, three teenagers huddle shoulder to shoulder, trying on frames and giggling. At LensCrafters, the store brims with six customers who are carefully examining the offerings or chatting softly with salespeople.

It's only when I gaze across the corridor from LensCrafters that I get my first physical evidence that something is awry in the Fashion Place Mall. Knighton Optical is closed, its metal gates shut tight, its eyewear cases empty, its fluorescent lights dark. This is exactly the confirmation I came here to find. Thanks to my research, I know that LensCrafters, Sears Optical, and Sunglass Hut are all owned by the same company, the Italian eyewear conglomerate Luxottica. The closure of Knighton means that at least for the eyewear business, the Fashion Place Mall has been monopolized.

Many historians will trace the end of the Consumer Age in the United States to the September 2008 Meltdown of Wall Street. That's certainly a reasonable way to look at the world, if your focus is on the financial foundations of the Great Global Bubble. Even if it didn't quite match the duration of the musical *Cats* on Broadway, the era of the Bubble certainly provided Americans with quite a run. For more than fifteen years, beginning in early 1993, we were allowed to act out the role of "global" consumers in chief, our fickle fingers flinging favor across the face of the earth, the slightest alteration in our tastes repositioning merchant fleets and reordering nations. In exchange for this service, we were rewarded with mountains of merchandise that seemed to flow into our homes via conveyor belt.

The reason I am standing in front of the shuttered entryway of Knighton Optical is to offer a slightly different take on this history. In my view, the "global system" plumbed by Bill Clinton and the other global utopians in the 1990s was unsustainable from the moment of conception, being nothing more than a Ponzi-like pipeworks for cycling an ever greater flow of dollars every year from the tills of Chinese and Japanese manufacturers into the wallets of U.S. consumers, who were expected to flush them right back again. This all worked just fine until one day, when all the debt in the system finally topped the levees.

In my alternate history, the Consumer Age in the United States actually ended years ago, with the overturning of the laws that prevented a company like Luxottica from monopolizing the sale of eyewear in our fashion malls and along our main streets.

Luxottica is certainly not the only dominant player in our malls. One reason I felt so at ease as soon as I entered the Fashion Place is that almost all the stores and brands looked so familiar. This is a familiarity that stretches across both space and time. Not only are these the same stores—Ann Taylor, Brookstone, J. Crew, the Gap—that I can shop in today in South Florida (or in any major city in the country, for that matter), they are also largely the same stores I shopped in when my friends were coifing themselves like Duran Duran. There's a simple reason for this, which is that during the same two decades that saw the dramatic rise of the Wal-Mart–style trading companies, the U.S. mall was colonized by a very few big retail corporations, each of which controls a cluster of stores.

What Luxottica provides is one of the more dramatic illustrations of the march to monopoly. Until the 1980s, anyone buying glasses in the United States was likely to stroll into one of the thousands of small stores run by individual and independent opticians and optometrists, who purchased their wares from dozens of suppliers and who often fashioned frames right on site. Yet almost as soon as the Reagan administration made clear its intention to overturn our antimonopoly laws, a few people began to use chains like LensCrafters and Pearle Vision to take the business of these independent entrepreneurs and craftsmen.

The backers of Luxottica did not enter the retail fray in the United States until 1995, when they bought one of these premade consolidation machines in the form of LensCrafters. In 1999, the Italian firm began to expand in earnest, buying the Ray-Ban brand from Bausch & Lomb. In 2001, Luxottica bought the Sunglass Hut chain of nineteen hundred stores. Then three years later it delivered its knockout blow, seizing control of Cole National, which owned Pearle Vision, as well as the optical departments at Sears, Target, and JCPenney. (Luxottica also runs the optical departments at Macy's and other Federated stores.)

Not that Luxottica stopped there, however. In June 2007, the company picked up the U.S. eyewear company Oakley for a modest $2.1 billion, an acquisition made nicely affordable by the fact that Luxottica had for years used its control of retail outlets to choke Oakley slowly to death. That deal also brought Luxottica three more retailers, including Bright Eyes and Sunglass Icon, the main competitor of Sunglass Hut.

Now, if you're the kind of consumer who has a bit of spare change jangling in your pocket, you probably don't buy your glasses at LensCrafters or Pearle Vision, let alone Target or Sears. This is fine with Luxottica, because the company has plenty of other ways to capture your custom. Luxottica began life as a manufacturer and still controls the distribution of much of the world's eyewear to what few independent stores remain. Not only does Luxottica sell products under its own name and that of Ray-Ban, it also makes what is sold under such names as Dolce & Gabbana, Donna Karan, Ralph Lauren, and Tag Heuer.

That means there's a very good chance that you will find yourself dealing with Luxottica even if you buy your glasses at a fancy boutique in Beverly Hills or on Fifth Avenue, or if for sunglasses you favor your local REI or the fly fishing shop in Livingston, Montana.

Nor is it easy to escape Luxottica if you fly across the ocean. Along with its crosstown, family-owned, less expansive-minded "rival" Safilo, Luxottica has ranged to the far corners of the world to protect its Italian base of operations from Chinese and other Asian competition (or at least those imports not controlled by Luxottica). In Europe, in Australia, even in China itself—where the company runs four separate chains—there's a good chance that you'll end up buying your eyewear from Luxottica.[1]

This strategy proved to be a fine way to make money, at least when times were good. In the first year after its purchase of Cole, Luxottica smashed its all-time record profit margin. Of course, the question for us is not whether this system serves the interest of an Italian family and its allied clans and retainers, but whether it serves the interests of the American consumer and citizen. To try to answer this, I wander outside the mall and cross the highway to the Spectacle, one of the few independent optical shops still in business in Utah.

Here I am greeted by the owner, John Cottam, a trim and young-looking man with a bushy mustache and graying hair. Cottam's store reminds me of the independent businesses I knew as a kid in South Florida. The room is big, open, airy, and full of light. And with Cottam himself, I am in luck. Not only is he full of insight into his business, he is also a bit of a celebrity craftsman. When Cottam first opened his own shop more than thirty years ago, he was living in Las Vegas, and his ability to craft custom frames soon won him orders from such eyewear icons as Elton John, Slappy White, and even 1970s-era Elvis himself. Cottam also developed a nice sideline bending frames for films, and he is most proud of his work for *Blade Runner*.

Cottam has brought his two sons and one daughter-in-law into his business, not because he is in any rush to retire but because until recently it seemed like such a good way for his family not to have to work for wages. However, it doesn't take long for him to tell me that he's a bit scared these days. Twice now, he whispers, he cut off purchasing from Luxottica because of the way they treat small businesses like his, but also twice now, he was forced back into Luxottica's corral, because the people who control that corporation used it to buy up yet another business or a few of the brand names that people expect to find in an independent store.

Luxottica's capture of Oakley, Cottam says, amounted to a sort of checkmate, for it left him with no practical way not to do business with the Italian firm. Cottam has been on his own for a long time, and he does not like to admit that he might need help. But he's never seen anything like Luxottica before, and he no longer knows how to escape its reach.

At various points in this book, we will talk in greater depth about the vitally important symbiotic relationship between the consumer and the small producer, the small farmer, and the independent craftsman like John Cottam. What I want to emphasize here is that the choices presented to you in the American mall, and the price competition you perceive, is increasingly a facade that is engineered by one or a few firms. The people who run these firms do not respond to any market, and do not learn from consumers, competitors, or upstart innovative craftsmen. Instead they sit atop a hierarchy, from which point they govern entire systems, manipulating everyone inside their fences, including the consumer. The point is not the improvement of overall social welfare but merely their own bottom line.

In Hollywood, if we peer behind the storefront on a movie set, we merely see scaffolding. The point of the storefront is to hide nothing. In the malls and along the main streets of Salt Lake City, Atlanta, and Minneapolis, however, if we peer behind the Hollywood storefronts that have been erected by the monopolists, we actually see something. What we see is not merely the central factory applying different labels to the same cans, nor is it merely the elimination of all opportunity as all the independent craftsmen and farmers and entrepreneurs are chased off their properties and transformed into employees and clerks. What we see is power, structured in a way that determines what we buy and when and how.

In the last chapter, we learned that there are monopolies just about everywhere in the United States today, and these monopolies do not eliminate competition but rather redirect competition so that it takes place between the very rich and all the rest of us. In this chapter, my intent is to show you how the rich use these immense institutions to govern our real economy and that one way they hide this governance is by conjuring up an illusion of choice and an illusion of competitive pricing.

My intent here is also to deepen our understanding of how these monopolists destroy the machines and the skilled workers on which we all depend, by looking at the real physical effects of the "Always Lower Prices" that they promise, and to deepen our understanding of the politically destructive results of such concentration of power.

The Law of Variety

Until the Meltdown of 2008, the average American certainly could be excused for believing that we live in a "paradise of choice," in the words of *Wired* magazine editor Chris Anderson.[2] That's what our eyes told us, anyway. America was the land of the endless shopping aisle, the 24/7 checkout line, the sky-high pile of T-shirts and televisions. That's also what our "experts" kept telling us. Robert Reich, Bill Clinton's secretary of labor, assured us in a 2007 book that U.S. consumers "have more choice than ever before, and can switch more easily to better deals."[3] Barry Schwartz, a psychology professor at Swarthmore College, has even insisted that we have *too many* options.[4]

Before the Meltdown, the sheer number of decisions we were presented with did often feel paralyzing. There were not enough days in the year to sample all of the delights whipped up by the industrious food engineers at places like Ruby Tuesday, California Pizza Kitchen, and the Olive Garden. Nor enough hours in the day to play all the video games, listen to all the songs, view all the videos, or press all the buttons on all the gadgets and gizmos that were set before us. Just to sort through our closets, organize our basements, and dig to the rear wall of our storage units would have taken weeks. It sometimes seemed that life would have been so much easier if whenever we clicked on some item on a Web site, UPS had delivered it straight to the landfill.

Some of this perception was based on fact. Over the last two decades or so, Americans with money enjoyed an expansion not merely of apparent choice but often of real variety. Consider our food economy. Globalization connected us with farm fields and orchards in strange and sunny lands. A new wave of alternative farmers presented us with organic tomatoes, rounds of goat cheese, plumper hens. Superstar chefs befoamed and betruffled our restaurant food. Stores like Whole Foods muscled in next door to the sterile and cheerless Safeways.

Yet even as all this activity was taking place at the margins, the center of the nation's economy was undergoing an even more profound transformation, one that is already well on its way to undoing many of our most important gains. To understand, let's first look at one of the greatest gustatory success stories, the craft beer movement, and its relationship to the corporations that govern our beer industry. Doing so will deepen our understanding of the relationship between power and illusion, and it will make very clear what is really responsible for what real choice we do still enjoy.

The modern era of beer in the United States began October 14, 1978. That was the day the American people, acting through Congress, restored to ourselves our right to brew beer at home without a license. Suddenly we were free to decide all on our own which malted barleys, roasted barleys, and hops to blend into the boil. Suddenly we could sit on the floor of our own kitchens and stare at our carboys as the domesticated fungi we call yeast transformed the sugars in our worts into alcohol, in a mad, swirling frenzy.

There is no way to credit one political act more than another with the reawakening of an American palate long since accustomed to the industrial pabulum churned out by Kraft and Wonder and Hormel. Yet all the home-brew experimentation, all the millions of efforts to reconnect with skills and techniques long ago locked away in distant factories, surely played a big part in leading Americans also to rediscover the charms of sturdy breads, pungent cheeses, and flavorful vegetables.

We know that all the myriad efforts to decipher the secrets inside the can resulted, over the next two decades, in an explosion in the numbers of breweries in our land. Before Prohibition, about fifteen hundred companies brewed beer in the United States. Immediately after the repeal of Prohibition, the number of breweries might have been even higher. However, by the eve of World War II, the number had fallen to about 750, and by 1978, the business of making beer had been consolidated into 42 corporations, the great majority of which produced industrial lager. Today, thirty years after Americans made themselves free to brew beer at home, the total number of companies licensed to make and sell beer in the United States is almost back to the pre-Prohibition level.[5]

Yet when you add up all these new brew operations, their total effect on the nation's beer industry remains quite small. Just before the Meltdown, the United States was producing more than 210 million barrels of beer per year. Of that total, all the microbreweries and brew pubs together accounted for less than 4 percent. Meanwhile, among the industrial brewers, consolidation never stopped. Since 1978, we have witnessed the vanishing, as independent companies, of Stroh's, Schaefer, Carling, Schlitz, Pabst, National, Olympia, Ranier, Lone Star, Schmidt's, Hamm's, Rheingold, Genesee, Piels, Mickey's, and Falstaff, along with many of the beauty pageants, local sporting events, and food festivals these companies once supported. With the merger in 2007 of Miller and Coors, under the direction of South African Breweries (SAB), and the takeover in 2008 of Anheuser-Busch by InBev, the United States, a nation of more than three hundred million people, was basically reduced to reliance on a world-bestriding beer duopoly, run not out of Milwaukee or St. Louis but out of Leuven, Belgium, and Johannesburg, South Africa.[6]

How does this roll-up of control over U.S. industrial beer operations affect you and me? After all, if we walk into our local supermarket, we are presented with a bewildering array of options bursting from the refrigerated case. Do you like straight-up lager? You can choose between Budweiser or Michelob. Do you prefer something lighter? There's Bud Light or Busch Light. Perhaps you want a European brew. Stella Artois and Grolsch beckon. Do you favor a flavor from Asia? Pick up a six-pack of Kirin or Tsingtao. Maybe Mexican will make your day, in which case you can choose between the tropical party offered by Corona and the more robust and hardworking Negra Modelo. Perhaps you're hankering for an old beloved brew from back home, like Rolling Rock or Widmer Brothers. No problem, they beckon patiently, in their smooth, cold, condensation-dappled bottles.

Then again, every single product listed here is either manufactured by or allied with Anheuser-Busch InBev. Never mind that there are dozens of labels arrayed on shelves that stretch at least a hundred feet, and if you stop to read all the ingredients, it would take hours to make it to the other end of the aisle. Every decision about what hop flower to blend in and when, what grain of barley to toast, and even what calorie to put where was made directly or indirectly by a single corporation, with a single integrated laboratory operation, with a single bottom line.

On television, Anheuser-Busch InBev likes to run advertisements suggesting that the company is really a community of jolly brewers who live and breathe and ooze beer and who would never ever put less than eight pounds of two-row pale malt into your India Pale Ale. In reality, such decisions are made by the most desiccated of accountants, who are armed with software systems that automate the tasks of scrimping, hedging, doctoring, and supplanting what is natural with what is chemical in a hundred million barrels of beer all at once, in a process long since distilled to 200-proof ruthlessness. And in reality, Anheuser-Busch InBev, as immense as it is, itself is under the sway of even bigger powers, like Wal-Mart, which has shown no compunction whatsoever about dictating to its suppliers what ingredients to use and where.

Over the years, I have spent a lot of time talking to people who brew for a living. In the early 1990s, this was a community filled with great dreams, one of which was to play by the rules of free enterprise and to beat Budweiser and Miller and Coors and Molson by pouring a better product into your glass. Today it is a community in which just below the surface there prevails a sense of frustration and often outright fear. This is reflected most dramatically in the fact that no one with real capital on the line will say a bad word (on the record) about Anheuser-Busch InBev or South African Breweries—and with good reason.

Everyone in the industry knows what happened in 1996 when Anheuser-Busch decided to take Boston Beer, which brews Sam Adams, down a notch or three.

For reasons still not entirely clear, the giant firm unleashed a devastating, multifront assault by armies of lawyers, lobbyists, and marketers who accused Boston Beer (to the government and to the public through the media) of deceptive packaging. Anheuser-Busch then followed up with an even more devastating second assault, in which it locked Boston Beer products out of the immensely powerful distribution networks that it controls.

Ultimately, an arbitrator rejected all of the megafirm's contentions, and Boston Beer survived to brew another day, but the company, less than 1 percent the size of Anheuser-Busch, was left on the verge of bankruptcy. Meanwhile, sales growth in the craft beer industry as a whole, which had been perking along at a very robust 25 percent per year, plummeted to zero.

In the years since, a truce of sorts has reigned between the megacorporations and the craft brewers. For a while the titans even seemed to acknowledge that the craft brewers served the interests of the industry as a whole, by setting a price umbrella and by leading the war against wine. Yet now that the roll-up of the rest of the beer market is all but complete, there are growing signs that the megacorporations are once again turning their sights onto the craft beer makers. Once again, key raw materials like hops are suddenly in short supply, and the distribution channels, even more consolidated than in 1996, are suddenly and without explanation closed off.

Most disturbing, the megacorporations are venturing much more aggressively into brewing and controlling their own craftlike beers. In the past, big brewers tried their hand at darker, hoppier, fuller, more bitter brews only rarely and with little success. In recent years, however, Anheuser-Busch has begun to brew something it calls American Ale. The company has forged strategic alliances with existing craft breweries like Redhook, Old Dominion, and Wild Goose, pushing their products through its powerful distribution system in exchange for a bigger cut of the profits. Anheuser-Busch also has begun to brew what are essentially *stealth* beers, such as the "organic" brews sold under such labels as Stone Mill Pale Ale or Wild Hop Lager. The label claims these beers are bottled by Green Valley Brewing of California. The real power behind the venture is Anheuser-Busch InBev, of Leuven, Belgium.

The most important lesson for us to take from this story is not what the megacorporations are doing to the craft brewers but why they have not yet wiped them entirely off the map. The reason we still enjoy as much real variety in the beer and wine we find in our communities has nothing at all to do with our power as consumers, with the natural functioning of any free market, or with our own discerning palates.

On the contrary, as we have seen with Menu Foods and with Luxottica, neither our power as consumers nor any natural functioning of a free market is, in and of itself, sufficient to guarantee two of anything, or even one. The only way to prevent any group from using a corporation to shut down all the open markets in which we freely exchange our own products with one another is through the law.

So it is with beer. The only real protection that all the hundreds of small brewers in this country enjoy—the only real force that keeps Anheuser-Busch InBev and SAB from rolling up these tiny pockets of profit and distraction—is the Twenty-First Amendment to the Constitution. In the process of overturning Prohibition, the authors of the amendment returned the power to regulate trade in intoxicating liquors to the individual states, many of which in turn passed the power on to the individual county, city, or town. The result was then, and still is now, a plethora of regulatory approaches and an intricate mosaic of powers that so far have proven impossible even for the immense world-spanning corporations to control entirely.

The interlocking system of small dealers that this bounty of regulatory approaches protects is the only thing that enables a beer drinker in Peoria to buy a bottle (or six) from the brewer of his or her choice in Vermont or Oregon. Just as it is this system that also enables the wine drinker in Peoria to interact with the small winemakers of Napa, the southern Rhone, Priorat, and Mendoza. It is this system of regulation alone that, at least for now, continues to guarantee even to the smallest brewer and winemaker the opportunity to enter a real open market in order to set his or her wares before you, the American consumer. It is a system of regulation the absence of which would surely leave us under the complete power of two, or maybe even one, international corporation run by and for the sake of financiers only, who would be just as happy to make money selling you T-bird in a jug or Swillwaukee juice in a tall-boy can.

It is also a system of regulation that is opposed by all of today's big trading and retail powers, including Anheuser-Busch InBev, SAB, and Wal-Mart. This plethora of regulatory approaches that was spun out by the American people, in all our backwoods wisdom, back in the 1930s is, these great corporate powers insist, not "efficient." In court after court, in state after state, they demand that these laws, which have helped to protect the greatest explosion of variety in the modern United States, be rationalized and simplified, to enable them (so they promise) to save the consumer a penny here and maybe a penny there.[7]

Thus, even this little patch of paradise, as tiny and shaded as it is, may soon be paved. Not that you will likely notice, though, because by the time Anheuser-Busch InBev dispatches the bulldozers, they will surely have taken the art of concocting the faux cornucopia in the cold case to the next level of perfection.

The Illusion of Choice

In the United States, the idea that a particular economic activity or even the economy as a whole might require some sort of sovereign to organize activity from the top down to ensure maximum "efficiency" traces back at least to the Gilded Age, after the Civil War.[8] It was then that the railroaders, exhausted from interminable rate wars among themselves and from increasingly stronger assaults from the customers they abused, began to dream of a control more powerful than the loose cartels and pools they had relied on up to then. The idea became a reality in the late nineteenth century, when the banker J. P. Morgan took upon himself the task of using his financial power to organize and "rationalize" (make efficient) first the railways and then, through his control of the railroads, many other industries, and then to run these industries in such a way as to maximize the manufacture of cash.

The reason I bring up Morgan's power here is to help us to understand the true political nature of the more faceless political powers behind the Hollywood storefronts in today's malls and behind the cold cases in today's supermarkets. In the next chapter, we will look at how the application of top-down power results in the destruction of variety and quality, not merely in small firms like Menu Foods but also in such immense operations as Coca-Cola, Nestlé, and Kraft.

Here I simply want to make sure that we fully appreciate the scale and the scope of these powers, by looking at one of the largest of these entities, Procter & Gamble. I also want to make sure that we appreciate fully how this firm, as immense as it is, interlinks with and is largely governed by an even more powerful and more central economic director, Wal-Mart. Doing so will enable us to understand how over the last generation a few people among us have resurrected Morgan's centralized planning state—mostly without our even noticing the fact—and now use this private state to direct most of our consumer economy. This is a private state that uses its power to maximize not any particular social good but only the production of cash. It is also a state that, thanks to modern information technologies, is able to direct power far more extreme than ever before and to focus that power far more exactly than was ever imagined by Morgan.

To start, let's consider a few of the sales figures that Procter & Gamble has been able to rack up since its 2005 takeover of Gillette. As a percentage of the total U.S. market, P&G controls the following:

- More than 75 percent of men's razors
- About 60 percent of laundry detergent
- Nearly 60 percent of dishwasher detergent
- More than 50 percent of feminine pads
- About 50 percent of toothbrushes
- Nearly 50 percent of batteries
- Nearly 45 percent of paper towels, just through the Bounty brand
- Nearly 40 percent of toothpaste
- Nearly 40 percent of over-the-counter heartburn medicines
- Nearly 40 percent of diapers.
- About 33 percent of shampoo, coffee, and toilet paper[9]

As striking as some of these numbers are, they tell only part of the story.[10] That's because Wal-Mart and a few other giant trading companies are so powerful that, at least for the time being, they do not fear further concentration in their supply base. On the contrary, they routinely force giant suppliers like P&G to form overt cartels with their direct competitors.

Individual retailers used to draw up their own merchandising plans, in which they would decide for themselves—based on their sense of the tastes of their local community of customers—which brands to promote, how much shelf space to devote to each, which products to place at eye level, and so on. These days, Wal-Mart, Target, and other big retailers have adopted a philosophy of control called *category management*. Under this system, these retailers name a single supplier to serve as a *category captain*. This supplier is expected to manage all the shelving and marketing decisions for an entire family of products, such as dental care.[11]

The retailer then requires all the other producers of this class of products—these days, usually no more than one or two other firms—to cooperate with the captain. The consciously intended result of this tight cartelization is a growing specialization of production and pricing among the few big suppliers who are still in business. This means that

Procter & Gamble's actual market share of many specialized items is much higher than the above numbers suggest.[12]

It's not that Wal-Mart and category copycats like Target cede all control over shelving and hence production decisions to these captains. The trading firms use the process mainly to gain more insight into the operations of the manufacturers and hence more leverage over them, their suppliers, and even their other clients. The goal is not merely to increase the "efficiency" that they claim derives from eliminating competition. It is also to understand how these companies produce what they produce and hence how they engineer their own profits. This knowledge then enables the traders to capture a larger share of those profits for themselves. That's why in recent years, these big firms—Wal-Mart, especially— have begun to dictate to the producers what ingredients to put into their own branded products, how to package them, and how to price them.[13]

Wal-Mart, for instance, has told Coca-Cola what artificial sweetener to use in a diet soda, it has told Disney what scenes to cut from a DVD, it has told Levi's what grade of cotton to use in its jeans, and it has told lawn mower makers what grade of steel to buy.[14]

And don't think that such consolidation within the Wal-Mart system makes it easier for new small manufacturers and retailers to rise up and compete. The exact opposite tends to be true. In the process of working together to manage the production and distribution of, for example, dental products, P&G, Colgate, and Wal-Mart tend to find it a very easy task to learn whatever they need to know about any firms that muddy the clarity of their semisocialistic vision of top-down industrial monopolism and then to take steps to isolate and eliminate them.

This helps to explain why Tom's of Maine, the maker of natural toothpaste and other personal products, sold out to Colgate-Palmolive in 2006.

Indeed, since Wal-Mart and its subject producers perfected this form of control, almost all lines of business in our consumer economy have been remade according to the principles espoused by John D. Rockefeller when he was building Standard Oil into an omnipotent and omniscient power in the world of petroleum. This technique boils down to presenting the owners of midsized and smaller companies, like Oakley or Tom's of Maine, with the "option" of selling their business to the monopolist in exchange for a "reasonable" sum determined by the monopolist. In the case of Standard Oil, this was usually far less than the total capital originally invested. The alternative for the smaller companies was then, as it is now, to see their investment crushed to nothing.[15]

This was the message delivered to many of the companies that in recent decades managed to develop big businesses seemingly outside the reach of the Procter & Gambles, Krafts, and Gillettes of the world. Consider the following:

- Ben & Jerry's, the Vermont ice cream company that reshaped the industry, was swallowed by Unilever in 2000.
- Cascadian Farm, one of the most successful organic food companies, sold out to General Mills and was promptly transformed into what its founder calls a "PR farm."[16]
- Stonyfield Farm and Brown Cow, organic dairy companies from New Hampshire and California, respectively, separately sold control to the French food giant Groupe Danone in February 2003 and were blended into a single operation.
- Glaceau, the company behind the brightly colored Vitamin Water and one of the last independent success stories, sold out to Coca-Cola in 2007.[17]

The practical result is a hierarchy of power in which a few immense trading companies—in control of and to some degree in cahoots with a few dominant supply conglomerates—govern almost all the industrial activities on which we depend, and they back their efforts with what amounts to police power. This tiny confederation of private corporate governments determines who wins and who loses in this country, at least within our consumer economy.

Do you think it's hard to get your child into Harvard? Try getting a new product onto the shelf of a big chain of stores in the United States.

And so, the American consumer—living in a nation of more than three hundred million people in fifty states, stretching from the Redwood forests to the Gulf Stream waters, from the Caribbean tropics to the ice fields of the Arctic, from the bodegas of San Antonio to the village shops of Maine—is today served by Standard Beverage Company, Standard Cookie Company, Standard Potato Chip Company, Standard Personal Care Company, and even Standard Organic and Alternative Foods Company. Then there's Standard Software Company, Standard Personal Computer

Company, Standard Microprocessor Company, Standard Discount Store, Standard Department Store, Standard Electronics Store, Standard Bedding Store, Standard Eyeglasses Store, Standard Ticket Service, and Standard Live Entertainment Company.

The one thing that seems to be missing from this list is Standard Oil Company. Despite the Clinton administration's best efforts to stitch Rockefeller's octopus back together again—through the merger of Exxon with Mobil, BP with Amoco, and Chevron with Texaco—the oil refining industry is *still* more diversified and competitive than most other big industries in the United States.

The Price of Control

Throughout this book, you won't read many complaints that monopolies charge high prices. This may strike you as strange. After all, you probably learned in school that the main reason people forge monopolies is to raise prices and make themselves richer. The politics of pricing is, in fact, a key to understanding the fantastic concentration of power in our economy but not necessarily for the reasons you think.

Numerous failings of imagination and law have contributed to the centralization of control over so many of our once open marketplaces. None, however, played a greater role, or unleashed greater destructive power, than the common misconception that Always Lower Prices are always better for us. That's why I want to take a moment to look at what *price* really means, the laws we use to determine who holds the power to determine a price, and how these people are able to wield that power.

Our first challenge is to come to grips with the fact that most prices are entirely arbitrary and political in nature. We are taught that the price of a particular item in a market is the product of a sort of automatic, self-regulating, natural process in which producers adjust supply to meet demand. In fact, the actual process of matching supply and demand does, technically, work pretty much as Adam Smith, the author of *The Wealth of Nations*, explained.

In any open market that is populated by many small buyers and many small sellers, if the producers try to raise their prices high enough to make themselves richer than their neighbors, other producers expand production or enter the market until prices go back down. If the prices fall below what an individual producer needs to sustain his business, *and* his home, the producers will cut production and in some cases exit the business entirely until the prices rise.

The problem lies not in the explanation of the dynamic but in the belief that the price that results is not political in nature. Even in a world like that imagined by Adam Smith, both the number of producers in any market system and the total amount of product are the result of innumerable political decisions. The ultimate purpose of every public market is, as we will see in chapter 4, to regulate how different groups in society compete with one another. This in turn requires the people who regulate the market to set a limit on the size of the market's participants.

The total amount of product that is brought to market, meanwhile, reflects an incredibly complex set of political decisions about what activities a particular society invests in. For instance, whether a government builds (or approves the building of) a road to a particular tract of timber or a port near a particular mine helps to determine the amount of lumber and copper that the participants in those markets can bring to market.

The political nature of a price is even more clear in systems in which power has been concentrated. In such cases, the price takes on the attributes of a tax. Henry Osborne Havemeyer, who in 1887 consolidated seventeen sugar refineries into the trust that eventually gave birth to Domino Sugar, stated the basic truth succinctly when he said, "Who cares for a quarter of a cent a pound?"[18] Translated into the world of real political economic actions, what Havemeyer meant was that he did not intend to use the power he had amassed over our supply of sugar to gouge us suddenly and violently. Rather, he intended to collect his quarter of a penny tax from us quietly and steadily, the same way our local governments collect a few pennies from us quietly and steadily every time we buy a Slurpee at 7-Eleven.[19]

That's why when I do speak of sudden spikes in prices, my point is not to bemoan any particular price as wrong or to celebrate any other price as right. It's to use the sudden spike (or sometimes crash) of a price to indicate that some individual or group wanted that price to move and enjoyed enough power to move it.

That's also why for most of our history, the ultimate point of our antimonopoly laws was not to prevent one company of men from charging "too much" for, say, cotton or vegetable oil. It was to prevent that company of men from using its corner on the supply of some item to increase their political power relative to the rest of us in a more or less permanent fashion.

To understand this, consider how Havemeyer's hold on sugar translated into the realm of politics. For many decades, every time an American sprinkled some sugarcane crystals into his or her tea, Havemeyer and his family became just a bit richer and hence a bit more politically powerful than you and me.

The same is true today of people like Bill Gates. Whenever we buy a product that includes any work done on a Microsoft system (which is just about every product, including the iPod), we direct a little more money to Mr. Gates and his family, which means that every day his political power, relative to you and me, grows greater. Sometimes he uses his power for unimpeachable causes, like fighting malaria in Africa. Other times he uses it in ways that directly affect the distribution of power here in the United States, such as when he erects foundations that work to undermine the right of individual teachers to organize unions.

Our next challenge is to understand that Always Lower Prices can also serve as one of the most powerful weapons in the war for control of any economic activity. To do so, it helps to divide economic activity into two distinct forms of enterprise. On one side, let's put the actual producers of goods and services, such as the people who grow grain and make shoes. On the other side, let's put the intermediaries who in a geographically dispersed market help to connect the producer with the consumer by transporting and retailing the grain and the shoes.

Note that there are two very different ways to price the products that flow through such a system. The first way is to let the producer of the grain or the shoes set a price at which to sell to the consumer and then prevent the intermediaries from changing that price and the producer from using different prices to discriminate among potential traders and retailers.

The second way is to let the people who stand between the producer and the consumer set whatever price they want for the product as it passes through their control. And further, to let these intermediaries, and/or the producers, set different prices for the exact same product and thereby discriminate among potential partners, if they so choose. In other words, to allow Procter & Gamble to offer better prices to the corner grocery on Main Street than to the corner grocery on Commercial

Street, in exchange for certain unfair favors. Or, in the obverse, to allow Wal-Mart to *demand* better prices from Procter & Gamble than what the producer gives to Target, in order to gain an unfair advantage in the competition for customers.

The difference in political outcome of these two pricing systems could hardly be more extreme. Protecting the producer's right to set the price of a good or a service results in dynamics very similar to Adam Smith's ideal market. Even though our modern marketplaces are physically extensive, and even though many intermediaries put their hands on the goods as they pass from producer to consumer, protecting the producer's right to set the price of a good or service means that the producer and the consumer make all the key decisions about the price, in dialogue with each other.

The producer sets the price high enough to avoid any degradation of the product as well as of his commercial *and* personal properties. The consumer reacts to that price in ways that discourage the producer (unless it is part of a cartel) from raising prices high enough to attract new competition. One of the biggest benefits of such a pricing system is that the activities of the producer and the retailer remain entirely distinct. Producers focus on competing with other producers for the consumer's favor. Retailers focus on competing with other retailers—not least by offering a greater variety of top-quality products—also for the consumer's favor.

The ability to use prices to discriminate among potential partners, by contrast, results in relentless and highly complex warfare, not only of producer against producer and retailer against retailer, but of producer against retailer and vice versa. The fact that the various actors can use prices to discriminate among their partners means that producers and retailers engage in ceaseless efforts to forge and reforge alliances with each other in ways that give them advantages in their competition with their horizontal rivals. Yet these alliances rarely remain harmonious for long, because the producer and the retailer must always seek to avoid being captured by their "ally."

One result of this second type of pricing system is to blur the activities of the producer and the retailer and trader, to the point where it becomes impossible to tell who is who. Another result is swift consolidation among the ranks of producers and retailers, as an early advantage from a well-structured alliance tends to snowball.

That's why for most of our history we have made sure that the power to set prices sat squarely in the hands of the producer. We did so consciously, to protect the properties of the producer *and* to avoid concentration. We did so also because we knew that such a system would result in far greater variety; it would enable the John Cottams of the world to focus not on protecting themselves from multidimensional predation but rather on perfecting their crafts.

The first time that anyone tried to shift the power to price away from the producer to the retailer and trader was in 1911. A slight majority on the Supreme Court—apparently taken by the "progressive" thinking of that era—rejected a suit by a drug company named Dr. Miles Medical against one of its distributors, which it accused of setting prices on its products too low. The majority, impressed by the fact that the actions of the distributor had resulted in a lower price for the consumer, rejected the complaint of Dr. Miles.

However, the decision triggered a slashing dissent by Justice Oliver Wendell Holmes, and it is worth quoting because it distills perfectly the traditional thinking on why to outlaw price discrimination.

"I cannot believe," he wrote, "that in the long run the public will profit by this court permitting knaves to cut reasonable prices for some ulterior purpose of their own, and thus to impair, if not to destroy, the production and sale of articles which it is assumed to be desirable that the public be able to get." Sure enough, the Supreme Court soon admitted it had erred, and in 1918 it largely restored the power to set prices to the producer.[20]

The *Dr. Miles* decision also led the American people, during the New Deal era in the 1930s, to direct Congress to greatly reinforce the laws that outlawed price discrimination by either the retailer or the producer.[21]

Thus, price discrimination remained illegal until the mid-1970s. In later chapters, I will discuss the mind-set of the "progressive" movement of the early twentieth century, especially its antipathy to competition and open markets and its fascination with socialized systems of production. I will also look at the thinking of the *neo*progressives who gained power in the Democratic Party in the early 1970s. What is important here is merely to note that during the neoprogressive revival, Congress in 1975 undid the entire structure of pricing policy that had been erected in the previous centuries when it passed a law called the Consumer Goods Pricing Act, which at last legalized price discrimination.[22]

The goal of those who promoted the act was laudable. They believed that big manufacturers like Procter & Gamble had become too fat and lazy. Yet rather than take on the giant conglomerates directly, such as by using antitrust law to make them smaller, the neoprogressives apparently decided that it would be easier to empower retailers to serve as "countervailing" powers able to exert more pressure on the producers.

Though all but forgotten today, the Consumer Goods Pricing Act must be credited with setting into motion the fantastic concentration of power in the hands of the giant retailers and trading companies that we have witnessed in the last generation. The decision six years later, in 1981, to all but suspend enforcement of our classic antitrust laws only accelerated the process. Perhaps the biggest proof of the lack of wisdom of the act is that the consolidation of power among the retailers eventually provided an excuse for round after round of consolidation among the very producers that the authors had originally set out to weaken, like Procter & Gamble.[23]

Which brings us to a set of laws that are closely related to price discrimination: our *common carriage* laws. These hold that certain businesses—especially those with a real or a de facto license to provide a vital service to the general public—must be kept open to all potential customers on a fair basis. The provider of the service cannot discriminate among users, either by denying service to some and not to others or by charging different people different prices. The ancient Romans applied the concept to inns and ships. The English applied it to cabs, ferries, toll roads, mills, bakeries, surgery, tailoring, and breweries. In the United States in the nineteenth century, we extended it to steamboats, telegraphy, and eventually railroads.

Today we usually view common carriage in personal terms and focus on the fact that these laws guarantee equal treatment for all when we do business with an airline or a telephone company, for instance. Yet in effect, our common carriage laws are among the most important of our antimonopoly laws, not because of how they protect us as consumers but how they protect us as producers. That's because if we allow the provider of an intermediary service to discriminate among producers who all depend equally on that service to reach their buyers, the provider of that service soon captures not merely most or all of the profits in the system but also political control over the producers themselves. That's why Charles Francis Adams warned in 1871 that the failure to stop monopolists from using railroads to discriminate among producers was a one-way trip to "Caesarism" in America.[24]

I bring up common carriage here because it helps us to complete our understanding of the nature of the power enjoyed by Wal-Mart and a few other giant retailers. These firms are now so big that their control over their own shelving systems essentially replicates the power once enjoyed by our nation's biggest railroads, before we extended our common carriage rules to that business. When Wal-Mart threatens to deprive a producer of access to its shelves, the effect is no different from when Jay Gould refused to carry Pennsylvania Bluestone to New York. The threat is existential in nature. Wal-Mart possesses the ability to kill at will, which means that its power to govern the political economic systems under its control is entirely despotic in nature.

Add this to what we learned in chapter 1, that driving prices down can degrade the products on our shelves, and to what we will learn in the next chapter, that such a combination of powers results in the stripping out of entire economic activities, and the picture is clear. Always Lower Prices is always an express trip not merely to rule but also to ruin.

A Market of One?

The Whac-A-Mole of contemporary truisms is that new information technologies make us free by melting down all the existing political and economic power structures. Read such books as *The World Is Flat*, *Free Agent Nation*, *Wikinomics*, *An Army of Davids*, and *The Work of Nations*, and you will be informed that the Internet is undermining China's authoritarian government, IBM's ability to protect its core businesses, and the power brokers who control both the Democratic and Republican parties.

A common corollary is that these new technologies—the Internet, especially—have created a marketplace of almost infinite size in which the modern consumer has far more pricing power than ever before. The basic idea here is that, as we trip down the sidewalk fingering our iPhones or captain our laptops from comfy chairs in cafés, we pass through portals that lead to the furthest antipodes of possibility.

Who needs the Fashion Place Mall? The modern Main Street has been shrunk to the size of a candy bar. Yet inside the new virtual Hollywood storefront there is so much more than ever before. To click through this portal is to arrive immediately at everything everywhere all the time. Even better, because we arrive in the form of a mob of limitless dimensions, prices fall before us like dandelions under an elephant's foot.

One of the more ambitious looks at the intersection of technology and markets is a book called *The Long Tail* by Chris Anderson. By eliminating the "tyranny of locality," he wrote, the Internet makes possible "markets without end."[25] Anderson made clear that his thesis applied mainly to the "media and entertainment industries," whose products can be digitalized or (as in the case of a physical book) people can wait a few days to receive. Anderson used the term *long tail* to refer to the hundreds of thousands of songs, books, and movies that never would have reached the shelf of any local real-world store but that a would-be buyer can easily find online today.

Anderson does not imply that the Internet brought these products into existence. Even in the sepia-toned days of the early 1990s these products existed, and people managed to find such items by using telephones, mail-order catalogs, fax machines, and interlibrary loans. What the Internet did, Anderson wrote, was to enable us to link to these isolated specialized items instantaneously and therefore to radically increase our consumption of them. This, in turn, Anderson insisted, encouraged the production of more specialized items.[26]

I do not question the general contention that the Internet makes us free in important new ways. Nor do I question that the Internet connects us to vastly more information and products than we could have found at any moment in any one place in the pre-Internet world. What I reject is the idea that these new technologies liberate us and empower us in all respects rather than only some.

My own take is that, just as Charles Francis Adams observed of railways, even as these new technologies free us from certain physical constraints, they also concentrate commerce in ways that enable a few to manipulate that commerce more easily than ever before, not only to increase their own wealth but to increase their power relative to the rest of us.

If anything, today's technologies pose political threats to us as individuals and as a society that in key respects are potentially far more dangerous than any described by Adams in the 1870s. What has melted down is the old system of checks and balances. Who has been truly liberated are the few who sit atop these new powers.

When we do admit to fear about the reach of the Internet, we tend to speak of how these technologies erode our privacy. We imagine the government reading our e-mail or tracking the articles we read, or we imagine some group of identity thieves grabbing the information they need to drain our bank accounts.

Yet this focus on privacy may actually hide the full scale and scope of the challenges we face. We must also look at how these new technologies affect our political economy as they result in the rise to power of new forms of trading companies, retailers, and content delivery systems that are not covered by any pricing law or any common carriage rules. To do so, we must look at two closely interlinked facts about the Internet, one that is obvious and one that is entirely new.

The obvious fact is that commerce on the Internet tends to collapse into near monopoly even faster than commerce in the real world. Precisely because the Internet eliminates the "tyranny" of locality, it eliminates most of the physical obstacles to centralization, such as the price of real estate. The result is consolidation beyond anything we have ever seen in the physical world, often in the form of a single superdominant entity—Netflix, Amazon, iTunes—that also tends to enjoy real cost advantages over real-world rivals.

Monopoly online poses the same problems that it does in the real economy. We see the same lopsided balance of power between the retailer and the producer. We see the same black-hole economics at work in the form of an accelerating degradation of the producers who are caught under these powers—or, to put it another way, an ever faster shriveling of the long tail.

The prices we see online may appear cheap, at least in relation to their real-world counterparts, but the costs reflected in these prices are incalculable. Anderson thought that what he saw online was a market. What he saw, in fact, was a few delivery infrastructures that give to their owners great if not complete freedom to manipulate the commerce that passes over their "rails."

This is true not merely of online megaretailers. It is also true of telecommunications and cable companies like AT&T and Comcast, which still retain the ability to discriminate among the producers of content who depend on their systems.[27] And it is true of online search engines; after all, the rankings on a search page are really just another form of shelving. Over time the almost inevitable result will be an ability to exert control over the producer that, for certain products—especially information products—outstrips what even Wal-Mart can accomplish.

The entirely new fact is that the monopolist in the digital world enjoys a power that the monopolist in the physical world does not. This is the ability not only to isolate producers one from another and to discriminate among them but also to isolate consumers from one another and to discriminate among them.

Politically, this is of profound importance for society.

To understand why and how, consider the prices we see on the shelves of the Wal-Mart in Prescott, Arizona. As we know, monopolization within the supply system means that these prices are increasingly arbitrary. Yet no matter how arbitrary they are, the prices are exactly the same for absolutely every consumer who crosses the threshold of the Supercenter. No matter how rich or poor one is, how well educated or how severely challenged, how politically connected or fanatically hermetic, everyone pays the same price at the scanner.

Although there is a vast asymmetry of power between the private planners and the public as a whole, the public is empowered by its knowledge of what it, as the public, must pay. In other words, when it enters the doors of Wal-Mart, the public is still treated as a mob and retains some remnants of the powers of the mob. If various members of the public don't like the price they see in front of them, they can join together and complain to both the private and public authorities, who do enjoy some power to take actions that will change the price.

In the digital world, by contrast, the companies that control the delivery systems can treat every individual consumer in a perfectly unique fashion. Every member of every community can be dealt with separately. From one house to the next, from one office desk to the next, from one bleacher seat to the next, from one airline seat to the next, the prices delivered via digital means may vary immensely. Such discrimination among different consumers goes by a variety of names: dynamic pricing, personalized pricing, customized pricing.

On the surface the idea that a business discriminates among customers can seem so innocuous that many firms—like automotive insurers—have begun to advertise the fact that they do so, to attract customers who believe that they will be among the select few who benefit from such discrimination. The political result, however, is that the asymmetry of power is complete. In such a relationship, the public no longer has any idea of what it, as a whole, must pay for any particular item. In other words, the various members of the public no longer have any interests in common. In the digital world, the mob is atomized. There is no public.[28]

In the first volume of *Democracy in America*, the French political philosopher Alexis de Tocqueville wrote that the most perfect authoritarian regime combines "centralized government" with "centralized administration." Such concentration, he wrote, "accustoms" men under such power "to set their own will habitually and completely aside; to submit, not only for once, or upon one point, but in every respect, and at all times. Not only, therefore, does this union of power subdue them compulsorily, but it affects their ordinary habits; it *isolates* them and then *influences* each *separately*." (Emphasis added.)[29]

The rise of private corporate governments that combine the ability to discriminate among the producers and the consumers in our society is just such a union of "centralized government" and "centralized administration." The main thing that can no longer be concentrated is our will as a people.

Thus, the next time you hear the word *price*, imagine not a well-oiled system of supply and demand that is regulated by markets; instead, imagine a tax, imposed on you with a greater or lesser degree of subtlety, by the rich. Imagine not an open negotiation but an act of subterfuge and coercion, of automated baiting and switching, of perfectly personalized pilfering. Imagine not a normative device forged by the dealings of people in an open market; instead, imagine a finely honed wedge to separate neighbor from neighbor, friend from friend, and parent from child.

When you hear the word *price*, imagine Big Brother. Only our Big Brother does not stare at us from a cold camera on the wall. Instead, he looks right at us through our own online searches and hence looks through our own eyes. And our Big Brother does not glare darkly from posters. Rather, he hovers like an angel in our souls—privy to our innermost wishes, darkest sins, and silliest weaknesses—and conjures for us the perfect solipsism in which to laze away our dollars, our days, and our liberties.

3

The Crystal House

There's still an element of chaos on Seventh Avenue and 38th Street in Manhattan, the rough center of New York's Garment District. On a gray February day I stand on the southeast corner of the intersection before noon, watching trucks and taxis roar through the traffic light, buffeted by the crowds who rush along the sidewalk. Nearby stores are stocked with a dazzling variety of tools and materials with which to cut and assemble clothing: buttons and beads, rhinestones and ribbons, scissors and sequins, tyrolese tape and tracing paper, feathers and piping, industrial sewing machines and industrial dress forms, tulle and muslin, chiffon and spandex. The floors above hold the people who work these items. I raise my eyes from the storefronts and catch sight of a cutter or a sewer, apparently on a break, staring back at me, next to a line of naked male mannequins sporting 1970s hairstyles.

This is a scene I know well. In the mid-1980s I worked as a warehouse-man and truck driver for the Custom Shirt Shop, a national cooperative of tailor shops, which kept a sprawling and junk-crammed loft on the eleventh floor of 37 West 37th Street. Forty years earlier my mother's mother worked as a jobber in the millenary business, running orders from retailers to cutters and sewers. Growing up, I was treated to stories of mobsters battling labor unions, of the black market for nylon stockings and panties sewn from misappropriated parachute silk, of small fortunes made, and—in the case of my family, at least—of small piles of savings lost.

For decades, the Garment District was one of world's great open markets and one of the great open production systems. It was also the archetype of the industrial metropolis, a roughly twenty-block world of factories in the sky, so vibrant that it required few protections other than local zoning laws.

Manufacturers began to gather here in the 1920s, attracted by new steel-framed fireproofed buildings, rail and road terminals, and the migration of retailers from the Ladies' Mile on Broadway to Fifth Avenue. The district soon became the center of a production system that linked pieceworkers on the Lower East Side and factories in New Jersey, Connecticut, and Pennsylvania to thousands of independent stores and small chains across the nation.

Much of the product was retailed right at the edges of the district itself, passing through giant department stores like Bonwit Teller, Bergdorf Goodman, Bloomingdale's, Saks Fifth Avenue, Gimbels, Lord & Taylor, B. Altman, and Macy's.[1] Not that production here was aimed solely at the luxury and mid markets. In his autobiography, Sam Walton wrote of making yearly pilgrimages from Arkansas to midtown Manhattan to buy in bulk for Wal-Mart.[2]

Manufacturing in the Garment District survived crackdowns on sweatshops, automation, and the spread of cutting and sewing to Alabama, the Caribbean, Guatemala, and China. Costume designers from Broadway theaters, wealthy Long Islanders shopping for wedding gowns, and working-class families from Washington Heights preparing for *quinceaneras* all helped to keep the district in the business of cutting and sewing. So too did New York designers who relied on the tiny factories here for small runs of luxury apparel and to meet surges in demand for a hot item.

When I worked on 37th Street, the streets were jammed with food carts serving workers from Russia, China, Korea, Israel, the Dominican Republic. Laborers from housing projects in the Bronx and Harlem apprenticed with skilled artisans from Brooklyn and Elizabeth. Sidewalks were often impassable as racks of dresses moving east collided with racks of dresses moving west. Most people entered buildings through the loading dock, where they rode freight elevators hundreds of feet up to the shop floor. In the afternoons, trucks clogged 37th and 38th Streets from Fifth Avenue to Ninth Avenue, parking in three of the four lanes. It was a rare feat to reach the West Side Highway without whacking another truck's mirror.

Today the Garment District is not what it was even a decade ago. One of my favorite buildings is 1407 Broadway, a forty-two-story green and red office and industrial tower erected just after World War II, based on a design by Ely Jacques Kahn. The building directory still lists more than two thousand individual tenants. But the great ecosystem that made up the Garment District is collapsing fast. Many of the older industrial buildings are half vacant, and their windows increasingly bear signs for yoga studios and dance lessons.

The district was never immaculate, but many buildings have crumbled almost beyond repair, and a growing number are being demolished.[3] You can still buy a slice of kosher pizza, but most of the tiny storefront synagogues have closed. Some recent comers, like Ben's Deli on 38th Street, look as if they've been here forever. The Stitch Bar & Lounge, regardless of the name, is alien. New York Zippers & Trimmings still sells YKKs and ribbons. But the future seems to lie two doors west, at the Zipper Factory Tavern and Theater, which advertises contemporary burlesque.

Where I really notice the difference is on the sidewalk and the street. As I stand on the corner, my eyes watering from the cold, I don't see even one dress rack. Of the few laundry carts I spot, most are filled not with jeans and skeins of cloth but with deliveries of catered foods. The storefronts where you could load up on overstocks and odd jobs display high-end—and imported—French and Italian fashions. The great fleet of double-parked trucks has all but vanished.

Change is the way of the world. It would be absurd to perpetuate artificially an industrial activity that people do not want or need. But what is taking place here has little to do with what people want or with the natural working of some "market system." Rather, it has a whole lot to do with the use of the institution of the corporation by the rich and powerful to extend their dominion over our markets and our lives by taking control of activities that until now were organized in open market systems.

To understand the nature of the shadow that has fallen over the Garment District, we have to stroll only three blocks south, to the northwest corner of Macy's at Broadway and 35th. The building has long borne the words "the World's Largest Store," but since construction was completed in the 1920s, this has referred only to the fact that under this roof there are about two million square feet of retail space spread over nine floors.[4] These days, however, Macy's claim can also refer to the fact that it is the world's largest chain of department stores. For the myriad companies and people of the Garment District, this change in the definition of what makes Macy's big makes a world of difference.

The old Macy's company first opened stores outside New York in the 1920s, but the company remained a bit player in U.S. retail until the 1980s. That was when financiers—freed up by the recent radical changes in antitrust law—began to move big-time into the department store business, to concentrate power. Old Macy's itself did not survive long.

After a valiant effort to protect its traditional ways, the store was taken over in 1994 by Federated, a holding company based in Cincinnati, which also controlled such one-time independents as Bullock's, Burdines, Bon Marché, Bloomingdale's, and Jordan Marsh. Then in 2005, Federated grabbed May Department Stores, which over the years had corralled such names as Marshall Field's, Lord & Taylor, Filene's, Hecht's, and Wanamaker's. Thus the Macy's name now applies to a chain of more than nine hundred stores that stretches from sea to sequined sea.

The effect of the May acquisition was especially dramatic. With that one swoop, the financiers who engineered the deal destroyed much of the remaining competition to merchandise the slacks, dresses, blouses, and sport coats designed and produced by America's remaining clothiers. They also radically reduced the overall amount of space that was devoted to selling these items, wiping about a third of the total length of shelving available for "designer fashion items" right off the map, in part by closing many of the stores they had seized.[5]

Through the governance system we call Macy's, these financiers captured the power to direct, rationalize, and determine who wins and who loses in an industry that until recently was among the most dynamic and open in the world. Even though the process has been playing out for years, the effect of the takeover of May was sudden and extreme.

Walking up Broadway to 41st Street, you come to the offices of Liz Claiborne. This was the first company founded by a woman to break into the Fortune 500, and it is still controlled by its founders, with the exception of Claiborne herself, who died in June 2007. Yet in April 2007, the firm's managers learned just how radically the Federated-May merger had altered the landscape of power.

Liz Claiborne executives had developed a new product line for JCPenney, and they expected Macy's executives to complain for a few moments about the "promiscuity" of this act but then get down to business as usual. Macy's actual response, however, was sharp, brutal, and without precedent. Macy's CEO told Liz Claiborne that it had lost its "most favored nation status," and he immediately slashed his buying from that firm by millions of dollars.

Liz Claiborne's quarterly earnings plummeted 65 percent, and the company's stock has been one of the most miserable performers on Wall Street ever since.[6]

It is unlikely that Liz Claiborne Inc. will fail. The company is too powerful in its own right, with annual revenues above $5 billion. And in the event, the management team swiftly put into motion a plan to lessen the firm's reliance on Macy's, mainly by opening hundreds of branded stores that will allow it to interact directly with consumers.

Other big names, however, are finding life in the world of mega-Macy's much tougher. Wander over to 601 West 26th Street, and you will come to the headquarters of Tommy Hilfiger. Here the story is one of complete submission to the new power: in September 2007, the designer agreed to sell his signature clothing line only through Macy's. The deal required Tommy Hilfiger to pull its merchandise entirely out of competitors like Bon-Ton and Dillard's. The *New York Times* called the deal a "coup" for Macy's—and indeed, the bigger company managed in essence to capture all the equity built up over decades in this one brand.

Hilfiger himself said it was Federated's takeover of May that made the exclusive deal "compelling and logical."[7] More accurate would be to call it a logic born of compulsion. Fewer retailers stocking fewer shelves means fewer independent producers.[8]

The crash of business activity after the financial Meltdown of the fall of 2008 has accustomed us to the sudden smashing not merely of capacity but also of variety, such as the number of different types of cars that General Motors manufactures. Yet as we see in the Garment District, such smashing began many years before the Meltdown, and even if the smashing was more controlled before, it was just as wholesale in nature.

In this chapter I want to do three things. First, detail some of the changes in organizational structure within our political economy that contribute to such smashing; second, examine the dynamics of such smashing within our large conglomerates; and third, sketch out the ultimate results of allowing our financiers to use corporations to rationalize production activities not merely in a twenty-block community like the Garment District but across the face of the entire world. The single most important result is the transformation of many of our most vital industrial systems into *structural monopolies*, in which even the most mundane of activities is made "too big to fail."

The Industrial Estates

The idea that allowing a few among us to concentrate economic power across an entire market can result in the destruction of many of the producers within that market is not new. Adam Smith bemoaned the economic devastation wrought in India by the nabobs who controlled the British East India Company monopoly. In the early 1930s, the Harvard economist Edward Chamberlin showed that the corporate enclosure of an industrial activity, when combined with unregulated competition between the different powers in that system of production, can result in the slow starvation of an entire system. Judge Richard Posner, in 1978 when he was still a law professor at the University of Chicago, explained that the concentration of power in a single buyer can result in that buyer forcing suppliers to engage in a "process of disinvestment" in "productive assets" and hence the undermining of even the most basic of industrial systems.[9]

In this section I want to continue our discussion of how we managed in the past to avoid such destruction of the machines and skills on which we depend, even when we allowed power over a particular activity or marketplace to be highly concentrated. One way, as we saw in the last chapter, was to protect the ability of the producer to set the price for his or her own products. Another way was to guarantee all producers equal access to such monopolized services as railway transportation.

Here I want to begin to look at the main *institution* we have used to protect our industrial and scientific arts and to pass them from one generation to the next: the industrial corporation itself. Specifically, I want to look at the intent, character, structure, and legal nature of the classic industrial enterprise that dominated the U.S. economy through most of the mid-twentieth century: the great oligopolies like General Electric, U.S. Steel, DuPont, IBM, RCA, Xerox, 3M, John Deere, Eli Lilly, Boeing, Caterpillar, and Westinghouse, as well as, of course, General Motors and the other automakers.

Like Macy's and Wal-Mart today, these firms exercised direct control over the actual people who made the goods and provided the services. Unlike Macy's and Wal-Mart and the other mega-retailers, the old industrial enterprises did so in ways that generally resulted in the protection of these producers and the machines and systems they had devised.

Let's start by looking at Ford Motor Company. For much of the last century, the automaker provided the general public with our iconic image of the industrial corporation. And Henry Ford himself provided America's industrial managers with what was arguably the single most important model of organization. This was something called *vertical integration*, and it meant that a particular enterprise tried to produce almost all the main components of its product in-house, in its own factories. Until Ford, most manufacturers purchased parts from outside suppliers and relied on informal, contracted labor. Ford's goal was to mass-produce inexpensive automobiles, and after a couple of experiments, he soon decided that outside suppliers were too expensive and untrustworthy.

Initially, Ford lacked the capital to handle all production in-house, but after the phenomenal success of the Model T, he began to design his dream organization on a patch of land outside Detroit called River Rouge. Although he never managed to produce 100 percent of the content in his vehicles, by the late 1920s Ford had come remarkably close to building a self-contained complex wherein to transform coal, iron ore, and other raw materials—offloaded from ships at one end of River Rouge—into finished cars.

Not all industrialists followed suit, but most big enterprises did. Thus the U.S. industrial sector as a whole came to be characterized by immense operations that aimed to master every step and every activity in a particular production process. IBM, for instance, bragged for years of manufacturing even its own screws. The result, especially after antitrust law began to be applied with more vigor in the late 1930s, was that most industrial activities were replicated many times over in the United States. Every automaker, for instance, manufactured its own piston rings and alternators. And to ensure that no human or natural act ever shut the main assembly line, the automakers often divided the production of such items between at least two different factories.

During these years, American society came to rely on these giant industrial enterprises to provide many of the basic services we generally associate with government. Some services were social in nature, such as the collection of income taxes, the provision of pensions, and the management of health care. Some were political; as we will see in chapter 7, America's international energy and mining companies usually worked very closely with Washington.

The most important services were intellectual in nature.

One vital task performed by these giant firms was to process information. In open-market systems, individual producers—such as weavers with their looms at home—receive most of their information directly from the market from which they buy their raw materials, and from the market into which they sell their finished products. The giant industrial enterprises, in contrast, had to internalize much of the task of processing information just as they internalized more and more market interactions.

In many ways, the firms that succeeded in the twentieth century were those that did the best job of transferring information up and down the vertical chain of production activity. One of the best pictures of such a system was drawn in 1946 by the political economist and management theorist Peter Drucker in his book *Concept of the Corporation*. Drucker devoted entire chapters to describing how the hundreds of thousands of individuals who then worked for General Motors gathered, transmitted, and made sense of the information flowing along their assembly lines and across their desks.[10]

These giant firms also served as America's main economic planners. Managers and engineers consciously structured the twentieth-century industrial enterprise to plan for the development and improvement of the products they manufactured and the manufacturing processes they governed. This in turn required them to coordinate such activities as the development and introduction of new technologies, the design and construction of the necessary production systems and external infrastructures, the education of workers and consumers, and the gathering and structuring of the capital necessary to power all these tasks. Although this may seem to be what Wal-Mart does nowadays in our consumer economy, the difference is that the integrated manufacturers looked much further into the future, and did so across many more planes of economic activity.

A third basic intellectual task managed by the classic U.S. industrial enterprises was to reduce risk within our production system. The fact that managers could actually walk up and down a line of production tended to make this task relatively easy. The fact that each company competed against at least a few rivals that manufactured more or less the same basic product provided a real incentive to ensure that one's own system never broke down.

One result was that even when managers decided to rely on an outside supplier for some component, they tended to divide the contract among a few different companies. Another result was that when managers or engineers noted a systemic risk outside their own control, they worked with colleagues at other companies to convince the government to take action.

In 1953, President Dwight Eisenhower named General Motor's CEO Charles Erwin Wilson to be his first secretary of defense. In a Senate hearing on his nomination, Wilson—who was known as "Engine Charley" to distinguish him from GE's then CEO Charles Edward ("Electric Charlie") Wilson—told the world that "for years I thought what was good for the country was good for General Motors, and vice versa." Although that "vice versa" at the end of the sentence struck a sour chord with Americans, especially after reporters rewrote the comment to read "what's good for General Motors is good for the country," the gist of the statement reflected a vitally important underlying reality: that for most of the twentieth century, American society and the American industrial enterprise had advanced hand in hand.[11]

This was no cowboy capitalism. Through the heart of the twentieth century, the U.S. industrial enterprise functioned as a highly specialized, largely bureaucratic, *social* institution that had more in common with the government of a large city than a personal private business like a farm or an independent grocery store. Indeed, in 1967, when economist John Kenneth Galbraith published his greatest work on the relationship between the industrial enterprise and society, he titled his book *The New Industrial State*, and he centered much of his analysis on the idea that the political economies of the United States and the Soviet Union were evolving, albeit from different directions, toward the same basic largely *socialized* structure.

There were many problems with the twentieth-century U.S. industrial system, not the least of which were industrial-scale pollution and waste, and the reordering of the landscape and of civil society to serve the needs of the industrial apparatus rather than the citizen per se. Yet overall, the system did two things very well. First, it divided and distributed the political power to govern these activities between distinct public and private institutions, which it did by setting these governments into competition with one another and keeping them in competition. And second, it protected and ensured the perpetuation of our most important physical systems of production as well as the skills and the knowledge necessary to complete these tasks.

Number One or Number Two

So how did we go from a political economy centered around production-oriented firms like General Motors and General Electric to one centered around trading-oriented firms like Wal-Mart and Macy's? And let's be clear: we are not talking about a transfer of relative power, in which one type of company shrinks in size while another type of company grows. What we have witnessed over the last generation, alongside the emergence of the trading company, is the complete transformation of the industrial company itself, to the point where even such heavyweights as GM and Boeing have taken on many of the attributes of the trading company.

Today's big industrial companies are still not as "flat" as Wal-Mart, but they are far less vertical in their organization than they were even a decade ago. With companies like Macy's capturing de facto control over producers like Tommy Hilfiger, and with GM and Boeing having outsourced most key production work to outside suppliers, the once sharp line between the industrial enterprise and the trading company has for all intents vanished.

In this section, I want to look at who transformed the classic American industrial enterprise into a Wal-Mart–like trading company and why they did so. This metamorphosis is one of the most dramatic events in our recent political economic history. It is one of the most important events to review in depth, if we are to make sense of how today's production systems work, and sometimes do not work.

The first stage of this transformation took place in the 1980s, when the professional, salaried managers who then controlled most big firms began to adapt their manufacturing operations to a legal environment that had been radically altered by the revolutionary changes in antimonopoly law in 1981. Perhaps the best way to understand this stage is to focus on Jack Welch, who was CEO of General Electric between 1981 and 2001 and who was one of the more brilliant managers of his era. Of Welch's many insights, the key one for our purposes came right at the beginning of his time in the corner office, in December 1981. That was when, in a speech to a ballroom full of Wall Street analysts, he demonstrated just how well he understood the license he had just been given by the Reagan administration's de facto suspension of antimonopoly law half a year earlier.

A "central idea" would guide GE during his reign, Welch said. Managers would make every business unit in the giant conglomerate into "the number one or number two leanest, lowest-cost, worldwide producer of quality goods and services." In cases in which GE was not *already* number one or two, and did not have a technology that would allow it to grow swiftly to one or two, Welch said the company would get there some other way, or else sell off or close the unit.[12]

Like many revolutionary statements, Welch's speech made little impression at first. In his memoir, Welch wrote that he left the hotel ballroom convinced that his performance had been a "bomb."[13]

It became a lot easier to understand exactly what Welch meant during the next few years as he illustrated his concepts with real-life actions. The most dramatic and iconic of these followed GE's 1985 takeover of the television pioneer RCA. This deal took place when Americans' fear of Japanese industrial competition was rising fast, and Welch assured Congress that he intended to create a national champion in television production. His plan, he said, was to merge RCA's TV division into GE's, then upgrade the technology and manufacturing processes of the combined operation.

It took only a year, however, for Welch to drop the ruse and orchestrate instead a masterful swap with his counterpart at France's Thompson Electronics. In exchange for Thompson's medical device business, Welch traded away the combined television manufacturing capabilities of both RCA and GE in a no-cash deal.[14]

In two strokes, Welch remade multiple world-spanning industries. The rationale behind his moves was simple: concentrate power, avoid direct competition with firms backed by mercantilist states (as Japan's electronics companies were), and focus on industrial activities that could be protected through interaction with regulators (Thompson's medical device business) or the Pentagon (RCA's defense business, which Welch kept).

In so doing, Welch helped to set the pattern for the great Wall Street merger boom of the 1980s. Although we remember that era mainly for the cash-printing shenanigans of private equity firms like Kohlberg Kravis Roberts & Co. and junk-bond master Michael Milken, there was also a real pattern to the deals. The general modus operandi was to break apart the huge mixed conglomerates that had been assembled in the late 1950s and 1960s—when "mature" manufacturers like RCA had expanded from their core activities into such businesses as renting automobiles, publishing books, and boxing up TV dinners—and then reassemble the parts in ways that better linked like to like.

Welch was a highly capable engineer, and his vision of industrial organization was that of a rational manager. His goal was to reduce competition as much as possible, to enable himself more easily to strike a balance among his various responsibilities as CEO. Highest on the list in the years after the election of Ronald Reagan was to pay a fat dividend to investors. However, in the eyes of Welch and other managers and engineers of those years, the goal was also to continue to produce the machines and systems humans need to live and to continue to develop innovative new technologies.

In the mature industrial environment of the 1980s, the consolidation pursued by Welch often weakened the systems over which his firm exercised power. He cut overall capacity, thinned out supply bases, culled skilled workers, and reduced the incentive to innovate. Nevertheless, he did so with some degree of care, and thereby managed to keep GE atop the world market in everything from locomotives to jet engines to powerplant turbines to electricity-generating windmills.[15]

In other words, Welch's approach still involved some risk to capital. Which is why his model would soon be tossed aside.

The second stage of the transformation of the manufacturer into a trading company played out mainly in the 1990s and the first decade of the twenty-first century. Managers at industrial firms during these years responded to two further revolutionary changes in the environment of law and regulation in which businesses operate. First was the retreat of the U.S. government from the strategic management of international trade, as exemplified by the creation of the World Trade Organization (WTO). Second was the centralization of power over the corporation in the hands of the financier, which we will discuss in depth in chapter 8.

These two sets of radical changes in law, combined with the ongoing revolution that had been triggered by the changes in antimonopoly law a decade earlier, presented corporate managers with an incredibly complex, varied, and constantly shifting set of influences, opportunities, and threats. One result is that no one character towers over the second act in the way that Welch dominated the first.

Another result is that we saw a remarkable variety of business models, all of which played off the trading company model. Let's consider a few.

Dell Computer grew to be the biggest personal computer (PC) maker in the world by avoiding manufacturing almost entirely and focusing instead on assembling components imported from Asia and on marketing. The model, as CEO Michael Dell admits, was not the one perfected by IBM in its heyday, but the one perfected by Sam Walton. The only real distinction between Wal-Mart and Dell is that whereas Wal-Mart displays the wares it imports in a "big box store," Dell assembles the wares it imports in little boxes.[16] Dell's import business proved so successful that it soon destroyed the PC manufacturing operations of both IBM and Compaq and forced the much larger Hewlett-Packard to transform itself from a manufacturer of components into more of a trading company importer like Dell.

IBM's managers, seeing their PC business bulldozed by Dell, promptly put these lessons to work in their own business. In this case, they transformed a firm that once boasted of producing almost every component in its famous mainframes into one that generates most of its revenue by managing for other firms the processes of selecting, installing, operating, and hosting information management systems. The new IBM also employs and manages the engineers who do so.

Earlier this decade, Boeing executives conceived one of the most audacious outsourcing efforts of the modern era, seeking to apply a Dell Computer–like systems integration model to the construction of its next-generation 787 Dreamliner passenger aircraft. The basic goal was to rely on outside suppliers to manufacture entire subsections of the plane—accounting for more than 90 percent of the value of the aircraft—and then to snap these together at a final assembly plant in Everett, Washington.

Another extreme outsourcing effort was that of General Motors. The process began in 1994 when the company first began to consolidate in-house components manufacturing operations into a single unit, Delphi. Then in 1999, GM spun off that unit as an independent firm. In the years immediately after, Delphi itself worked diligently to sell off or shut down erstwhile GM factories in the United States and to replace their product with items sourced from joint-venture operations in Asia, especially China, and increasingly from outside suppliers there. During these years, GM spun off or replaced the work of hundreds of thousands of engineers and workers.

Even Welch at GE got into the game, as he also opted to outsource a huge portion of his company's work in the late 1990s. But he did so with a special twist, transforming the conglomerate into one of the world's most sophisticated providers of outsourcing *services*. It was GE executives, for instance, who pioneered much of the outsourcing of back-office information-processing operations to India, almost single-handedly establishing the companies and protocols that now dominate the business.

The person who comes closest to serving as the poster boy for the second stage of the transformation of American manufacturing, however, is Tyco CEO Dennis Kozlowski. You may remember that Kozlowski was hauled off to prison a few years ago for misappropriating $400 million in funds. Yet Kozlowski's key industrial legacy was the construction of a $40 billion corporation that specialized in forging monopolies over U.S. marketplaces for everything from catheters to fire sprinklers to clothes hangers, and then eliminating the U.S. producers of these products by outsourcing production offshore.[17]

The difference between the classic twentieth-century industrial firm and these new stripped-out traders in and marketers of industrial items cannot be overstated. One of the most important distinctions between the industrial philosophy of executives like Henry Ford or even Jack Welch and executives like Dennis Kozlowski is their attitude toward competition. Ford and Welch sought to limit competition along both the vertical and horizontal axes. Kozlowski, in contrast, sought to suppress competition only with Tyco's horizontal rivals, mainly by buying them and forging monopolies. His model aimed to use the power he captured over the entire industrial activity to extract capital from the smaller firms and the individuals who own the actual machines and do the actual work of making things.

Which helps to answer the question *why* the financiers have imposed such structures on our production systems. Suppression of horizontal competition is exactly what gave exeuctives at Tyco, Boeing, and GM the ability—just like Wal-Mart—to pit supplier against supplier, and worker against worker, and community against community, for the benefit not of society as a whole but merely of the financiers who now controlled these industrial estates. Unlike a generation ago, the purpose of these firms is no longer mainly to make things, nor to plan how to keep making things, nor even to understand how things are made. The purpose of such firms is to engineer rivalry among the actual people who make things in a way that results in a more rapid generation of cash in the accounts of the rich. The result is often a grinding down of the real properties—the machines, skills, systems—society has entrusted to the care of these institutions.[18]

From the point of view of the financier, such schemes often work well, for a while. Eventually, however, such schemes run up against the physical and financial limits of the real-world properties and structures themselves. Not that such strip mining is necessarily a one-way trip to bankruptcy. As we have seen with our recent bailouts, if the financiers do a good enough job of monopolizing—hence, socializing—these industrial systems, they may eventually be able to call on the public state itself to deliver them yet more cash.

The Smashing

To get a sense of the actual dynamics of such strip mining of our industrial systems by our financiers, let's look at how the process operates within some of our largest consumer product conglomerates, which, like every other major "manufacturer," have also been transformed to a great degree into trading companies. A good place to start is a recent *Wall Street Journal* article titled "After Buying Binge, Nestle Goes on a Diet."[19]

According to the reporter, the cycle of destruction starts with a little "shopping spree" in which the managers gobble up other companies and brands. In the case of Nestlé, which is already the biggest food company in the world,[20] recent examples include Dreyer's ice cream and Gerber baby foods (acquisition of which gave Nestlé an 80 percent share of the U.S. baby food business).

The next stage occurs when the conglomerate's managers become aware of the predicament that naturally results, as such M&A frenzies yield "megaliths" that are "bigger than ever, and now need to be rationalized" (not least to pay off the immense debt the financiers merged into the new enterprises they forged, to pay their own upfront "fees").

This leads to the third stage, in which the managers cut production capacity and product variety in a process sometimes called "SKU rationalization" (SKU stands for "stock-keeping unit," which is the individualized code that is applied to every item for sale in a store). In the case of Nestlé, this rationalization played out as the outright elimination of *one-fifth* of all the company's products in 2006, followed by another 10 percent cut in 2007.[21]

The fourth stage takes place when company managers reinvest some of the money that has been freed up by this frenzied smashing of capacity and variety. Some they use to fund "innovations," like "leaner" versions of existing lines of ham. Most they set aside for the next round of acquisitions (and payments to the financiers), as the now "leaner" Nestlé is ready once again to "absorb acquisitions down the road."

Now look at the world's second largest food company, Kraft. Here we see the same basic cyclical pattern of buying up and closing down. Take, for instance, the company's merger with Nabisco, a deal brokered in 2000 by Kraft's parent company, Philip Morris. At first, Kraft managers were able to report many "synergies" as they integrated such new product lines as Oreo cookies, Planters Peanuts, and Shredded Wheat into existing channels designed to distribute Oscar Mayer wieners, Grey Poupon mustard, Gevalia coffee, and Velveeta "cheese product." Indeed, *Forbes* was soon celebrating Kraft managers for "leading the charge" in a "brutal industry." Soon thereafter, however, margins began to tank and Kraft began to cut. This included 39 plants, 13,500 workers, and roughly 25 percent of Kraft's entire suite of products.[22]

Once this rationalization was accomplished, Kraft, just like Nestlé, went right back to bingeing. One special target was crackers and biscuits. The company laid out $7.2 billion for Groupe Danone's biscuit division and $1.1 billion for a major line of United Biscuit products. But the company also had a sweet tooth; in September 2009, Kraft offered $16.7 billion for the British candy maker Cadbury.

This dynamic of destruction results partly from the fact that the people who direct Nestlé and Kraft enjoy such unfettered freedom to buy or otherwise eliminate their rivals. But it is important to recognize how top-tier trading companies like Wal-Mart speed the processes of destruction. One of the main ways they do so is to dictate that the suppliers reduce what they charge Wal-Mart for certain items to levels that do not leave the suppliers with sufficient revenue to care for their own operations. (Wal-Mart, we should keep in mind, does this not for the sake of the American consumer but to enable itself to temporarily increase its own profit margins.)

Consider, for instance, the effects of such sudden deflationary impulses on the world's largest rubber products company, Newell. The story here starts in 1998, when the managers of Rubbermaid, which had long been one of the nation's "most admired corporations," agreed to be purchased by their longtime rival Newell. As one executive put it at the time, Rubbermaid was "caught in a vise between higher raw-material costs and a downward spiral in pricing," imposed by "discounters like Wal-Mart."[23]

The result was a new conglomerate that dominated the production of plastic garbage pails, Cephalon pots and pans, and Sharpie pens.

Yet it was soon clear that no matter what products the new bigger Newell dominated, the consolidation with Rubbermaid had brought little relief from the pressures of Wal-Mart. In 2003, *Fortune* magazine, in an article titled "One Nation under Wal-Mart," described how Newell's then CEO spent four weeks a year walking through Wal-Mart stores, how the firm consulted with Wal-Mart on the design of every product that would be sold through the retailer, how one division president gave every new employee a copy of Sam Walton's biography, and how Newell employees had decorated the company's Bentonville, Arkansas, sales office with photographs of Sam Walton. Yet even such abject toadying did not earn Newell whatever dispensation it needed to keep the hound at bay. So beginning in 2004, Newell's CEO took out his hatchet. Over the next two years he hacked away 20 percent of the company's brands, twenty-seven of its eighty-one plants, five thousand jobs, and more than a hundred thousand SKUs.

As soon as Newell executives sensed anything like stability, did they build up cash reserves to resist the next assault? Not on your life. Just like Nestlé and Kraft they went on a spree. In 2008 this included Aprica, the Japanese manufacturer of baby strollers, and Technical Concepts, a maker of public restroom equipment.[24]

Much the same story played out at Procter & Gamble after the company grabbed its once mighty rival Gillette in 2005. So too at Circuit City, which in early 2008 was celebrated in an article for the fact that its "shelves have been cleared of merchandise with ho-hum sales to focus on blockbuster sellers."[25] So too at, of all places, Macy's, which in the summer of 2007 was itself rumored to be a buyout target. Then between December 2007 and February 2008, the giant retailer announced plans to shut stores in seven states and to slash twenty-three hundred jobs. In February 2009, it cut another seven thousand jobs.

One of the basic goals of every merger, no matter what the deal makers say in public, is to eliminate a few "redundancies." Yet in the past, the process of cutting tended to continue for only a while. Years before the Meltdown of 2008, however, something else began to happen throughout the American economy. Firms like Nabisco and Kraft are already extremely consolidated—they are, to a large degree, conglomerations of monopolies and near monopolies. Yet not only are these monopolists unable to protect their operations (or uninterested in doing so), but the pace of destruction within these systems has been accelerating.

A growing number of firms, like Nestlé, have for all intents been transformed into immense rationalization machines, destroying product variety and diversity even as they absorb many of their competitors. Which, of course, had they remained independent, would (at least in theory) have acted to fill the very niches that such wholesale destruction leaves behind.[26]

The Monopolist

In the previous sections, we looked at the physical effects of *top-down* monopolization and rationalization of entire systems. In the rest of this chapter, I want to show how monopolization can also proceed from the *bottom up*. I also want to show how such bottom-up monopolization—by rendering even mundane activities "too big to fail"—can leave entire production systems fantastically fragile and make them subject, just like our post-Glass-Steagall financial systems, to sudden cascading collapse.

I will do so first by looking at who makes the systems fragile and how, in order to put a human face on a process that can otherwise seem overly abstract (and therefore perhaps almost *natural*). Then I will look briefly at the financial and physical effects that such structural monopolization can have on complex systems by reviewing one industrial crash that did not happen and one that did. I will then examine how we often see the same sort of hyper rationalization in systems that the government regulates directly or indirectly. Last I'll discuss what it means for our well-being—even survival—when such rationalization is imposed upon the "global" industrial system as a whole.

For our first task—to understand who has driven so much of this monopolization of our industrial supply bases and why—we are in luck; we can turn to an industry with which we are relatively familiar: the making of automobiles. In so doing, we can take advantage of the fact that here we skirt the shores of Serendip. For not only did the Reagan administration set this process of monopolization into motion, it also provided us with perhaps the single best personification of the process in a man named David Stockman.

Older readers will remember that Stockman first made his name when President Reagan tapped him to direct the Office of Management and Budget. Only thirty-four years old at the time, and hence one of the youngest cabinet officials ever, Stockman almost immediately got himself into trouble when he told reporter William Greider, in an interview on Reagan's policy of giving tax cuts to the rich, that "none of us really understands what's going on with all these numbers."[27] In 1985, still in government, Stockman was even more honest, admitting in a speech to the board of the New York Stock Exchange that the Reagan administration had employed "accounting gimmicks, evasions, half truths and downright dishonesty in our budget numbers."[28]

Such a record of accomplishment was highly valued on Wall Street, and Stockman went on to a very successful career, first at Salomon Brothers, then as a founding partner at the Blackstone Group.

Right from the start, Stockman seemed to have a special fascination with the automobile industry. In 1979, he was the only member of the Michigan congressional delegation to oppose the first federal bailout of Chrysler. Then, very early in his time at Blackstone, he began to take a direct interest in the automotive supply business.

Indeed, Stockman's ties to the firm that would prove his downfall—Collins & Aikman (C&A)—can be traced to 1988, when Blackstone took a position in C&A's then parent company, Wickes. In the early 1990s, Stockman carved C&A out of Wickes, then set out to refine the lines of business organized under the C&A brand.[29] (One of the more suspect maneuvers involved arranging for C&A to sell one subsidiary for $100 million to Blackstone, which then promptly shut down that unit.)[30]

As we saw earlier in this chapter, by 1999 GM, Ford, and Chrysler were all ready to accelerate their efforts to outsource their parts-making operations. By this time they had bundled much of their in-house parts-manufacturing activity into new entities with names like Delphi and Visteon. The moment had come, they claimed, to spin those units off as independent operations. In other cases, they said, the moment had come to simply shut down in-house production and buy the parts instead from outside suppliers like Johnson Controls and Lear.

In pursuing this "dis-integration" of their operations, the big automakers often claimed to be seeking merely to compete with their Japanese rivals like Toyota, many of which had adopted forms of "virtual integration" in which most parts are made by outside "captive" suppliers. Yet the U.S. companies also made clear that they had no intention of insisting on Japanese-style industrial "monogamy," in which big firms, like Toyota, insist that their outside suppliers avoid any relationship with their direct competitors. On the contrary, the Big Three actuallypushed their newly spun-off parts makers to also supply their rivals. Doing so, they said, would result in greater "efficiencies" across the system as a whole and, hence, cost savings for the customer.

Let's take a moment to make sure we understand what exactly our automotive executives were promoting in the late 1990s. Until this point, these firms had been more or less completely vertically integrated and, hence, largely discrete from one another. Each firm was composed of productive units that served only the firm itself. This meant that GM, Ford, and Toyota North America each made its own wiper blades and alternators or relied on suppliers who did so for that one company alone. Now, by contrast, the Big Three offloaded as many of these operations as possible, as swiftly as possible, and they urged all their suppliers to rationalize their operations among themselves to as great a degree as possible.

For a bounding (if not-so-young-anymore) financier like David Stockman, this was the opportunity for which he had been waiting since coming to Wall Street. This was more than just a chance to buy up some of the hundreds of small and midsize industrial firms that were being orphaned and sometimes bankrupted in this revolutionary reorganization of Detroit. This was a de facto license to create miniature monopolies, as the big automakers had abandoned all the old rules by which they had imposed competition within their industrial systems.

And so Stockman now upped the ante, professionally and personally, by launching his own investment fund, Heartland Industrial Partners, into this chaotic industrial environment. His goal was simple: fashion small supplier firms into monopoly powers that would enable Stockman and his partners to get rich fast by charging more for less.

In short order, Stockman used Heartland to shape four holding companies. In addition to C&A, these were Metaldyne, Spring Industries, and TriMas. In each case, the strategy was the same: use a branded company as a shell into which to load a slew of similarly oriented producers— or, as one consultant put it, "to consolidate subsectors" in order to put together "a dominant position" in one or a few industrial activities.[31]

Of these four efforts, C&A was the most audacious. Stockman used the firm to consolidate a position supplying cockpit assemblies, seats, flooring, and door panels to more than 90 *percent* of all cars manufactured in the United States—including the operations of the Japanese transplants—and hence at least the potential to exercise real power over the operations of the branded automakers.

Stockman was so sure of his plan that in the summer of 2003, even as C&A's stock was plummeting, he took direct control of the company as its CEO. As he explained his move to the *New York Times*, "since the vision for this company was originally mine . . . now was the time to step in myself and really bring this together, bring some intensity, a heartbeat to the company."[32]

In the spring of 2005, the huge debt that Stockman had loaded onto C&A to fund his spree, combined with years of price cutting by the automakers, had resulted in an extreme cash-flow crisis in the company. And so, with bankruptcy looming, Stockman finally made the play that he had spent so many years preparing, acting at last on his threat to use the power he had consolidated to shut down the big boys if he did not get the cash he demanded. His initial target was Chrysler, specifically the assembly plant that produced the Chrysler 300, which at the time was being touted as "Detroit's hottest car in years."

The threat to shut down one of the Big Three resounded throughout the industry. As one writer put it, "such a warning is the auto industry equivalent of a nuclear weapon—rarely threatened and almost never used."[33] And in the end, the threat worked. Chrysler swiftly agreed to come up with $65 to $75 million in price increases and low-cost loans—and that was just in the near term. In all, C&A won promises from Chrysler for $335 million in price hikes and subsidized loans. Nevertheless, Stockman somehow goofed the timing of his auto parts putsch. Or maybe he once again got lost in his numbers. Whatever the reason, on May 17, 2005, C&A was forced to file for bankruptcy, and Stockman found himself no longer on the Street but just on the street. Soon he found himself in court, charged with securities fraud and conspiracy for misrepresenting the magnitude of C&A's crisis to his shareholders.[34]

For our purposes, what Stockman bequeathed us was, first of all, a finely drawn sketch of the new landscape of power, extortion, and terror in our *structurally monopolized* yet still *competitive* U.S. automotive industry. Look closely, and you can see how Stockman updated the old Mexican standoff, for at various points he managed to force the Big Six—Chrysler, GM, Ford, Toyota, Nissan, and Honda—to stand around and stare at one another, wondering who would pay the most to bail out their common supplier.

The Stockman shakedown also illuminates for us the terrible destruction that can result among the people who actually produce things during such an event. Small firms like the fabric maker Unifi were financially
battered, and skilled workers like those at C&A's three plants in Rantoul,
Illinois, ended up without jobs.[35] Not that this dissuaded similar plays.
On the contrary, Stockman's innovative approach to the industrial holdup
inspired other firms to do much the same thing, such as when the wheel
manufacturer Topy threatened a few months later to shut down GM.[36]

The Stockman shakedown also shows us the limits of such schemes.
No matter how big a share of the market C&A rolled up, the firm was
still a bit player. Given a little time, the *really big* boys can almost always
out enjoin a relatively small operator like C&A and thereby hold off the
holdup artist. They can also almost always outbet a small operator like
C&A in the capital markets, where, in a game that traces back at least
to the days of Jay Gould, they can unleash their brute financial power in
ways that neutralize or even euthanize the upstart.

That's exactly what happened here, for Stockman's C&A corner was
soon broken to pieces. A few plants were brought back under the direct
control of several of the Big Six automakers. Others were taken over by
other auto parts firms. Some, once their activities had been replicated
elsewhere, were closed. The rest? They ended up in the hands of more
patient monopolists, like Wilbur Ross.[37]

The Hydra

Over the centuries, human beings have proven to be remarkably adept at
devising techniques to run complex systems safely. We long ago learned
to build airtight compartments into our ships and circuit breakers into our
electrical systems. For more than sixty years, until the repeal of the Glass-
Steagall Act, we engineered our financial systems to be safe through such
physical measures as separating the speculator from the bank and requir-
ing the bank to hold specific levels of cash reserves. The Internet itself
was, at least in its conception, structured specifically to ensure the flow
of information around even the largest physical glitch. As we will see in
chapter 8, the division of agricultural land into personal private plots is
perhaps the earliest instance of human beings engineering a social system

to isolate failure. It is not a stretch to regard the separation of powers in the U.S. government as yet another method that humans devised to protect complex systems from the failure of some one part.

In the past, such compartmentalized structures were often developed through trial and error, often in response to a catastrophe. In recent decades, however, the people who engineer our complex systems have been able to benefit from a growing body of literature on the subject. One of the first people to systemically study how humans structure complex systems to be safe is my friend Charles Perrow. In his book *Normal Accidents*, Perrow, a professor of sociology at Yale, looked at such questions as how humans keep nuclear power plants from melting down and airliners from colliding.

Other important studies take the form of firsthand reports. In recent years, we have seen a number of excellent works that warn of how failure to build compartments and circuit breakers into our financial systems set the stage for catastrophic cascading failure. Among those sounding such warnings are Nassim Nicholas Taleb, author of *The Black Swan*, and Richard Bookstaber, author of *A Demon of Our Own Design*.

Almost no one, however, has written about such forms of risk in our industrial systems. The most obvious reason is that few people view industrial activity as organized into actual systems. And indeed, the vertical integration of most large manufacturers, combined with antitrust enforcement, meant that as a society we could until recently generally count on having a number of entirely distinct systems charged with the same basic task, competing with one another. This meant that if something went wrong anywhere, not only was the problem naturally isolated but any incompetence could be punished, as other teams of people stood ready to help fix the problem, if need be.

This is no longer the case. Over the last two decades, many industrial activities were, in fact, reorganized into extremely complex systems in which production processes are very "tightly coupled" to one another, a structure that makes them subject to cascading collapse. One of my main goals in *Cornered* is to help us begin to understand how this revolution happened and what it means.

To do so, let's continue our study of the automotive industry. Here, if anywhere it would seem, is an industrial activity marked by extreme competition, where failure can be isolated and punished. In the United States, after all, more than ten firms compete for our attention, and they do so with great vim and gusto. In fact, however, the combination of a *top-down* disintegration of firms like GM with a *bottom-up* consolidation of suppliers by players like David Stockman has resulted in a growing *structural monopolization* of the supply base of this entire industry.

The result, as we noted earlier, is an organization that increasingly resembles the structure of the ancient Greek monster the Hydra. We see many heads—GM, Ford, Chrysler, Toyota, Honda, and Nissan. But below the heads, these firms increasingly all share a single "body" composed of even more monopolized suppliers like C&A and Metaldyne. Although the vehicles these firms sell all look different and all have different names, more and more of the actual components come from the same factories.

Not that this Hydra structure originated in the automotive industry. It was in the electronics industry where we first saw such a bottom-up monopolization of an entire supply base. Microsoft and Intel are, of course, the classic examples of suppliers capturing monopoly positions in this industry, yet over the last two decades we have seen almost the entire electronics system consolidated along similar lines. In more recent years, the model has been applied—usually due to pressure from financiers—to industries as varied as chemicals, metals, and even (as we saw in chapter 1) cat food.

Whatever its provenance, the key fact for us is that the Hydra model poses many huge and unprecedented problems. One, as we will discuss in chapter 6, is that such systems tend to become ever less permeable to innovation, as consolidation increasingly enables even relatively small suppliers to block new and better ideas that may in any way threaten their established position within the system. A second problem is financial, namely that the combination of extreme competition among branded firms like GM and Toyota with monopolization among smaller firms in the supply base can unleash dynamics that result in the bankrupting of all players in the system.[38]

Here, however, I want to focus on the fact that this Hydra structure violates every principle we ever learned about how to engineer complex, socially vital systems to ensure that they remain safe in the long run. And I want to make sure we fully understand the nature of the *physical* risks created by such bottom-up monopolization—or *communalization*—of entire industrial activities.

The main problem is that where traditional industrial systems enabled us, as a society, to isolate failure and to damp down shock, the combination of monopolization of suppliers with "just-in-time" inventory of components and finished goods means that today's systems transmit shock instantly to all players in ways that ensure that a failure anywhere can result in a sudden failure everywhere. To understand how this works, let's look first at an industrial crash that did not happen, then at one that did.

The story of the industrial crash that did not happen traces back to the terrifying days after the collapse of Lehman Brothers. By then it had become evident that both General Motors and Chrysler were, for all intents, already bankrupt. It was at this point that Congress first began to debate whether to bail out the two firms. And so it was at this point that Alan Mulally, CEO of Ford, went to Capitol Hill to request just such help for his *rivals*.

The automotive industry, Mulally explained, is "uniquely interdependent." This was particularly true, he said, "with respect to our supply base, with more than 90 percent commonality among our suppliers. Should one of the other domestic companies declare bankruptcy, the effect on Ford's production operations would be felt within days—if not hours. . . . Without parts for the just-in-time inventory system, Ford plants would not be able to produce vehicles."[39]

On its face, this was a remarkable request. In American capitalism, after all, the leaders of a big company are supposed to celebrate the collapse of their rivals. Yet here was a desperate plea from one big firm to save one of its biggest and, according to prevailing economic theory, most dangerous competitors.

There was a simple reason Mulally made this request, however: the operations of Ford and General Motors had, to a very large degree, been merged.

As I mentioned in the preface, Mulally's request was soon seconded by Toyota. It was also supported by an exhaustive study by the Center for Automotive Research (CAR). Any sudden and uncontrolled bankruptcy of GM and Chrysler, CAR warned, by cutting off the flow of cash to suppliers that were already on the verge of bankruptcy themselves, could well trigger a "bottom up failure" of the entire North American automotive industry.[40]

The reason this industrial crash did not happen was precisely because the Bush administration did, in fact, loan GM and Chrysler $17.4 billion in December 2008. This kept the two firms out of bankruptcy court long enough to allow Ford, Toyota, and the other automakers and parts makers to prepare for the eventual bankruptcy of those two firms, which they did by building up their stocks of parts and cash and stabilizing the finances of key suppliers. And when the Obama administration's Automotive Task Force did bring the two erstwhile giants into bankruptcy court, it managed to complete the process of shedding debt in an astoundingly short period of time.[41]

Now let's look at an industrial crash that did happen. To do so, we must turn to Japan and to Toyota.

Most of us know that Toyota makes some of the world's highest quality and most technologically advanced cars and trucks. What is important here is that the company has long been renowned among manufacturing engineers for having devised one of the world's most efficient production systems. Toyota developed what it calls its production "philosophy" in the cash-strapped Japanese economy just after World War II. The lack of capital led the company to bypass the more expensive vertical integration model of the classic U.S. industrial firm in favor of a looser form of "virtual integration" with an array of small suppliers. Although Toyota did not technically own these small firms, it had sufficient power to prohibit them from supplying Toyota's competitors. To save yet more money, Toyota managers did not require these suppliers to build back-up operations, and they added a just-in-time parts delivery system that all but eliminated the giant inventories that characterized the U.S. automakers.[42]

Toyota always set strict limits on how far to push this system, which its own engineers sometimes referred to as "fragile production." The company did not trust long lines of supply, so when it expanded production to the United States and Europe, it generally did not ship parts from Japan but instead arranged for the construction of a new cluster of suppliers near the new assembly lines. Toyota also generally continued to insist on exclusive relationships with its "outside" suppliers. The result was that even though the Toyota system was extremely stripped out, compared to the classic U.S. model of production, it and the other Japanese companies that followed similar models remained largely isolated from one another.

In 1997, the Toyota system was put to its first big structural test when a fire destroyed a factory that manufactured brake valves. The sudden loss of this tiny component demonstrated three things. First, Toyota's system really was fragile, for the absence of this one part shut down the company's entire Japanese operation for more than a week. Second, the fragility did not appear to threaten the financial well-being of the company; on the contrary, the savings over the course of one year from

Toyota's super lean system far outweighed the cost of this one shutdown. Third, the company's manufacturing operations were still largely discrete from those of its rivals—no other big companies were affected by the fire or, for that matter, by the shutdown of the entire Toyota system.[43]

On July 16, 2007, an earthquake measuring 6.8 on the Richter scale ripped through the small city of Kashiwazaki, in Niigata Province on Japan's west coast. Compared to the Kobe earthquake of 1995, which killed more than six thousand people and shattered one of Japan's most important industrial cities, the event was minor. Though the Kashiwazaki quake killed eight people and knocked down hundreds of buildings, the damage was highly localized. Within a day, however, all ten of Japan's big vehicle manufacturers had shut down their assembly lines. Kashiwazaki, it turned out, was the home of a small company named Riken, which in the previous few years had come to dominate the production of the piston rings that are built into most of the internal combustion engines assembled in Japan.

In the summer of 2008, I spent two months in Japan interviewing dozens of industry engineers and managers and government officials about the lessons they took from the Kashiwazaki quake. One thing I learned is that both government officials and automotive engineers—including at Toyota—concluded that this Hydra form of industrial organization poses unacceptable dangers to society and must be restructured to be more resilient. (At the time I was in Japan, officials there had not yet determined how to engineer such a restructuring.)

The officials and engineers also agreed on something else, which was that the *impetus* to reorganize the Japanese auto industry into this highly unstable Hydra structure did not come from within Japanese corporations or from within the Japanese financial system. Rather, it came from the United States. The Japanese automakers and parts suppliers adopted this model to remain competitive with GM and Ford, and under pressure from such suppliers as Johnson Controls, Lear, and Collins & Aikman.

A decade ago, a failure anywhere hurt only one isolated cluster of companies in an industry. Today, thanks to financiers like David Stockman, even the smallest of failures can hit an entire industry at once and hence the entire society that depends on that industry. A decade ago, the firms that were not affected by the breakdown could help the firm or firms that suffered the blow. Today, thanks to financiers like David Stockman, all stand or fall together.[44]

The Industrial State?

In 1967, when John Kenneth Galbraith predicted that the U.S. and Soviet systems would converge into a vaguely democratic and vaguely socialistic "industrial state," he did not present his vision as either economically or politically utopian. Even so, his concept was mildly reassuring. The production of our most vital goods, after all, would be overseen by a class of highly trained scientists and public servants. And even if this class was not entirely disinterested in nature, rule by such a technocratic elite seemed far less dangerous than the obvious alternatives, namely, rule by power-hungry party apparatchiks or avaricious financiers.

Such visions of state direction of our political economy fell out of fashion long ago, not least because our financiers did such a good job of training us to celebrate avarice. Over the last year or so, however, a swelling number of people—in Washington as well as in such capitals as Brussels and Beijing—began to call for a far more bureaucratic approach to running our political economy. We have seen this in the debate over how to stabilize our financial systems and in the debate over whether and how to salvage GM and Chrysler. The basic idea is that even if state direction of the economy does not generate swift growth, it does result in a far more safe and stable system. The basic assumption here seems to be that elimination of the profit motive will result—almost naturally—in more "sober" and "professional" decision making.

Before we conclude this chapter, I want to tell two short stories. The first recounts an instance in which the U.S. government *did* enforce our antitrust laws in an effort to restructure industrial activity. The second recounts an instance in which an agency of the U.S. government *did* use its purchasing power in ways that affected the structure of private industry. Doing so, I believe, will clarify that the question we face is not *whether* to settle the power to direct our political economy in private *or* public hands, but rather *how* to ensure that the power of both the public state and the private corporation is directed in ways that result in the structuring of production systems to be safe and resilient.[45]

Consider first the system we rely on to synthesize vitamin C. As most of us know, vitamin C is essential to human life. It enables our bodies to manufacture a protein named collagen, which is a key component in bones, teeth, and cartilage. Most animals make their own vitamin C, but humans don't. Until the industrial age, humans took in vitamin C when we ate certain fruits and vegetables and uncooked meat. When deprived of such foods, we are liable to get scurvy, a disease in which the body literally breaks down due to a lack of collagen. Gums become spongy, muscles lose their tone, teeth fall out, skin splits open.

We have known for many centuries that eating citrus seems to prevent and cure scurvy. The trouble with citrus is that the supply of fresh fruit is limited. That's why in 1880 U.S. chemists began to extract citric acid from the juice of oranges and limes. The process proved expensive, however, especially because the supplies of the most common raw material, citrate of lime, were largely controlled by a rapacious Italian cartel, the Camera Agrumaria. Scurvy therefore remained common well into the twentieth century, with huge outbreaks among European soldiers and civilians on both sides during and after World War I.[46]

The big breakthrough came in 1931, when an American biochemist—Charles Glen King—finally isolated the molecule we call vitamin C.[47] This immediately set off a race among firms including Merck, Roche, and Abbott Laboratories to synthesize vitamin C in bulk. Nevertheless, after four years a pound still cost $3,415 wholesale. Then Charles Pfizer & Company of Brooklyn perfected a fermentation-free method of production. By 1938 the price of a pound was $44. By the 1970s it was $4.50. This enabled us to blend vitamin C into our industrially processed foods almost as freely as we blend fluoride into water. And so we made scurvy all but vanish from rich nations, even among children who gag at the sight of a fruit or a vegetable.[48]

Now let's jump to the late 1980s. That's when a cartel of private firms, mainly from Europe, allied with U.S. financiers to capture control of the U.S. market for industrial vitamins. Between 1988 and 1992 this cartel grew to include twenty-one chemical manufacturers based in seven nations, and it governed the manufacture of at least sixteen different vitamin products. Once the cartel was complete, the members promptly raised their prices. Indeed, they did so in such a blatant way that they attracted the attention even of the Clinton administration, which tended to smile benignly upon the actions of almost any monopolist.

The government's investigation, made public in May 1999, resulted in formal actions against cartel members in at least nine other countries and more than a hundred private lawsuits. One firm, Roche, paid $954 million in fines. Another, BASF, paid some $500 million. In the specific instance of vitamin C, the government was able to trace a conspiracy at least as far back as 1991, when Hoffman–La Roche began to coordinate operations with Archer Daniels Midland (ADM). As part of that cartel agreement, ADM apparently delayed construction of a next-generation vitamin C plant that it had long planned for the U.S. market.[49]

The investigation of the vitamin cartel was a big and important victory for our antitrust enforcers. Every regulator who took part in the case has a right to be proud. The problem lies in what our government did next. Which was, precisely, nothing. The assumption, it seems, was that now that the cartel busters had done their work, the "market" would take over, and the supply of vitamins would swiftly return to "normal."

Yet the firms that participated in the original vitamin cartel did not, in fact, rush back into the business of making and selling vitamins to Americans. Almost the exact opposite happened. In the specific case of vitamin C, ADM decided not to open its long-planned, next-generation plant. Hoffman–La Roche, meanwhile, actually decided to sell off its plant in Belvedere, New Jersey—the last vitamin C plant in the United States. The Dutch chemical firm that bought the plant, DSM, then decided to shut down all vitamin C production there and to concentrate work at a plant in Scotland.[50]

One reason these corporations acted this way was that by the time the antitrust investigation was complete, most of the giant companies that blend vitamin C into the processed foods sold in the United States had turned to Chinese suppliers. And these Chinese firms, whose own cartel was for some reason ignored by the antitrust enforcers, priced their vitamin C so low that the European and U. S. chemical manufacturers saw no reason to compete with them. Now jump to 2007. That's when the Chinese suppliers of vitamin C, finally confident of their dominance of the U.S. market, jacked up the price they charge American buyers by 400 percent.[51]

And so, one of the great achievements of U.S. scientists and industrial engineers in the twentieth century—one that made the American people more healthy and more independent of foreign powers—was undone. The French chemical engineer and historian Fred Aftalion wrote that Pfizer's achievement in the 1930s "freed America from the shackles of the European" citric acid cartel. In the 1990s, U.S. financiers delivered us right back into the hands of the European cartel, which promptly abandoned us to the Chinese.[52]

Now let's take a moment to look at how our government has managed our supply of flu vaccine in recent years. Here we see not one but two huge regulatory failures. The first was another failure to apply antimonopoly law at all, in this case to the U.S. pharmaceutical industry. This left the financiers who run these corporations free to whittle down the number of firms able to manufacture flu vaccine from more than a dozen in the 1960s to two by 2004. This also left them free to cut the number of firms equipped to manufacture vaccines of any kind from twenty-six to four, also by 2004.[53]

The second failure, which I want to focus on, was in the Centers for Disease Control's (CDC) procurement system. This system was put into place originally to guarantee that some public servant was watching over supplies of the medical products we use to prevent contagion. The basic idea is that even in cases where antitrust authorities fail to ensure productive competition, government agencies can often throw around their procurement funds in ways that ensure a multiplicity of suppliers.

That's what officials in Britain did during that same 2004 flu season. Even though monopolists have run 10 Downing Street for the last generation, in much the same way they have run the White House, the Health Ministry in London spread its purchasing of flu vaccine across five companies.

Yet in recent years, the CDC, even though it is responsible for ensuring supply to a far larger population, stopped spreading out its purchases. Instead it *concentrated* purchases in only two companies, and allowed those two companies to *concentrate production* in two plants.

The initial result of such concentration was a series of shortages. In 2003, for instance, flu vaccine supplies ran short early in December. This followed the seven shortages of children's vaccines in the previous four years. These were shortages not of fancy new concoctions but of our old, basic vaccines for tetanus, chicken pox, measles, and diphtheria.

Then in October 2004 British health officials shut a long-troubled plant in Liverpool that had been controlled by the California-based corporation Chiron. Because U.S. health officials had contracted Chiron to supply half of the nation's flu vaccine but had allowed the company to locate *all* production in the Liverpool plant, the result was a sudden and massive shortage of flu vaccine right at the beginning of flu season.

The CDC tried to convince other vaccine makers to step in, but none had any excess capacity; thanks to the years of working to make the system more "efficient," all were running their lines full out.

So doctors had no choice but to ration shots, which meant that a lot of people who wanted vaccinations did not get them. Five years later, it's still not clear how many Americans died because of this breakdown. Fortunately, the flu strain that year was especially mild.[54]

From these two stories, I believe we may draw three conclusions. First is that to guarantee the safety of our food and drug systems, we must keep in mind that one of the most important steps is not to hire more inspectors or regulate more harshly. The easiest way to ensure that we get what we need, even when someone makes a really big mistake, is simply to use our antitrust laws and other antimonopoly powers to *compartmentalize* these systems in different companies that operate different manufacturing plants located in different places and run by different management teams.

Second, except in cases of clear natural monopoly, concentration is almost never cheaper than competition in any respect. Time and again our government regulators and procurement officers justify concentration by claiming that one or two is all we can afford. Yet in the long run, not only does monopoly entail higher social costs, not least by posing far greater dangers of disruption, it also almost always results in higher prices for our goods. The catch is that a large portion of these higher prices is passed on to us through the IRS.

When the Bush administration took action in May 2006 to avoid any repetition of the flu vaccine fiasco, for instance, it did not use antitrust law nor procurement coercion to alter the behavior of our pharmaceutical companies. Instead, it simply used our tax dollars to bribe five firms—three of them from Europe—up to $299 million apiece ($1 billion in all) to develop new flu vaccine production techniques and then to build new flu vaccine plants in the United States.[55]

Third, and most important, when it comes to the physical safety of any production system, the debate over whether to govern that system through public or private institutions is largely a red herring. What matters is not who runs the system but how the system is structured. How a system is structured is, in turn, largely a matter of whether the people who regulate the system use their power to promote "efficiency" unto monopoly or resiliency and redundancy through competition. Whether any team of regulators promotes efficiency or resiliency is, in turn, largely a result of whether those regulators have fallen into the intellectual framework set by the monopolists. Or rather, whether these regulators have been transformed into tools of the monopolists.

Built to Break

On page 1 of *The Wealth of Nations*, Adam Smith illustrates the central principle of his political economics with an example taken from, in his words, a "very trifling manufacture": the making of pins. "One man draws out the wire," he writes, "another straits it, a third cuts it, a fourth points it, a fifth grinds it at the top for receiving the head." In all, Smith counts eighteen different operations, then estimates that such specialization boosts productivity at least 240 times over what the same number of men, each working alone, could accomplish.[56] Ever since, Smith's image of wealth achieved through specialization of labor has served as perhaps the central vision for organizing economic activity, at least among the English-speaking peoples of the world. Which is not surprising. After all, a 24,000 percent jump in productivity is a powerful argument.

This is also one of the main reasons that many people today believe so strongly in "free trade" among nations. Opening all borders, they are convinced, is the fastest way to increase the size of the population in which such specialization of labor can occur; hence, it is the fastest way to enrich all people everywhere.

There are two problems with this reading of Smith. The first is that Smith's intent was not to maximize trade among nations, nor was it to maximize wealth among all people everywhere. His goal was to increase the wealth of *his nation,* and thereby increase the ability of the citizens who have a *stake* in that nation to use the powers therein to serve their own interests, often by protecting themselves from *other groups of people in other* nations.

The second and even bigger problem is that circumstances change. When Smith published *The Wealth of Nations* in 1776, he hoped merely to promote greater trade among English counties. Today, more than 230 years and two industrially powered world wars later, our world production system itself has come to look much like one giant pin factory.

Every few months the opinion pages of our newspapers swell with impassioned pleas to our representatives in Washington not to stumble down the path to trade "protectionism." The slightest hint that Congress or the administration might alter a comma in NAFTA, or might insist that a few of our own tax dollars in our own stimulus bill be spent in our own hometowns, is met by apoplectic warnings of a second coming of Smoot-Hawley (the 1930 tariff act that raised taxes on imported goods and that, in one of their more blatant perversions of history, is blamed by the free traders for plunging the world into depression).

The reality today is that the industrial systems of the nations of the world are already tied together so intimately that it is all but impossible to restore our national industrial autonomy, even if that's what we really wanted to do.

The problem is not that we are doomed to live in an interdependent world, however. As we will see in chapter 7, a deeply interdependent system can be made, if we choose to enact the laws necessary to restructure industrial activity accordingly, almost perfectly safe, physically and politically. The trouble is monopolization. Or rather that, as our financiers did with the systems we devised to produce vitamin C, flu vaccine, and piston rings, so too have they done with the systems we devised to produce semiconductors, industrial chemicals, pharmaceuticals, medical devices, metals, even our food. Sometimes on their own and sometimes in alliance with mercantilists abroad, our financiers exerted their power in ways that transformed the world industrial system—taken as a whole—into an intricate network of operations made "too big to fail."[57]

The problem is that in such a structurally monopolized world-spanning industrial system, every key worker in every nation must show up for work every day. The problem is that we have been made to depend on single distant semiconductor foundries, single distant data entry operations, and single distant piston ring plants just as intimately as we depend on Citibank and all the other financial institutions that we now recognize are "too big to fail."[58] The structure of such a system, combined with the nature of man and the whims of nature, all but ensures that there will come a day when we do not have access to one of these keystone operations. Which means that it is a system all but guaranteed to collapse in a precipitous and potentially catastrophic chain reaction.

This is no mere theory. In addition to the Niigata earthquake, we have seen many times already what happens to such structurally monopolized cross-border industrial systems when those borders close, as they inevitably sometimes do. On September 11, 2001, we saw our automotive and electronic industries shut down in hours. After an earthquake in Taiwan in September 1999, we saw our computer industry toppled in a matter of days. Nor is it very hard to imagine what would happen if there were ever another war on the Korean peninsula. Or if ever India and Pakistan launched nuclear weapons at each other, as they threatened to do in 2001 and 2002. Or if a major epidemic ever disrupts everyday business and normal cross-border trade, as nearly happened in 2003 with SARS. Or if the Chinese people ever again decide to shut down business as usual to fight for freedom, as they did in Tiananmen Square in 1989.

We even have a model that shows what can happen to a society when an industrial system based on single sources of production breaks apart, in the devastating industrial crash that followed the breakup of the Soviet Union in 1991.

These are not the sorts of crashes that the Federal Reserve or the U.S. Treasury can fix. Unlike cash, industrial parts are not fungible.

When we were sold the concept of globalization in the 1990s, we were assured that the new system would be safer and more resilient than the system it replaced. And so it could have been. Instead, we stopped enforcing our antimonopoly laws and allowed our financiers to rationalize our political economy as they alone saw fit. This meant putting every industrial activity over which they had control into what they alone believed was the perfect place—from which to leverage money and power. Often these places were simply too few in number and too far away.

All the opulent chaos of an open marketplace, in which people truck and barter free of top-down direction and control, was eliminated, often to a degree that would have gladdened Joseph Stalin. We were locked inside a crystalline house, with every atom of every wall rationalized to the point of perfect brittleness, by men so mad for cash that they continue today to attack the foundation of our house with picks and shovels and sticks of dynamite.

Leviticus tells us:

> When you reap the harvest of your land, you shall not reap to the very corners of your field, nor shall you gather the gleanings of your harvest. Nor shall you glean your vineyard, nor shall you gather the fallen fruit of your vineyard; you shall leave them for the needy and for the stranger.

I guess we skipped that passage. The reckoning is yet to come.

4

The Market Masters

It's just before noon in September, and I am wandering among the stalls at the downtown City Market in Kansas City. The display tables are nearly invisible under mounds of tomatoes, squash, green beans, eggplants, and cut flowers, and just walking between the rows of vendors is hard work. The ground is cluttered with piles of immense orange and white pump-kins, late-season watermelons, and red and yellow chrysanthemums. The aisles are jammed with families burdened with bags of greens, college students sipping coffee while considering carrots, and white-haired reti-rees gently fondling apples. Everything seems right with the world.

This scene takes place every Saturday from early spring to late fall on a two-acre plot near the Missouri River. As I quickly learned, however, this scene does not just happen naturally and harmoniously. Ever since I walked into the market at 5:30 a.m., I've been talking to vendors, and it took only a few conversations to fill my notebook with stories of jeal-ousy and resentment, of grudges new and old, of feelings of inadequacy and failure, of whispered accusations of conniving and cheating. Greed, abuse of power, laziness—I've heard all alleged this morning.

The City Market, like all real markets, is a microcosm of human society, an arena of pushing and passion that requires close and con-stant oversight and policing. Adam Smith wrote that human beings have a natural propensity to "truck and barter."[1] We also have a natural pro-pensity to establish rules to govern our trucking and bartering as well as institutions to enforce the rules. The most important of these institu-tions is the market.

People have been selling and buying on this spot for more than 150 years, since a local landowner deeded the property to the city for the express purpose of erecting a public market. Physically, there's nothing special about the City Market. Most vendors display their produce—and items like homemade cakes, jams, and honey—in one or two of 180 stalls that stretch through three open-air pavilions. Low-slung buildings that date from the late 1930s—and that now house restaurants, stores, and a museum—surround the market on four sides.

In the 1960s, the market almost closed when consumers began flocking to shiny supermarkets and a new six-lane superhighway cut off Kansas City's old downtown from the rest of the city. Beginning in the early 1990s, however, Kansas City boosters began to view the market as one of the centerpieces of their efforts to redevelop central Kansas City. Until the collapse of the housing market, nearby blocks had been filling fast with renovated loft apartments, upscale gyms, and restaurants.

Ron Fahrmeier is one of the farmers in town this Saturday. I catch Fahrmeier, a big man in overalls, just as he sets a bulging box of tomatoes onto his table, and he speaks to me slowly at first as he catches his breath. This is his first year selling at the City Market, and he says that he has found it easier than he expected to build up steady business. The foray into raising and selling produce marks a major late-career change for Fahrmeier, who spent most of his thirty or so years on the farm raising row crops like corn and soybeans. Even though at this moment the price for commodity crops is soaring, he tells me that he plans to stick with vegetables. In recent years, he was able to sell enough produce to local grocers to lure both of his sons back to the farm, including one with a young family. Selling in the market has increased his income even further, he says.

Nevertheless, Fahrmeier readily admits that he often feels nervous and fretful at the City Market. Today, for instance, the problem is that the price of tomatoes and zucchinis is lower than he expected. When asked why, he nods toward one of the stores that surround the market pavilions. Only local farmers are allowed to sell in the stalls of the market, and these farmers have to raise at least half the food they sell. Fahrmeier and his family grew everything on his tables except the apples, which he carries to market for a neighbor.

At the nearby stores, however, most of the produce was trucked in from industrial farms in California and Florida. Those vegetables were picked at least a week ago, whereas Fahrmeier harvested most of his produce yesterday. The trucked-in vegetables look similar enough and fresh enough to fool many buyers, however, so the low prices charged by the stores depress what the local farmers at the stalls can charge.

"You have to deal with the market," Fahrmeier says. "You are governed by what is around you." That's why he would like to see the stores expelled entirely from the City Market. But Fahrmeier is also confident that in time he will be able to outsmart those vendors. Next year he plans to bring different varieties of vegetables to market that will be more easily distinguishable from the industrial-grown produce. He also plans to paint some new signs over the winter to explain to the buyers why they should view his products as superior.

At another stall, Fred Messner is in a less sanguine mood. Messner is a wiry man, his eyes blue and steely under a wide-brimmed cap, and at first he doesn't seem to have much about which to complain. His face cocked into a half grin, Messner says that he makes a fine living at the City Market, selling much of his produce above the going rate. He says this is because he's a good salesman and has built up a robust base of regular customers. Another reason is that Messner and his wife have worked hard to stay ahead of the trends in food fashion. After they quit growing row crops in Missouri in the 1980s, they raised organic vegetables in California and organic citrus in Florida.

When they returned home, they were among the first in Missouri to win organic certification. More recently, Messner says, he began to "move beyond" organic, after he concluded that the government had allowed big corporations to dumb down the organic regulations. Messner now engages in "biodynamic" farming, which he describes as an "intense application of organic practices that, first off, the feds don't have their fingers in."

Messner is anxious because he knows that the only way to ensure that a market works for both the farmer and the consumer is to remain vigilant against people who break the rules. Messner has been selling at City Market for more than fifteen years, and he says he's seen a lot of dirty dealing. One year, a man hauled in immense loads of tomatoes from Tennessee and sold them from twelve different stalls spread throughout the market. Another year, a man trucked apples from Texas, then convinced otherwise legitimate vendors to sell them as their own.

Last year, Messner says, the state of Missouri hurt the market when it cut a successful program that gave poor families coupons to buy fresh produce. Messner also dislikes vendors who dump unsold vegetables too early in the afternoon. Nor is he fond of gardeners and hobbyists who earn good salaries at city jobs and who sell at the market mainly for fun. A form of competition that Messner does welcome wholeheartedly, however, is the emergence of new farmers' markets in and around Kansas City. The fact that a popular producer like him has more options each weekend, he believes, increases his leverage with the people who make the City Market.

To discover whether this is true, I wander away from the market stalls and into a nearby building. There I find Stephanie Spatz-Ornburn, a longtime executive at the City Market who on this Saturday is serving as the "market master." When I arrive, Spatz-Ornburn, a slim blond woman dressed in a loose jacket, is talking animatedly on a landline telephone while her cell phone rings. She soon joins me in a second-floor conference room, where we sit next to windows that overlook the market. Yet before she manages to close the door, two vendors appear, and her phones ring again.

Saturdays are like this, she says, finally relaxing. Vendors start lodging complaints and requests before dawn, and they don't stop until the market closes in the late afternoon. On this day Spatz-Ornburn must deal with complaints about lighting, where temporary sellers have set up their tables, about a delay in getting a new slot. She also hears about a man who sold chickens and eggs before dawn from a truck parked on the street, about a couple caught selling puppies from a blanket, and about loud music early in the morning. Spatz-Ornburn has worked at the market for more than ten years, and she says that it used to be much worse. She hands me the forty-page *Vendor Handbook*. In general, she says, the more detailed the rules, the fewer the complaints. "People need to see the rules in writing, or they will fight about everything."

Yet the rules are also always in flux, she says. That's because it is a never-ending challenge to devise a balance that serves farmers, consumers, and the market itself. Many farmers want to restrict the market only to people who grow 100 percent of what they sell, as many other farmers' markets do, but Spatz-Ornburn says that the City Market wants to continue to make room for farmers who supplement their sales with produce from other local farms. This is partly to increase the variety of the foods that are available to local consumers.

The main goal is to provide an outlet for the many Amish families who farm north and east of Kansas City but who, because they don't own trucks, can't make it to town on a Saturday. As a compromise, the City Market has redoubled its inspections of local farms to make sure that the farmers who trade in others' produce really do raise at least half of what they sell.

And so, in this small square in the center of a city in the middle of the United States, we observe most of the basic functions that open and public markets serve in our society. Some of these are obvious; others are less so. These include the following:

- *Supply*. Producers from the countryside transfer food directly to consumers in the city without passing through the hands of a middleman.
- *Pricing*. The farmers and the consumers work out how much a local tomato, for example, is worth to Kansas City consumers on any given Saturday.
- *Transparency*. The rules of the market are public, and so are all the efforts to manipulate these rules, as much as possible.
- *Innovation*. To increase sales, the producers learn to differentiate their offerings from one another.
- *Protection*. The rules of the market shield the farmers from better-capitalized competitors and cheats.[2]

Our stroll through the City Market also allows us to begin to identify the most important characteristic of open and public markets—and the central point of this chapter—which is that there is no such thing as a "free" market. All real markets are political institutions in which market "masters" regulate economic competition among different groups within a society. This includes competition between the producer and the consumer over such issues as price and quality. It also includes competition between the producer and the trader and between the small-property holder and the financier.

The ultimate function of a well-regulated open-market system is not to ensure an "efficient" distribution of resources. (One thing Wal-Mart proves is that, at least for a while, nonmarket systems can be made reasonably efficient through the use of terror.) Rather, the ultimate function is to reveal, harness, and direct power within a society in order to ensure the widest possible distribution of *political* freedom and the greatest possible degree of political and economic stability.

For individual producers like Fahrmeier and Messner, the well-regulated market protects their freedom to work their personal private properties safe from predatory competition and authoritarian private or public governance. This protection of these physical properties, in turn, helps to protect the society that depends on these properties for its own well being. In the first three chapters, we saw that the failure to regulate corporate power wisely and well can result in the wholesale destruction of real properties and liberties. The same thing is true when we fail to regulate markets in ways that protect them from manipulation and predation by distant financiers.

Markets and Freedom

In the last generation, we have been taught to believe in a philosophy of what is sometimes called "free-market fundamentalism." As we noted in the preface, this philosophy is designed not to illuminate real-world phenomena but to hide the real-world use by the rich of such man-made institutions as the corporation and the marketplace—and sometimes even our own governments—to seize our properties and our liberties. In this chapter and the next, my goal is to reconnect us with our traditional understanding of how markets operate and what purposes they serve, to thereby restore our ability to use markets to help protect our most important political interests.

In the following pages I will sketch a political economic history of the United States that will show us how we evolved our institutions over the last two centuries to protect our open markets. Then in the next chapter, I will look at how the Chicago School operators who are responsible for the free-market fundamentalist philosophy managed to substitute such a fantastically different definition of *market*, one that enabled the rich to use their corporations and their banks to destroy or pervert most of our most important actual markets and, in the process, capture many of our properties.

The first step is simply to recall that at the time we were founding our nation, the American people staunchly opposed not only the monopolization of soul by any one church, or political power by any one man, but also commerce by any one company. Let's do this by turning to a story we all know, the Boston Tea Party.

This story began in May 1773 when the British Parliament passed the Tea Act, which eliminated taxes on tea imported to England and then exported to North America. The act also allowed the British East India Company to bypass the existing system of markets and traders and sell directly to individual American consumers, at prices far below those that independent merchants could charge. In exchange for this bargain-priced tea, the British Parliament expected Americans finally to end their long and sometimes violent agitation against direct taxation.[3]

As we all know, the Tea Act did not work as intended. The colonists did not respond as mechanistic consumers thankful for lower-priced leaf. Instead, we expanded what had been a rebellion against government taxation into a rebellion also against the monopolization of a public market activity by a private corporation. The most dramatic act took place on December 16, 1773, when the Sons of Liberty slipped aboard three ships in Boston Harbor and tossed forty-five tons of British East India Company tea into the water.

The anger that led to the Boston Tea Party was not solely an American phenomenon. It was part of a wider rebellion in the British world of the late eighteenth century against the abuses and unfair privileges enjoyed by the East India Company in relation to smaller producers and shopkeepers—a rebellion that in the coming years would be championed in Parliament itself by the political philosopher Edmund Burke.

Nor was the anger that was expressed in the Tea Party isolated in time. Rather, it was part of a long chain of antimonopoly agitation that traces through U.S. and English history back to the Statute of Monopolies in 1623, the Case of Monopolies in 1602, and ultimately to the Magna Carta in 1215. This history illustrates that the Tea Party was not merely, or even mainly, a drama of national independence, but one of individual independence.

When they confounded the British East India Company in 1773, the Americans succeeded precisely where their great-grandparents in England had failed a century earlier, during the great enclosures of agricultural land at the end of the English Civil War. In doing so, the founders set the stage for the central achievement of the American Revolution: the overthrow of an aristocratic social structure characterized by the direct or indirect enthrallment of most citizens to a patron or master.

As historian Gordon Wood has written, the free and open markets created by the Revolution "liberated men" from the "intricate networks of personal loyalties, obligations, and quasi-dependencies" that had dominated life in the colonies, and indeed life in most European nations for hundreds of years.[4]

We will discuss in more detail in the next chapter how today's monopolies affect us as entrepreneurs, professionals, and workers. The reason it is important to recollect here how the American Revolution redefined the concept of personal "independence," is that the newly free American people tied their new independence to the erection and protection of open markets.

To be "independent" in an aristocratic and feudal society, a man had to control a big enough stock of land or capital to be free of any need to beg favor of any other man. In other words, independence in an aristocratic society was a function of having many others work for you and depend on you. The Americans of the Revolutionary generation redefined independence as the freedom of *every* farmer, worker, and trader to contract with *anyone*, or not, within open market systems.[5]

The Scottish historian Thomas Carlyle later termed this form of interaction the "nexus" of "cash payment," by which he meant that individuals could now sell their products and labor for money, then use that money to buy whatever they wished, wherever they wished, with no regard for proper aristocratic relations.[6]

James Madison put it better, in a 1792 essay in which he focused not on the medium of exchange but on what was being exchanged and how. There is no "just government," he wrote, "nor is property secure under it, where arbitrary restrictions, exemptions, and monopolies deny to part of its citizens that free use of their faculties and free choice of their occupations, which not only constitute their property in the general sense of the word; but are the means of acquiring property strictly so called."[7]

In other words, labor is a form of property, and citizens have a right to work their property without restriction, and to trade their work with others in open and public marketplaces free of interference by others. The creation of such a property-based, money-lubricated, open market system was central to the goal of ensuring citizens the freedom to withhold work, to choose their own business partners, to move to another town or another state, and to never be forced to beg favor of another person.

To understand more fully the attitudes against monopoly in the early United States, consider another event of 1776: Adam Smith's publication of *The Wealth of Nations*. Although Smith was an Englishman, his work was partly a product of the U.S. colonial reality, as told to Smith by American friends such as Benjamin Franklin. Smith's work, in turn, exerted a huge influence on the founders.

Smith reserved a special place in the netherworld for monopolists, especially but not solely those of the East India Company. Monopolists, he wrote, raise prices, suppress wages, distort investment, unsettle international relations, pervert the functioning of markets, and are "enemies of good management." Then, his eyes fixed squarely on the East India Company's predations in India, Smith wrote that monopolists sometimes destroy men, governments, and nations. Any law, he concluded, that aids the monopolist—and all monopolies are direct or indirect products of law—"may be said to be all written in blood."[8]

The Harnessing of Power

The early United States was a small, weak, and scattered nation surrounded to the north, the west, and the south by the military and commercial empires of Britain, France, and Spain. The early Americans therefore understood that if they were to keep their republic, they must have rifles, cannons, ships, and clothing. This meant that they must have factories and skilled craftsmen and inventors, which meant that they must devise institutions to concentrate capital and people. This in turn meant that they must accept limits on some open markets, in the form of government monopolies and partial or complete private corporate monopolies.

The next step in reconstructing traditional political economic thinking in this country is to understand how early Americans managed to consolidate sufficient political economic power to master these complex industries and also managed not to be consumed by that power. The debate over how to manage the public and private industrial corporations that were deemed necessary to survive in a world of warring states was one of the most important in the history of our nation.

The challenge of figuring out how to keep corporations in political harness is almost perfectly analogous to the challenge of figuring out how to keep a standing army in political harness. An industrial corporation can be an incredibly powerful institution, in which legions of men, capital, and know-how are amassed. Such forces, the early Americans understood well, could be put to use in domestic competitions between regions or between classes just as easily as in military competition with other nations.

Secretary of the Treasury Alexander Hamilton was the first to outline an integrated argument about how to concentrate the economic powers that were necessary to arm and protect the nation, in his "Report on Manufactures," published in December 1791.[9] The report proved to be one of the most influential works in the political economic history of our nation, yet its initial reception was less friendly. This was due largely to the fact that Hamilton elsewhere made clear that he expected such corporations, even as they manufactured the arms that the nation needed to protect itself, would also serve to empower a new American aristocracy by enabling a few men to control and profit from the economic activities of their compatriots.

Hamilton made this intent clear when he established America's first inter-state alliance of would-be land, industrial, and trading lords—what came to be known as the Federalist Party. He also made his intent clear when he used his position as secretary of the treasury to design regulations that would help his well-off friends and allies. The most infamous instance was when Hamilton structured a tax on whiskey to give rich distillers a big price advantage over the average independent farmer.[10]

This in turn led to his single most notorious act in office, which was to raise and lead an army of thirteen thousand men to put down a rebellion against the whiskey tax by free farmers in western Pennsylvania. This made it obvious to the American people that if we were to keep our independence as individuals, we would have to continue fighting here at home against men who wielded not merely industrial estates but also sometimes the power of the federal government.

Jefferson, Madison, and their followers were no utopian agrarians, as they are often derided by those who seek to justify and impose top-down corporate control over our markets and our selves. If anything, it was they who, along with their fellow Democratic-Republicans, took Hamilton's "Report on Manufactures" most to heart, and who emerged as the true promoters of the industries that were necessary to protect the liberty of the American Republic.

It was Jefferson, we should remember, who introduced Americans to the concept of building rifles from identical interchangeable parts, in an act that jump-started what came to be known as the "American System" of industrial production.[11] It was also Jefferson who, during the Napoleonic wars, signed the radical Embargo Act, which outlawed all exports from the United States to Europe in a move that forced U.S. traders and bankers to shift capital into manufacturing goods.

And it was Madison who, after the War of 1812, took the first steps to implement Hamilton's vision for national industrial development, again often in opposition to U.S. traders, bankers, and planters. A generation later, it was the Democratic-Republican Andrew Jackson who threatened the use of armed force against South Carolina planters who refused to pay the tariff of 1828, which was designed to protect domestic industries, and who then signed the protective tariff of 1832.

The Democratic-Republican Party, not Hamilton's Federalist Party, was the true "producerist" party in the early United States. It was the Democratic-Republicans who ensured that we developed the industries we needed to keep ourselves free from foreign domination, even as they simultaneously helped us to devise the political economic institutional balances that would enable us to keep ourselves free *from* these new and necessary industrial powers.

It was, in fact, the Democratic-Republicans who best understood the two fatal flaws of the Hamiltonian aristocratic vision. First, that the line between the manufacturer and the trader is very thin and that industrial lords would, whenever they thought it served their interests, shut down even the most vital production systems and replace that production with imports. Second, that in any society as decentralized as America in those years, the natural competition among aristocrats from different regions would result in the rise of factions among the rich. If left unchecked by the people as a whole, some of these factions would choose to empower themselves by selling off their homemade monopolies (and the people governed within them) to foreign sovereigns. Some of these factions would, in other words, in their competition for gold and precedence, betray the republic itself.

Indeed, this vision animated the most famous fight against monopoly during that era. This was President Jackson's "war" against the Second Bank of the United States—which he called a "hydra of corruption" because of the many interlinking monopolies that grew from it.[12] It is not clear that Jackson was right in the particulars; Madison was a strong supporter of a central bank, and in 1819, Jefferson deplored the lack of any coherent control by any legislature over the issuance of money.[13]

But the battle against the Second Bank is important because Jackson and his allies were so clearly aware of how the power of monopolized capital—if not jealously regulated by the people—could be used to determine industrial and agricultural winners and losers in ways that would undermine both democracy and republicanism.

And so during the first half of the nineteenth century, the citizens of the young United States made themselves free to use their state legislatures to ensure that their markets were open and well regulated and that the incorporations of power necessary to achieve any particular large-scale project were limited in scope and duration. That is, the citizens of the United States ensured that we alone, as a people, would be masters of our own markets and that we alone, as a people, would be masters of our corporations.[14]

The result of the experiment was clear by 1840, when the French political thinker Alexis de Tocqueville published the second volume of his famous study of American democracy. In one of his more inspired passages, Tocqueville wrote:

> The United States of America have only been emancipated for half a century from the state of colonial dependence in which they stood to Great Britain; the number of large fortunes there is small, and capital is still scarce. Yet no people in the world has made such rapid progress in trade and manufactures as the Americans: they constitute at the present day the second maritime nation in the world; and although their manufactures have to struggle with almost insurmountable natural impediments, they are not prevented from making great and daily advances. In the United States the greatest undertakings and speculations are executed without difficulty, because the whole population is engaged in productive industry, and because the poorest as well as the most opulent members of the commonwealth are ready to combine their efforts for these purposes. The consequence is that a stranger is constantly amazed by the immense public works executed by a nation which *contains, so to speak, no rich men.* The Americans arrived but as yesterday on the territory which they inhabit, and they have already changed the whole order of nature for their own advantage. They have joined the Hudson to the Mississippi, and made the Atlantic Ocean communicate with the Gulf of Mexico, across a continent of more than five

hundred leagues in extent which separates the two seas. The longest railroads which have been constructed up to the present time are in America. But *what most astonishes me in the United States is not so much the marvelous grandeur of some undertakings, as the innumerable multitude of small ones.*[15] (emphasis added)

In Britain, Friedrich Engels ran a factory in Manchester and used some of his profit to support Karl Marx, who was scribbling away in the reading room of the British Museum, distilling the horrors of the industrial revolution in that aristocratic land into his utopian and ultimately cataclysmic vision of massed human power.[16] The United States, in these same years, bred Ralph Waldo Emerson, Henry David Thoreau, Walt Whitman, and Samuel Colt.

The British waged an admirable yet slow and sporadic campaign to eliminate slavery in their overseas colonies, with the rather glaring exception of the "crown jewel" governed by the private British East India Company, where slavery was transformed into debt bondage. The American people, meanwhile, were steeling themselves for an apocalyptic war at home against the last great corporate power—that of the slave-owning planters—led by that most noble child of our democratic republic, Abraham Lincoln.

Meet the New Boss

It may seem strange that the bloodiest war in U.S. history—fought by the most free people in the modern world to destroy the power of the last great landlords—opened the door to monopoly, hierarchy, and the mass impressment of citizens into industrial estates. Yet that is exactly what happened during and after the Civil War, due to the interaction of three factors.

First, during the war itself, northern governments directed massive investments to certain industries, resulting in unprecedented concentrations of machinery and capital in the United States. Second, the people who controlled these corporations and banks used their new power to win huge changes in law, at both the state and the federal levels, that cleared the way for them to extend these corporations across state lines. Third, the rapid spread of new technologies and transport services like the telegraph and the railroad enabled corporations to operate effectively over much wider geographical areas. In combination, these changes empowered a swelling legion of men to escape the reach of the state legislatures that we had always used to protect ourselves from predation by the powerful.

What was most stunning about the crushing of our first democratic republic was not that it took place but how swiftly the event unfurled. By 1871, a mere six years after the end of the war, the pioneering railroad regulator Charles Francis Adams—the grandson and great-grandson of U.S. presidents—was able to write that "our great corporations are fast emancipating themselves from the State, or rather subjecting the State to their own control." The men who rose to power during these years included Cornelius Vanderbilt, Jay Gould, and Jim Fisk. They did so mainly by using control of the steamships and the railroads to, in the words of Adams, "make levies . . . upon the whole business of a nation."[17] They also, as we have seen, used the power that railroads gave them over U.S. marketplaces to create property at will, in their own hands, as Gould did when he took over the building-stone business in New York.

This first stage of consolidation, in the years immediately after the war, is perhaps the premier episode of pure laissez-faire capitalism in the North Atlantic world. Many industrial and financial lords—in charge of some regional monopoly—battled among themselves for precedence, using whatever means they found at hand. This ranged from organized armed conflict in the streets and in train terminals to fantastic battles in the stock market and legal struggles in our legislatures and courts that involved machinations, speculations, and corruptions more audacious than anything ever seen in any modern nation up to that time.

The second stage of consolidation began in the 1880s as men like Andrew Carnegie and John D. Rockefeller began to roll up control over particular industrial activities, not merely across a region but across the entire nation. To justify such complete elimination of competition, this second generation of post–Civil War monopolists came bearing a new vision, which was that the cutthroat competition in the years after the war was needlessly "wasteful" and "inefficient." Yet their tactics were largely the same as those of their predecessors, albeit better capitalized. Much of the success of men like Carnegie and Rockefeller was, just like Gould and Fisk, due to their ability to master the railroads and leverage the power of those monopolies. In some cases, like steel and oil, the institutions they created were truly immense. In other cases—such as the making of wooden matches, shoes, and cigarettes—the results were more modest, though no less important for the entrepreneurs and the workers who were accustomed to earning their livelihood in what had been open-market systems.

History books tell us that since 1776, no king has ruled in America. But in the political economy of the late nineteenth century, the banker J. P. Morgan established himself as, for all intents, the central sovereign over America's industrial lords. Morgan used his control over Wall Street to rationalize—or, in the lingo of the day, "morganize"—not merely the U.S. railroad industry but also the production of such diverse products as electrical machinery and farm equipment and the provision of such services as telephony, urban trolleys, and coastal and trans-Atlantic steamships. Although Morgan never managed to capture control of Rockefeller, he did capture Carnegie, and for much of two decades he ruled the heights of the U.S. political economy with near complete freedom to create and destroy property as he alone saw fit.

During these years, the American people strove tirelessly to rebuild our democratic republic, especially by seeking to rebuild at the federal level the regulatory powers we had once exercised through our state governments. Our first big victory came in the form of the Interstate Commerce Act of 1887, which we designed to prevent financiers from using the railroads to control our markets. The second was the Sherman Antitrust Act of 1890, which we designed to prevent financiers from using industrial corporations, or "trusts," to capture and manipulate our markets.

The failure of both of these laws—and the outright perversion of the Sherman Act, which the barons turned against the cooperatives of the small entrepreneur and the unions of the working man—inspired a growing number of American citizens to focus on more direct forms of control. This culminated in the capture of the Democratic Party itself in 1896 by a movement directly descended from the old Democratic-Republican party of Madison and Jefferson, and the nomination for president of William Jennings Bryan, one of the great antimonopoly preachers in American history.

Yet just as the American people reconsolidated their own political position, just as we the people gathered sufficient power to seize our government back from J. P. Morgan, we found ourselves contending with a brand-new political figure in the person of Theodore Roosevelt.

Most histories present Morgan and Roosevelt as archenemies and depict Roosevelt as a great "trustbuster." And when Roosevelt first used the Sherman Antitrust Act, in 1902, it was indeed against the Northern Securities railroad trust recently forged by Morgan himself. To be sure, there certainly were great differences between the two men, as we will discuss in a moment. But from the point of view of the American people, these differences were less important than the similarities. Such as that Morgan and Roosevelt were both members of the same elite, and neither was fond of sharing power with the common people. On the contrary, both strove to centralize power within—and their personal authority over—the U.S. economy. Both men were, albeit in different ways, economic autocrats.

When Roosevelt aimed his Justice Department at Morgan's Northern Securities railroad trust, his goal was not to restore the people's markets. It was to demonstrate—to Morgan and to the rest of us—that a new boss had arrived, and he worked not on Wall Street but in the White House.

The "Progress" of Man

For any history of American political economics, Theodore Roosevelt's presidency (1901–1909) is one of the most important yet least understood periods, as was, for that matter, the Progressive Era that Roosevelt so often seemed to personify. It was during these years that Roosevelt and his allies established many of the practices that enabled Americans to govern the vast new powers that had been consolidated by Morgan and his allies. It was also during these years that an elite came perilously close to establishing a permanent authoritarian control in the United States through the fusing of public and private government.

Unfortunately, our lack of a clear understanding of what took place in these years impedes our ability to make sense of what is taking place today, for the political and intellectual legacy of those days continues to be used, both consciously and unconsciously, to justify the consolidation of power in America today. My aim in this section is therefore to identify some of the main ideas that animated Progressive Era thinkers, then identify some of the legacies of the era, both good and bad, especially those that affected our attitudes toward open markets.

Of all the animating ideas, the most striking—at least, from a contemporary viewpoint—was that the progressive elites saw themselves as engaged in a task of "socializing" basic economic functions.

The word *socialism*, in and of itself, is of little practical use in any political discussion. Every society, by definition, socializes certain risks and certain benefits by sharing them among the entire population or some large group. Every society also centralizes control over certain activities and leaves other forms of control in the hands of individuals. The key political question of any moment is always what mix of risks and benefits to socialize, and among what groups, and what activities to centralize and where to situate that control.

Nevertheless, there is much to be learned from how the word *socialism* was used by the progressive elite and the industrial lords of the era. Both, for instance, favored centralized, top-down, largely autocratic control over most of the industrial activities in the United States.

One way to understand how the word *socialism* was perceived a century ago is to consider the following question and answer by J. P. Morgan's number two man, George Perkins. "What is the difference between the U.S. Steel Corporation, as it was organized by Mr. Morgan, and a Department of Steel as it might be organized by the Government?" he asked. Morgan might be the private ruler of this industrial government, Perkins acknowledged, but he insisted that the result of this rule was not merely beneficial to all of society but was, at bottom, no different from the same sort of rule settled in the state itself. Morgan's rule amounted, Perkins said, to nothing less than "socialism of the highest, best, and most ideal sort."[18]

And, indeed, Morgan does, as we saw, deserve to be remembered for centralizing control over a number of vital economic activities in the United States and for using that control to "socialize" many of the risks to the capital invested there. His acts of monopolization enabled financiers to pass on to the common people the results of bad decisions or simple laziness in the form of higher prices, lower quality, and less innovation. His acts of monopolization also concentrated the power to govern many industrial systems in a single group, even a single person, with the power to determine all. Indeed, Morgan, for all intents, erected the world's first modern *planning* state. Although it was headquartered on Wall Street and not Washington, and although the aim was to maximize production of cash and not tractors, the practical accomplishment was basically the same as that achieved later by the Bolsheviks in Russia.

Where Roosevelt and other members of the progressive elite differed from Perkins was that they did not view Morgan's approach to centralization as sufficient. On the contrary, they tended to view Morgan's centralizing efforts as dangerously incomplete in nature, both because the power he consolidated was not held by the "public" state itself and because his techniques were antiquated. The first problem was easy to overcome. Soon after Roosevelt took on Morgan in the Northern Securities case, he established the Bureau of Corporations to more or less directly run the U.S. economy through the act of regulating private corporate institutions.

The second problem—that Morgan's approach to governance was too old-fashioned—takes us to the second animating idea of the Progressive Era elite, which is that science could lead us to a truly ideal form of social organization. The goal of Roosevelt and the progressives was to erect a *better* planning state, one that was geared to maximizing the production not of cash but of material items (although none of the progressives ever quite figured out how to decide which items).

The progressives' faith in their ability to use science to control human economic and social activity—indeed, to perfect the human animal itself—exerted a huge influence on the shaping of America's political economy in the twentieth century. For our purposes, two outgrowths of this belief are most important. First was the creation of a professional bureaucracy to run industry and business, in the form of technocratic managers trained in rational methods of control. This included the entirely new level of middle management, made up of efficiency engineers, timekeepers, auditors, bookkeepers, inspectors, and production planners, many of whom were enamored of such newfangled worker-control regimes as the time and motion management techniques of Frederick Winslow Taylor.[19]

The second key result of the progressives' faith in scientific control was their dismissal of the institution of the market as a wasteful and even dangerous archaism. In the words of the journalist Walter Lippmann, one of the more elegant voices of the progressive elite, organizing activity within market structures resulted in a "chaos" and "welter" of profiteering by inefficient "small competitors" and other "men on the make."[20]

The Progressive Era elite transformed the U.S. economy and political economic thinking in many other ways as well. Many of the changes they introduced would later be ratified or adopted by the reformers of the New Deal era. These included the following:

- Government has a vital role in ensuring the safety and quality of foods and drugs, guaranteeing the safe and fair treatment of workers, and raising the quality and accountability of government itself.
- The skills, technologies, and machines that are held within the great industrial enterprises must be protected from the predations of financiers.
- The workers within the industrial enterprise should be empowered to form labor unions to enable them to negotiate on an equal basis with the financiers.[21]

Yet the Progressive Era elite also left us with many extremely problematic legacies. In addition to the complete dismissal of the vital political and economic roles played by open market systems, these included:

- The failure to understand the value and purpose of fostering a sense of ownership over vital physical properties.
- The de facto ratification of top-down authoritarian planning.
- A dangerous fixation on efficiency, institutionalized in the practice of a new social science, economics.

Of all the legacies of the Progressive Era, perhaps most dangerous was the belief that the mere application of scientific method by highly trained technocrats obviated the need to engineer political institutions to direct and deflect power. Many progressives truly believed that humans were on the verge of discovering, through the application of science, the secret forces and invisible laws that ruled human society and the individual human animal, in much the same way that we had earlier discovered the laws that ruled the planets and their moons. This in turn led them to believe that science could somehow sterilize the act of control of the human individual of any and all human taint.

If this materialistic philosophy sounds vaguely Marxist, it should. In one of the more influential books of the Progressive Era, mathematician and electrical engineer Charles Proteus Steinmetz, who had once served as General Electric's chief scientist, informed the world in 1916 that he was a "dues-paying member of the Socialist Party." He then went on to assure his readers that the engineers of the world were in the process of uniting to form an "industrial government" parallel to the political government in Washington and the other capital cities of the world. To achieve this end, Steinmetz wrote, the engineers intended to use the corporate governments now under their control. This new industrial government, he wrote, would have "an authority greater than the world has ever seen," one that was "not maintained by a police force, but based on mutual co-operation for everybody's interest."[22]

Even after the end of World War I, and even after the Russian Revolution, progressives continued to be fascinated by visions of corporatist combinations of public and private power, engineered in the name of maximizing efficiency and hence the output of material goods. During the 1920s, the leading advocate of such thinking was none other than Herbert Hoover. Although today we remember Hoover as the ultimate laissez-faire man, due to his supposed decision to let events in the financial system take their own course after the stock market crash of 1929, he was actually one of the most interventionist presidents in U.S. history.

Hoover even had his own political economic philosophy, which he based on progressive ideals and which he developed first as a planning czar during World War I and then refined during a long stint as commerce secretary. He called his idea *associationalism*, and the basic idea was that capital, labor, professional managers, and the state should all work together in a network of supercartels to fix everything from prices to production runs to profits.[23]

During this long era, the American people watched in bemusement and sometimes horror as the financial, political, and technocratic elites fought among themselves over how best to rule the rest of us. The people, who still held significant power within the Democratic Party, often allied with the progressive and technocratic elites to improve the safety of products, the protections for workers, and the regulation of natural monopolies like railroads and streetcars. Yet the majority of American farmers, small businesspeople, and workers stood in staunch opposition to the progressive elite's vision of a command-and-control approach to organizing the U.S. political economy.

Whereas the progressives truly believed that human institutions could be structured to direct both society and the individual to act in a rational and enlightened manner, these small holders, operating squarely in the democratic republican tradition of Madison and Jefferson, insisted that human institutions must be structured not to promote "growth" but to protect society and the individual from the passions and madness (and "scientific" fads) of their fellows. Herbert Croly, who in 1909 published one of the main primers on progressivism, faulted Jefferson for having failed to establish a "set of *efficient* institutions" to govern the U.S. economy.[24] When the populist reformer and later Supreme Court Justice Louis Brandeis read this statement, his reaction was that this was exactly the point.

During the long decades between the end of the Civil War and the New Deal, the American people managed to break through the chokehold of the centralizing elite only once, when they elected Woodrow Wilson president. A former president of Princeton University, Wilson has never been recognized as one of the more natural populists in the United States. And in fact, the onset of World War I forced Wilson to adopt emergency economic measures that led to the centralization of control and planning. However, in the year and a half before the war shattered the world economic system, Wilson and his allies in Congress did manage to pass a remarkable suite of reforms that aimed at reestablishing and stabilizing an open-market political economic system in the United States. This included passage of the Clayton Antitrust Act, establishment of the Federal Trade Commission and the Federal Reserve System, and a constitutional amendment that cleared the way for the first income tax that took more from the wealthy than from the middle class.

Wilson also left us with one of the finest vocalizations of how the American people viewed the progressive elite's alternative to Morgan's private director state. During the 1912 campaign, Wilson faced not merely the sitting president, the Republican William Howard Taft, but also Theodore Roosevelt, who after four years in the wilderness had returned as the head of the Progressive Party, nicknamed the Bull Moose Party. The former president, Wilson said, "proposes to use monopoly in order to make us happy. And the project is one of those projects which all history cries out against as impossible. . . . These gentlemen are not proposing the methods of liberty but are proposing the methods of control. A control among a free people is intolerable."[25] The American people, in other words, did not want a private boss or a public boss. They wanted no boss at all.

The Restoration of Republic

When Franklin Roosevelt became president in 1933, one of his first acts was to sign the National Industrial Recovery Act (NIRA). The United States was at one of the worst points in the Great Depression, and the act gave Roosevelt unprecedented powers to regulate and reorganize the whole economic system. The tool that Roosevelt came up with was the National Recovery Administration (NRA), and its flavor was distinctly militaristic. The NRA was designed to follow economic practices "perfected" by Hoover and the other production czars during World War I, and Roosevelt named a U.S. Army general to oversee the agency.

One of the general's first actions was to suspend the antitrust laws, to allow firms to work together openly to set wages, prices, and practices. The NRA, in other words, took the corporatist approach of the progressives, now so finely honed by Herbert Hoover, to its logical conclusion, which was something uncomfortably akin to what Benito Mussolini was then promoting in Italy.

In the last generation, Americans have been taught to remember the New Deal as an era of big government, big industry, big labor, and, ultimately, big social policy. This is at best a half-truth that serves the interests of both the neoprogressive "left" and the neofeudal "right." One side wants to use the federal government to tax the American people and decide for us how to spend our money. The other side insists that we must shrink the public state almost to nothing and instead allow the financiers to use their private corporations to tax us and decide for us how to spend our money.

What determined the real character of the political economy that we put into place during the New Deal era was the conscious act of rejecting the NIRA's corporatist top-down approach to governing. This rejection was led not by big business nor by the progressives in Roosevelt's government. On the contrary, both the big business and progressive elites—along with members of the Socialist Party—tended to applaud the NRA's blending of public and private government and the centralization of control. What they fought over was who would hold the levers. The rejection of the entire corporatist approach, meanwhile, was led by people from both parties, who used Congress, the courts, and various perches within the administration to decentralize control in both the government and the private sector, for both economic and political reasons.[26]

It was the Supreme Court that drove the final stake into NIRA with a 9–0 decision in 1935. The justices essentially adopted an argument that was first expressed eight years earlier by Justice Brandeis in a similar case. The essence of the earlier argument, which Brandeis made in a dissent, was that to focus too much on efficiency was a good way to destroy liberty.

"Checks and balances were established in order that this should be 'a government of laws and not of men,'" Brandeis had written. "The doctrine of the separation of powers was adopted by the convention of 1787 not to promote efficiency but to preclude the exercise of arbitrary power. The purpose was not to avoid friction, but, by means of the inevitable friction incident to the distribution of the government powers among three departments, to save the people from autocracy."[27]

To complete our history of American democratic republicanism up to 1981, what I want to do here is to look at how the central animating idea of the New Deal–era reformers—to maximize freedom for the individual citizen—shaped their overall goals. I will do so by looking at two specific sets of policies, then by listing a few important actions that illustrate how the New Deal era was characterized mainly by policies designed to fortify our systems of checks and balances, protect the personal private properties of the average citizen, and distribute power to the people.

The set of New Deal–era policies that marked the most complete rejection of the political economic approach of both Morgan & Co. and the progressive elite was the wide-ranging effort to protect the small entrepreneur and the farmer from distant billionaires wielding chain stores and agricultural trading corporations. These laws came in a remarkable variety of shapes and sizes, and they ranged from the crop price support systems of the 1930s to the establishment of the Small Business Administration in the 1950s.

Of all these, the one that left us with the clearest statement of political intent was the Robinson-Patman Act of 1936. The purpose of the bill, the authors made clear in its preamble, was "to protect the independent merchant, the public whom he serves, and the manufacturer from whom he buys" from the use of price to discriminate among different partners.[28]

As we saw in chapters 2 and 3, there are many excellent economic reasons to outlaw or control giant trading firms and retailers. These include their tendency to strip entire systems of their profits and thereby harm the machines, technologies, and people under their power. The authors of Robinson-Patman went out of their way to make sure we understood that although they were aware of this problem, their goal was not economic but political. The point of the law, they wrote, was to "protect the weak [from] the strong." The "public interest" was best served not by efficiency but by keeping "trade and industry divided among as many different parties as possible."[29]

A second New Deal–era set of policies that completely inverted the goals of the financial lords and would-be bureaucratic lords were those that aimed to protect local business communities. Some of the clearest statements on why to do so can be found in a debate in Congress in 1950 on whether to outlaw mergers. Senator Estes Kefauver of Tennessee, speaking on behalf of the law that would bear his name, said that "the control of American business is steadily being transferred . . . from local communities to a few large cities in which central managers decide the policies and the fate of the far-flung enterprises they control. Millions of people depend helplessly on their judgment. Through monopolistic mergers the people are losing power to direct their own economic welfare."[30]

An even more eloquent statement came the year before from Supreme Court Justice William O. Douglas, who decried the "effect on the community when independents are swallowed up by the trusts and entrepreneurs become employees of absentee owners." The result, Douglas wrote, in a case that focused on how big oil companies were capturing control of independent gasoline stations, "is a serious loss in citizenship. Local leadership is diluted. He who was a leader in the village becomes dependent on outsiders for his action and policy. Clerks responsible to a superior in a distant place take the place of resident proprietors beholden to no one."[31]

Such goals help to illuminate the overall intent of the institutional changes that were put into place by the American people during the New Deal era. In instance after instance, the reforms aimed not to lower prices for consumers but to fortify systems of checks and balances, create systems of personal and local ownership, and force large governmental institutions, both public and private, to compete. Consider a few other of the better known reforms (some of these will be discussed in more detail in later chapters):

Industrial competition. Beginning in the late 1930s, Franklin Roosevelt's antitrust team established a policy of engineering competition among large enterprises whenever possible, either by breaking them into pieces or by forcing them to turn over key technologies and markets to their rivals. The ultimate point of competition was not to lower prices but to keep necessary concentrations of power always off balance. Or, in the lingo of the era, the goal was "competition for the sake of competition."

Industrial ownership. Congress and the administration accepted the Progressive Era idea that the financier's power over the industrial firm must be counterbalanced by technocratic managers and labor. Then they fortified the new system by treating the counterbalancing classes as forms of owners. They also established another set of owners—the small investor—who up to this point had been largely powerless.

Stable commodity markets. Congress and the administration established systems of regulation, such as through the Commodities Exchange Act, to ensure that the prices of grains and other agricultural commodities were established not by speculators but by the producer and the consumer interacting in open exchanges.

Democratic banking. Through government oversight and support, the chartering of different forms and classes of banks, and the compartmentalization of different activities in different institutions, Congress and the administration at one and the same time stabilized the financial system and democratized access to capital.

Open innovation. Roosevelt's antitrust team devised a system of enforcement that forced large industrial firms to share their key technologies with any comer. This approach, which was kept in place until 1981, produced the seed ideas for thousands of startup companies, many of which grew to be major powers in the world economy.

Realistic trade. Before World War II the Roosevelt administration waged an aggressive campaign to break overseas cartels and to prevent U.S.

firms from colluding with foreign enterprises in ways that would harm the interest of individual U.S. producers. After the war, American presidents through Reagan enforced trade law in ways that fostered deep industrial interdependence yet still effectively prevented financiers wielding trading firms from wiping out entire U.S. industries or from manufacturing artificial dependencies on overseas powers.

It would be irresponsible to deny that the New Deal–era reformers left much work undone. Their failure to put checks on the autocratic power of the corporate managers and the labor bosses is especially troubling. However, we must also recognize what the reformers of the New Deal era achieved, which on balance was nothing less than the wholesale reconstruction of the institutions that guided the flow of power though our society in ways that ensured the protection of individual private properties whether defined as skills, labor, or land.

It was the political equivalent of one of the immense hydraulics projects of the era, but rather than seek to construct a single all-purpose political dam, average Americans in the New Deal era used a myriad of laws to build a complex network of canals, levees, ponds, and diversions that distributed the power throughout the entire country in ways that made it hard for that power to be turned, once again, against them. Maybe the water did not turn such immense turbines, but it had been tamed to a point where any individual citizen could make use of it, right in his or her own backyard.

Indeed, the New Deal–era reformers managed to replicate what the first democratic republican movement had achieved in the early United States, and to do so in the much more challenging environment of the mid-twentieth century. At the same time we concentrated the industrial forces necessary to protect the American people in apocalyptic conflicts with industrial-powered totalitarian societies, we erected a political economic framework that successfully protected the individual citizen from being crushed by the weight of these same industrial powers, in complete contrast to what happened after the Civil War. We did so by ensuring that the people who worked in our great industrial enterprises enjoyed freedom from arbitrary rule, and we did so by restoring the old internal frontier, in which any citizen who did not want to work for someone else could still afford to open a small and independent business. We did so, in other words, by restoring a political system organized, as much as possible, around open markets.

The Pit

While we are still in Kansas City, let's take a brief look at a very different type of market, one for an agricultural commodity. For many Americans today, the "pits"—where traders shout out orders for grains, hydrocarbons, metals, and equities—are what best exemplify the idea of a market in action, as the surging chaotic energy we see among the buyers and sellers seems to direct and redirect the flow of great rivers of wheat, oil, copper, and cash across the face of the earth. Kansas City is home to one of the last such markets, the "open outcry" exchange for hard red winter wheat. It is located here because the thin rocky soils of neighboring Kansas are ideal for this highly valued bread grain.

The wheat pit is located in the offices of the Kansas City Board of Trade, in a modern office building near the upscale Country Club shopping plaza. It takes my eyes a few minutes to adjust from the shining cloudless midday sky to the muted lighting and wood-paneled hallways. Yet on this day, the action in the pit itself is quite heated. The price of a bushel of wheat is spiking, and when I enter the room the traders are gathered in a frenzied scrum, shouting and gesticulating wildly as they flash coded hand signals in one another's faces.

After a few moments, the madness suddenly dies down to an almost shocking calm, and men who a moment before were literally red in the face mill about, calmly chatting, staring aimlessly, doodling on pads of paper. Then, as some bit of news from the outer world flashes into the room via computer monitor or landline phone, the riot picks up right where it left off.

During the quiet periods I study the sartorial choices of the traders. Most dress in candy-colored jackets and shirts—some adorned with flowers, black-and-white checks, even tie-dyed prints—to help them more swiftly identify friend and rival. About five minutes before the closing bell, all the distinct colors and patterns dissolve into a blur as the traders throng, scatter, surge up the sides of the pit and cascade back down, a Bedlam loosed. One group even tumbles to the ground, where, in a heap, they continue trading.

My main focus in this book is on corporate monopolies and the dangers they pose to the delicate engineering of our complex production systems and to the fragile balances of our political systems. Yet just as such a work requires that we understand open markets and how they are monopolized, it also requires that we understand commodity markets and how they monopolize and are monopolized.

In chapter 7, we will look in more detail at how the markets for oil and other hydrocarbons are shaped—and intentionally misshaped—by companies of men who use corporate and banking institutions, pure financial power, and even our government regulators to achieve their end. Our task here is to take advantage of the relatively simple nature of the market for red winter wheat to understand the history and the role of commodity markets and to get some idea of the systemic dangers posed by our failure to regulate these wisely and well.

Commodities like gold and equities have been traded at national exchanges for centuries, in cities like London and Amsterdam, but the formal commodity market for agricultural products is a relatively recent invention. Well into the mid-nineteenth century in the United States, farmers packed their wheat, corn, and other grains into sacks that usually carried the name of their farm. The farmers (or a local merchant) then carried the sacks to a local market, where the grain was priced based on such factors as its plumpness and cleanliness. A single lot of grain might make its way through a series of such markets from a western state to an eastern city many hundreds of miles away. The openness of this system made it very hard for one trader to monopolize a market for very long. Indeed, the traders often found themselves cut out of the system entirely, as buyers in the cities routinely formed long-standing relationships with particular farmers whose product they trusted.

Beginning about 1850, however, traders began to break open the individual sacks and mix their contents into the great rivers of "commodified" grain we see today. The ostensible reason was to take advantage of three new technologies: the railroad, the telegraph, and the steam-powered grain elevator. The new system did offer advantages to society, mainly in the form of lower prices due to greater automation. However, it also meant that bakers ended up with much less control over the quality of their breads, because the almost infinitely varied production of millions of individual farms was reduced down to four basic grades of grain.[32]

The new system also, with astonishing swiftness, concentrated wealth and the power to govern in the hands of a few well-capitalized companies of men able to erect the largest grain elevators, and thence to even more powerful groups of capitalists, who used their control over railroads to capture control of the grain traders.

Most to our purpose here, the new system also shifted the power to price grain away from the farmers and the bakers who were scattered across the country and concentrated that power in the hands of financiers in a few metropolises, especially Chicago. Under the old system, every shipment was priced from a rough local benchmark and reflected a myriad of factors, including long-standing personal relationships. This resulted in a huge variety of prices at any given moment across America.

Once the traders began to use the new centralized pits to "discover" prices, these prices began to serve as great impersonal and imperial beacons that were able to regulate trade across the entire nation and to some degree across the entire world. The inability of an individual farmer to escape such an imperial price system is, indeed, one of the main reasons that men like Fred Messner and Ron Fahrmeier continue today to abandon row crops in favor of selling produce directly to the consumer.

We should therefore view a commodity market as a sort of master market. By concentrating the pricing process in one place, the organizers of a commodity market essentially monopolize the pricing process. A society might consciously accept such a centralization of the power to "discover" prices because, in theory, this can result in an extremely stable supply as the production of millions of farms is distributed from the same virtual pool. Such a market may also seem to promise more stable pricing, as farmers and bakers all around the world look toward the same one marker. Indeed, except for speculators armed with piles of capital, the only things that can disrupt such a market are natural disasters like storms and floods and political disasters like wars and strikes. On a day-to-day basis, not even a new technology can push the price of a bushel of wheat very far in one direction or the other.

In fact, however, as we will see in more detail in chapter 7, the centralization of so much power in one place often increases volatility. It does so by dramatically raising the stakes that are in play at any given moment, and hence the temptation for the powerful to risk their capital on speculation rather than on making things or providing services.

Such centralization also makes the job of the speculator much easier. In the old decentralized system, it was hard for a speculator to corner more than a tiny portion of the grain that passed through the interlocking system of markets. Any enterprising person with a wagon or a boat who was able to bring new physical grain to market could break the corner. In the new system of commodities, the fact that all grain is, in theory, blended into a single great sea would seem to make it even more difficult to corner the supply. Yet in fact the opposite is true, because most of the grain is never actually traded on the centralized market. The act of transforming the grain into a commodity means that the market participants no longer have to look at every single lot of grain. Instead, they need merely price a representative portion of grain—a few buckets out of the sea—and then apply this price to all grain everywhere.

The supply of grain that is actually traded can be minimized in a number of ways. One is to trade only the grain that passes through a particular transfer point. Another is to trade only the grain that is delivered at a particular time. Because the amount of grain that will pass through a particular gateway in a particular period is quite limited, this greatly reduces the amount of money required to form a corner on the "forward contracts" that represent this grain in the market.

To make the task even easier, traders with credit can immensely amplify the reach of their own capital. As the pioneering financial buccaneer Jay Gould once explained, "A man with $100,000 of money and with credit can transact a business of $20,000,000." And Gould knew what he was talking about. In the fall of 1869, he and his partner Jim Fisk cornered the supply of gold in New York and triggered one of the worst panics in the history of Wall Street.[33]

Commodity markets are political in much the same way that open retail markets like the City Market are political. In the act of regulating who can participate in the market and how, the masters of these markets favor certain classes of participants and disfavor others. A commodity market can be designed to simultaneously serve the interests of both the small farmer and the individual consumer, such as by empowering the farmers to earn enough money to remain on their farms year after year while also restricting their ability to combine in ways that enable them to gouge consumers. To help ensure such an outcome, the market master might, for instance, outlaw certain types of trading and perhaps certain types of traders. Or the same market might be designed to serve the interests mainly of the financier in the city, such as by eliminating the limits on how much leverage a trader can bring to bear in the market or by allowing traders to use inside information (which today is actually a common practice on many commodity markets).

In the century and a half since financiers created the modern commodity market, Americans have proposed many ways to ensure that such systems serve the interest of the producer and the consumer rather than the financier. At one extreme is the "ever normal" granary, in which the government or a private monopoly functions basically as a form of bank that, through the careful buying and selling of supplies, fixes the price of grain in much the same way that the Federal Reserve fixes the price of the dollar by buying and selling currency and debt.

The idea for such a grain bank dates at least to the book of Genesis, when Joseph convinced Pharaoh to gather and store grain during the seven years of plenty to ensure an adequate supply during the seven years of famine.[34] Genesis also instructs us about one of the main dangers in such a system, which is that the power of such a centralized bank can easily be abused. Joseph released the grain to the hungry farmers only in exchange for their land.

The danger of such abuse is one reason that Americans ended up with a variety of less strategic, ad hoc, and sometimes downright sloppy approaches to regulating supply—such as by taking land out of production or simply paying farmers when the market price is too low. The danger of such abuse is also why, beginning in the 1920s, Americans imposed direct federal control over the commodity markets in the cities through a series of actions that culminated in the formation of the Commodities Futures Trading Commission and through a series of regulations that restricted how financiers could wield power in these markets.

A complete picture of our system for regulating trade in commodities is beyond the scope of this work. We would have to look at how different markets and exchanges compete and interact and at the effects of the massive consolidation among these exchanges in recent years. We would have to look at the regulatory changes that led to the creation of global prices and at the political pressures that forced individual nations to attune their internal economies to these market prices. We would have to look at the shift of trade away from open outcry markets, which by their very design facilitate the exchange of information that makes it easier to identify who is moving a market and how, to electronic exchanges, where all is silent and mysterious.

Finally, we would have to look at the long series of changes that began under George H. W. Bush and accelerated under Bill Clinton, made in the name of deregulating our commodities markets and making them more "free." These reforms opened the door ever wider to "investment funds"[35] and simultaneously liberated traders to move their business away from the well-lighted, well-regulated public marketplace into "dark markets," where immense masses of power can more easily be hidden from all eyes.[36]

We must content ourselves instead merely with noting that the huge spike in the price of wheat from roughly $3 per bushel for many years to nearly $13 per bushel in the spring of 2008 was not the result of any natural or political disaster. Nor was it the result of the higher cost of energy or because people in China or India were suddenly consuming such vastly greater quantities of bread. Rather, it was because the cumulative changes made in the name of "deregulating" our commodities markets in the last two decades made it far easier for speculators routinely to manipulate the price of our wheat. Just as similar changes in the law made it far easier for speculators to manipulate the prices we pay for our oil, natural gas, cotton, rice, even ship bottoms.[37]

On the two afternoons that I watch the action at the wheat pit in Kansas City, the thrill that is transmitted by the soaring price of wheat is almost palpable. So too the sense of unease and foreboding among the regulars. One reason is simply that everyone here knows that higher prices for wheat come at a literal cost to the health and well-being of people around the world. Another reason is their fear of what will happen once the market reverses. None of the old-timers believe that the high prices will last, and they know that when the prices fall, it could take down many of their businesses along with the businesses of many innocent farmers.

Which brings me to my final point about the dangers that derive from having allowed a tiny few among us to so muddy our understanding of how markets operate. Which is that when it comes to our commodity markets, we should understand the term *free market* as not merely a cover for the few who wish to use corporations to enclose our open markets and direct the actions of the people they capture within their fences. *Free market* also means the freedom for an even smaller number among us to enrich themselves by speculating without limit on the price of the food we eat, in a process that not only starves millions of people in poor countries but also routinely smashes the plans and the properties of the farmers and other producers on whom we rely for the most basic goods.

5

In the Cockpit

Before 1980, the American advertising industry symbolized, at one and the same time, the polar extremes of the American psyche when it comes to entrepreneurship and work. At one extreme, the industry seemed to epitomize American verve and wit and clashing competitiveness, as compact, fast-moving, flush firms with names like J. Walter Thompson, Young & Rubicam, Ogilvy & Mather, and Leo Burnett duked it out for the television and magazine advertising accounts of America's corporate giants. At the other extreme stood "the man in the gray flannel suit"—the midlevel advertising executive—riding the same train every day at the same hour home to Westchester or New Canaan, where he would trade his briefcase for a martini and a round of bridge.[1]

Yet this seeming contradiction was in fact one of the better illustrations of the symbiotic relationship that long existed in American society between the entrepreneur and the salaried professional (or wage earner). Hunger for control, the desire to build a company, and the readiness to do battle defined the former. The willingness to do another person's work and to follow orders characterized the latter.

The wage earner may be just as creative and driven as the entrepreneur, yet he or she may prefer to devote his or her energy to running the school parent-teacher association, or mastering the oboe or wind surfing, or collecting Malawian stamps, or protecting a local creek from developers, or caring for an ailing parent. And so in the open-market system, the entrepreneur and the wage earner fit one with the other. Good employees could always land new jobs at one of their employer's many rivals. Which meant that entrepreneurs paid their employees a reasonable salary, showed them a modicum of respect, and allowed them to leave in time to catch the 5:25 train home.

I'm sitting in an Indian restaurant on the Upper West Side of Manhattan with a college classmate whom I will call Peter. After graduation, Peter and I both headed off to see the world, but whereas I kept wandering, Peter soon came back to New York to work on his art. To pay his rent and buy a few drinks, Peter gladly settled into the role of the man in the gray flannel suit at a big ad agency in midtown. Getting the job proved easy; there was no shortage of demand for a young man with an Ivy League education.

Peter worked by day, pursued his dream by night, won a few prizes for his art, and looked forward to at least moderate success. Then one day, Peter realized that his fervor to make art had ebbed away. For whatever reason, he now wanted a different sort of challenge. Perhaps, he figured, the time had come to move up the advertising ladder to a position in management.

As Peter was soon to discover, there were now a lot fewer potential pathways to the top than there had been when he started in the business. That's because the advertising industry had been remade in the last two decades by the same processes of consolidation that we have seen in so many other sectors of the U.S. economy.

The March 2005 purchase of the New York–based agency Grey Global by the WPP Group of London served to cap the nearly complete roll-up of the industry. A deeply American activity, which traces back to nineteenth-century New York and which until recently could count more than a score of big firms along Madison Avenue, had been brought under the control of three immense global conglomerates, or holding companies, with Omnicom Group and Interpublic Group joining WPP at the top.[2]

The rules of the game were now radically different. Although Peter heard of what seemed like a perfect job at JWT (the former J. Walter Thompson), the friend who told him about the position also urged him to check with human resources before sending over his résumé. That's because JWT was now under the same holding company as Peter's employer, and that holding company had imposed systemwide restrictions on where employees could move and what they could earn.[3]

The head of human resources did not prohibit Peter from applying. She merely told him that "you'd have to be pretty brave to do that."

In 1991, Robert Reich wrote *The Work of Nations*. This book is one of the first works designed to convince contemporary Americans that two supposedly natural processes—globalization and digitalization—had rendered the average American citizen largely powerless, whether working alone or as part of a group, to affect his or her political economy. I bring up Reich here because *The Work of Nations* also played a huge role in shaping how Americans—especially elite members of today's Democratic Party—have interpreted and responded to the radical changes over the last generation in the American workplace. Or, rather, have not.

Many of our fellow Americans, Reich wrote, would inevitably end up worse off in this new global and networked world—especially production workers, who would find themselves competing with laborers in Mexico and China. Yet Reich also claimed that the top 20 percent of the U.S. population (which pretty much covered everyone who was reading his book) would do fine. That was because globalization and new technologies like the Internet were melting down not merely the nation-state but also the corporation. This meant that those of us with specialized talents could look forward to a life far more free of top-down rule by private bosses.

Reich, who was rewarded for his intellectual exertions with a job as Bill Clinton's secretary of labor, said that what was happening was nothing less than the emergence of a new class, made up of scientists, engineers, lawyers, real estate developers, and advertising executives. The special skill of these "symbolic analysts," he wrote, was to "simplify reality into abstract images that can be rearranged, juggled, experimented with, and then, eventually, transformed back into reality." If anything, the revolution was already well under way. Demand for the insights of the symbolic analysts was growing so fast, Reich effused, that many were beginning to "have difficulty keeping track of all their earnings."[4]

Even better, this class could look forward to a world of ever greater degrees of freedom as the power that had been monopolized by the state and the corporation devolved back to the individual, or at least this particular class of individuals. No political fight was necessary. If we studied hard in school, then globalization and the information revolution would all but automatically take care of everything for us. It was evolution—nature's way.

And so, for a brief moment, members of America's educated elite imagined themselves as a sort of neo-Jeffersonian citizenry, magically reborn in the cockpit of personal private spacecraft poised to rocket high above all the fences, rules, and arguments of yore. Yet when the average symbolic analyst hit the ignition switch, the only sound was silence. For some reason, America's lords chose *not* to dismantle voluntarily the private governance systems they controlled in the form of their business corporations and banks. And for some reason, the elites who governed other nation-states, like China, chose not to voluntarily let go their levers of power, either.

The result is that today, a decade and a half later, we find ourselves in a "cockpit," all right, but in this cockpit there's no control stick in our hands. Our cockpit today is little more than a circle chalked on the ground, and the floor inside is strewn with sawdust. In this cockpit, the business at hand is not to soar high above the earth in a mighty capsule of ego but to scratch and scrape, claw and peck, and cluck in one-on-one combat with our erstwhile colleagues as the distant powers glance every so often in our direction, perhaps, until one contestant is left plucked and bleeding while the other struts on to the next round.[5]

Back in the 1970s, Johnny Paycheck scored a big hit with his song "Take This Job and Shove It." A lot fewer Americans today dare to sing along, at least in public, and this was true long before the Meltdown. The consolidation that has taken place at almost all levels in almost all sectors of our economy means that for a growing legion of Americans, the number of companies to which we can sell our labor, skills, and products is falling fast.

This is true if you have only a high school education; as a growing number of towns fall almost entirely under the sway of Wal-Mart, the only option for any worker who runs afoul of his boss is, increasingly, to move.[6] It is also true if you are a middle manager, a trained engineer or scientist, an optician in Salt Lake City, or an Ivy League–educated "symbolic analyst" in Manhattan, like Peter. It's even becoming true for the average lawyer, accountant, business consultant, and software engineer as the rich few among us increasingly use their fatly capitalized corporations to govern how, where, and for whom we work.[7] In the case of doctors, for instance, a 2006 study by the American Medical Association made clear that "consolidation among health insurers is creating near-monopolies in virtually all reaches of the United States."[8]

Not so long ago, most of us lived in a world where we could bring our skills to a real marketplace made up of many buyers as well as many sellers. Today, however, a growing number of us live in a world where one small company of men, or a few, have used their corporations to enclose entirely, or nearly so, the markets in which we sell our work. This use of the corporation to restrict how we use our hands, and minds, and wits to transform raw matter and fresh ideas into the goods and services of use and value to our fellow citizens amounts to a frontal assault on one of our most basic liberties.

Like all of you, I've spent a lot of my life thinking about work. I've certainly enjoyed more than my share of opportunities to compare and contrast the many varieties of American jobs. I've flipped burgers, and I've packed screws into bags and put those bags into boxes in a factory. With a pick and a shovel I have dug holes big enough to plant ten-year-old willows, and with a strap I have humped couches and pianos up and down five-floor walk-ups. I have spent eight-hour shifts loading sixty-pound trays of bread onto racks at a bakery, and eight-hour shifts lifting data off sheets of paper to put into computer databases. I've hauled lumber off trailers at a loading dock, nail-gunned studs to frame out walls, and lugged rolls of tar paper up ladders to rooftops blistering in the summer heat. I've pushed mowers for my dad's lawn-cutting business, run deliveries for a drugstore, refilled soda machines with bottles of RC Cola, and driven trucks full of prebuilt cabinets across the country. I've made change at cash registers, proofread signs at a printer, slopped paint on the walls of tenement apartments, and built props at a theater.

I've worked for multinational corporations and the tiniest of family businesses, in glittering midtown Manhattan towers and in South American shantytowns, as a top manager and the lowliest day laborer. I once organized a union, and I once reorganized a business. For most of my professional life I worked as a journalist. Now I spend my days at a think tank.

One thing I know is that most Americans, as we struggle through the present financial and economic crisis, are desperate for whatever job we can get and keep. Yet as we as a nation discuss how to create these jobs, it is vital to talk also about whom we ask to create them. That's because it makes a really big difference whether a job is created out of nothing by an entrepreneur with a new idea or merely shifted from the books of one giant company to another. The first act results in more, and in many ways better, jobs. The second may result in no net gain in the number of jobs, and often a big loss. That, after all, is exactly what happened when the people who govern our pharmaceutical industry used $31 billion of our bailout money to forge two megamergers that, as we saw in the preface, destroyed thirty-five thousand jobs.

If we want more jobs in this country, especially those that are better paying, one of the swiftest ways to achieve this is to enforce our antimonopoly laws. In the rest of this chapter, I will do two things. First, I will show you how power is exercised down upon two types of entrepreneurs in our land today: the restaurateur and the farmer. My goal is to examine whether such businesspeople can continue to perform the vital dual role they have so long played in our nation, which is not merely to take care of themselves and their families but also to provide many of the most important jobs for the rest of us.[9] Second, I will illuminate why life is now so hard for the average worker and entrepreneur by completing the answer to the question we framed in chapter 1: how such a well-educated and vigilant people missed such a fantastic political revolution right in the midst of our own political economy.

The New Sharecroppers

As we all know, the average American entrepreneur is not an Ivy League–educated advertising executive, a rocket scientist, or a doctor. The great majority of our entrepreneurs serve our communities by running one of the grocery stores where we shop, or one of the motels, garages, or pharmacies down the street. Entrepreneurs build our houses and grow the food we eat. They patch our roofs, unclog our pipes, and plant our trees. They feed us in their restaurants, drive us places in their taxicabs, and offer us reasonable mortgages in their community banks. They help us to fill out our tax forms, shop for life insurance, deliver our babies.

Some do their work in innovative ways. But the real value they provide, at least compared with a distant corporation that employs someone to perform the same services—is a sense of ownership and responsibility over the task, a knowledge of the local community, and a commitment to providing jobs for fellow citizens they actually know. This form of entrepreneurship is of immense social value.

For many, if not most, of us, the real American Dream is not to get rich but simply to be our own boss. This was certainly the case when I was growing up in Miami in the late 1970s. My friends and I didn't spend a lot of time talking about our parents' businesses and jobs. We didn't have to, because we would see one another's parents running the local pizza joint or tuning ten-speeds at the bicycle store. We knew who owned the apartment complex, the license tag agency, the auto parts store, and the plant nursery. The family who ran the summer day camp lived in a neighborhood just to the east. So did the couple who rented baskets of ferns to all the restaurants when no South Florida restaurateur could imagine a dining room without hanging baskets of ferns.

My best friend's father parked his Freightliner cab in front of his house and told fantastically romantic stories of losing his brakes in the Sierra Nevada. Garo Yepremian, when he wasn't kicking field goals for the Dolphins or throwing touchdown passes to Redskins linebackers, painted neckties by hand to sell at his haberdashery. No one ever got rich, at least not legally. But everyone got by. Success was a fiberglass fishing boat, a Corvette, a bigger house on the other side of the canal, or a trailer in the Keys.

So how are everyday entrepreneurs in this country faring today? When I set out to answer this question, the Meltdown was still months in the future. Even so, it swiftly became apparent that the answer was "Not well." We have seen how the consolidation of department stores crushes small clothing producers; how Luxottica's control over eyeglass manufacture and retail has all but destroyed the opportunity for small manufacturers, crafts-people, and independent optical shops; and how Anheuser-Busch InBev keeps craft beer brewers in a state of near terror. In the next chapter we will see how independent inventors, as ingenious as ever, are finding ever fewer pathways along which to bring their ideas to the rest of us.

The proof that America's entrepreneurs are in trouble is not merely anecdotal. Although it is extremely hard to find good statistics on entre-preneurship in the United States—in large part because the government years ago stopped keeping track in any realistic way—what statistics we do have are bleak.

Between 1948 and 2003, the self-employment rate in the United States fell from 18.5 percent to 7.5 percent. Even when we exclude farmers, the number drops from 12 percent to only 6.9 percent. Self-employment in retail fell from 38 percent in 1910 to less than 12 per-cent in 1990. Nor was this a slow and steady drop. In the 1980s alone, in the first years after the Reagan Revolution, the number plummeted by nearly a third. Nor do these figures separate the one-person consul-tant or contract worker from the person who runs an actual small busi-ness. In other words, the real figure is even lower. (A new study by the Organization for Economic Cooperation and Development ranked the United States as the second lowest of twenty-two rich nations in the percentage of workers who are self-employed, above only Luxembourg. Among the specific activities the United States ranked especially low in were small manufacturing [nineteenth], R&D in small firms [twentieth], and computer-related service employment [twenty-first].)[10]

No matter how shocking, numbers are always abstract. Figuring that the best way to get a sense of how the U.S. entrepreneur is faring was to speak with a few people on the front lines, I tracked down the owners of a few franchise operations in South Florida. A franchise might not seem to fit the definition of a true entrepreneur—a Cuppy's Coffee, after all, is not really "independent" in the same way as Toby's Coffee Bar in Point Reyes Station or Mocha Joe's in Brattleboro.

But for a growing number of Americans in places like Peoria, Purdue, and Pembroke Pines, franchising is not so much the easiest way to establish a small business, it is increasingly the only way. Americans are no less desirous or able today than they were fifty years ago to open Sarah and Michael's Diner rather than yet another Subway, but today's would-be entrepreneur quickly discovers that our nation's increasingly consolidated banking and commercial real estate systems greatly favor the franchise over the independent business, not least because the franchise model enables the bankers, and the bureaucrats in places like the Small Business Administration, to justify not investing more time or money on due diligence.[11]

And so I find myself chatting with John McCarthy about the Quiznos franchise he opened in North Palm Beach a few years back. Born in New Hampshire, McCarthy moved to Florida in the mid-1980s to manage mental health facilities. This is not work that makes a man rich, but McCarthy tells me that he did manage to save some money. One day he decided to use that money to set his son-in-law up with his own business. Although he originally considered some sort of independent operation, McCarthy soon concluded that the franchise route was more practical.

It seemed a simple quid pro quo. McCarthy and his son-in-law would put up the hard work, the capital, and connections in the community. The franchisor would bring to the table its brand, its tested menu, its large-scale purchasing operation, and its knowledge of health and zoning regulations. It would be a true partnership. And given that the Federal Trade Commission appeared to regulate franchising contracts closely, the whole endeavor seemed to offer little risk of getting cheated.[12]

McCarthy soon settled on Quiznos. Here, he believed, was a fast-growing company with a high-quality and unique product: the toasted submarine sandwich made with deli-quality meats. Better yet, Quiznos was already well known in South Florida—the first outlet had opened in 1993—yet there were still no shops in Jupiter, an upscale, beach-front community just north of Palm Beach. McCarthy was also attracted to the Quiznos story.[13] The company had been built by a young fellow named Rick Schaden, who had used his father's money to buy a locally famous Denver sub shop and in a decade had developed it into the number six ranking firm in *Entrepreneur Magazine*'s 2001 listing of franchise businesses, right behind such gold-standard operations as McDonald's, Subway, Taco Bell, and Jiffy Lube.[14]

What McCarthy's research missed, however, were the first big signs of trouble at Quiznos, such as the fact that one group of early franchisees had recently founded an association called Toasted Subs to organize their complaints on how Quiznos was treating them. Which was unfortunate, because McCarthy began to run into problems almost as soon as he signed a contract in August 2001 to open a Quiznos outlet and paid his $25,000 deposit.

Based on his conversations with the local Quiznos representative, McCarthy expected to build his shop on a brand-new centrally located strip mall. After six months of watching the grass grow, however, McCarthy learned that not only was there no plan to build any strip mall there, the lot wasn't even zoned for a fast-food restaurant.

McCarthy was furious. But when he went to complain, the Quiznos representative was so reassuring that instead of getting his deposit back, McCarthy plunked down another $25,000 for the rights to open a second Quiznos, this one in an industrial area on the edge of town. McCarthy tells me he feels silly now, but at the time there seemed to be a certain logic, composed of equal parts of hope and fear. On one hand, two franchises promised more money than one. On the other, Quiznos had a grip on McCarthy's first deposit and showed no signs of letting go. "You begin to feel that you have no exit," he says, "that you have to keep shoveling new money in to get your first investment out."

The second shop proved almost as difficult to develop as the first, and it did not open until April 2004. The effort sucked up more time and money than McCarthy expected; it cost nearly double the $60,000 in up-front costs that Quiznos had originally quoted to him. Moreover, from the very first day the sales numbers never added up. Quiznos requires that its franchisees buy all their food, equipment, and signage from the central corporation and that they pay a fixed percent of all sales (not profits) as a "royalty." This system enables the company to know, more or less, whether their franchisees are earning enough to survive.

But now McCarthy learned that even though Quiznos knew that he and his son-in-law were losing money big-time, it did not intend to adjust any of its charges or fees in the slightest. For a year and a half, McCarthy's son-in-law, who had a new baby at home, worked seven days a week, twelve hours per day, and earned no money. In October 2005, McCarthy shut his doors for the last time, though only after paying another $25,000 to his landlord to get out of his lease. "It was disastrous," he says now. "Absolutely disastrous."

Them's the breaks, right? Either you got it, or you don't, right? Ain't no free lunch in America, amigo, right? ('Cept what you can scrounge from the unsold stock, or if you're a banker, from the U.S. Treasury.) Well, yes, the nature of business does entail risk. And yes, the nature of business means that many small enterprises fail. And yes, many fail for excellent reasons, such as the incompetence or laziness of the entrepreneur. McCarthy himself admits that for a long time he thought that it was his fault he had lost all his money, that he had been somehow especially naive.

Then one day, after he accepted that his venture was hopeless, McCarthy asked a local real estate broker to sell the shop as a going concern. The broker showed him a list of more than thirty other Quiznos shops just in South Florida for which he was trying to find a buyer.

As numerous lawsuits and articles from the last four years reveal, if McCarthy was naive, he sure had plenty of company. Although Quiznos still presents itself as a submarine sandwich chain, there appears to be another side to the business model, which is that the firm is organized to function also as a highly sophisticated fleecing operation. Consider a few facts:

- In 2005, Quiznos Corporate admitted that 67 percent of the people who paid $25,000 deposits did not open a store within twelve months, which entitled the firm to keep their money. In all, about three thousand people who transferred at least $75 million in working capital to Quiznos never got what they paid for.[15]
- Quiznos Corporate was fully aware of the consequences of charging its franchisees above-market prices for raw materials and machinery. One company lawyer wrote in 2003 that 40 percent of all franchises were "not breaking even."[16]

- Quiznos Corporate has worked especially hard to keep all this a secret, unleashing its lawyers against any franchisee who dared to complain in public or who merely attempted to set up a system by which to communicate with other franchisees.[17]

These problems with Quiznos are not inherent in franchising itself. Running a franchise has never been easy or risk free, but the franchise industry is also home to many truly cooperative associations, which are structured not to make money for a central corporation but to help the individual franchisees succeed. To the extent that there has been a pattern in recent years, it is that *big financiers* have used *big corporations* to transform more and more of these franchise systems into a twenty-first-century version of tenant farming—with a twist.

In the old days, sharecroppers generally did not have to pay the rent until after the crop was harvested. Today's franchisees have to start paying rent long before they set foot on the land, and sometimes even when they never see the land. They have to keep paying rent when the crop fails, until they are bled dry. At that point, the landlord runs the bankrupt off the lot and moves the next sharecropper into his or her place.

Beginning about thirty years ago, just around the time that Ronald Reagan became president, rich Americans began to get a lot richer and middle-class Americans began to get relatively poorer. As this trend became clearer in the last decade, a veritable cottage industry developed in Washington to figure out why this was so.[18] Some reasons are obvious: the destruction of labor unions, tax cuts for the rich, the use of immense cross-border trading companies to pit working Americans against poor people in distant lands, the privatization of the U.S. Department of the Treasury. Yet almost no attention has been paid to the growing number of instances in which some of the redistribution of wealth from the middle class to the rich was affected by corporations purposely built for that task.

Consider a few of the facts about how the money in the Quiznos system was redistributed. Although it is impossible to find out how much money Rick Schaden has made from running Quiznos, because the company has been private since 2001, we do know that in 2000 his annual revenues topped $428 million, and his profit just from the resale of food to the franchisees topped $20 million. We also know that when Schaden sold part of the company to JP Morgan Chase and part to former Burger King CEO Greg Brenneman, he still kept control of the company.

Warren Buffett need not fear for his title as the richest American, but Schaden, we can be sure, walks our land with a bulging bag of boodle.

We also know that a man named Bhupinder "Bob" Buber opened two Quiznos shops in 1998 in Long Beach, California. Over the years Buber poured his entire life savings, more than $500,000, into this business. And we know that in November 2006, Buber locked himself in the restroom of a friend's store in Whittier and shot himself three times in the chest. We also know the content of Buber's suicide note.

"Quiznos has killed me," he wrote. "Destroyed my life. Destroyed my family life for the past seven years. They retaliated against me for trying to create a voice for the franchisees in the systems. . . . How can a common individual like me . . . with limited resources get justice?"[19]

The Paradox of Efficiency

All activity in our political economy takes place in an environment of law. This means that whenever huge changes take place in our political economy, it is because someone somewhere changed a law or how we enforce that law. In the United States there are two ways to change a law. The first way, which is what we study in civics class, is to debate the proposed change in public and then vote whether to approve it. The other way is to change it surreptitiously. Perhaps the most effective way to do so is to redefine the meaning of the words that are embedded in the existing law or to redefine or alter entirely the words we use to interpret the intent of the law.

We saw in chapter 1 that one reason it has taken us so long to notice the return of monopolists to America is because they long ago seized control of both of our main political parties. One of the ways the monopolists managed this feat was precisely to devise an entirely new philosophy of political economics that enabled them to replace one language system with another. Instead of the language of law and politics we have always used to illuminate how other people use political economic institutions against us, they substituted a language of math and mysticism that was designed specifically to hide such use of power.

Our next step is to understand exactly *how* the rich changed our language in ways that liberated them to use *our* corporations, *our* banks, and *our* markets to rule us. I place this discussion here, in the middle of a chapter on entrepreneurs and workers, precisely because our would-be lords have focused so much of their efforts to change our language on the very laws we use to protect the markets in which we exchange our work and ideas. I will concentrate on two of the most important changes they accomplished. The first altered how we enforce our antimonopoly laws. The second altered how—and, indeed, whether—we perceive monopolies.

Let's start with the term *efficiency*. In political debate, efficiency has long been a staple argument of those who defend absolute monarchs and dictators. To concentrate power in a single individual or a small group is said to be more efficient than scattering power among, for instance, different branches of government. In debates on economic governance, we can trace use of the efficiency argument back at least to the years after the English civil war of the seventeenth century. The newly empowered gentry often justified the seizure of common lands and the private property of independent farmers by claiming that the greater scale of operations would enable more efficient exploitation of the land.

In the modern era in the United States, efficiency was a favorite defense by industrial autocrats like John D. Rockefeller and financial autocrats like J. P. Morgan of their use of corporate power to arbitrarily determine particular political economic outcomes. The progressive elite, meanwhile, later turned efficiency into a veritable religion.

That's why the American people learned long ago to reject efficiency as either a goal or a means of public or private governance, and why we consistently rejected it for the first two hundred years of our nation. We understood that *efficiency* was a code word for top-down autocratic rule by the lords of the private corporate estates or the "public" state. Hence we rejected efficiency in the Declaration of Independence and again in the Constitution. We rejected efficiency when we wrote the Sherman Antitrust Act, then reiterated our rejection time and again in our other antimonopoly laws.

The Supreme Court unanimously rejected efficiency as an excuse for industrial dictatorship when it ordered the breakup of Standard Oil despite the fact that the company had lowered the cost of a gallon of kerosene by more than half. The Supreme Court unanimously rejected the efficiency argument again in 1935 when it ruled President Roosevelt's National Industrial Recovery Act unconstitutional. In every case, the American people embraced not efficiency but freedom and moved to protect that freedom through the erection of intricate systems of checks and balances designed to scatter power.

And yet, consider this chain of events from a generation ago. On January 20, 1981, Ronald Reagan assumed office as the fortieth president of the United States. On February 6, the *New York Times* reported that Attorney General William French Smith had chosen a law professor, William F. Baxter, to head the Justice Department's Antitrust Division. On February 13, the *Times* quoted Baxter as saying that he planned to "pursue an antitrust policy based on *efficiency* considerations."[20]

Consider also that this was no surprise to anyone who had paid any attention to the writings of the main economic philosophers of the neofeudal revolution. In the late 1950s, nearly half a century after the Supreme Court's decision on Standard Oil, a radical economics professor named John McGee published a paper in which he carefully resurrected Rockefeller's old efficiency argument.[21] In the early 1960s, the economists Milton Friedman and Alan Greenspan, along with other radical intellectuals at the Chicago School, spun out a string of essays that built on McGee's argument in order to attack antitrust law. Much of this work was quite strident: in one screed, Greenspan attacked antimonopoly law as a "jumble of economic irrationality and ignorance" and trustbusters as "naive" and "unrealistic." All of the essays hewed to the same basic message, that antimonopoly laws were not "efficient."[22]

The great leap came in the late 1970s when a law professor named Robert Bork figured out how to repackage the efficiency argument in entirely new language. Older readers will remember that Ronald Reagan nominated Bork to serve on the Supreme Court in 1987 and that the Democratic-controlled Senate rejected the nomination in a brutal political battle. One of the main achievements that helped Bork earn the nomination, and the main reason I bring him up now, is a book he published in 1978, titled *The Antitrust Paradox*. The authors of the Sherman Antitrust Act had not used the word *consumer* even once. The authors of the Clayton Antitrust Act of 1914, which strengthened the Sherman Act, did use the word *consumer*, but only once, and then peripherally.

Nevertheless, Bork began his book by asserting, "The only legitimate goal of American antitrust law" is to protect consumers by delivering lower prices to them.[23] He then identified his "paradox," which is that sometimes the enforcement of antitrust law interferes with the efforts of the managers of large corporations to devise more "efficient" systems of production and distribution, and this may result, at least in the near term, in higher prices. Bork then insisted that regulators should in the future measure any proposed enforcement of antitrust law by its likely effect on "consumer welfare."

This was a masterstroke of the sapper's art. Bork replaced a term—*efficiency*—that had always triggered a negative political reaction among a wide spectrum of Americans with a word—*consumer*—that had been carefully groomed and profitably used by the hippest of 1960s-era reformers, Ralph Nader.

This enabled Bork to roll out a magically simple chain of reasoning: if antitrust law exists to serve the consumer, and if consumers are best served by getting more for less, and if the best way to get more for less is to encourage business to be "efficient," and if the best way to be efficient is to build up scale and scope, then ergo, monopoly is the best friend of the consumer.

Bork then concluded with a direct attack on the idea that the American people might ever want to force these immensely powerful private corporate governments to compete, for *political* reasons. "'Competition,'" he wrote, "must be understood as a *term of art*, signifying *any state* of affairs in which the consumer welfare cannot be increased by judicial decree."[24] He emphasized that "any state of affairs" included cases of outright monopoly.

This new terminology enabled the neofeudal movement to leap swiftly beyond Baxter's straightforward use of the efficiency argument to something far more palatable. I was unable to determine whether Baxter himself ever used the term *consumer welfare* while he was in office. But many of the more ardent enemies of antitrust law did so from the very first days of the Reagan administration. And Baxter's successor as head of the Antitrust Division, J. Paul McGrath, used the term *consumer welfare* in his very first speech, in January 1984.[25]

The Invisible Fist

Our next challenge is to review how the rich repackaged the concept of laissez-faire in such a way as to make us all but unable to *see* when the few use their immensely powerful corporations to impose their will upon us. This was an even more significant achievement than their conjuring up of the concept of consumer welfare. The efficiency argument affects how we apply only one set of laws. The veiling of laissez-faire—basically, the argument that the rich should be allowed to rule our political economy in pretty much whatever fashion they wish—affects how we perceive every interaction in our political economy.

There is nothing new about the fact that the powerful few among us often claim a "right" to rule the rest of us, free from all interference. This belief is, quite understandably, a stock notion of the aristocratic mind. Nor is there anything new—and this is more to the point here—about the fact that the more autocratic aristocrats often attempt to package their claim in the language of liberty.

Historian David Hackett Fischer, who says that such thinking came to this country with the first Virginia planters, coined the term *hegemonic liberty* to describe the conviction among the powerful few that they enjoy a veritable "freedom to enslave" the many.[26] This line of thinking—modernized to include the trade and industrial corporation alongside the estate and plantation and dressed up in claims that such top-down control was vital to the national defense—greatly shaped the politics of many of those who, in our young republic, advocated various forms of aristocratic social structure.

Ever since, our would-be lords have dressed the term *laissez-faire* in far more fanciful guises. At various times they have presented their alleged right to rule as a "natural" right, a "divine" right, and, most successfully in America, a "property" right. Even before Charles Darwin published *On the Origin of Species*, in which he discussed the biological concept of natural selection, the British economist Herbert Spencer had coined the term *survival of the fittest*. Sure enough, many industrial and financial autocrats began to claim that their success was proof they had been constituted most "fit" to survive in the jungle of America's political economy. In other words, their "right" to rule—through force, if necessary—was literally bred into them. At no point, however, did any of these arguments come close to convincing the majority of Americans to let go of the institutions and laws we had established to protect ourselves from the predations of the rich.

To identify the exact terms that the powerful substituted for *laissez-faire*, I will turn to one of the most well-known theologians in this country, Harvey Cox, a professor at Harvard Divinity School. In an article he published a few years ago titled "The Market as God," Cox describes his journey from the cloisters of academia into the realm of business. There, much to his surprise, he discovered that the "lexicon of *The Wall Street Journal* and the business sections of *Time* and *Newsweek* turned out to bear a striking resemblance to Genesis, the Epistle to the Romans, and St. Augustine's *City of God*." Increasing numbers of

Americans, Cox noted, were coming to view "the market" as some sort of all-wise but largely mysterious mechanism able to determine—indeed, somehow insistent on the *right* to determine—who does what in the world and for how much. "Such is the grip of the current orthodoxy," Cox concluded, "that to question the omniscience of the market is to question the inscrutable wisdom of Providence."[27]

Cox did not, of course, mean that Americans today worship the market in the same way that people worship Jesus or Ganesha. He meant that an increasing number of us tend to react to changes in our economic status differently from the way we did in the past. Not long ago, when the people who control institutions like Wal-Mart, Archer Daniels Midland, and Tyson Foods used these immensely powerful private governments and massive concentrations of capital to enclose the markets used by citizens like Fred Messner and Ron Fahrmeier in Kansas City, many if not most Americans would have understood this to be a form of theft. Such enclosure of the public market, we knew, amounted to a taking of the properties of the citizens who used those markets, and often the reduction of independent entrepreneurs into dependent and powerless "employees" in top-down corporate systems. Even the elite often admitted as much, although they tended to insist that such theft was a necessary "price of progress."

Yet as Cox noticed, today Americans increasingly interpret such seizures as acts of nature, not all that different from an earthquake or a volcanic explosion. Rather than take to the streets to battle this destruction of our properties and our liberties, we sit passively. Rather than rip back the curtain to reveal the rich wizards of Oz pulling the levers of their corporations and refining their market-cornering trading formulas, we imagine a blind, mechanical, automatic process playing slowly out.

To understand how the rich and powerful managed to replace the "invisible hand" of the open market with the invisible fist of their autocratic institutions, we have to look beyond their co-optation of the word *market*. We must also look at the word they appended to it: *free*. It was the act of combining these two words into the term *free market* that transformed the market from a political tool that exists *within* human society into something that exists *over and around* human society, something that acts *upon* human society like a sort of mechanical god.

It was by combining these two words that the rich and powerful finally enabled themselves to transform the most brutal acts of men using corporations and massed capital, into the whims of a distant, blind, even vaguely just divinity. Karl Marx wrote in 1843 that religion is the "opium of the people."[28] America's lords, in perhaps the single most brilliant bit of linguistic legerdemain ever perpetrated in our nation, figured out how to transmute the scrim behind which they disguise their predations into the religion of the American people.

Our next task is to identify who did this, which is why we must take a look at the University of Chicago's departments of economics and law. As many of you may know, *Chicago School* is a term used to describe a philosophy of economics that was first pushed onto the national stage in the late 1950s. This philosophy holds that government interference with the private actors who run economic institutions like corporations, banks, and investment funds violates the liberty of these individuals *and* retards their ability to produce wealth—or at least cash and power for themselves. In other words, the Chicago School philosophy is laissez-faire served straight up. As we have noted, Chicago School sophists like Alan Greenspan and Robert Bork deserve most of the credit for resurrecting and repackaging the term *efficiency* as *consumer welfare*. Chicago School operators also deserve most of the credit for shaping the term *free market* as we understand it today.

This becomes clear if we look at who first used the term in modern fashion. It was not Adam Smith. *Free market* appears but once in *The Wealth of Nations*, and only then in the phrase "open and free market."[29] Nor was it Alfred Marshall, the pioneering advocate of "scientific" economics. In Marshall's 1890 work *Principles of Economics*, the term appears just once.[30] Nor was it either of the Austrian-born economists—Friedrich Hayek and Joseph Schumpeter—whom the Chicago School sophists claim to hold in highest regard. *Free market* appears only once in Hayek's 1944 work, *The Road to Serfdom*, and only then in a quote from Max Eastman, whom Hayek calls a "pathetic . . . old communist."[31] Schumpeter does not use the term at all in his 1942 work, *Capitalism, Socialism, and Democracy*.[32]

The work in which the term *free market* does play a starring role is a 1962 collection of essays by Milton Friedman, the economist who is the single most important shaper and promoter of the Chicago School ideology of laissez-faire. In that work, titled *Capitalism and Freedom*, Friedman uses *free market* more than two dozen times, and he generally does not use it in the technical ways that Smith and Marshall used it.

Rather, he uses it to paint a picture of a mechanism that serves humanity as a dispassionate determinator of economic outcomes and a beneficent bringer of bounty, hence something very unwise to interfere with.[33]

Capitalism and Freedom is a slim book, and many of the essays are not so much well-developed arguments as compact catalogs of assertions. Yet the work is dense with an entirely new and highly sophisticated political language, designed specifically to hide the use of power within our political economy by the rich. Friedman accomplishes this through the very act of subverting our traditional political economic language of law and politics. In addition to the term *free market*, this includes (as we will discuss in more detail in chapter 8), the assertion that the business corporation is not an institution of governance designed to regulate a marketplace and the property within it; rather, the corporation is a property itself that exists within the market. *Capitalism and Freedom* also includes an early effort to redefine *privatization* as *deregulation*.[34]

Friedman's ultimate intent in his book is made most clear by his discussion of antimonopoly law itself. Friedman's own putative hero, Friedrich Hayek, was a great defender of engineering competition wherever it "can be created," and he believed that doing so should be one of the foremost goals of government policy. Enforcement of antimonopoly law against great private powers, Hayek wrote, was not merely smart economics but one of most "obvious tasks" of governance.[35] In *Capitalism and Freedom*, in contrast, Friedman states that the American people should never be allowed to use our antimonopoly laws to impede any effort by rich people to combine their capital and employ the resulting political power as they alone see fit.

Not that Friedman favored repeal of our antimonopoly laws. On the contrary, he advocated leaving the laws on the books so that they can be *redirected against* the American people whenever we might try to protect our liberty and our property from the predations of the rich by, say, organizing a professional organization, a small-business association, a cooperative, or a labor union.[36]

In other words, even while preaching that the richest and most powerful among us should have absolute freedom to unify their powers with one another and with the state, Friedman advocated denying the exact same right to citizens like you and me. Friedman's *Capitalism and Freedom* deserves to be recognized for what it is: the most effective profeudal manifesto in the English language since the restoration of monarchy in Britain more than three hundred years ago.

The Two Roads to Serfdom

In December 1938, as the world spiraled toward a second world war, Robert Jackson, a future Supreme Court justice who was then serving as President Roosevelt's solicitor general, concisely linked the socialist and laissez-faire visions.

"It is strange," wrote Jackson, who later headed the U.S. prosecution of Nazi war criminals, "that one view of centralization of wealth and its control is shared by both the intelligent socialist, who wants to remake our society, and by the unenlightened capitalist, who wants shelter from every social control. What the extreme socialist favors because of his creed, the extreme capitalist favors because of greed."[37]

In the decades after World War II, this lesson, which we the American people had for so long preached to our business and intellectual elites, seemed at last to stick. The examples of countries like Italy that had taken Hoover-style corporatist associationalism a step too far were enough to convince two generations of Americans of all classes that a vigorous antimonopoly policy was central to maintaining a free nation. For the next half century, the concept of competition for the sake of competition enjoyed strong bipartisan support, and some of the most sophisticated enforcement took place under Presidents Dwight Eisenhower and Richard Nixon.

When the Chicago School operators in the Reagan administration announced their intent to overthrow our antitrust laws, senators from both parties defended the laws on the grounds that their purpose was not to lower prices but to protect the independent entrepreneur and to prevent a few among us from using our political economic institutions to concentrate power in their own hands.

To complete our task of answering why the rich were able to overturn our antimonopoly laws so easily, we must look at who within the Democratic Party supported this coup and why. The history of the takeover of the Republican Party by a radical neofeudal wing of the elite wielding the language so carefully fabricated by the Chicago School sophists is well known, so I am not going to recount those details here.

Far less understood is what happened during these same years to undercut support for antimonopoly law within the Democratic Party. When the neofeudal revolutionaries arrived in Washington with their doctrine of efficiency, why did so many Democratic academics, like MIT economist Lester Thurow, prove to be such valuable allies?[38] And when Bill Clinton became president in 1993, why did almost no one in his administration object when he not only let stand the basic outlines of Reagan's antimonopoly policy but also set about encouraging further "rationalization" in almost every sector of the American political economy?

The answer rests on two intrusions into the Democratic Party that took place during the 1960s. The first was Ralph Nader's consumer crusade. Although at the time this seemed to be an entirely newfangled popular movement, in reality it was the incarnation of an idea that had been envisioned by the progressive elite more than half a century earlier. In 1914, Walter Lippmann, in a long passage in which he sketched the outlines of a plan to make the public the "determining voice in government," predicted that the consumer "interest" was "destined to be stronger than the interests of either labor or capital." No matter the movement's origin or underlying philosophy, the initial message of the Naderites—that laws should be passed to ensure that manufacturers deliver safe products, like cars with seat belts—from the average citizen's point of view was a very good thing. Much more problematic was the second stage of Nader's campaign, when he and his followers, under the banner Public Citizen, began, just as Lippmann had urged, to cry "out against the 'high cost of living.'"[39]

Right through Lyndon Johnson's presidency, the Democratic Party had remained the primary tool of the small farmer, the small-business owner, and the individual worker—in other words, the American producer. That's why until this point the party had focused not on lowering prices—which as we have seen are largely arbitrary and political constructs—but on increasing the freedom of the small producer to protect his or her own income, within the limits set by the dynamics of open market systems. In many specific cases, the Naderite stance on antitrust was dead on. Yet as the Democratic Party elite increasingly adopted Nader's proconsumer language and fixation on lowering prices, the party leaders became increasingly open to the idea that concentration, efficiency, and privatization (under the guise of deregulation) were the best way to serve the nation's populace. Or put another way, the "consumer" movement foundered on its own intellectual contradictions.

The second intrusion into the Democratic Party was a reconstituted progressivism, now sometimes referred to as *democratic socialism*. The most well known, intelligent, influential, and honest of the democratic socialists was the economist John Kenneth Galbraith, who during these years updated many Progressive Era concepts by putting them in new frames, like that of "countervailing power." Like their progressive brethren in the early twentieth century, this neo-socialist elite tended to be strong supporters of democracy, in the sense that citizens should be free to choose their own representatives.

But also like their brethren early in the century, the neo-socialist elite tended to dismiss the importance of economic freedom, defined as the ability of an individual citizen to work his or her own properties free of predation or direction from above. Many also tended to favor restricting the power of the people and their representatives to act within our own political economy. Indeed, the neo-socialists of Vietnam-era vintage, just like their role models, tended to advocate management of the economy by a select and centralized group of "scientific" economists and other "experts," entrusted with the task of enforcing "efficiency" in the name of producing ever greater piles of stuff. That's why Galbraith, in such books as *Economics and the Public Purpose*, did not merely dismiss the importance of antimonopoly law—which of course shifts power from elites to smaller and more democratically scattered actors—but actively waged war against the very idea of antimonopoly law and indeed of open markets.[40]

My purpose here is not to assign blame to any one group for our present economic and political woes but to complete our effort to understand the meaning and the provenance of the words we use today and to illuminate the ideas that continue to shape our thinking and guide our decisions. One of the clearest ways to do so is to highlight the fact that the two main groups that came out in 1981 in support of overthrowing our antimonopoly laws were the operators of the Chicago School neofeudal philosophy, descended more or less directly from J. P. Morgan, and the democratic socialists, descended more or less directly from the classical progressive movement, best personified by Theodore Roosevelt, circa 1912.

In an introduction written for the second edition of *The Antitrust Paradox*, Robert Bork, after patting himself on the back for sparking the "revolution," admitted to being still mystified as to why the "socialists" had decided to abandon "this branch of law," by which he meant the regulation of competition.[41] I quote this statement to illustrate that

Bork himself never fully understood the distinction between the democratic socialists (like Galbraith), who always opposed antitrust, and the
democratic republicans (like Supreme Court Justice Louis Brandeis),
who believe that antimonopoly law to be—within the scheme of laws
designed to govern economic relations in the United States—perhaps
the single most important bulwark of liberty.

Which in turn means that Bork apparently did not understand (or
simply refused to admit) how much his "free-market" laissez-faire friends
had in common with their "socialist" antagonists. Which also means
that he did not understand (or refused to admit) the role he played in
bringing off a very harmonious conclusion to the century-long interne-
cine battle for precedence between the progressive patrician "left" wing
of America's elite, with its vision of top-down, semiauthoritarian state-
directed socialism, and the more classically feudal "right" wing, with its
vision of top-down, semiauthoritarian private direction of our economy.

Anyone who has paid even the slightest bit of attention to the
debates of the last forty years about how to govern America's political
economy might reasonably conclude that John Kenneth Galbraith and
Milton Friedman are polar opposites. No two ideals could be more different, or so it often seemed.

On one side there was Galbraith, the persistently prodding prophet
of socialism, teaching that all relationships in our political economy are
political in nature, that efforts to erect markets will lead only to grief,
and that control should be turned over to a professional technocratic
elite. On the other side stood Friedman, the smiling and avuncular yet
stubborn and sophistical defender of "free-market" capitalism, teaching
that there was little that any politician could ever do to improve the natural workings of the unfettered "free market."

Yet if we go back to the early 1990s and trace the effort by such "progressives" as Robert Reich to import Chicago School concepts into the
mainstream of the Democratic Party, such as through *The Work of Nations*;

And, if we look at the similarity of the thinking in both wings of the elite
about the desirability of allowing immense investment funds to organize,
rationalize, and direct our economy, to maximize the manufacture of cash;

And, if we look at the similarity of thinking in both wings of the elite
about the desirability, of allowing giant retailers and trading companies
to organize, rationalize, and direct activity within our real economy in
order, supposedly, to drive down prices;[42]

And, if we look at the similarity of thinking in both wings of the elite on using immense trading corporations to pit Chinese machine operators, Indian software engineers, Mexican doctors against American machine operators, software engineers, and doctors to drive down wages;[43]

And, if we look at the similarity of thinking in both wings of the elite on using new technologies—no matter how coercive—to increase *efficiency* and *productivity* by counting every one of our keystrokes, tracking every move we make on our delivery routes, and timing how fast we swipe groceries across checkout scanners;[44]

And, if we look at the similarity of thinking in both wings of the elite on the value of using shame to govern us, through such tactics as rating in public the performance of every individual doctor, teacher, and dairy farmer, without any mechanism for appeal;

And, if we sift through the wreckage around the great bank bail-out and recollect how two teams of men from Goldman Sachs—one in control of each party—traded our Treasury Department back and forth between themselves and used it to bail each other out:

Then it is reasonable to conclude that the time has come for the American people to accept a hard truth, which is that *both* of our political parties are now run by people who view us not as sovereign citizens who command them but as nude and sometimes rude animals who must be fed, clothed, employed, entertained, exercised, disciplined, and, once every four years, herded by beaters into a voting booth.

And it is reasonable to conclude that the time has come for the admirers of John Kenneth Galbraith and the admirers of Milton Friedman to accept another hard truth, which is that although these men may have directed us down two seemingly different roads these last forty years, both roads led us to the same feudal estate.

The Politics of Milking

To understand just how tough it is to be your own person in our "land of the free" today, I decided to visit one of America's last remaining *yeoman* farmers (which is what independent small-property holders used to be called in the days of Thomas Jefferson). Don't get me wrong; I am not one to get all romantic about working the land. My father grew up sharecropping corn and strawberries outside Plant City, Florida, and his sister later married a man who could afford to buy some of that land and to lease a lot more from the phosphate companies.

As I was growing up, I spent long and educational days at my uncle's farm. Home life was much improved: the farmhouse had screens and indoor plumbing. But work was still tough. My uncle's hands were so rough and calloused he could barely pick a pencil off the table. In the winter, the farm was strikingly beautiful, a land of mossy oaks and blue springs, a fine place to smack runt potatoes with a baseball bat, or just sit and listen to the grown-ups crack jokes, cackle, and hack. In the summer, though, as we dug post holes in slick black mud, blinded by sweat and choking on mosquitoes, the farm seemed about a mile beyond the gates of hell.

My search for a contemporary yeoman has led me to the small dairy of Ronald Hazelwood, outside the town of Elizabethton in Carter County, Tennessee. Ronny, as he prefers to be called, is not a big man. But he stands straight as a post under a flowering cherry tree in the front yard of his meticulous white-painted home, telling me about the business of farming in America in the early twenty-first century. His dairy is named Watauga Valley Farms, and the red walls of the barns glow in the sun a few hundred yards beyond his fence. It's a glorious day in early spring, and the view is almost enough to wipe the memory of Florida summers from my mind.

Hazelwood owns 125 acres on the floor of the Siam Valley, below a looming mass of rock called Lynn Mountain, and today the trees are flush with light green and maroon leaves. The land here was so rich, and the landscape so beckoning, that this network of valleys was one of the first west of the Blue Ridge Mountains to be settled by Europeans, particularly by a rabble of rebel farmers who were fleeing North Carolina's colonial government in 1771. Ronny's family has farmed nearby for as long as anyone he knows can remember. Ronny bought this dairy in the 1970s, and his father bought the farm where Ronny grew up in the 1940s. That was because the family's old homestead was flooded when New Dealers dammed the Watauga River upstream and made a big lake.

Ronny tells me that he wants to pass his dairy on to his son, Michael, who is now standing at his side. But he's growing increasingly doubtful that there'll be much to pass on. Ronny lists a litany of challenges, ranging from the price of feed and diesel to taxes and the constant flux of health regulations. His real concern, however, is the lack of places to sell his milk. Not long ago, there were a number of small processors who were eager to buy what Ronny's seventy cows produce each day.

Consolidation in the milk business has eliminated most of these, and Ronny now depends on a single bottler in Asheville, North Carolina, who dispatches a truck across the mountains to pick up his milk along with that produced by three dairies nearby. It's not good to depend on only one buyer, Ronny says, but when I ask him if there isn't some local market where he can sell his milk, he laughs. Everyone locally shops at Wal-Mart, he says, because that's the only place to shop. And all the milk there—although it's sold under such labels as Great Value, PET Dairy, and Mayfield—comes mainly from one company, called Dean Foods. And Dean Foods is not interested in dealing with small dairies like Ronny's.

This is not the first time the American farmer has come up against monopolists. First there were the landlords. Then the engrosser at the local market. Then came the railroads and the speculators in the old commodity exchanges. Then the big slaughterhouses and the modern grain traders. Over the years, though, the farmers did win a few battles, such as passing the Interstate Commerce Act, the Grain Futures Act, and the Packers and Stockyards Act. The farmers also won for themselves the right to organize themselves into cooperatives, which for a time proved especially useful to the dairy farmers.

No matter what the laws on the books say, however, the words have no meaning if the government ignores them or the courts intentionally misinterpret them. And so in recent years, the cooperatives the dairy farmers have so long used to protect themselves found it harder and harder to survive. Immense private firms like Dean Foods seemed always to have access to more money. The cooperatives tried to keep up, by merging and by borrowing to upgrade their plants and systems. But without government help, competition between the cooperative of the farmer and the corporation of the financier is a race the farmer is destined eventually to lose.

And over the last generation—under Reagan, Clinton, and both Bushes—that help from the government stopped coming. And so the old story played slowly out once again. The big loans the co-ops took on themselves meant big loan repayments. And in hard times these big repayments meant delinquency. Eventually, even the biggest cooperatives ended up, somehow or another, in the hands of the financiers. In some cases, like the immense cooperative Farmland Industries, the financiers scattered the constituent pieces among private firms.[45] In others, such as the Dairy Farmers of America, the financiers merged a number of cooperatives into a single super-"cooperative," which they could more easily use for their own purposes.[46]

Over the last twenty years, the path was cleared more completely than ever before for corporations to seize control of the nation's hog-raising, chicken-raising, and cattle-raising businesses (although the independent cowboy still holds out in pockets here and there across the plains).[47] One of the most dramatic such roll-ups of power took place in dairy; Dean Foods and Dairy Farmers of America now split roughly 80 percent of the business. Given that the two work together in more or less open collusion, they form what in essence is a single private government that determines who gets to milk cows in America and who doesn't.[48]

Ronny Hazelwood knows he's not on their list.

Markets are made, and markets have masters. The question we face today in this country is whether we shall ever again master the political art of making markets serve the will and the interest of the average citizen. Or shall we instead yield our markets forevermore unto small companies of private men, and let them serve as our masters.

On my way out of the Siam and Watauga valleys, I figure I should pick up a bottle of whiskey to help me ponder this question. A whiskey distilled in Tennessee seemed an especially fitting souvenir of my visit here. It was, after all, the rebels who settled these valleys in East Tennessee who inspired the whiskey rebels in western Pennsylvania in the first years of our constitutional government. Yet as soon as I walk into a liquor store in nearby Johnsonville, I learn that I am out of luck. My only choices, the clerk tells me, are Jack Daniels and George Dickel. But the shelf where the George Dickel used to sit is empty. The clerk is not sure why. Only thing he's heard is there was some problem at the distillery.

Only later did I find out why the great state of Tennessee, home to Andrew Jackson and once one of the corn alcohol capitals of the world, could offer me only one whiskey—Jack Daniels—which in recent years has been watered down to a pathetic 80 proof to make it more "efficient" to distribute. Turns out that the George Dickel distillery fell into British hands when it was purchased by Guinness in 1987. Then in 1997, the merger of Guinness and Grand Metropolitan brought Dickel under the control of the immense London-based transnational Diageo, which also runs the Johnnie Walker, J&B, Smirnoff, Gordon, Crown Royal, and Bushmills brands.

Then in 1999 Diageo—which at the time had a contract to distribute Jack Daniels in Europe—decided there was too much Tennessee whiskey for sale in the world, so it shut the Dickel distillery for four years. Diageo did such a sloppy job of managing this shutdown that the result was empty shelves, which did not so much raise the price of Dickel as send drinkers in search of other distillations.[49] Not that, frankly, this mattered all that much to the financiers, as the duopoly of Diageo and Brown-Forman still maintained sufficient control over the distribution of whiskey in America to keep most would-be newcomers locked out of our stores.

We've fallen a ways since 1773. Back then we took up arms against a British corporation for monopolizing our imports of Chinese tea. Now we let a British corporation govern our own production and sale of our own whiskey in our own land.

Kind of takes the fun out of shouting yeeeee haawww, don't it?

6

Lightning Escapes the Bottle

The online postings are filled with terror, anger, guilt. Many plead for advice or merely a prayer. The postings are from nurses, medical technicians, and sometimes doctors who were stuck by a used syringe or another sharp medical device on the job.

The accidents happen suddenly and unpredictably—perhaps a patient coughs, or a used needle rebounds off a trash can—and they can be deadly. Every year about six thousand medical workers come down with HIV or infectious hepatitis from such accidents, and dozens end up dead. That's bad enough, but many hundreds of thousands live in uncertainty—maybe for just an hour or two but often for weeks or months—as they wait to see if they were infected. As one nurse, who was stuck on May 17, 2008, wrote online, "I don't want to risk giving anything to my husband, so our whole family is pretty much going crazy with fear."[1]

Thomas J. Shaw is sitting across from me, holding an ingenious device that would have kept this nurse safe, as well as most of the other medical workers who are stuck by syringe needles each year. The device looks like a regular syringe, but when Shaw pushes the plunger all the way down, the needle vanishes faster than the eye can follow, retracted up into the plastic tube.

But Shaw was not able to put this safety syringe into the hands of many American nurses. Nor is he allowed to even interact directly with most other health-care workers in the United States, or with the procurement offices at most hospitals or clinics. That's because the market for syringes in this country is more or less owned by one company, Becton, Dickinson and Company.

Monopolies are forged, as we have seen, to shift power from the many of us to the few of them. Some monopolies force Americans to pay with more than money.

Shaw is literally red in the face with rage. In researching this book, I spoke with many angry people. Shaw's anger is deep and pure, a slow-burning fury like something out of the Pentateuch. When he's calm, he's a pleasant man. He spends his days in a small white-walled office in a large glass-encased building that bears the name Retractable Technologies, across the street from a new school in the town of Little Elm, Texas. The setting is almost idyllic. But start Shaw talking about Becton, Dickinson and his eyes pierce right through this world to somewhere beyond.

The difference in the price of a traditional plastic disposable syringe and one of Shaw's safety syringes is a few pennies at most, and the cost could be lowered by higher production runs. That's why Shaw is sure that the monopoly he fights is run by people who are fully conscious of the results of their actions. "They kill people for money," he says.

Nor do the old-school plastic syringes manufactured by Becton, Dickinson kill only through accidental sticks. They also kill when they are intentionally reused, because unlike the glass syringes of old, plastic syringes cannot be sterilized. The intentional reuse of disposable syringes has long been a huge problem in poor lands, especially in Africa, but also in much of Asia.

In the late 1990s, studies showed that every year about 10 million people around the world contract AIDS or hepatitis through the reuse of syringes and that as many as 1.8 million of these eventually die. Since then, a strong push by international health groups has reduced the number somewhat, largely by flooding these lands with safer syringes, including many manufactured by Retractable. Yet right here in America, where Becton, Dickinson controls about 90 percent of the market, the situation may actually be getting worse. In 2008, Las Vegas officials shut a clinic where the owner had instructed the nurses to reuse disposable syringes to save money. This practice exposed as many as forty thousand people to the hepatitis C and HIV viruses.[2]

Not so many years ago, Shaw had faith in our system. In the United States, he was told, a citizen enjoyed the liberty to think up a better idea and bring that idea to the open market, where his or her fellow citizens would have the liberty to choose for themselves what works best. In a case like medical devices, in which the individual consumer is not the actual buyer, professionals armed with good information would act on their behalf, also in the open market. Thus Shaw began his journey in innocence. After seeing a late-night news report on needlestick injuries, Shaw, who was trained as an engineer, began to imagine a better syringe. One day he inserted a spring into a plastic tube and confirmed that a syringe could in fact be made almost perfectly safe. By 1992, armed with a grant from the National Institutes of Health, he thought he was on his way.[3]

That's when Shaw began to learn how America's political economy really works these days. He learned that Becton, Dickinson was loathe to invest significantly on upgrading its plants; financiers rarely see much reason to retool an operation that enjoys a functional monopoly. He learned that what money Becton, Dickinson had spent abroad in recent years—in China, India, and Brazil—was on factories to house the same old machines that stamped out the same old disposable syringes. He learned that Becton, Dickinson had gobbled up one of the first designs for a safer syringe, then priced that model so high that few bought it.

He learned that Becton, Dickinson was able to get away with these actions because it had all but captured the parts of the U.S. government that were supposed to protect Americans from such misuse of economic power. Indeed, of all the lessons Shaw learned, it was this that made him most furious. If you want to see Tom Shaw really become upset, ask him not about Becton, Dickinson but about the U.S. Congress today, which he calls a "subsidiary of the health-care monopolists."

Not only did Becton, Dickinson manage to capture a monopoly, it managed to get that monopoly all but licensed by our government.

Back in the 1950s, Becton, Dickinson was merely a powerful company, the leading U.S. manufacturer of glass syringes. The firm had enough clout to shape the market for syringes but not enough to police every corner. Indeed Becton, Dickinson faced constant assaults on its position, ranging from an antitrust suit to an all-out war for the home market against a Japanese firm named Terumo.

Becton, Dickinson survived, but it clearly could be hurt. This meant it certainly had to work to stay ahead of the curve; as new ideas for a better syringe could enter the market through any of hundreds, if not thousands, of hospital doors. Then in the mid-1980s Congress gave Becton, Dickinson—and other medical-device monopolists such as Baxter, Tyco, and Johnson & Johnson—a brand-new wall behind which to shelter their already immense power. This was an institution called the group purchasing organization, or GPO.

The GPO was created by a few well-meaning members of Congress who wanted to enable independent hospitals to negotiate better deals with medical suppliers. The idea seemed simple enough: allow the hospitals to link their purchasing operations to get bulk rates. To make the deal even better for the hospitals, the legislators required the suppliers to pay the operating expenses of the GPOs through administrative fees. The result was the formation of hundreds of GPOs, each often composed of no more than two or three hospitals.

Then four things happened. First, the GPOs began to merge. The top two, Novation and Premier, Inc., now control upward of 65 percent of all hospital purchases, while the top seven control 85 percent. Second, suppliers like Becton, Dickinson and Johnson & Johnson transformed the administrative fees they had to pay to the GPOs into a slushy system of kickbacks to bring the interests of the top executives of the GPOs into closer alignment with the interests of the suppliers. (In just one year alone, Becton, Dickinson paid Novation $1 million in "special marketing" fees.)[4]

Third, the GPOs themselves, now flush with money, began to target hospital executives with various forms of favor. Fourth, the GPO executives began to target Congress, using their vast pots of cash to chase all would-be reformers away.[5]

By the time Shaw was ready to bring his revolutionary retractable syringe to the open market, there was hardly a semblance of market to be found. Becton, Dickinson was protected not merely by its own immense powers but also by a great outer wall, which it shares with Johnson & Johnson, Tyco, Baxter, C. R. Bard, and others. The GPO system has been transformed into a veritable cooperative of monopolies, a common front, a hardwired cartel.

It is a monopoly as powerful as any government health-care monopoly could ever be: able to all but dictate what hospitals will buy, hence what will be used to treat patients.[6] But this monopoly is private, run for profit, nontransparent, and not accountable in any way to the public. Since one of the best ways for any monopoly to keep life cushy is simply to chase away new ideas, like Shaw's, for as long as possible, that's exactly what happens.

These days, many hospital buying agents won't even dare to talk to Shaw for fear of upsetting their more powerful suppliers.[7] Furthermore, these buyers can tell the nurses and the doctors at their hospitals that they *do* buy "safe" syringes—as long as those devices carry the Becton, Dickinson label. What the buying agents don't tell the people who depend on them is that the Becton, Dickinson devices—which require a health worker to pull a plastic tube over the needle in order to sheath it—pose a few problems: They cost more. They do not deal with both the needlestick and the needle reuse problems simultaneously, the way Retractable's device does. They require more special "training."[8] Most important, the fact that they do not work automatically and require health-care workers to move their hands over the needle means these so-called safety devices actually *cause* many needlestick injuries.

One day Shaw realized that he too had to play politics, and play hard. After some time as an eager and successful inventor and some time as an increasingly frustrated salesman, Shaw recast himself as an activist. And his success over the last decade—in Congress, in court, and in the media—has left him even more pessimistic than before about the prospects of his country. Consider a few of his accomplishments:

- Long, detailed articles in the *San Francisco Chronicle*, the *New York Times*, and *Business Week*, even a report by Mike Wallace on *60 Minutes*.
- Four sets of hearings in five years in the Senate antitrust subcommittee.
- Confirmation from numerous other lawsuits by other inventors whose journey to market was stopped short by the monopolists and their GPOs.[9]
- Independent tests that repeatedly found Retractable's device to be superior to any safety syringe offered by Becton, Dickinson.[10]
- Victory in court in 2003 over the GPOs Novation and Premier and over the syringe maker Tyco; another victory in 2004, in the form of a $100 million payment by Becton, Dickinson to Retractable.[11]

And yet, life goes on almost unchanged. Nearly a decade after Congress passed, thanks in part to Shaw's work, the Needlestick Safety and Prevention Act of 2000, Becton, Dickinson continues to push old-fashioned disposable syringes. Or for those who prefer to buy a safety syringe, their expensive and flawed alternative. Shaw's invention, meanwhile, remains all but excluded from the U.S. "market."

Actually, I misspoke. A few things have changed.

A study by a team of Massachusetts health officials—virtually the only independent study done since the Needlestick Safety and Prevention Act—shows that the total number of needlesticks is not declining. What is growing is the percentage of needlesticks caused by unsafe "safety" syringes.[12]

In late 2006, Novation and Premier merged their e-commerce operations into a single company called Global Healthcare Exchange, or GHX. This brought more than two-thirds of the market under the direct control of what is, for all intents, a single private supercartel.[13]

Becton, Dickinson, during this period, managed to increase its share of the U.S. market for syringes from about 70 percent of the total to about 90 percent. And thanks to the fact that it charges more for its "safety" syringes, the growing use of them—even though the Massachusetts study indicates that they have no positive effect on safety—means that Becton, Dickinson also increased what it earns for every unit it sells.[14]

Finally, more than fifteen years after Shaw came out with his retractable syringe, Becton, Dickinson finally began to market a similar device—after which it promptly sued Shaw for patent infringement.[15]

And so was the American innovator served in the early years of the twenty-first century.

From Land to Man

"Yet I cannot forbear adding a few observations on M[r]. Muschenbroek's wonderful bottle." It was with these words that Benjamin Franklin began his first letter to the English cloth merchant and horticulturalist Peter Collinson in 1747. The correspondence led to the publication of a book by Franklin, in London in 1751, that transformed the debate on the nature and properties of electricity, transformed how Europeans saw their American cousins, and transformed Franklin into America's first celebrity in the Atlantic world.

The Pieter van Muschenbroek of whom Franklin wrote was a Dutch scientist, and two years earlier he had constructed what came to be known as a Leyden jar. This was a glass jar filled with water, into which he had inserted a brass wire attached to a device that generated an electrical current when he turned a crank. In those days, science was a very hands-on art, and when Muschenbroek applied his own to the bottle, he suffered a terrible shock. In doing so, however, he discovered that his jar had somehow stored the electricity generated by the hand crank. Muschenbroek believed that the water itself held the charge, and it was this theory that Franklin disproved through a careful series of experiments. Franklin also set the world on a path toward the useful exploitation of Muschenbroek's device as he amplified its power by bundling multiple jars together in what he called a *battery* (until then a military term for a group of cannons).[16]

American business enterprise and, indeed, the American national enterprise itself can, with a little literary license, be said to have taken life from this spark. Europe remained the center of scientific research into the twentieth century, but for two hundred years after the founding of the United States, it was Americans who took the lead in distilling science into practical devices and pragmatic systems.[17] In the early nineteenth century, the same basic set of technologies and ideas was available to all nations of the Atlantic world. The British combined these ideas with capital and the institution of the corporation in ways that enabled them to revolutionize the production of textiles, china, steel, and locomotion.

Yet the United States, with fewer people and a less developed infrastructure, caught up fast, and it did so not merely by replicating European models but often by improving on them in ways that opened entirely new paths. It was in the United States, for instance, that people first mass-produced the pistol, the reaper, and the sewing machine, as later we first mass-produced the lightbulb, the automobile, the electric refrigerator, and the personal camera. So swift was the intellectual progress of America's innovators, that by the middle of the nineteenth century, before the Civil War, Europeans had begun to write of a distinct "American system" of production.[18]

My main aim in this chapter is to detail how the present structure of power in our political economy makes it far harder than it should be for the American inventor and innovator to introduce new and better ideas to the rest of us. I will detail some of the ways that the rich use corporations and patent law to direct power against the inventor and innovator and some of the biggest dangers that such assaults on the American innovator pose to us now, both as individuals and as a society.

First I want to identify why this country proved so friendly to the inventor and innovator for so long. Two factors stand out. The first is that until relatively recently in America, there was no concept of what we have been trained to call "intellectual property," which in turn implies that the reason we saw so much innovation on so many fronts was precisely because the ideas were not "protected."

And in fact the founders did not view human ideas as a property at all, in the way they viewed land, capital, or the skills of an individual. This is evident in the Constitution, which specifies that patent monopolies and copyright monopolies must be awarded for "limited times" only and specifically "to promote the progress of science and useful arts."[19] It is also evident in the actions of the founders. Ben Franklin, whose inventions include the circulating stove, the lightning rod, and the bifocal lens, never patented any of his ideas and refused offers to help him do so. Instead, in his autobiography he wrote that "as we enjoy great advantages from the inventions of others, we should be glad of an opportunity to serve others by any invention of ours, and this we should do freely and generously."[20]

Perhaps the clearest statement came from Thomas Jefferson, who in the 1790s served on the first U.S. Patent Commission. In a letter written in 1813, Jefferson roundly condemned attempts to build fences around any idea or innovation. Once uttered, he wrote, an idea can never be subject to "exclusive appropriation." Human invention "cannot, in nature, be a subject of property." Jefferson granted that a society may *choose* "to give an exclusive right to the profits arising from [an invention], as an encouragement to men to pursue ideas which may produce utility." He even made clear his belief that such a choice was sometimes wise, because some ideas are of such value to society as to be "worth to the public the embarrassment of an exclusive patent." However, he emphasized that government should be extremely careful in granting such privileges.[21]

In practice, this meant that an American inventor could not hope to hold very long on to his or her idea, which increased the urgency of working on it. It also meant that there was little incentive for men wielding corporations to use patents to buttress their power by seizing the ideas of other people and locking them away.

The second reason that the United States proved so friendly to the inventor and innovator is that we interacted with one another in open markets. By overthrowing a political economic system organized around private estates run by landlords and industrial lords and erecting in its place a system organized around the free exchange of goods and services among individual citizens, Americans created a system that also furthered the introduction and development of new ideas.

In the aristocratic systems in Britain and on the Continent, an individual with a better idea had to run a gauntlet of power, in which the idea was vetted by and often stolen by those atop the political hierarchy. The American system, in contrast, enabled anyone and everyone to bring an idea to the rest of the nation, to be accepted or rejected on its merits. This unleashed vast new energies from the average individual. By linking citizens together through open public markets that were unmediated and untaxed by any lord, Americans radically amplified the total number of interactions and exchanges that could take place in society.

The resulting explosion of innovative ideas had a huge political effect. That the success of our political structure could be measured not merely in terms of personal freedom but also in terms of material wealth and the introduction of new ideas posed immense challenges to the rulers of European nations. Not only did it mean that the American experiment would not pass swiftly from the scene, it also meant that in at least some material respects the American political system was a superior form of organization.

In fact, the U.S. experiment did in time change political economic thinking in much of the world. In nineteenth-century Europe, we must remember, most political economists operated within the zero-sum framework erected by Thomas Malthus, a demographer who taught at a British East India Company training college. Malthus's basic theory held that population growth in Europe would result in an inevitable and ineluctable decline in the welfare of the majority of the people.[22] This was because there were already more people living in those nations than the land in those nations could support.

Published in 1798 amid the utopian-tinged social chaos in France, Malthus's theory was pressed into immediate service by those who preferred to believe—or at least contend—that no political rearrangements could ever improve the lot of the average person. In time, Malthusian theory came to serve as a useful excuse not to take action even in times of acute crisis, such as famines in India and Ireland.

Americans, by contrast, even though we tended to accept that the distribution of power in society was a zero-sum equation, rejected the idea that there was any limit to the sum of material wealth that men and women, free to use their hands and minds, could create. In a sense, the phenomenal economic successes in the United States resulted in the replacement of the economics of Malthus, with its fixation on the limits of natural resources, with a political economic vision that focused on nurturing and rewarding human resourcefulness. Put another way, we reoriented economic thinking away from land to man.[23]

Or as Ralph Waldo Emerson put it in 1878, "It is not the plants or the animals, innumerable as they are, nor the whole magazine of material nature that can give the sum of power, but the infinite applicability of these things in the hands of thinking man."[24]

The Power of Patents

On September 4, 1882, Thomas Edison ordered an employee to flip a circuit breaker at a power plant on Pearle Street in Lower Manhattan. Copper wires buried under the cobblestones carried a direct current into the offices of the *New York Times* and other newspapers near city hall, where Edison's men had strung a few hundred of his new incandescent lightbulbs. Edison himself was standing not with any mere editor or publisher, however, but with J. P. Morgan. He now closed a switch and released current into another hundred or so bulbs strung through the offices of Drexel, Morgan & Co., and the filaments immediately began to throw off heat and a soft white steady light. The time had come to put Ben Franklin's bolt of electricity to use in illuminating the world. Edison, one of the great showmen as well as inventors of the nineteenth century, knew just where to perform, which was in front of the most powerful capitalist of the day.[25]

By the time Edison took the stage, the modern corporate form had already been introduced in the United States to govern such distance-spanning networks as the railroad and the telegraph. To light the world, however, required an organization unlike any that had been built before. When Edison demonstrated his bulb in 1879, he was following in the steps of many inventors. Thanks to its carbon filament and its high-quality vacuum, Edison's bulb was superior. But just as Edison's predecessors had found, bulb alone does not a lighting *system* make. Anyone planning to weave incandescence along the avenues and into the cul-de-sacs and attics of the world also needed switches, fuses, regulators, and dynamos. This implied a big, well-equipped laboratory and a team of engineers able to work closely with one another. And factories with machines and workers. And trained marketers and salespeople. It required, ultimately, a corporation to govern this incredibly complex operation. And a lot of money.

It also required restricting the power that the men who provided the money could direct at the inventors. Edison had long before learned to place strict limits on what the providers of money could demand. Some years earlier he had designed a radically improved telegraph machine, a work that brought him his first big payoff. Of greater value was that the work brought him an education in the ways of big business, as his patents became a pawn in Jay Gould's attempt to roll up control over America's railroad and telegraph systems.

Even after Edison gained personal fame with his invention of the phonograph in 1877, he refused most offers of outside investment. This came at a cost. Sometimes Edison had to choke off one business to feed another, or shut one promising line of research to pursue another that promised a quicker profit. What was important, though, was the freedom to work on the projects of his own choosing without any cash-mad financier glaring over his shoulder.

Despite the splendid light show at Drexel, Morgan & Co., Edison did not get the deal he wanted from Morgan himself, so Edison Electric continued to earn its way through sales. In fact, Edison now launched a counterattack against the moneymen, kicking Wall Street types off his board and replacing them with scientists, engineers, and inventors.[26] His grand venture required capital—and protection from the capitalist.

Someone somewhere would have eventually electrified the world, but the great leaps that gave the electrical revolution a democratic and American face were made possible largely by the fact that Edison, along with archrival George Westinghouse and the brilliant scientist Nikola Tesla, managed for a few short years to avoid the grasp of Morgan and the other moneymen and so were able to experiment wildly in ways that transformed both technologies and business models with astounding swiftness.

As it turns out, we owe electrification not merely to Edison, whose vision was flawed by his stubborn rejection of alternating current to transmit electricity over long distance. We owe it also to the fact that Tesla left Edison's employ and allied himself with Westinghouse, who enabled him to prove that alternating current (AC) was far superior to direct current and to design and build the world's first AC motor.

In the end, all three men were brought to the ground by Morgan. Edison fell first, in the panic of 1892, when Morgan engineered a takeover of Edison Electric—and Edison's electrical patents—by Thomas-Houston and named the new firm General Electric. Westinghouse, gravely weakened by the same panic, fell next, when Morgan cornered him into turning over his precious horde of AC patents to a patent pool, where Morgan's men at GE could govern their use.

Tesla's fate was the most tragic. A natural loner, he had quit Westinghouse but continued to conjure up fantastic technologies. In 1901, when Tesla was desperate to raise capital to experiment with a radio system, Morgan snookered him into selling a 51 percent interest in all his patents, which Morgan promptly pocketed forever.[27]

And so the days of wild creation came to an end. Edison himself, as the walls he had built to protect his work were falling during the final amalgamation, put it best, telling one of the moneymen: "If you make the coalition, my usefulness as an inventor is gone. My services wouldn't be worth a penny. I can only invent under powerful incentive. No competition means no invention." And thus it proved, as Edison soon largely abandoned his work on electricity and as major technological advances in that field slowed dramatically.[28]

We like to tell ourselves that, technologically, we live in the best of times. And certainly there is much reason to be proud of our accomplishments. We look to the heavens and see robot rovers on Mars. We look in our driveways and see new hybrid technologies in our cars. We look in our own hands and see magical devices that empower us in phenomenal ways. Every day, it seems, we read of great leaps in raw science.

In just one month in 2008, scientists in Sweden captured the first image of an electron, researchers at IBM measured how much force it takes to nudge a single cobalt atom over a platinum surface, and scientists at Fermilab came closer to confirming the existence of the theoretical subatomic "God particle." Every day, we witness revolutionary changes in how we interact with one another. We spend hours at a time in dream spaces, building cities and fighting wars in landscapes that exist only on some server somewhere. We collaborate in real time with colleagues in India, China, Russia. We cooperate in the editing of an online encyclopedia that can be adjusted to reality moment by moment.

Yet these are also the worst of times. The average American is just as likely to be struck by a bolt of inspiration today as two hundred years ago and just as willing to invest the perspiration to bring that idea to the attention of other Americans. In many industrial activities, however, that task is now far tougher than a mere generation ago. In just the last few years, the amount of power that can be brought to bear upon an individual inventor like safety-syringe maker Tom Shaw has grown immensely.

Recently I read a report in the *New York Times* that the introduction of new and better drugs to treat non-Hodgkin's lymphoma was being hindered by "market-driven forces that can distort medical decisions." The problem, of course, is precisely the opposite. It is that there is *no* market, because we have ceded to the rich almost complete license to use the institution of the corporation to determine whether a better drug will be introduced. The "forces" the reporter saw are the powers of a private corporate government, which in this case simply paid doctors to use other, lesser drugs instead. It is vital to keep in mind that there is nothing inherently wrong with private corporate government and con-cenrated capital; both, for instance, have often been used to empower the individual inventor. These days, however, both the corporation and concentrated capital are more generally used to suppress the introduc-tion of new ideas, even in cases when a new idea could save lives.[29]

Most contemporary writing and thinking in America on innovation focuses on the number of years of protection offered by a patent or a copy-right. The general assumption—or rather, the largely unopposed assertion—is that longer periods of protection serve the interest of the inventor. Yet the real intent of many of those who promote stronger patent and copyright laws is something quite different: to enable the people who control corpo-rations to increase their power over entire human activities by giving them more direct control over the human ideas on which these activities stand. Just as Jay Gould—who among his many innovations in freebooting also pioneered modern patent litigation—demonstrated with Edison's telegraph patents. And just as Morgan demonstrated with Edison's lightbulb patents.[30]

Quieting the Mind

In January 2009, the U.S. Court of Federal Claims cleared the way for Zoltek, a manufacturer of carbon fiber, to sue Lockheed Martin for infring-ing on one of its patents during construction of the F-22 Raptor fighter jet. The problem was not that Lockheed Martin had manufactured the prod-uct in question—carbon fiber sheets with "controlled surface electrical resistivity." Rather it was that the defense contractor had purchased the product from a Japanese supplier that, Zoltek claimed, had copied its idea without permission. The decision marked a major reversal by the court, which in 2003 had thrown out a suit by Zoltek for the same instance of alleged infringement, though in that case lodged against the government.[31]

On the surface, the lawsuit may sound like good news. A citizen came up with an idea, which was then stolen by a foreign firm, and then a U.S. government contractor took advantage of the theft in a sort of indirect form of eminent domain. Now there will finally be justice for the inventor, right?

Well, the case is a lot less clear if we look at it through the eyes of a citizen who is protected by those F-22s. And it gets even hazier if we look through the eyes of a citizen who relies on any of the many advanced products made with these particular carbon fiber materials, which include jet turbines and windmill blades. And if we look through the eyes of an inventor who wants to use such materials for an entirely new idea, the picture is downright foggy.

That's because in actual fact, the people who control Zoltek and its patents have shown themselves to be masters of keeping the price of their carbon fiber up by keeping the rate of production down. Indeed, the company's production is sold out three years ahead of time—and has been since 2005—and Zoltek shows no interest in licensing its technology to any other firm.

Thus, contrary to the claim that longer patent terms help the inventor, in this case at least, the protection of a claim harms numerous real-life inventors of other products, as well as U.S. citizens who stand to benefit from new and improved products.

Not that this bottleneck strategy serves no one. The big winners include two New York hedge funds that hold large stakes in Zoltek, one of which is now under investigation by the Securities and Exchange Commission for insider trading. And these hedge funds will continue to win for as long as the case against Lockheed Martin (or a similar case by Zoltek against the government for construction of the B-2 stealth bomber) remains unresolved. That's because the legal uncertainty that the lawsuits create makes it dangerous for any U.S. manufacturer to turn to any alternative sources of carbon fiber—even though Zoltek's production is sold out.

Wal-Mart is perhaps the most well-known company that, through sheer size, governs the work of producers in ways that sometimes result in the destruction of the ability of our fellow citizens to bring new and better ideas to the rest of us. The people who run Wal-Mart do not consciously intend to suppress innovation. On the contrary, company managers often try to use the firm's immense power to *force* their suppliers to innovate, by, for instance, developing and introducing greener technologies and techniques. Unfortunately, these efforts to "greenwash" the company's immense power—and Wal-Mart chieftains have made it clear this is exactly their intent—often backfire. This is what happened, for instance, after the titan promised to introduce compact fluorescent lightbulbs to every U.S. household by forcing suppliers to cut their prices to levels determined by Wal-Mart, rather than to compete with one another as they saw fit. Prices did go down. So too quality, often precipitously.[32]

In a growing number of other cases, however, the people who control our corporations act with full consciousness to retard or destroy innovation in the activities they control. Take, for instance, Intel, which enjoys a roughly 90 percent share of the market for one of the most basic forms of microprocessors in our computers. Even though the firm's managers devote an immense amount of their monopoly profits to branding the company as a leading "innovator," they also devote a huge portion of these same monopoly profits to attempts to kill their only rival in the manufacture of these products, Advanced Micro Devices (AMD), a company that is often actually the lead innovator in microprocessors.

And let's be clear, Intel did not achieve its original monopoly position through innovation. Intel was, for all intents simply handed the monopoly by another firm—IBM—after that titan came under antitrust pressure in the late 1970s. Also pertinent is the fact that Intel, when it received this immense boon from IBM, agreed to share the market with AMD and other firms precisely to avoid monopoly. Intel's predations against AMD have been so extreme that in the last three years Intel has lost antitrust cases in Japan, South Korea, and Europe. (Unfortunately, the law enforcers appear to have arrived too late to save AMD and its team of innovators. In April 2008, AMD managers cut 10 percent of the company's workforce. In early 2009, they began to break AMD into pieces.)

If you can't beat 'em—or if you prefer, for legal reasons, to avoid the brutal approach taken by Intel—you can always buy 'em. Consider the software company Oracle. For years, CEO Larry Ellison preached that buying another firm was "a confession that there's a failure to innovate." Then, in early 2008, Ellison made a rather snappish confession. After buying one of Oracle's main competitors, he declared, "It's crazy to say you will only grow through innovation."

Ellison was not alone in doing this; the entire software industry has shifted from a model that emphasized the creation of new products to one that emphasizes charging more for existing technologies, then using these funds to buy up any new ideas that might challenge their power. This same basic model—in which one company or a few companies essentially govern technological development for an entire human industrial activity—increasingly holds true in other arenas, such as biotechnology and alternative energy. In both of these cases, once small startups have demonstrated the viability of their concept, the rule is to sell out almost immediately to the established governor of the human activity in question.[33]

Another way small companies of men protect their capital and their positions is to prevent society from traveling down an alternative technological pathway. A generation ago, firms often did this by hiring the best and brightest scientists and directing them to work on certain projects and not others. These days the task has become much easier, as more and more public research universities allow corporations to more or less direct the work of their scientists, even though they are technically on the public payroll.

One of the more audacious efforts was masterminded by the hydrocarbon monger BP, which in February 2007 announced plans to spend $500 million in ten years to support the Energy Biosciences Institute at the University of California in Berkeley. The deal, brokered by physicist Steven Chu, since named by President Obama as secretary of energy, gave BP some influence over the research agenda at all twenty-five labs run by the institute, which range from the Lawrence Livermore National Laboratory to the University of Illinois at Urbana-Champaign.[34]

One of the easiest ways for groups of financiers to reduce competition among the corporations they control is to share key technologies. In J. P. Morgan's day, the result was called a patent pool. Today it is often called a technology *alliance*. One of the more dramatic recent examples of such an alliance was brokered in 1993 by Vice President Al Gore, who wanted the then Big Three automakers to mass-produce cleaner and more efficient cars. At the time, many in the Clinton administration contended that the best way to convince the corporations to serve the public's interest was not to make threats but to offer rewards.

The result was a program called Partnership for a New Generation of Vehicles (PNGV), and the idea was to give the carmakers technologies that were developed in public laboratories, as well as license to share these technologies among themselves. PNGV did in fact result in the design of a new vehicle architecture—the electric hybrid. The program also illustrated exactly why financiers are so enamored of the patent-pool model; PNGV ended up stifling innovation on alternative technologies precisely by eliminating technology as a source of competition. The U.S. firms that participated in the patent-pool arrangement did not bring even one hybrid automobile to market by the target date, not least because the alliance enabled them to determine that their rivals had no such plans. By contrast, the two firms kept entirely outside the patent pool and hence kept in fear—Toyota and Honda—managed to develop not only their own technologies without any help from government labs but also brought those technologies to market in affordable cars.[35]

Then there is the old *standard* approach to retarding technological advance. Basically, this involves representing your particular set of technologies as the *only* way to manage the task at hand, by declaring it to be the *standard* solution. This is essentially what Microsoft declared in court in the late 1990s when states' attorneys general forced the Clinton administration to bring an antitrust suit against the firm.

Standardization is not, in and of itself, a bad thing. On the contrary, some form of technological standardization is often the only way to develop certain complex systems. The issue is *who* determines *how* the activity will be standardized, and for how long. As the editors of *Engineering Magazine* explained the conundrum in 1911, the challenge is "to suppress the folly of individualism, which prefers sliding down a rope to using the standardized staircase, and yet not suppress the benefactor of standards who can evolve the escalator."[36]

In many cases, such as television technology, standardization was managed not by a private firm but by our federal government. The difference between letting a firm like Microsoft—or Cisco or Oracle—declare its approach to managing a task to be the "standard" and having our government manage the task is often the difference between a top-down authoritarian system and an open market.

Not that the people who control corporations need always take aggressive measures to suppress, restrain, or redirect the work of the inventors and innovators among us.[37] The mere act of capturing monopoly control over a particular human activity results almost automatically in sharp reductions in investment in related ideas.

Sometimes we see the effects within the walls of the corporation. After former GE CEO Jack Welch pioneered the creation of duopolies in the early 1980s, he pioneered the gutting of the great laboratories that were once the pride of our big industrial firms. These two facts are closely related. After Welch had his duopoly strategy in place, he soon realized that such control over the market meant that GE did not have to improve products so swiftly. In 1981, GE was the fourth biggest U.S. industrial firm and one of the top spenders on research. By 1993, GE had become the most profitable big company in the United States, but it had fallen to seventeenth place in spending on research and development (R&D).[38] Managers at firms ranging from IBM to 3M to United Technologies soon followed Welch's lead.[39]

Sometimes we see such effects outside the walls of the corporation, in the venture capital community. A good example is the medical device industry since the consolidation of power by the GPOs. A few years back, Bess Weathermen, then the managing director of the investment bank Warburg Pincus, spelled out the effect that cartels like these have on investments in new technologies. In a Senate hearing,[40] Weatherman said that "companies subject to, or potentially subject to, anti-competitive practices . . . will not be funded by venture capital. As a result, many of their innovations will die, even if they offer a dramatic improvement over an existing solution. Permitting this innovation-stifling practice is unnecessary and counter to what we believe should be a fundamental role of the government: enhancing health by making new or improved products widely available as quickly and efficiently as possible."[41]

The Monopoly Innovation Myth

The Austrian economist Joseph Schumpeter famously wrote that an industrial company that achieves a de facto monopoly with an entirely new product *sometimes* takes *some* of the superhigh profits it earns from the monopoly and invests those funds in efforts to improve that product in order to keep ahead of potential competitors. According to Schumpeter's theory, the firm then takes the monopoly earnings from this second spurt of innovation and reinvests them in yet another round of R&D—and so on and so on.

Schumpeter admitted that many monopolies do have an "injurious effect" on the "long-run development of output," and he emphasized that his argument "does not amount to a case against state regulation." But he wanted his readers to believe that some monopolies, in his marvelously concise description, "largely create what they exploit."[42]

Schumpeter's defense of the large-scale firm was not radical or even especially original. By the time he published these musings in 1942, even many of the more hard-core populists had long since accepted the need for at least some industrial concentration. At the time Schumpeter wrote—right after the Great Depression and during World War II—no serious policy maker in the United States questioned the need for some concentration in the production of metals, chemicals, energy, heavy machinery, and electronics.

What made Schumpeter's statement on innovation stand out is what can be achieved with a few small edits, especially deletion of the word *some*. Indeed, the reason his statement has now become the standard view of the matter is that—with prudent pruning—it enables the Chicago School operators to declare, in effect, that "monopoly is more innovative than competition." Which in turn implies that the fastest way to innovate is to forge monopolies.

No matter what the prevailing theory might be, the actual history of antitrust shows quite clearly that one of the most effective ways to speed innovation is not to leave the monopolists alone with their monopoly. On the contrary, it is to disrupt the ability of any one group of people to use a corporation or a hold on some patent to rule a particular industrial activity. The proof lies in an almost forgotten policy innovation pioneered by the groundbreaking team of trustbusters that was installed by Franklin Roosevelt during his second term as president, after he was forced to abandon his flirtations with corporatism.

Whereas Schumpeter seems to have imagined the innovation process he described as a sort of natural process, built into the genetic makeup of the institutions themselves, Roosevelt's team of trustbusters, led by Thurmond Arnold, understood that a bit of political prodding from the outside was often necessary. That's because a series of extensive studies of industrial firms in the United States in the late 1930s had revealed that scientists and researchers working for many industrial monopolies and oligopolies had in fact developed slews of fine new ideas in the company labs. In case after case, however, the companies had chosen not to bring these ideas to the American people.[43]

Consider AT&T. Over time this immense, government-sanctioned monopoly developed Bell Laboratories into one of the nation's great manufactories of new ideas. During World War II, AT&T scientists and engineers helped to develop radar, and they rolled out the world's first automated antiaircraft gun.[44] Yet in peacetime AT&T was notorious for its failure to blend new technologies into the telephone system that it controlled.

In 1939, the Federal Trade Commission cited the monopoly for sitting on such ready-for-market innovations as automatic dialing, office switchboards, and new handsets.[45] In 1952, antitrust officials finally took action. But unlike the later push against AT&T that resulted in the breakup of the firm, the trustbusters of 1952 opted to leave the corporation whole *if* AT&T agreed to share some of its technologies with the general public. One of these ideas was called the "electronic transistor." Today we call this idea—which AT&T gave away to thirty-five U.S. and foreign firms—the "semiconductor."[46]

Or consider the Radio Corporation of America (RCA). This corporation also started life as a government-sanctioned monopoly, built around a pool of patents gathered from other firms. In this case, the purpose was to master such electronic arts as radio and television, originally for national security.[47] For a while RCA was extremely innovative. The company introduced the first color television in 1939 and pioneered the video-guided bomb during World War II. Like AT&T, however, RCA tended to sit on technologies, not least because it enjoyed such an immense advantage in the market over any potential rival.

Here too the trustbusters opted to help Schumpeter's theory along with some real-life poking and squeezing. In 1958, they forced RCA to reveal its basic radio and television technologies—about twelve thousand patents. Among the firms that picked up some of these technologies were small, eager electronics manufacturers named Zenith, Sony, and Phillips.[48]

Although huge antitrust cases like these are now so rare that they'd rate a lot national coverage, such actions were so common at the time that they attracted little attention. The first high-profile use of such tactics took place right at the end of World War II, when trustbusters targeted Alcoa, which had long defended a complete monopoly on aluminum. Not only did the government manufacture brand-new competitors for Alcoa by selling aluminum plants built during the war to companies like Kaiser and Reynolds, it also forced Alcoa to share its technologies with these newly minted rivals.

During the next thirty-five years, the trustbusters applied this basic approach to scores of big industrial firms. And so the world was treated to the secrets behind the lightbulbs of GE and Westinghouse, the cellophane and nylon of DuPont, the glass of Hartford-Empire, the titanium of National Lead, the photocopiers of Xerox, the software of IBM, and the shoemaking technologies of United Shoe Machinery, among many others.[49]

In a sense, we can view the basic innovation policy that was institutionalized by the New Deal–era trustbusters as largely Schumpeterian in nature, but with a very big twist, in the form of government compulsion.

Until the Chicago School operators finally killed the policy in the early 1980s, our trustbusters used this *Schumpeterian squeeze* to force the people who controlled our biggest corporations to spill tens of thousands of technological "source codes" into the world. A study in 1961 counted 107 judgments between 1941 and 1959 that resulted in the compulsory licensing of forty thousand to fifty thousand patents, a number equal to nearly 10 percent of all new patents granted during this period.[50]

Nor did such squeezes result only in the sharing of ideas and the opportunity for new firms to work with them. The squeezes also led many of the giant monopolists to invest more in real R&D themselves. Although Schumpeter imagined that monopolists naturally reinvested in R&D to maintain their advantage in the marketplace, in the real world, the monopolists often decided that it was easier and cheaper to invest their monopoly profits not in new ideas but in buying protection from Congress or in bankrupting rivals. In many cases, the monopolists undertook real innovation only after the government used its antitrust powers to create new rivals.

DuPont, for instance, after it was targeted for a patent squeeze, "concluded that its generation-old strategy of growth through acquisition was no longer politically feasible." In the view of industrial historian David Hounshell, the government's antitrust case "unquestionably led to DuPont spending more on fundamental research."[51]

As a technique to accelerate the dispersion and advancement of technology, the Schumpeterian squeeze proved so successful that it led Harvard industrial historian Alfred Chandler to shift his whole method of analysis. Through his long and celebrated career, Chandler had largely ignored the effect of antitrust enforcement on the organizational decisions of U.S. industrial managers. But in his final book, *Inventing the Electronic Century*, Chandler looked in depth for the first time at the development of the technologies that undergird our modern information society, and suddenly the real intent of the postwar trustbusters became clear to him.

These were not Jacksonian hillbillies out to chop the beast to pieces with a broad axe; rather, they were husbandmen who were carefully trimming the giant trees that shaded the land and then sowing the newly sun-kissed soil with seeds that sprouted into firms with names like Intel, Compaq, Dell, and NVIDIA. Surveying the wonders of the personal computer and the Internet, Chandler praised this policy in the most extravagant terms. The "middle-level bureaucrats" of Thurmond Arnold's antitrust division, he wrote, were nothing less than "gods" of creation.[52]

Even though monopolists exert power over almost every one of our key industries today, in ways that suppress and distort real innovation, we should not despair entirely. There is still one area where our monopolists have managed to keep the fires of creativity burning brightly: in the workshops of the image makers tasked with conjuring up new ways to disguise their predations. Consider, for instance, a recent survey put out by the consulting firm Booz Allen Hamilton. Singling out many of the monopolists we've come across in this book—Illinois Tool Works, Eaton, C. R. Bard, Parker Hannifin—the authors noted a stunning statistic.

"For five straight years," they wrote, "these companies have each invested *substantially less* in R&D than their industry peers—56 percent less on average. Yet from 2000 through 2005 they consistently exceeded their competitors in seven critical performance measures—sales growth, gross margin percentage, gross profit growth, operating margin percentage, operating income growth, total shareholder returns, and market capitalization growth."

Like all consultants worth their salt, the Booz Allen gurus coined a new term to describe this new business model they had "discovered." These monopolists, the gurus concluded, had mastered the art of "high leverage innovation." Translated, this means new ways of charging more for less.[53]

One Best Way?

In July 1927, Henry Ford shut down his assembly line and sent his workers home. The era of the Model T was over, and it had ended not with a whimper but with a crash that reverberated throughout the world of industry. When Ford launched the Model T in 1908, he introduced the world to the wonders of mass production. Americans had used assembly-line methods for years to carve up cattle, to store industrial-stewed soup in cans, and to cut and sew clothes, but Ford's new car revolutionized the pace and nature of life in the United States, and the secret seemed to lie in the art of mass production itself. Ford's assembly line enabled him to introduce the Model T at a fraction of the price of the craft-built cars then on the market, and further refinements and increasing scale enabled him to keep cutting the price year after year.

Fordism is often portrayed as being profoundly American, and Ford's industrial system did democratize ownership of the automobile. Yet Ford's system was also a product of the same Progressive Era in which many members of the U.S. elite envisioned a future in which a "standard" car would putter along on Standard Oil, carrying people fed by General Mills through a landscape lit by General Electric. In fact, there was something about the machinelike nature of the new production society that Ford founded at his River Rouge plant, as well as about Ford's own hierarchical and authoritarian nature, that appealed deeply to such bounding young regimentarians as Joseph Stalin and Adolf Hitler.

For our purposes here, however, the most important aspect of Ford's system was the tremendous economic flaw at its heart: even though it was possible to refine individual industrial processes on the Ford assembly line, it was essentially impossible to adjust such a huge and rationalized organization, as a whole, to fit changing times. Henry Ford had long believed that his Model T was the perfect car. Then one day it wasn't, and the perfect production system that had stamped out more than fifteen million copies of that car was transformed into so much scrap.[54]

As we look over our modern industrial landscape—rationalized over the last generation in such a dramatic fashion by firms like Microsoft, Intel, Oracle, and Wal-Mart—and consider how, in the coming years, we shall develop what is new and better and then do so again and again, it is vital to keep in mind the experiences of Ford as the world around the firm changed, ever so gradually, year after year.

Ford's final fall was truly stunning. In 1920, the Model T accounted for more than 90 percent of all cars sold in the United States, but that number began to fall swiftly as other firms applied the arts of mass manufacture to newer suites of technologies. Then in the mid-1920s,

GM's launch of the low-priced Chevrolet and the Dodge Brothers' new Plymouth set into motion the sudden collapse of the entire Model T system.

What allowed Henry Ford to get back into business was that he had $90,839,000 in the bank. This enabled him to design an entirely new car—the Model A—and to outfit an entirely new assembly line. The Model A was a fine car and a huge hit with drivers, yet in all of 1928 Ford was able to produce only 633,000, fewer than half of the number of orders he took. Ford did top Chevrolet in deliveries in 1929 and 1930, but by now GM was flooding the market with new vehicles under such names as Pontiac, Buick, and Cadillac, as well as a new generation of Chevys. In 1931, Ford lost his lead for good.

Not that GM's production model was built to last forever, either. After the war, that company began to treat all its different lines more like one integrated whole. This helped to set the stage for the 1970s, when the flexibility of Japan's modest twelve proved more than a match for America's sclerotic Big Three.

On the surface this story may seem to support those who argue that government does not have to intrude in such industrial activities, because new rivals emerge "naturally." It is also possible to argue that the simplicity of the Model T served an important purpose, which was to expand the market for cars much faster than would have happened otherwise. I do not question that the Ford model illustrates that there are real benefits to developing one way of doing something and then doing that thing over and over and over. What I want to do here is focus on what happens when people decide they need or merely want to move beyond such a system.

Just as such extreme standardization offers certain short-term benefits, over the long term, extreme standardization is the source of huge and even fatal weaknesses, the gravest of which is the danger of a precipitate economic or physical collapse from which recovery may be difficult, if not impossible. In the case of the automobile industry around 1928, there were a number of smaller competitors that had been building up sufficient know-how and power to challenge Ford. Unfortunately, this is not always so.

In fact, in a growing number of instances in which vital systems have been truly monopolized, there are few firms or even no firms waiting in the wings ready to step in. This is true of many of our overly standardized computing and communications systems, which have been made vulnerable to potentially devastating viruses. And this is true of many banks and insurers like Citibank and AIG, where the rotting carcasses of these intricately tentacled creatures swiftly corrupted entire systems. The risk of failure in these systems, in other words, has been completely *socialized*.

As we look at today's industries and systems, it is clear that in many cases we cannot assume that the collapse of one company that has been made "too big to fail" will automatically result in another company moving into the space that has been left vacant. Even if there is a company with the know-how necessary for the task, it may well lack the scale and the scope to step swiftly into the shoes of a dead monopolist. Such systems simply cannot be made as safe as those in which power and knowledge are compartmentalized among at least a few big firms.[55] This is true both physically and economically. Even when failure in such systems results in the punishment of, say, bondholders, it does not create a space for new ideas.

In earlier chapters we looked at how the forging of truly immense trading companies like Wal-Mart, which are able to control the activities and profits of an incredibly wide array of firms under their sway, amounts to the erection of a private planning state in the heart of America. We also looked at how these powers more or less directly determine what it is that we consume, entirely outside of any market mechanism, and at how these immense institutions tend to use their powers in ways that degrade the systems under their power.

What I want to do here is to push forward our understanding of how planning and innovation actually takes place in a society that is increasingly controlled by monopolists. To do so, I want to look at two instances in which a single company of men has captured the power to determine, to a great degree, the pathway (property) along which we are allowed to "progress."

The first case involves Procter & Gamble. A recent *Wall Street Journal* article described how the managers at the firm, after they took control of Gillette in 2005, decided to devote a huge portion of their R&D funds to devise ways to, as the writer put it, better "unite toothbrush [and] toothpaste."[56] In other words, one of the world's biggest corporations—which already sells us more than 50 percent of our toothbrushes and 40 percent of our toothpaste and which colludes more or less openly with its main competitor, Colgate, through a process known as *category management*—has decided to lift from our shoulders the burden of selecting our own toothbrush and our own toothpaste as separate items, by combining Oral-B and Crest into a brand-new "suite of products."

There are many reasons why this little case should disturb us. As consumers, we see P&G further restricting our choices under the guise of giving us new options. As inventors and innovators, we see ourselves excluded even more completely from a production system that should never have been closed in the first place. Yet the dangers posed by such incipient dental despotism are also clearly limited in scope. They are political, not physical, and in and of themselves they are relatively minor. I include this example not as a call to arms but merely as a symptom of what is taking place throughout our political economy.

A more sublimely terrifying example is the genetic monopolization taking place throughout our food systems. As we have seen, immense corporations like Cargill, ADM, Smithfield, and Tyson have captured control over most of the once-open agricultural market systems in the United States. They have done so up to now mainly through horizontal expansion of the borders of their corporations, to a point where they basically gain direct control over the actions of farmers who, traditionally, interacted with the rest of us through the medium of more or less open markets. In recent years, however, these Goliaths have greatly expanded their efforts to modify the actual genetic materials in our livestock and grains.

Such systems of genetic monopolization serve them in three ways: First, they increase revenue by automating agricultural activity with one-seed-sows-all-fields cotton and corn and one-size-fits-all-hooks hogs. Second, they raise even higher the barriers that prevent other companies from entering the same field. And third, they fortify their control over the individual farmer. Indeed, agricultural companies like Tyson and Smithfield tend to organize their physical poultry- and hog-processing operations in ways that lock the "farmers" who grow their products for them into relationships of extreme dependence that often result in the transference of wealth from the individual to the people who run the corporation.

Farmers who work within Tyson's or Smithfield's systems not only can't sell their highly specialized product to anyone else, they must also buy the whole "suite" of food and drugs they need to bring their chickens and hogs from incubator to slaughter. It is a system, in other words, designed to transform free farmers into employees and, hence, into debt peons.

What is important for us to understand here is how far this process of genetic monopolization has progressed. Already, more than half the crops grown in the United States have been genetically monopolized by corporations with proprietary seed lines. This includes 70 percent of our corn and nearly all of our soybeans. Giant powers—especially Monsanto, which sells more than 90 percent of such seeds—are fast pushing genetic monopolization into our cotton, squash, canola, even papayas. In this country, in the not-too-distant future, Monsanto expects to spread its genetically monopolized corn across more than a hundred million acres, or roughly a third of all planted cropland in the whole nation.[57]

Genetic monopolization does often increase yields, temporarily. But it also hugely magnifies the risk of a Ford-like or Menu Foods–like or Windows virus–like collapse. That's because the result is the wholesale destruction of the great heterodoxic pools of genetic material that our forefathers and foremothers built up with such care over so many centuries, precisely to empower our society to adapt to the changes that take place every day in our natural environment.

The dangers and limitations are not merely physical. Such genetic monopolization also binds our minds—training us to think in terms only of one variety of crop, one way of raising pigs, one organization for growing chickens. We lose the ability to imagine the necessary next.

At this time of sudden and strange changes in our climate and environment, this is a big deal. Free human beings seek to identify the perfect seed for every place and moment. Monopolists force us to standardize what should be left free, to centralize what should be left local. They do so not because it is good for us, but for profit and power only. At the very moment when we most need flexibility, we instead allow ourselves to be directed to make our systems ever more rigid, brittle, and simple. At the very time when we need to all but feel our way forward, we find our way blocked by gargantuan planning states bereft of any conscious planners. Rather than link ourselves to all our scientists and farmers through an open-market system designed to transmit not merely goods to their right place but also ideas, we tie ourselves to one way of thinking only, and one thought alone, one "best" way devised by some one inherently fallible human being.

The Wave of the Past

On the morning of December 6, 2005, surfers around the world woke to stunning news. The night before, seventy-two-year-old Grubby Clark had locked the doors of the factory where for more than forty-five years he had overseen the manufacture of the foam blanks that form the center of the classic fiberglass-coated surfboard. Worse yet, Clark, who blamed overeager environmental regulators for his decision, had no plans to sell his business to anyone else; he had ordered his workers to smash his concrete blank molds and to cut his custom-designed glue presses to pieces.

When Henry Ford closed his factory eighty years earlier, other automakers were in a position to ramp up production fast. Clark Foam, by contrast, had enjoyed an almost complete monopoly, shipping as many as a thousand surfboard blanks every day to the small shops and garages where independent artisans would decorate the boards with dragons, manta rays, and sunbursts and then coat them in fiberglass. Now Clark was gone and there was no one to fill the void.

Up and down the coasts of America, the reaction was panic. Surf shops jacked up the price of boards in stock by hundreds of dollars, yet stocks soon sold out. The problem is that glassed boards don't last forever or even for very long. They break when dropped and sometimes even just when they're ridden hard. Within days a deep sense of gloom settled on the world community of surf riders.[58]

Michael Caldwell was among those who cursed loudest that day. A longtime fin designer, Caldwell had spent much of the previous five years in western Australia experimenting with a totally new idea: the flexible surfboard. A curvier board allows a surfer to cut sharper turns on a wave, whereas a flatter board allows a surfer to plane faster in front of the wave. Why not, Caldwell thought, combine both shapes in a single adjustable board? When Caldwell finally had a design ready for production, he took his idea to Clark. Although he had been tempted to set up his own company, Caldwell concluded it would be wiser to share his idea with the existing monopolist, not least because Clark had long since earned a reputation as one of the most cutthroat competitors in the United States. As it proved, Clark embraced the idea, introducing Caldwell's board only two weeks before making the sudden decision to shut his doors.

Dan Mann, by contrast, ordered a chunk of expanded polystyrene (EPS) foam to shape in his garage the afternoon after he heard of Clark's rampage. A master glasser, Mann had long chafed at the low margins in merely finishing boards and had been looking to expand into other lines of board work. As soon as he heard Clark Foam had closed, Mann knew this was his chance. "The gloves were off everyone," he says. "Minds were opened—consumers' minds and manufacturers' minds. And I knew marketers' minds would follow."

Mann sits to my right at a long table in the office of a small factory building in the western end of San Diego. He is lanky, and his blond hair is long. In his mid-thirties, he looks like the very icon of a California surfer, his eyes glowing brightly in his deeply tanned face. To my left sits Caldwell, his clothes tattered, his face unshaven. Well into his fifties, he looks like someone you might find manning the cash register of a package store in Barstow. Three years ago, Mann and Caldwell did not know each other. Now they constitute the yin and yang of Firewire, the company that has done more to rethink the nature of the surfboard than any group of people since Duke Kahanamoku bombed to shore on a sixteen-foot koa-wood torpedo.

If you imagine the surf industry to be a mellow communal dude culture, you'd be radically wrong. Caldwell and Mann tell me the history of the industry back when Grubby Clark dominated blank making, and the basic story line is not much different from John D. Rockefeller's roll-up of the oil business. Within a few years of starting his foam works in the 1950s, they tell me, Clark had developed both the industrial techniques and the business acumen that put him in front of all other blank makers and enabled him to stay there.

On the front end, Clark delivered predictable quality blanks at a reasonable price and at a steady pace. On the back end, Clark enforced his dominance with the ability to crush any glasser who experimented with another person's blanks, not least by cutting off that glasser's supply of Clark's high-quality, mass-produced blanks entirely. One result was a long period of technological stasis. By the end of the 1970s, surfboards had all but ceased to change. For decades, the main choices for wave riders was whether to buy a long board or a short board, and what sort of cobra or shark to have stenciled under the glass.

In the days after Clark's closure, the industry descended into chaos. Mann was anything but alone in rushing to seize a bigger chunk of the surfboard business. Within weeks, dozens, if not hundreds, of men and women were making and selling blanks. New ventures sprouted up and down the coast of California and as far afield as Australia, Mexico, Alabama, and Argentina. Many—including some of Clark's former employees—tried to replicate Clark's product. A growing number began to experiment with new materials and techniques.

Firewire combines two techniques to make the boards flexible. The first was developed by a man named Nev Hyman in Australia and relies on balsa rails along the edges of the board. The other is Caldwell's idea, which was to insert carbon rods into the center of the board itself. Caldwell started off with the shafts of golf clubs but has since moved up to custom-ordered rods made from the highest grade carbon fiber. Mann, meanwhile, is the material master; he ensures that the foams and coatings that make up the bulk of the board are both flexible and durable.

Most larger production runs are done in a company factory in Thailand. But Southern California is where the world's richest surfers live, so the Firewire team does most of its development here, along with most of its high-end and test production runs. The factory itself is very active. As Mann, Caldwell, and I speak, young men run into the office to ask them technical questions, then run out. Down the hall, a giant cutting machine drones as it automatically shapes foam into the desired size and shape. The loading dock is filled with boxes destined for surf shops in Kailua, Santa Cruz, Nags Head. A rack in a back room holds some of the developers' more far-out ideas, like a board with a sort of wah-wah peddle on its tail, to allow a surfer to increase curvature with whiplash speed.

Four years into the post–Grubby Clark era, most of the early ventures to replace his business have vanished. It's not that the business is reorganizing around any new standard board or component, however. Firewire, despite its revolutionary ideas and deep-pocketed investors, faces many other new well-funded companies with high-quality, often highly innovative boards. And all kinds of variations have yet to be fully tested, and new variations continue to emerge.

Then there's the fact that many riders prefer old-school Clark-style hard boards. Indeed, Caldwell admits to mixed feelings about the demise of Clark Foam. His joint venture with Grubby would have made him more money more swiftly, he feels, because it would have leveraged off an existing monopoly. But Caldwell also knows that his joint venture with Clark would have meant huge opportunity costs. Once Grubby Clark decided that a technology was sufficiently mature, he would lock it down for mass manufacture, and that was that. The time for tinkering would be over.

One day soon, Mann and Caldwell say, firms like Nike and Adidas will likely pony up big money and make a play to dominate the surfboard business.

Not because there's much money in making the boards themselves, but because there's really big money selling surf-style clothing and other products. For every serious surfer, there are maybe hundreds of people who buy surfer togs, from Albuquerque to Moscow to Dubai. Yet no matter how much big brand money comes into the board business, Mann and Caldwell tell me they are increasingly convinced no one will ever again be able to shut down innovation in the industry the way Grubby Clark did. At least eight or ten big companies will stay in the game, so there will always be a pathway for new ideas. Anyway, that's what they hope. And that's why I told their story, because I figured it was time for a little hope.

It's 5 p.m. and time to close. Some Firewire workers head home, while others drive to the beach to play with next year's models. After waiting for traffic to break, I scream up the coast, as the sun sets in an explosion of color only slightly more spectacular than the conjurings that can erupt in what Emerson once called our "practical democracy."[59] Or for that matter, a hibiscus flower on a long board.

7

The American Piece

A few miles south of the muddy and red Cimarron River, in a land of galloping windswept hills halfway between Oklahoma City and Tulsa, a haphazard grid of listing buildings and weedy lots goes by the name Cushing. A century ago the land hereabouts brimmed with oil, and in 1915 a rush of drillers punched thousands of holes through the earth's crust into what was then America's biggest known underground lake of crude.

For a while, some 30 percent of the nation's high-grade oil flowed from nearby wells. Then the oil began to tap out, and the money and people moved on. What they left behind was a scattering of black derricks, which still rock slowly in the ranchlands, and America's most important hub of oil pipelines and tank farms. That's why, when the New York Mercantile Exchange (NYMEX) decided to start an oil futures market in 1983, it chose Cushing as the price settlement point for West Texas Intermediate crude.

I drive across Skull Creek, pass a cluster of three shuttered gas stations, and stop at the corner of State Road 18 and Main Street. It's lunch time, and I opt for the Homestead Family Restaurant over McDonald's or the EZ Mart. Back when Oklahoma was known as the Indian Territories, these hills were reserved for the Fox and Sac nations. Then President Harrison opened the reservations to settlers, who stampeded south from Kansas and north from Texas in a series of chaotic and dusty land rushes.

The owners of the Homestead are proud descendants of original "sooners"—the sobriquet earned by settlers who snuck early onto Indian lands—or so the photographs on the wall above my table tell me. But from what I can see, there's not much rushing here anymore. My meat loaf and mashed potatoes are set on the table by a waitress who uses a dish cart as a walker, and my after-lunch tour of Main Street discovers a town dominated by retirement homes and hospices. The most intense competition I see is between two stores that rent hospital beds and home oxygen tanks.

It's not until I park on a hilltop south of town, where scudding clouds cast perpendicular shadows across the land, that I get a good view of what brought me here. Behind a fence and a sign reading "SHINN PENCE TANK FARM," I see dozens of immense oil tanks, their steel sides rusted but their tops painted a pristine white. Scores more tanks rise from fields to my right and left. In all, these tanks, which hold up to 575,000 barrels each, cover about nine square miles around Cushing, and on any given day they contain between 5 and 10 percent of the U.S. crude oil inventory. Four companies operate them. Two—British Petroleum (BP) and Enbridge—operate most of them.[1]

I am standing, in other words, smack in the middle of America's "market" for oil. And if such evident concentration of control over pipelines and holding tanks does not lend itself easily to the idea that this is an *actual* market, that's one of the three main points of this chapter. The second is that the intricate network of industrial and political systems designed to extract, refine, and distribute energy is also one of the foundations of the whole system of international governance established by the United States after World War II. It's not just oil that is redistributed through the so-called market set atop the knot of pipelines that interconnect here, it's also political power. Which leads to my third point—that how we regulate this so-called market affects not merely the price we pay for oil but also the price we pay to keep our nation free and at peace.

And so we arrive at the final third of this book. In the first three chapters, we looked at how the present environment of law encourages the consolidation of economic and political power in ways that result in the destruction of the machines and the skills on which our society depends. In the middle third of the book, we looked at how these powers affect us as individuals who bring our products, our labor, and our ideas to market. In the next three chapters, we will look at how this consolidated power deranges our world system, our scientific and engineering systems, and our political system.

By *world system*, I mean the set of institutional arrangements that American leaders put into place after World War II to encourage the nations of the world to cooperate through peaceful, liberal, commercial activity rather than to compete through mercantilism and militarism. To discuss this topic effectively, I believe it necessary to speak of this world system as an American-imposed "imperial" system. In doing so, however, we must be careful to avoid entirely the language of both the contemporary left, which tends to depict empire as an unrelieved history of rapine, and of the right, which tends to view empire entirely through the lens of military power.

My intent is, instead, to present our postwar empire as an audacious, albeit flawed (as all human creations are to some extent flawed) experiment in enlightened self-interest. The American empire was, in my view, a system that supplemented, and to some degree supplanted, the use of military power with the use of financial power, and power directed across international systems of production and supply, like that of oil. It was a system of relatively hands-off rule, based on a highly realistic acceptance that humans are not always guided by our better angels. It was, ultimately, a system designed to regulate competition among nations, and it was based on many of the principles that we had developed to regulate competition among citizens at home.

As we have seen throughout this book, simply calling something a market does not make it so. In the case of a system like oil—which is both industrial and political in nature—calling it a market merely leaves those who actually believe this fiction vulnerable to those who know it to be a lie. To believe oil to be a market is to grant a de facto license to the men who wield capital, the corporation, and the nation-state to use the powers inherent in those political institutions to derange our world system at will.

Before we move on from Cushing, I want to take a moment to make it clear that in the United States, until very recently, almost no one understood the system that delivers us our oil to be a *market*. In the case of Cushing itself, for a short while in 1915 there was, in fact, a true open market here, with independent drillers hauling oil in barrels and wagons to town, where a multitude of traders bid for the sun's fire resting within.[2]

In fact, the American people could have organized the activity of oil drilling and refining into a form of open market, had we wished. We could have done so even after John D. Rockefeller rolled the U.S. oil business into a nearly complete monopoly, integrated vertically from well to store shelf and pump. And for a while it seemed we might try. In 1906, Congress passed a law that brought interstate pipelines under the common carrier rules that we have traditionally used to protect the small producer taking his or her product to market.[3]

Yet by 1911, when the Supreme Court ruled 9–0 to uphold the government order to break Standard Oil into thirty-four independent companies, no one spoke much of trying to keep any oil "market" open to the Jed Clampetts of the world. We see this in the ruling itself, where the word *market* does not appear even once; what does appear, seven times, is the word *competition*. We see this also in Congress at the time. Even as the people rose in anger against J. P. Morgan's bank trust and demanded that power over money be returned to the people, when it came to oil most populists accepted that the industry required some degree of control and concentration.

There was a clear sense that the extraction and refining of oil were activities industrial in nature and hence there was some social value in scale and scope. In the case of Cushing itself, so the thinking went, it was better that a few large companies like Gulf and Texaco concentrate the capital to build clean and efficient pipelines and refineries than that thousands of citizen drillers erect rigs in their yards and haul the crude to market in whatever conveyance lay at hand.

As we have seen, Americans never developed any strict formula about how to structure and regulate complex industrial systems like oil. In the case of oil itself, we even rejected two of the more obvious models. We did not attempt to regulate oil as we were in those same years regulating telephony, as a single integrated monopoly. Nor did we attempt to regulate oil as we did our electric utilities. We cut up Standard Oil along state lines, but we did not turn the resulting pieces over to state regulators. If anything, our approach to oil bears more resemblance to the approach to oligopolies developed by Thurmond Arnold's trustbusters in the 1940s. The goal was to replace straight-up monopoly with a cluster of vertically integrated oligopolies that more or less replicate one another's capabilities and that competed with one another somewhat.

The newly independent oil companies were expected to integrate drilling, pumping, transport, refining, and distribution, much as Standard Oil had, in whatever way they thought best to keep the supply stable and the price low. The price of oil was not really expected to adjust as, for instance, the price of wheat was expected to adjust, according to the size of the crop. On the contrary, the goal was to keep the price steady or, rather, to bring it slowly down as the oil industrial system grew in size and sophistication, much as Henry Ford had slowly brought down the price of the Model T.

The system was regulated not by market mechanisms but indirectly at many points by political actors. The general expectation was that higher prices at the pump should reflect higher real costs and not a desire by the rulers of these utilities for more money. How the oil company executives achieved their price was not important. As with sausage making, all that mattered was the result.

One of the more interesting coincidences in oil history is that the American people broke up Standard Oil and established this new order at home at the very time that many other nations were forging national champions to ensure their supply of oil in case of conflict. The most important example was the British Parliament's decision in June 1914 to take a 51 percent stake in the Anglo-Persian Oil Company (renamed the Anglo-Iranian Oil Company in 1935 and the main parent of British Petroleum) and transform it into a de facto arm of the Admiralty.[4]

It is important not to make too much of this difference, however. The American experience was distinct because at the time we were an oil exporter and hence saw ourselves as a land of producers. Yet beyond the border, our government did not really view the international political economy of oil all that differently than the British government did. Even though privately run, firms like Standard Oil of California (later renamed Chevron) and Standard Oil of New York (later renamed Exxon) came to serve almost as extensions of the U.S. government, organizing and integrating drilling, distribution, and diplomacy in nations like Mexico, Venezuela, and later Saudi Arabia. Well into the 1960s, these activities were intended not to secure oil to burn in the United States but to provide oil to other nations—like Japan and Germany—so they didn't feel obliged to go get oil for themselves.

In other words, through most of the twentieth century, the U.S. oil companies served a dual governance role. At home they were semiutilities, charged with managing all the necessary steps in delivering high-quality gasoline to our filling stations. Abroad, along with a few mining and fruit companies, they were the prototype of what we could come to know as the multinational corporation. They were central actors in our government's efforts to strengthen the United States and neutralize and win over our potential foes. In other words, the oil companies domestically enjoyed attributes of government, while internationally they served as an unofficial arm of government. The oil system was about as far from being a *market* as any system can be.

Squeeze Play

As we've seen repeatedly in this book, the sleekest revolutions are won not at the barricades but in the dictionary. So it proved with our energy system.

In previous chapters we saw how one of the foundations of the revolution achieved by the Chicago School operators was to redefine *market* to mean not a vital political institution but a natural, superhuman mechanism. In this section I want to look at how these operators transformed the oil *system*—which for most of the last century we viewed as a human-run industrial and political mechanism—into a market. I also want to make clear what they accomplished in doing so. First, they *depoliticized* the actions of the oil corporations, the oil speculators, and even to some degree, the producer cartel, the Organization of the Petroleum Exporting Countries (OPEC). Second, they put into place the arrangements and mechanisms they needed to manipulate the price of oil almost completely free of any political control.

Our story here begins in the early 1970s, when two rebellions upset the informal balances that in some instances dated to before World War I and forced lawmakers to rethink the entire structure of the domestic and international energy systems. The first rebellion took place mainly in the Middle East, after the Yom Kippur War in October 1973 provided Arab leaders with an excuse to declare an oil embargo on the United States and the Netherlands. For decades the price of oil had been determined through the negotiation of long-term contracts and, for all intents, had been dictated by a buyers' cartel supported more or less openly by that supermonopoly, the U.S. government. Although the producer countries had long chafed at this arrangement, they only now managed to bring their actions into alignment. OPEC, the newly empowered cartel (which had been formed in 1960), promptly called a production strike, thereby shifting the power to set the price of oil from the buyers to the sellers, who promptly quadrupled the price of crude.

The strike, or oil embargo, set the stage for the second rebellion. This took place in the United States, as executives at the vertically integrated oil companies did not merely fail to smooth out the resulting wild swings in the price of oil but actually took advantage of the chaos to pile up windfall profits.

For our purposes, the more important rebellion was the second, or rather the *reaction to* the great cash grab by the oil executives. The best solution would have been for our government to impose a windfall profits tax and to tighten regulatory control of these utilities. Yet many members of Congress were so angry that instead they began to explore ways to reorganize the entire energy system to lessen the power wielded by these institutions.

Beginning in 1975, liberals in particular floated a variety of plans to slice up the oil companies along both horizontal and vertical lines, by separating pumping, refining, and retailing. The idea was to have many smaller, more specialized companies trading petroleum products in a series of open and transparent exchanges. For the first time in more than half a century, reformers began to imagine reorganizing the oil system into a network of "markets." Nothing came of this effort, however; to no one's surprise, the managers of the oil giants proved adept at using their new wealth to block the restructuring and the taxes.[5] Then, as they relaxed their grip, the issue died away.

The next act began after the Iranian Islamic Revolution in 1979 and the Iraqi invasion of Iran in 1980 cut the world supply of oil dramatically. The Carter administration responded—like the Nixon administration before it—with price controls and a system of rationing designed to ensure that Americans of all classes would share the pain fairly. The practical result was panic buying, long lines, and angry citizens, many of whom voted in November 1980 for Ronald Reagan.

As we know, Reagan brought to power with him the Chicago School operators, and it was they who promptly took the next two key actions in the long series that resulted in the rebranding of our industrial oil system as a *market*.[6] First was to remove all price and allocation controls on oil and instead let the oil companies ration supply by raising prices. What this did was accustom buyers to the idea that the price of oil, which had been more or less fixed for decades, should move up and down.

The far bigger change began in October 1981, when the administration allowed the New York Mercantile Exchange (NYMEX) to establish a market in gasoline "futures." This set the stage for NYMEX to establish, in June 1983, the first futures contract for crude oil, based on the trading of West Texas Intermediate. At the time, neither action struck the public as big news, and on the surface there was no obvious reason they should have. As we saw in chapter 4, people have used futures contracts, which are merely agreements between a seller and a buyer to exchange a certain quantity of a commodity at a certain price on a certain day, for hundreds of years.

Yet in fact, NYMEX had broken entirely new ground. Up to this point, futures exchanges had been used almost solely to regulate naturally volatile markets like those for farm products, in which production is a function of fickle weather.

Until the 1980s, no one saw much reason to use this tool to regulate the exchange of oil or natural gas, precisely because these energy systems, being industrial in nature, were so stable. Except in cases of political upheaval, the nature of the infrastructure required to extract, deliver, and burn most hydrocarbons ensured that day-to-day changes in supply tended to be minimal. Most buyers and sellers therefore preferred to establish long-term contracts, each of which was able to reflect a myriad of political factors, including discounts for new sources of supply expected to be brought on line during the course of the contract. The point was stability, predictability.

There was, by contrast, a need for a "spot" market, in which commodities available for immediate delivery are exchanged. In the case of oil, the spot market had long been of marginal importance. What was sold on the spot market were mainly loose shipments of crude and refinery overruns of gasoline rendered excess by some sudden drop in demand. At most the spot market accounted for 8 percent of sales in crude, usually much less.[7]

In a sense, the spot market in oil serves the same role as an outlet store. The products on the shelves change from day to day. Sometimes great deals are to be had, and sometimes the shelves are nearly bare. The idea that the price on the spot market on any particular day would necessarily affect the price of long-term contracts is as absurd as saying that the price of a single dusty pair of size 12 sneakers at Marshall's will affect the price that Foot Locker pays for the full range of next year's models it contracts to buy from Nike. And in fact, during its first few years of life, the market for West Texas Intermediate futures remained a minor factor in the oil system, which was still shaped almost entirely by the political acts of nation-states and energy corporations.

The next big change came in 1986, when Mexico introduced an idea called *formula pricing* for its oil exports. The idea was that the delivery of the oil would still be covered by a long-term contract, but the price of the oil covered by the contract would change at set intervals in reference to some external marker. In this case the marker, or benchmark, was to be the price on the NYMEX market for West Texas Intermediate. The price of a barrel of Mexican crude would now be adjusted up or down based on its quality relative to West Texas crude, and the price would also be reset at predetermined times over the course of the contract. This could be once a month. Or, as in the case of some contemporary pricing formulas, it could be day by day, even shipload by shipload.

When Mexico introduced formula pricing, a glut of new oil brought on line after the 1979 supply shock had collapsed the price of a barrel below $10. This helps to explain why this change received almost no attention in the U.S. news media.[8] Even after every other major oil supplier followed Mexico's example and adopted formula pricing over the next two years, the news barely rated a mention in the press.

Thus the modern oil "market" was born. It doesn't take much effort to identify at least four bottlenecks that the creation of this so-called market did nothing to eliminate. The first is OPEC, which continued to control a supply bottleneck and hence to enjoy some ability to dictate prices through unified action. The second bottleneck is formed by the giant oil companies themselves; oil must be refined, and control over the refineries that encircle the United States gives firms like ExxonMobil and BP considerable ability to crimp supplies, especially given their efforts in recent years to cut the capacity of these refineries.[9]

The third bottleneck is that gasoline must be distributed to the people who drive cars and trucks, and the same basic group of refiners also controls an intricate network of distribution bottlenecks. The fourth is that just as supplier nations have the ability to restrict supply at will by closing their borders, other nations, like the United States, can use various forms of force to divert or cut the flow of oil at will. This is the military-power bottleneck.

The redefinition of the oil system as a "market" was one of the great political revolutions of the last generation. In a few short years, the responsibility—and the political onus—of pricing oil and gasoline were shifted away from real people, and real corporations, and real governments to a "neutral" mechanism that was presented as entirely nonpolitical in nature.

Yet this is only half our story. Because even after the formula pricing system was perfected, the NYMEX market, where West Texas crude futures were traded, was still a relatively well-regulated public market, and well-regulated markets tend to result in very stable pricing, which means they are of little value to the financier and large-scale speculator.

The final necessary step in transforming the oil system from a tool of our society as a whole into a tool of the rich alone was therefore to *deregulate* the market that had now been perched like a cherry atop this quadruply cartelized heavy industry. Commodities markets themselves, as we saw in chapter 4, are also simply another form of bottleneck by design, and they too can be easily crimped or squeezed. To clear the way for such crimping and squeezing, however, the regulators must be removed from the exchange, the trades must be removed from under the noses of the regulators, or some combination of the two.

And so, over the decade after the introduction of formula pricing, Chicago School operators in the administrations of George H. W. Bush and Bill Clinton and in Congress, imposed a series of "reforms" of our market regulations designed to give the financier and large-scale speculator more and more control over this fifth bottleneck. Consider the following changes that transformed a system originally geared to deliver steady predictable prices into one of the most volatile pricing systems the world has ever seen:

- In 1988, European and Middle Eastern suppliers, along with corporations like BP and traders like Goldman Sachs, organized an alternative market for oil futures in the lightly regulated International Petroleum Exchange (IPE) in London, around trade in Brent crude and oil from other North Sea wells.[10]
- The NYMEX market itself was opened to investments by giant retirement and hedge funds, an act that radically increased the amount of money that was available to those who trade in futures contracts.
- Fund managers like Goldman Sachs and Morgan Stanley as well as other floor traders were allowed to trade on their own account,

thereby creating a class of participants who benefited immensely from volatility.

- The vertically integrated oil giants like BP and Shell were allowed to buy as well as sell oil on the market, which transformed them from utilities into traders and speculators.
- The vertically integrated oil giants such as BP and Shell were— just like the grain trader and shipper Cargill—given license to use inside information in their trading activity. In BP's case, this means its knowledge of what exactly is *inside* all the storage tanks it controls at Cushing, which it can combine with its knowledge of how much oil it plans to deliver from *inside* its North Sea wells.
- Congress and the Clinton administration greatly loosened the limits on how much borrowed money traders could use to buy contracts, which further amplified the power that could be concentrated on any set of contracts.
- Congress and the Clinton administration in December 2000 freed traders to complete their trades outside the public marketplace, in back rooms and especially in electronic exchanges, where neither the government nor any other market participants were able to see what these powers were doing.[11]

The result is an electronic forum that allows professional traders and speculators to bring massive amounts of cash—massively amplified (in good times) through leverage—to bear on the artificially limited number of contracts in play. The result, in other words, is an almost automated system of squeezes or corners, not over the oil itself but over the supply of paper futures. The numbers are astounding. In mid-2008, Chris Cook, a former head of market supervision for the IPE in London, estimated that investors were then piling $260 billion atop the less than $6 billion in Brent contracts that were made available in any one month.[12]

This means that—at least when supplies are relatively tight—a few traders enjoy the power to raise or lower the price of the entire world supply of oil with great freedom and even for long periods with great security. They do so entirely outside the reach of any market regulator other than, as in the days of Jay Gould, other traders.

The initial result of these reforms was to create a lot more activity on the oil market, with the price spiking up and down from day to day, the mere activity itself manufacturing billions of dollars for the traders.

Yet looked at over the long term, the price of oil actually remained remarkably stable from 1988 to about 2004, other than a few spikes occasioned by real-life supply shocks like the Persian Gulf War in 1991 and the September 11, 2001, attacks. The price continued, in other words, to reflect the fact that the extraction and distribution of oil was still, at bottom, an industrial and political system. It was only in 2004 that the people who run our oil "markets" decided the time had come to show off exactly how their new automated cornering mechanisms could manufacture really big money. The result was the truly fantastic increase in oil prices that lasted until July 2008, when the price of a barrel of oil reached nearly $150, surpassing the previous record, set in December 1979.

Yet this fact does not even begin to do justice to the originality of the speculators' achievement. The run up in price a generation ago required an actual cutoff of supply by the Iranian revolutionaries. This time, the speculators managed to beat the old price record even though there was *no cutoff of supply*. They did so by manufacturing their own supply shock—in oil futures.[13] And then they renewed that shock month after month after month.

And so America's oil system was transformed into perhaps the single finest example of what happens to a people who are taught to see a "market" system where there really is no market whatsoever.[14] In place of a set of utilities designed, however imperfectly, to stabilize the supply and price of oil for the American people, and to promote and protect American interests around the world, we substituted a chain of exploitation opportunities that cedes to foreign states, immense private governments, and financiers the power to routinely crimp supply at the well, the port, the pump, and on the trading floor.[15]

It is the world's most perfect shell game, in which the fault for soaring prices always lies under someone else's walnut. And in which none of the main participants has any real interest in preventing the other participants from applying their various squeezes, for they all live more or less harmoniously under the same flexible price.

When it comes to commodity markets, the term *free market* means merely the freedom for the speculators to speculate, hence the freedom for the financier to derange. The trouble here is that, unlike in the markets for gold or cocoa beans, the derangement of the oil system affects just about everyone and everything. In the event, the result was a massive shift of wealth—and hence power—out of our hands. Not merely to a few financiers in New York and London, but often to the least savory actors abroad, in Tehran, Caracas, Moscow. The result, in other words, was a massive destabilization of the whole world system that a more intelligent (or at least less easily bamboozled) generation of Americans built with such care and patience in an attempt to prevent any recurrence of industrial-powered war.

Rule and Reason

There are three reasons it has been so hard for practical, realistic Americans to make sense of our nation's empire. First, our empire is different in nature from any other empire imposed since the modern European nation-state was shaped more than half a millennium ago. Second, those who understand how our empire actually works rarely speak about it in public, and when they do they use language that is nearly impossible for the layperson to understand. Third, the nature of our empire changed radically in the early 1990s, and the imperial institutions were put to entirely different tasks, namely, the enclosure and exploitation of the American people. Our most important initial task therefore, is simply to understand how our empire was originally designed to work, and to what end, so that we can begin to understand how its institutions have been turned against us.

In this section I want to make clear the exceptional nature of the American empire by looking at the exceptional nature of the American concept of empire. One way to do so is to identify the three factors that combined to shape a very unique sense among early Americans of our nation's place in the world.

First was that our economy was not watched over by any jealous human sovereign, which meant that individual Americans were free to trade as they alone saw fit, with whom they alone chose. Second was that we organized our own domestic commerce around a system of open markets, and we tended to seek similar relationships abroad. Third was that we tended to view the ideals on which we founded our nation as of universal appeal, much as Christians or Marxists see their ideals as universal in nature. This often led us to believe the best way to achieve our goals in the world was not through arms but through a combination of peaceful exchange and political evangelization.

America was also a physical empire. We used force to seize vast swaths of land from Native American nations and from Mexico. Outside North America, however, we tended to operate on a very different set of principles, ones that distinguished us from most of the other expansive nation-states across the Atlantic. Whereas the agents of Spain, France, and Britain (and later of Germany, Japan, and Russia) sailed into foreign ports intent on imposing direct control, most Americans strongly opposed colonies overseas.

This was not necessarily because Americans operated on a superior moral plane. On the contrary, our approach to international relations jibed well with our interest as citizens of a democratic republic.[16] Overseas colonies often proved to be semilawless lands where the most ruthless could concentrate economic and political power that translated into real power back home, as the British discovered when the newly enriched Nabobs of the British East India Company returned from the subcontinent loaded with plunder, which they promptly swapped for property and power.[17]

A good way to understand the exceptional nature of the American approach to empire is to look at the practical result of two of the most important nineteenth-century statements of U.S. principles: the Monroe Doctrine and the Open Door Policy. The Monroe Doctrine headed off a scramble for control over the newly independent states of Latin America, recently broken free from Spain. The Open Door Policy in China slowed a scramble for colonies in China that had already resulted in the tearing away of large swaths of Chinese territory by Russia, Japan, France, Germany, and Britain.

In both instances, the U.S. stance served the interests of other peoples, in Latin America and in China, by helping to protect them from foreign rule. In both instances, our stance also served our interests, by enabling us to avoid the monetary and human costs of formal empire and yet to enjoy the benefits of trade. Put another way, no trade monopolies oppressed those peoples, and no trade monopolies excluded us.

It is easy to point out hypocrisies, especially in Central America and the Caribbean, especially in instances where we allowed multinationals like the United Fruit Company to function as de facto trading companies not terribly different from the East India Company. Yet the single most traditional imperial venture of the United States—in the Philippines—was less a violation of our prevailing set of principles than a pragmatic, realistic illustration of them.

Almost no members of the McKinley or Roosevelt administrations, or of Congress in the years after the Spanish-American War, saw much glory or gain in ruling that distant, scattered, and largely undeveloped archipelago. What they did see was the great harbor of Manila, where they imagined basing a naval squadron that would be charged with policing the predations of the old colonial powers along the China coast.

The colonization of the Philippines is therefore an instance in which the United States used its power to head off the consolidation of far greater and potentially more threatening powers. When Franklin Roosevelt, in 1935, promised the Filipinos independence, the United States became the first nation of the Atlantic world to volunteer to free a colony.[18]

In 1944, when the Roosevelt administration gathered hundreds of financial officials and bankers from around the world at the Bretton Woods Resort in New Hampshire, it was clear that the United States would emerge as the greatest victor in World War II: largely unscathed, immensely wealthy, fantastically powerful, by some estimates home to more than half of the industrial capacity in the world. For thirty years the old colonial powers had staggered from one cataclysm to another. Even Britain was practically bankrupt.

To an extent greater than at any moment since the final defeat of Napoleon in 1815, the world was a tabula rasa. Which meant the United States held sufficient power to establish pretty much whatever sort of economic system we wished and to impose it on the nations assembled. We could, for instance, have designed a truly centralized imperial system to concentrate all power and profit in our own hands.

What we imposed instead was a system organized around liberal trade among nations envisioned as largely independent of one another and of us. The only major restriction was that these nations were not to be regarded as free to use force on one another, or to impose monopolies on other peoples, or to use monopolies against us. Indeed, one of our main demands was that the British, the French, and the Dutch unwind their own monopolistic imperial systems.

When we talk today about the Bretton Woods institutions, we tend to focus on the World Bank, the International Monetary Fund (IMF), and the gold-backed monetary system that lasted until 1971. All played immensely important roles in resurrecting, ordering, and governing the international economy in the decades after the war. But these were not the institutions that most clearly revealed the political intent of the American vision of empire.

To understand the true nature of what the Americans of that generation envisioned, we must look at the Bretton Woods institution least studied today: the International Trade Organization (ITO). Although it is sometimes linked rhetorically to today's World Trade Organization (WTO), the differences could not be more extreme. The purpose of the WTO is to force nations to harmonize their laws in order to make it easier for immense trading companies, run by private actors for private profit, to transfer property from one nation to another.

The ITO, by contrast, was an intricate mechanism designed to harmonize the external trade of a particular nation with the employment levels and labor standards within that nation. It was designed to do so through the realistic regulation of marketlike international exchanges, built to integrate the functioning of these national systems. And it left to each individual nation-state the wherewithal to protect its own small and medium size businesses as it alone saw fit.[19]

The vision of empire that Americans formalized in these documents was a radical departure from all the imperial systems that existed before the war, and it was also radically different from the imperial system that was imposed after the war by the other main victor nation, the Soviet Union. The ultimate goal of the system was not top-down control but creation of a federation of responsible republics. The system was perceived to be self-regulating only to the extent that any human organization can be said to be self-governing. Like all real market systems, it was to have a master, the United States. And like all true market systems, it was designed to force the master to serve the interests of the participants. In other words, at the very height of our power, we devised a system that set strict limits on what we could demand of our neighbors.

The U.S. World System

In recent decades, we have been trained to use vague and outright deceptive language to describe how nations and peoples interact. The term *globalization*, for instance, blurs together trade, technology, finance, and culture to the point where it is of no practical political use whatsoever. The "soft" power versus "hard" power frame that is popular among academics is in some ways even more confusing, because the division it implies is largely false; some exercises of commercial and financial power can be far more destructive than some exercises of military force.[20]

It is far easier to understand how nations interact with one another if we break these relationships down into four distinct planes of power. The most obvious way nations project power against one another is, of course, through the use or threat of military force, and at any given moment this is the most compelling form of power. A second way nations project power is through the strategic use of information and ideology; this can mean anything from the laws that regulate trade in Hollywood films to the limits on foreign ownership of a nation's news media to the reiteration of democratic truisms at an international summit. A third way nations project power is through finance, which includes everything from international monetary policy to fiscal policy to the politics of the World Bank and IMF.

The fourth plane of power, and the one that most concerns us here, is what we may call the international political economy of supply and production. This includes the management and structure of the systems we rely on for our raw materials and energy, as well as processed factory goods and information.

The goal of the United States in establishing the Bretton Woods system and the United Nations system was to fashion an international institutional architecture that would lead the nations of the world toward harmonious commercial interaction. And, when additional prodding was required, the institutional architecture was designed to enable us to project power across the last three of these planes in ways that would, we hoped, avoid the need to resort to military force.

In the event, two challenges soon emerged to the Bretton Woods system as it was originally conceived. First, the ITO proved difficult to establish. The main problem was that the open drafting process resulted in a bloated, exception-ridden document known as the Havana Charter. This in turn led the Republican-dominated Senate to make clear that it would not approve the charter, at least not without a big fight.

The second challenge was the Truman administration's belief that the Soviet Union did not intend to participate in our new world system as a constructive actor but that instead it planned to push toward conflict in Europe and in Asia. This second factor was especially important, for it led the Truman administration to conclude that the economies of western Europe and East Asia had to be rebuilt far more swiftly than originally planned. Thus, less than half a decade after the original Bretton Woods plan, the Truman administration began to work on a second-generation vision of empire, which would prove in certain respects to be far more radical than the first.

The new approach first took shape in a debate on whether and how to rebuild German industry. For centuries, nation-states had been structured around more or less self-contained military-industrial complexes designed to manufacture the arms that enabled the state both to protect itself and to capture the raw materials and overseas markets it required to keep the process going. After the war, both the U.S. Treasury and the French government promoted plans to strip most or all industry from Germany so that the country could never rearm, hence never again venture abroad in search of plunder and power.

This all changed after the United States decided that the Soviet Union, so recently our ally, now posed an imminent threat. The plan became to rebuild German industry, both to give West Germany's restive workers something to do and to harness the know-how of German scientists, engineers, and machinists into the new anti-Soviet alliance we had begun to build.

What made the plan revolutionary was the decision not to rebuild German industry as a stand-alone national system but to *blend* the German industrial system with that of other European states into a single, common, integrated whole. The idea was that if western Europe's biggest nations essentially *shared* control of certain key resources and activities, then none among them could rearm without the others being able to prevent it. Many in Europe objected to this idea—especially, at first, the French. But the United States had two big arguments in its favor.

The first was strategic: such deep integration was a way to tie down German industrial power even as it was built back up, by giving nations like France some direct hold over the Germans. The second was financial: it was U.S. money that was paying to rebuild Europe, mainly through the Marshall Plan. As it proved, the French soon came to embrace the idea, especially once it was restated by their own foreign minister, Robert Schuman. The result was the European Coal and Steel Community, which brought the mines, the mills, and the metal markets of West Germany, France, Italy, Belgium, the Netherlands, and Luxembourg under joint control.[21] And the result was to set into motion the process that over the next half century would lead to the European Community, the European Union, and the euro.

The biggest difference between our original Bretton Woods vision—of independent nations organized around market systems—and what we actually constructed in Europe was that we ended up organizing certain key industries into a common cross-border shared system. U.S. officials imagined a sort of United States of Europe, and they introduced a sort of physicalized Interstate Commerce Clause to make it happen. If you read a book like Thomas Friedman's *The World Is Flat*, you get the impression that "industrial interdependence" among nations is an entirely new and entirely *natural* phenomenon. In fact, we can trace extreme cross-border industrial integration back more than sixty years. And unlike in Friedman's take, industrial interdependence was not the result of the workings of any organic free-market, efficiency-seeking mechanism. It was imposed, for the most strategic of reasons, by our government in Washington.

The U.S. government did not stop with Europe. The Truman, Eisenhower, Kennedy, and Johnson administrations applied the same idea over the next twenty years across much of Asia. As in Europe, the main goal was to promote industrial and financial integration, with economic "efficiency" seen merely as an important by-product. And as in Europe, the U.S. planners who reshaped the international political economy of Asia initially imagined blending the economies of the two main adversaries, China and Japan.[22] But after the Maoist revolution took China out of the equation, the Americans came up with a new approach, which called for the United States itself to serve as a sort of hub for Asia's industry. Rather than blend the economies of Asia into a largely self-contained bloc like Europe, the plan was to merge them more or less directly into the U.S. economy. As it had done in Europe, the U.S. government rarely insisted that U.S. corporations control the resulting trade relationships directly. On the contrary, the government often forced U.S. corporations to transfer market share as well as technology to their Asian competitors. The goal was not centralized control but a complex industrial interdependence that would make it hard for any of these Asian nations ever to take up arms against the United States.[23]

Industrial integration was never the only tool we used to bind nations together. We also wove complex systems of military cooperation, and we built or consolidated a myriad of physical, intellectual, and political systems: in communications, transportation, law, accounting, and engineering, and of course, in the supply of energy, raw materials, and food. In the process, we "outsourced" much of the decision making itself to international institutions such as the IMF and World

Bank, and especially the Organization for Economic Cooperation and Development (OECD).

The mechanisms did not automatically result in harmonious cooperation among peoples. But they did enable U.S. presidents to repeatedly instruct the world in how these new webs of production and supply could be used to achieve very dramatic, almost militarylike political ends without the use of military force. The most famous instance came in 1956, after Egypt nationalized the Suez Canal, and Britain, France, and Israel responded by invading Egypt. President Eisenhower, who had opposed the invasion, responded by threatening to crash the British pound, and he worked with Saudi Arabia to impose an oil embargo on both Britain and France.

The U.S. government also repeatedly used these webs to counter attempts by the nations within the system to erect industrial monopolies. One of the most successful instances was orchestrated by President Reagan in 1987, when he imposed a tariff to punish Japan for attempting to monopolize the production of certain electronics components, and arranged for U.S. computer makers to shift their purchases of such items away from Japan to suppliers at home or in other nations.[24]

The idea that a semiliberal trading system can be imposed on much of the world may seem paradoxical. Yet when the Bretton Woods ideal proved unattainable, the United States resorted to far more direct—sometimes coercive—means to engineer the decentralized, commerce-based, cosmopolitan empire we envisioned. The effort was realistic, practical, result-oriented, and self-consciously political. The aim was to regulate competition among nations run by self-serving elites in much the same way that the federal government regulated competition among corporations run by self-serving financiers.

The ultimate result was, as one European historian put it, "empire by integration."[25] It was an empire organized around two great hubs, one in Europe and one across the Pacific. It was an empire that completely reorganized the economies of some of the biggest nations of the world. And it was an empire that resulted in the complete reorganization of America's own political economy as well. Jobs were traded away, although we rarely allowed entire skill sets to be moved abroad. And a great deal of new wealth was created, for the overall system was marked simultaneously by both more cooperation and greater specialization of labor, on one hand, and more competition, on the other. By almost any measure, the experiment proved to be phenomenally successful in achieving its central aim, which was the promotion of peace and prosperity among nations that until recently had been engaged in cataclysmic industrial-powered war.

Yet the system never overcame two interlinked flaws. The first was that none of the new institutions was ever charged with looking at the effects that such radical reorganization of industrial activity might have on the structural stability of our production systems. The assumption was that the professional managers of our large industrial enterprises would watch for any large-scale risks and that antimonopoly policy would guard against dangerous concentration. The second flaw was that the people who conceived this imperial system never entirely trusted the people of the world—or even the American citizen—to support such high levels of integration, so they developed a habit of hiding their actions from the very people they believed they were serving.

Perhaps some secrecy was necessary. After all, the idea that some American workers should pay for empire with their jobs might have sparked a political reaction. Similarly, the necessary compromises were not always easy for people in other nations to swallow. Yet the failure of our Cold War–era leadership to speak honestly with us about these revolutionary international arrangements prevented citizens in Western democracies from keeping track of the need always to ensure that the production and supply systems that had been extended across these borders were engineered, physically and politically, in ways that made them safe over the long run. It also prevented us from protecting these remarkable political achievements, after the Cold War ended, from the predations of our own financiers.

Derangement

In 1989, America's world system delivered perhaps its greatest achievement: a peaceful end to the Cold War. China was the first to fall, or so it seemed, after thousands of pro-democracy protesters occupied Tiananmen Square in late May. Although hard-liners responded by killing hundreds if not thousands of unarmed civilians on June 4, many concluded that the Maoist regime was doomed. Then in November the Soviet empire in Eastern Europe collapsed as popular revolutions overthrew regimes from East Germany to Romania.

For most Americans, the revolutions were both exhilarating and deeply unsettling. People felt joy for the liberation of Eastern Europe, and immense relief from the gnawing fear of nuclear war. But the end of the Cold War also begged the question "What next?"

Sure enough, the end of the Cold War loosed numerous power plays. Iraqi leader Saddam Hussein seized Kuwait. Slovenia and Croatia declared independence from Yugoslavia. Japan and Europe broke from the United States and rushed to invest in Communist China. Yet the most important power play took place right in the United States. Financiers, with remarkable swiftness, moved to seize control of the levers of power of our world system. In a sense, this marked the beginning of the second stage of the revolution set in motion when Reagan's election in 1980 carried the Chicago School operators into power. Their aim now was to consolidate their political economic power over the whole world.

Among U.S. government officials, the entirely new set of institutional arrangements established in the early and mid-1990s, through the signing of agreements like NAFTA and the WTO, is often called by the eminently sober name Bretton Woods II. And some members of the Clinton administration did truly seem to imagine that these deals—rather than simply opening the United States and a few more easily gulled or steamrolled nations to the predations of the financiers—were a natural next step for the system that was pieced together with such care after that 1944 meeting in New Hampshire. The goal, the Clintonians assured us, was to adjust and perfect the old system mainly by expanding it out another ring or two so that it could begin to work its magic of integration, stabilization, and liberalization on another set of worthy nations. Mexico was to be a special project of the United States, while Eastern Europe was entrusted to Brussels and Berlin. The central target of the strategy was China. Here all the liberal democracies were to work together, in a noncompetitive way, to ease this great but troubled society into the "community of nations."

In the rest of this section, I want to focus on how the financiers sold this complete replumbing of the world system to the American people. Their success in making this sale is undoubtedly one of the greatest of the many sophistical achievements of the Chicago School operators, right up there with the creation of the concept of a "free market."

In retrospect, the speed with which the grand U.S. financiers—or rather, the intellectuals in their service—reshaped our perceptions of the revolutionary events in Beijing and Berlin in 1989 is remarkable. In fact, the Marxist regimes in China and Russia collapsed because the leaders there could no longer hide the evidence that the U.S. system—which by then had been extended to half of the world—was vastly superior to their own, politically and economically. And in the early days after the German people tore down the Berlin Wall, this was indeed one of the main story lines used to explain this revolution.

Yet even before the Berlin Wall actually fell, the Chicago School operators succeeded in establishing a second and parallel story line, which they now amplified and fleshed out day by day. What shattered the Soviet system, they claimed, was not a complex system of governance that required strong participation by the state. What had shattered the Soviet Union was nothing other than "capitalism," "free trade," and the "free market." Therefore, what all the nations of the world needed—and this included the United States itself—was a more powerful capitalism, freer trade, and freer markets.

Almost as stunning was how swiftly the intellectuals working for the grand financiers managed to produce relatively complex arguments designed to convince the American people to accept the idea that our entire international system—so soon after delivering its great victories over the communist regimes—must now be entirely overhauled. One of the first such works was a book called *The Borderless World* by McKinsey & Company consultant Kenichi Ohmae. To understand the central message the financiers were broadcasting to the world, let's look at a key section.

Ohmae's work, which hit bookstore shelves in mid-1990, concludes with what he called a "Declaration of Interdependence Toward the World" that serves as a fine summary of his central set of arguments. The "security of humankind's social and economic institutions," Ohmae wrote:

> lies no longer in superpower deterrence but is rather to be found in the weave of economic and intellectual interdependence of nations. As such, we believe that the interlinked economy:
> - Enhances the well-being of individuals and institutions;
> - Stands open to all who wish to participate in it, mainly through the deregulation of trade;
> - Creates no absolute losers nor winners, as market mechanisms adjust participating nations' competitiveness rather fairly through currency exchange rates and employment.[26]

There is no evidence that a single American statesman in the period between 1944 and 1991 believed for a single moment that the international political economy was a self-regulating system. Yet Ohmae, for all intents, claimed exactly this. In essence, Ohmae, a Japanese nationalist with a doctorate in nuclear engineering, told his audience of American businesspeople to: (1) get your government out of the way on trade, (2) get your government out of the way on finance, (3) get your government out of the way on jobs, (4) work with other governments to get your opponents to such changes out of the way, and (5) feel righteous when you do so, because you walk arm in arm with that great neutral mechanical judge, the good lord Market.

Ohmae's work was, in other words, about as pure a distillation as could be imagined of the language systems that Milton Friedman and company had developed to sell their neofeudal philosophy.[27] And just as the intent of the Chicago School preachers at home was to shift power from the public government to the private corporate governments and banks controlled by their patrons, so too was their intent here, at least as channeled by Ohmae.

Ohmae's book sold well to American businesspeople and financiers, yet it was not a work that could really affect mainstream opinion. Therefore, let's turn once again to Robert Reich's book, *The Work of Nations*, published a year after Ohmae's. For the average American, especially the average member of the Democratic Party, this work was perhaps the most influential introduction to the then newly concocted concept of "globalization," especially after the book became recognized widely as the "primer" for "Clintonomics."[28] In the future, Reich assured his readers that:

> there will be no *national* products or technologies, no national corporations, no national industries. There will no longer be national economies, at least as we have come to understand that concept. All that will remain rooted within national borders are the people who comprise a nation. Each nation's primary assets will be its citizens' skills and insights. Each nation's primary political task will be to cope with the centrifugal forces of the global economy which tear at the ties binding citizens together— bestowing ever greater wealth on the most skilled and insightful, while consigning the less skilled to a declining standard of living. (Emphasis in the original.)[29]

Reich's message, at heart, was almost exactly the same as Ohmae's. The U.S. government should: (1) get out of the way on trade, (2) get out of the way on finance, and (3) work with other governments to get our own opponents out of the way. Reich did differ with Ohmae on one point, however. Government, he contended, still had one role to play, which was to educate the American populace. Not to be citizens, mind you. Rather to be brighter, more eager, and more productive employees for the new "global" corporations.

Reich, in other words, essentially translated hard-core neo-feudal philosophy—after it had been dressed up in glittering new language by the Chicago School operators and after it was "globalized" by Ohmae— into a frame designed to capture the minds of the neoprogressive elite that now largely controlled the Democratic Party.

As it proved, one last bit of salesmanship was necessary. Even after the WTO had gone into effect, Congress still refused to let go of one very big lever over trade. This was the granting of normal trade status to China. Without such status, China was not guaranteed the same treatment we promised, under the WTO regime, to countries like Japan and France. And so it fell to Bill Clinton in 1997 to deliver a speech in which he laid out a new "strategy" to explain and guide our actions in relation to China. For a quarter century, American leaders since Nixon had been slowly integrating Maoist China into our world system, with great care, with great skepticism, and, up to this point, with great success. Now Clinton told us that such a slow steady careful course was no longer necessary.

Rather than rely on officials negotiating across tables, management of the relationship between the United States and China could now be outsourced to new technologies and the magical mechanism of the free market itself. The "Internet, fax machines, and photocopiers" (even the lowly "modem"), Clinton said, by exposing Chinese citizens to "people, ideas, and the world beyond China's borders," would make it increasingly difficult for China's rulers to maintain their "closed political system."

Meanwhile, he insisted, "growing interdependence will have a liberalizing effect on China."[30]

In other words, in place of the Madisonian principle that freedom, both at home and around the world, can be protected and developed only through the careful and conscious engineering of competition to enable peaceful and productive commerce among peoples, Clinton now substituted the idea that freedom was a materialistically determined function of machines and money.[31]

In actual fact, the result was to outsource management of our trade not to any "market" but rather to the men and women who ran private trading firms and banks. And given that these financial and industrial and resource institutions and systems were the same systems the U.S. government had long used to affect how money, grains, oil, and manufactured goods flowed from country to country, the "strategy" Clinton advocated amounted to nothing less than the unilateral disarmament of the United States.

And so, over the course of a few short years, we melted the plowshares of our postwar world system into pipe dreams.

The Octopus and the Spider

In Brussels in the fall of 2007, the European Union's commissioner for energy and commissioner for competition stood together to promote a plan to "unbundle" Europe's energy system and transform it into a "market." As Andris Piebalgs, the energy commissioner, put it, "We have moved a long way towards an internal energy market in the EU over the last 10 years. . . . It is now time to complete this process and ensure that the benefits of this market are real." The targets of the antitrust action that the two commissioners envisioned were Germany's E.ON, France's GDF SUEZ, and Italy's Eni. And Russia's Gazprom.[32]

In this section I want to look at how Russia and China manage their international energy systems and compare this to how the United States and the European Union manage our international energy systems today. Or rather, how our leaders don't.

On the surface, there was nothing out of the ordinary in this joint call by the two EU commissioners.[33] Indeed, their desire to restructure Europe's energy systems into a system of markets was, fundamentally, no different from what the liberal reformers in the United States imagined doing in the mid-1970s to Big Oil. It is important, however, to put this statement into context.

We must, for instance, keep in mind that it was made after Russia had engineered a phenomenal roll-up of control over the supplies of natural gas that Europeans had assumed would be available to them in the coming decades in the international "market." In the two years leading up to

Piebalg's statement, Russia had not merely stripped concessions from the Western energy firms that were operating in Russia's Far East, it had also struck state-to-state deals with Iran and *all* the natural gas exporters of North Africa.[34]

The result was simultaneously to suppress Russia's own production and to give Russia some say over the delivery and pricing of nearly 40 percent of all gas burned in western Europe.[35] In those same two years, Russia also made clear its willingness to use its control of gas supplies as a political weapon, repeatedly cutting off flows to punish an anti-Russian government in Ukraine.

If we view Piebalg's statement in this context, what seemed on the surface to be a hard-line threat against an array of big firms begins to sound a lot more like a last-ditch plea directly to Russia's then prime minister Vladimir Putin to cease the projection of power across these planes of supply and instead embrace the regulation of these activities by Western "market" systems. It didn't take long for Putin to make clear that however heartfelt the invitation, he did not intend to yield complete control to the speculators. On the contrary, less than a year later, Russia moved to complete its chokehold on Europe's supply of natural gas with its invasion of Georgia.

Ever since the collapse of the Soviet Union in 1991, the United States and the European Union had viewed independent Georgia as the best, if not only, gateway through which to pipe to the West the oil and the natural gas that is buried below the landlocked nations of Central Asia. The invasion of Georgia marked the final and most direct of a long series of efforts by Russia to project various forms of power down the Balkans and across the Caspian Sea in order to block any and all potential routes for those pipelines.

Not that our allies in Europe were entirely out of ammunition. On the contrary, after the invasion of Georgia, they set out to punish Russia by pulling billions of dollars in investments out of that country, in a move that did succeed in destabilizing that fragile economy. And in the event, this move was followed by a second, entirely unplanned assault on Russia's economy in the form of the financial shock waves unleashed around the world by the collapse of Lehman Brothers in September 2008.

Yet if you bet that such financial pain alone would be enough to lead Russia to play productively within the "market" system, you bet wrong. The Russians instead picked another fight with Ukraine in the cold, dark winter days of January 2009 and used this as an excuse to shut off the flow of gas through the Soviet-era pipelines that still deliver almost all of the gas consumed by the European Union's newest members in eastern Europe. Furthermore, Russia continued its pinpoint predations in the heart of Europe,[36] especially in Germany, through lavish and quite public payoffs to such high-profile leaders as the former German chancellor Gerhard Schroeder.

In the nineteenth century, John D. Rockefeller bought up long swaths of land at strategic points in Pennsylvania (often called "dead lines") to block independent drillers from building pipelines that would enable them to escape Standard Oil's control over the railroads. Rockefeller's goal, which he basically achieved, was to govern the entire U.S. oil industry.[37] What Rockefeller failed to achieve—largely because the American people rose up to oppose him with such energy and relentlessness for so many years—was control over our government.

We should view Russia's new energy octopus, therefore, as a far more daunting threat than any other energy power we, or our democratic allies in Europe, have faced. This is precisely because the Russian octopus so seamlessly fuses the power of an energy transportation monopoly with that of an immensely powerful state, the power of which Russia's tiny elite now uses with almost complete freedom to pick apart the centerpiece of America's postwar world system: the unity of western Europe.[38]

Not bad for a nation the wise men of the Clinton administration wrote off as a basket case in the mid 1990s and all but ignored as they kowtowed in Beijing.

Now let's look at China's energy strategy. And let's start by reviewing China's August 2008 oil deal with Iraq, under which the state-controlled China National Petroleum Corporation will be paid $3 billion over the next twenty-two years to develop and operate an oil field southeast of Baghdad. In and of itself, this is not a big deal. What makes it a big deal is what happened ten days later to a collection of similar service contracts that Iraq had been set to sign with ExxonMobil, Chevron, Shell, BP, and France's Total. On September 11, 2008, the Iraqi government cancelled negotiations, at least temporarily, after Iraqi parliamentarians protested the deals.

Let's make sure that we understand the symbolism of these two decisions. The Bush administration invested the lives of four thousand (and still counting) American men and women and nearly $1 trillion to grab control of Iraq's oil and, supposedly, to "free" the Iraqi people from a brutal dictatorship. The Iraqi regime created by this action then awards its first major oil service contract to a nation—China—that had been perfectly happy to deal with that dictator. The new Iraqi regime then topped this off by all but promising China far bigger prizes in the years to come. As one Iraqi oilman made clear, the deal marked the beginning of a fine friendship. "When [the Chinese] need oil," he said, "the Iraqi people will feel that China has done something for them."[39]

This pragmatic approach to trading money, goods, services, and information for what China needs has worked remarkably well politically for China's leaders and materially for China's people. Consider some statistics on world oil holdings. In 2007, PetroChina surpassed ExxonMobil as the world's largest energy company, as measured by market capitalization. In the previous year, China's Sinopec soared from number twelve to number five on the same list. Market capitalization mainly reflects the number of long-term drilling concessions that an oil firm has under contract, so these surges in rank were a good indicator of the success of these state-controlled oil companies in lining up new deals, at least compared to their Western competitors.[40]

Consider also a recent set of moves that China made in metals. As we saw in chapter 1, some of the most aggressive monopolists in recent years have been the people who control the Anglo-Australian company BHP Billiton. After BHP and fellow Anglo-Australian giant Rio Tinto began to raise drastically the price of copper a few years back, the Chinese government responded by turning the annual price negotiations into a state-to-state affair, insisting on direct talks with the Australian government, upon which leaders in Beijing can bring a far wider array of pressures than they can against the private mining companies. Not that Beijing failed to apply direct power onto the two companies; in March 2008, for instance, the Chinese government began to hold up approvals for imports of iron ore that the two firms had priced on spot markets.[41] Then in early 2009, after the world economic crisis collapsed the demand for copper and left Rio Tinto and BHP out of sorts, China unveiled a plan to invest $19.5 billion in Rio Tinto, in a deal designed to give the Chinese state a direct say in the firm's governance. When Rio Tinto shareholders later blocked the deal and instead agreed to a joint venture with BHP, the Chinese government said it would use its new antitrust law to block the deal and backed that up by arresting Rio Tinto's top Australian salesman in China.[42]

China's ability to project financial and industrial power across national borders to get what it wants—more financial and industrial power and more control over its systems of supply—is even more impressive if we consider the breadth of the country's efforts. China is active not merely throughout Africa and Southeast Asia but also in many of the South American nations that the United States so recently regarded as "strategic" suppliers of our energy and metals. Indeed, almost simultaneous with its investment in BHP, China announced plans to loan $39 billion to Brazil, Venezuela, and Russia to develop oil projects in exchange for a call on the oil produced. (In a similar vein, in September 2009, the Chinese regime revealed plans to ban outright the export from China of many "rare earth" metals, which are used to manufacture advanced magnets and electronic devices. Given that China has an almost complete monopoly over many of these metals, such a ban will have a big effect on certain forms of research and production in the United States, Europe, and Japan.)[43]

To support this world-spanning effort, China has developed what amounts to a complete international regime of aid, diplomacy, trade, and finance that exists *parallel* to the IMF and the World Bank and all the other half-ruined and largely corrupted apparatuses of our own post-war world system. China uses this parallel international system not merely to acquire long-term contracts for the supply of oil and metals but also to acquire power within the Western system itself. One way it does so is by purchasing votes in such semidemocratic institutions as the United Nations and International Monetary Fund, which China's leadership essentially buys from the many small nations that we, for all intents, ignore.[44]

Most impressive of all is China's ability to extend its reach right into our own political economy here in the United States. It does so thanks to the overarching structure of the Bretton Woods II system put into place by the Clinton administration in the early 1990s. For more than a decade this system settled into a balance wherein our financiers used money they borrowed from China to seize control of our manufacturing corporations, then used those corporations to transfer the machines, technologies, and jobs we had entrusted to their care from our shores to China. Which in turn forced Americans to ship even bigger piles of cash across the Pacific to pay for what we used to produce here. Which cash China loaned back to us through our own Treasury Department, mortgage companies, and credit card companies to enable us to build yet bigger houses and buy more Chinese products to pile into those houses, in a process that resulted in the gathering of yet more cash in China's coffers. Which China then loaned once more to our financiers to buy up more manufacturing corporations in order to manage the shipping of yet more machines and technologies across the sea.

China also reaches into our political economy through the giant trading companies themselves.[45] What is Wal-Mart, after all, if not the reincarnation of the British East India Company, albeit this time in the form of an export arm of the Chinese state?[46]

And how do our own leaders respond to this absolutely brilliant use of our own international system and our own corporations against us? Pretty much the same way the leaders of Europe respond to Russia's predations, in this case, by whiningly upbraiding the leaders in Beijing for not playing by the "rules" of our "global free market." Given that the Chinese know, just like the Russians, that when Western leaders say "market" they actually mean control by Western financiers and their batteries of private and public banks and other speculative mechanisms, they quite reasonably refuse. Far more effective is to instruct Western leaders like President Obama to apologize for whining and to "guarantee" the "value" of the Treasury bills the Chinese continue to purchase with our money.[47]

So, thirteen years after President Clinton's big strategy speech on U.S.-China relations, have "technology, " and "interdependence," and the magic of the "free market" actually resulted in any real liberalization of the closed (and, may we add, authoritarian) political regime in Beijing? Is China any closer to becoming a cooperative and productive participant in our global community? To answer that question, we might find it easier to alter the order of the words and ask instead: is the United States any closer to becoming a cooperative player in China's system?

When there's one web and two spiders but only one is awake, the result is one spider.

Plantation Nation

One of the clearest ways to understand the effects of a quarter century of rule over the United States by governments dedicated to concentrating power in the hands of financiers and foreign states is to look at what U.S. oil companies did as our troops fought in the streets of Fallujah and Baghdad.

First consider ExxonMobil. Or, more specifically, consider a 2007 article in *Business Week* that detailed how that company was "pumping cash, not oil." With gasoline prices at record highs, the article stated, the oil titan "ought to be drilling like mad and refining more of that black gold, right?" Yet it wasn't. "As it turns out, the world's largest oil producer thinks it is smarter to use more of its resources to buy back stock. The indirect result: increased pain at the pump for consumers."[48] The article made it clear that this was not a new problem. On the contrary, it traced this lack of interest in exploration and drilling to President Clinton's approval of Exxon's massive merger with Mobil in 1999. It was at that point that the company ceased to devote resources to expanding its overall reserve holdings.

Now consider Shell. In 2004, the company shocked investors when it revealed that in order to drive its stock price higher, it had vastly overstated the amount of proven oil and gas reserves over which it could claim control. The courts responded by ordering Shell to pay $470 million in damages to the shareholders who had been deceived by such lies. And to solve the problem going forward? Shell drew up plans to sink more new oil wells? And sallied out into the world to compete with Petro China for more concessions? Actually, no. Far easier was to ask the Securities and Exchange Commission, then run by the arch "deregulator" Christopher Cox, to loosen those reporting rules to make it easier for Shell to fudge again in the future, which is what it did in February 2008.[49]

In other words, as Russia used diplomacy and force to gain control of natural gas deposits in other countries, solely to increase its own political power vis-à-vis the European Union; and as China's authoritarian regime used American money and American trading companies and America's Bretton Woods institutions and America's military to lock in the oil supplies it will need to ensure its ability to displace the United States atop our own imperial mechanism; and as the Bush administration wreaked havoc across Mesopotamia in a disastrous and anachronistic attempt to ensure American control of oil in the Middle East, the corporations we have licensed to gather and refine the oil we need—erstwhile public utilities, erstwhile arms of our state—focused instead only on manufacturing cash for financiers.[50] Which they did with phenomenal success, setting a profit record in 2007 and promptly beating that record in 2008.

More impressive yet, these erstwhile public utilities did so even as they worked with speculator operations like Goldman Sachs to transform our "markets" into the very seat of their cartel, where for years now they have set prices in ways that enrich the few who control them, even though those same prices resulted, for long periods of time, in the shifting of immense power abroad, to our most cynical and hard sworn of rivals.

The people of the United States have a right to be enraged, but not with the Chinese or the Russians.[51] These regimes are merely filling the power vacuum created when the Clinton administration—in the act of embracing a mythical global market system—unilaterally disarmed our nation, by eliminating our ability to direct financial and industrial power against other nations, or even to use such powers to protect our most vital interests, the most important of which was precisely a liberal international system. If anything, the Chinese and the Russians are merely doing exactly what we in the United States should be doing, which is to fend off the predations of financiers who will smash states as recklessly as they smash productive enterprises.

But let's be completely honest with ourselves about the nature of these two societies. China and Russia may use the same tactics that we used until so recently, across the same webs of finance and industrial activity, and toward seemingly similar ends. China may even envision replacing us one day soon as the new hegemon at the center of a new world system.

Yet neither society has any recent tradition of a cosmopolitan decentralized empire. And given that both societies have proven unable to distribute power at home, there's no reason to expect them to do so internationally now. So let's not hold our breath waiting for any Munificent Maoism or Kompassionate Komissarism to resurrect the balances of our old world system or impose some twenty-first century Open Door policy designed to prevent our America from being carved into a mosaic of monopolies ruled from abroad.

As long as we do not defend our own political economic interests, all on our own, these two regimes will simply join the other peoples of the world in using our own institutions to carve out their particular pieces of America and Europe—until, that is, the hounds we so carefully locked away in our American Peace break loose once more.

8

Wreckonomics 101

A surreal painting still hangs in the entryway to Motorola's old headquarters in Phoenix, and sprinklers still chatter over trim lawns and spatter the trunks of palm and orange trees. But outside the concrete and tinted-glass building the fountains no longer splash, the three aluminum flagpoles are bare, and where a sculpture once stood remains only a concrete base.

As I poke at an intercom box, a smiling security guard rolls up in a striped compact car, pleased someone has intruded into her midmorning quiet, eager to tell me what she knows, which is mainly that the For Sale sign out front attracts few potential buyers. The day is clear and crisp, and sprays of red and white ocotillo flowers bounce in the breeze. Behind the guard, a parking lot built to hold a couple hundred cars stretches to a white perimeter wall. A perfect place to spin donut after donut after donut.

Instead I wheel south on Galvin Parkway to continue my tour of closed Motorola facilities. My next stop is an industrial building on South Diablo where the Motorola sign is covered with a fresh white canvas cloth that reads Emerson Network Power. Then I wind through Arizona State University's lushly landscaped Research Park, where the buildings once occupied by Motorola Labs and Motorola University now house a training center for a financial services firm.

Some miles farther south, in Chandler, I pull up next to Motorola's old semiconductor plant at the intersection of Price and Queen Creek roads, where I watch a dust devil twist and hop through the brush behind the building. Then I speed north to the "Hayden Campus" in Scottsdale. This was Motorola's first big facility in the area, an almost elegant building with hints of mid-century Vegas. The name on this sign? General Dynamics. By now I am exhausted, even though I bypassed many other sites—like the buildings that once housed the Semiconductor Components Group, the Semiconductor Products Sector, and Motorola's Iridium satellite phone system.

Less than a decade ago, Motorola was the biggest private employer in Arizona, with more than twenty thousand workers. The company was also the star of a classic mid-century American high-tech industrial development story. Founded in Chicago by Paul Galvin in 1928, Motorola carved a comfortable niche manufacturing radios for roadsters. Then, just before World War II, a Motorola scientist invented the world's first handheld walkie-talkie, and the company became a major supplier of gear and ideas to the U.S. military.

When the U.S. government began to plan for potential atomic war in the late 1940s, Motorola was one of the firms pressured to move its researchers and workers safely outside the range of Soviet bombers. A Motorola scientist who liked to vacation among the saguaro chose Phoenix, and companies such as GE and Sperry Rand soon followed. As local universities staffed their math and science departments, the Phoenix area became one of the country's most important centers for the electronics, space, and defense industries.[1]

The speed of Motorola's collapse was stunning. By 2007, the company's Arizona payroll was down to fifteen hundred, and Wal-Mart had long since replaced Motorola as the state's top employer.[2] Yet for the nation as a whole, the issue is not merely the loss of good jobs. Nor is it all the commercial real estate and ranch homes dumped on a depressed market. The issue, once again, is how we protect the systems, sciences, and industrial arts on which our lives depend—or rather, how we don't. Until a few years ago, Motorola was also one of world's most advanced manufacturers of many of the basic elements of our modern life, including semiconductors, satellites, lighting systems, failure-proof computers, airborne radars, and mobile phones, as well as a developer of advanced manufacturing and management techniques like Six Sigma. Many of these activities were sold off or transferred to other firms, but many were lost. Understanding why and how these vital activities were disrupted—sometimes destroyed—is crucial to our well-being, even our survival.

One factor we can largely rule out is "globalization." Motorola was one of the first U.S. manufacturers to establish plants in China. In much the same way that the Truman administration forced Paul Galvin to diversify from Chicago into Arizona, the Reagan administration twisted the arm of Galvin's son and successor, Robert, to "encourage" him to invest in China. This time, the strategic reason was to head off similar investments by Japanese or European concerns.

Motorola cooperated, and, in typical fashion, the firm's investment in the city of Tianjin proved to be one of the first highly successful foreign ventures in China.[3] For our purposes, this means that Motorola was long insulated from any sudden assault by another company with access to cheaper labor. To the extent that foreign competition did play a role in weakening Motorola, it came not from China but from mercantilist states like Taiwan and South Korea, where trade protections and generous state subsidies enabled Motorola competitors like the Taiwan Semiconductor Manufacturing Company (TSMC) and Samsung to undersell Motorola semiconductors and mobile phones.

What shattered Motorola was domestic competition. But this was not "horizontal" competition with firms that make the same or similar products. Rather, it was two forms of "vertical" competition. The first was with the companies that retailed Motorola's mobile phones, once one of the main sources of profit at the company. Until the latest round of consolidation among mobile providers, Motorola still had a lot of control over the pricing of its products. Not any more—today Motorola may manufacture the phones, but in the United States it is AT&T and Verizon that decide which phones to sell and what to charge subscribers; hence, they also decide how much profit, if any, Motorola will earn.[4]

The other form of vertical competition was even more devastating. This was competition between Motorola's scientists, engineers, skilled workers, and professional managers on one side of the corporation (and, of course, the citizens who depend on their work), and financiers armed with concentrated capital on the other. It is this competition that I want to discuss in this chapter.

A generation ago, many vertically integrated corporations functioned as communities of sorts, with everyone sharing more or less fairly in the work and the profits. If a company put out a better product and won a bigger share of sales, everyone could expect some portion of the winnings. If the members of the team delivered shoddy products or services, everyone took a hit.

Competition among members of the team did not vanish, of course. The industrial history of the mid-twentieth-century United States is replete with great battles between workers and managers for the exact same slice of the profit pie. Nevertheless, there was also a far greater sense of interdependence among the interest groups within the enterprise than is usually the case today. So it was for many decades at Motorola, where long-serving "Motorolans" were said to be "Galvinized," which meant they were guaranteed lifetime employment.[5]

As we have seen, the financiers began to take apart the vertical integration model that dominated industry in the United States almost as soon as the Chicago School operators in the Reagan administration eliminated the basic laws we had long used to regulate competition in the U.S. economy. As the financiers extended the horizontal reach of these corporations and cut loose their vertical operations, competition between the interest groups within the "classic" corporation grew much more extreme.

When companies like GM began to spin off certain production activities in the 1980s, a key goal was to weaken unions and drive down wages. Although the managers often said that such changes were necessary to compete with Japanese manufacturers, in actuality much of the cash that was saved went straight to the financiers. In this breaking up of the old industrial community, Jack Welch of GE was again one of the pioneers. In the early 1980s, he earned the nickname Neutron Jack for eliminating workers while leaving the buildings intact. He did so not to plow money into R&D but to fill the coffers of GE shareholders. The trouble is that when the managers at one firm take such an approach, investors expect the managers at other firms to do so as well. Thus, eventually, the pressure began to grow on Motorola's managers to follow Welch's lead.

One of the best ways to make sense of the shattering and shuttering of Motorola is precisely by considering the company's recent history in relation to GE. Both were long-established conglomerates that combined consumer lines of business with defense work, and both dominated certain technologies and products. But whereas Welch chose to keep his shareholders happy, even when it meant cutting into his treasured R&D, the Galvin family refused time and again to do so, preferring instead to try to empower Motorola's scientists and engineers to invent their way to profits. GE's industrial capabilities have, overall, declined in the years since Reagan took office, in some cases precipitously. Yet Welch and his successor, Jeffrey Immelt, managed—until 2008—to protect most of the firm's core business lines and capabilities.

The Galvins, in contrast, dramatically built up Motorola's capabilities on the strength of years of smart investments. Then, when a single round of R&D disappointed, they found themselves unable to recover their equilibrium, which left the Wall Street jackals free to tear their firm to pieces.

The turning point came in the mid-1990s. Motorola had become one of the hottest manufacturers in the world. It had beaten back a Japanese invasion on pagers, was rolling out an advanced line of cell phones, and was winning kudos for its Six Sigma business management system. It was also pouring big money into new ideas; in 1993 it invested $224 million more in R&D than the much larger GE did. For a while the strategy worked wonders and Motorola reaped the rewards. From 1992 to 1994, the price of a share of Motorola stock rose by 62 percent, 77 percent, and 26 percent. The price of GE stock, meanwhile, rose only 15 percent and 23 percent, then fell 2.7 percent. Motorola also added tens of thousands of jobs while GE continued to trim.

Then in 1995, GE's focus on cutting costs and grooming duopolies and monopolies began to pay off. Welch had by now beaten his R&D budget down to seventeenth place among big U.S. firms, yet GE now shot to the top position as the most profitable big company in the world. Thus it was GE's shares that soared, by 41 percent. Motorola, which missed its profit target by a hair, saw its shares drop 2 percent.[6]

To make matters worse, Motorola now found itself competing for funds with three newer business models, which were far more stripped down than even the Welch model at GE. The first was the pure trading company model, under which firms like Dell and Tyco would largely forgo R&D and simply repackage and resell foreign-made products and components. The second was the "innovation through acquisition" model, now raised to a high art by the Internet equipment monopolist Cisco. The third was the "Hydra" model, which spread swiftly through the electronics industry and resulted in the rise of highly concentrated and specialized powers—like the semiconductor foundry-services firm TSMC—that were able to price their wares below those of integrated and complex operations like Motorola.

By 1998, Motorola was feeling real pain. When a financial crisis in Asia hit sales hard, the Galvins finally began to retreat. Over the next five years they fired 60,000 of the company's 150,000 workers and spun off a whole semiconductor division. Once again, however, the company—whose reins had now been passed to Robert Galvin's son, Christopher—refused to share as much of this cash as the financiers demanded. Instead, the managers redoubled investment in new ideas and products, outpacing GE by more than $1 billion per year.

Christopher Galvin was not around to collect any winnings when this investment resulted in a final fit of engineering brilliance: the sleek RAZR flip phone. Long before that model hit stores, the financiers had engineered a putsch against Galvin, whom they faulted for being too "gentlemanly" and "academic." They also ordered the surviving managers to spin off another semiconductor business (which has since been picked apart by vultures). Yet even without a Galvin in the CEO position, Motorola's old spirit flared up one last time. When the RAZR proved to be a smash success and enabled Motorola to amass a huge stash of cash, Galvin's successor, Ed Zander, did not hand this money over to the financiers, as instructed. Instead, he set it aside to, as *BusinessWeek* put it, "remake the company into a master of innovation." By January 2007, Motorola's total cash on hand hit $11.3 billion.[7]

And so early in 2007, a man named Carl Icahn entered the scene to deliver the coup de grace to what was arguably the last classic R&D-focused conglomerate in the United States.

Icahn gained wide notoriety in the 1980s as a "corporate raider" after he grabbed and smashed Trans World Airlines (TWA). In recent years, Icahn's targets have included Time Warner, Yahoo!, MedImmune, and even Marvel Comics. Icahn's basic modus operandi is to buy up shares of stock until he owns a small percentage of the total outstanding, then use this position as a perch from which to demand a payoff. In the case of Motorola, Icahn slowly accumulated 6.4 percent of the company's shares. Then one day he ordered Zander to spend the entire $11.3 billion in cash to "buy back" shares from other investors. This would drive up the price of Icahn's holdings, which he could then sell at a big profit. The resulting battle lasted nearly a year. As is usually the case, Icahn got what he wanted, which was to have Zander fired, two buddies named to the board, and what was left of Motorola broken in two.[8]

And what did the American citizen get from all this? One of the last remnants of our twentieth-century industrial system—a corporate system that we designed and funded to protect and develop the technologies, skills, and systems on which we depend—smashed for quick cash.

In previous chapters we have seen how, in the half century after the Civil War, men used the institution of the corporation to enclose in their fences the people who actually make and invent the products and services on which we depend. We also saw how politicians outside the corporation and engineers inside it learned to use law and "management systems" to neutralize the power of the individual capitalist and slowly transform the giant industrial corporation into a semisocialized institution of immense economic value that did not threaten any political balances in our republic.

The story of Motorola illustrates how radically our attitudes have changed. In the 1980s, after the election of Ronald Reagan brought the Chicago School operators to power, men like Carl Icahn suddenly found themselves free to break up airlines at will, and men like Ronald Perelman found themselves free to use Michael Milken's "junk bonds" to grab healthy producers like Revlon and turn them into ruthless trading operations.

Yet the idea that any "barbarian"—as the new 1980s breed of financier was famously dubbed in a book about the takeover of RJR Nabisco[9]—would be allowed to grab and smash a keystone industrial firm like Motorola was still unthinkable. Just as no speculator would be allowed to seize the cash in the coffers of such corporations as, say, the city of Boston or Stanford University, no speculator was allowed to assault any vital U.S. industrial firm. To this day, such attacks remain unheard of in Japan, Germany, France, and South Korea.[10]

And yet in early 2007, when Icahn revealed that he was targeting Motorola, hardly anyone in the United States stood up to defend this industrial corporation to which we had entrusted so many vital activities and in which we had invested so many tax dollars. On the contrary, most "business" reporters on our newspapers and magazines applauded the assault and near destruction of this institution (and many of the skills, technologies, and techniques held within it) just as they applauded when Icahn brought his power to bear on Yahoo!. The final destruction of this once great industrial system was viewed as a healthy culling of a weak and sickly company. No matter how brutal, they said, the process was necessary to generate *real* wealth for the American people, in the form of cash.

There are many reasons today to believe that something is seriously awry with U.S. corporate capitalism, or even with capitalism per se. After the Meltdown of 2008 came close to burning up the whole world financial system and gutted such titans as Citibank and AIG, even the most conservative newspapers were filled with articles wondering, as the *Washington Post* did, if this was "the end of American capitalism."[11]

The story of Motorola illustrates that even if we manage to devise better ways to regulate our financial systems, our market systems, and our trade systems, we still will not have reached the core of the matter. Nor will we get there even after we begin once again to enforce our classic antimonopoly laws, and outlaw outright the sort of plain day plundering practiced by Carl Icahn and such copycat vandals as Daniel Loeb and Warren Lichtenstein.

As we have seen throughout this book, from Menu Foods to Luxottica to Macy's to General Motors and Toyota, the pressure from financiers to increase profits has resulted in an ever swifter monopolization (and socialization) of the industrial systems on which we depend. Even when we are down to a single source of supply, the financiers keep stripping. We have also seen that this pressure derives not from some genetic flaw in the organic makeup of these firms but from the *legal structure* of American capitalism itself. The American model of capitalism—of corporate monopolies supposedly "owned" by financiers who direct all their power to maximizing the production only of cash—builds vandalism right into the system.

Merely Money

In this chapter I want to complete our look at how capital interlinks, through the institution of the corporation, to the real world in which we live, in order to understand why nowadays we smash so many of the machines and technologies and systems we need to live. To do this I will focus on two main issues: how the rich reappropriated the institution of the corporation after we took it away from them in the early twentieth century, and how regarding the rich as the "owners" of these institutions lies at the heart of our present crisis.

Along the way we will see that the single biggest problem with the physical stability of our industrial and financial systems is that we have seated almost complete control over these institutions, and hence the real properties held within them, in a class of people whose interests are served not by building things but by breaking things. We will also see

how traditional American democratic republicanism, by distributing ownership and responsibility over real properties, is not merely politically safer
but also *physically* safer than our present approach of concentrating control in absentee "owners." Indeed, we will see how democratic republicanism is the only approach that enables us to protect and maintain over the
long term the complex systems on which our modern society depends.

Let's start by clearing away a few myths about American "capitalism."
There are many, and both by intent and happenstance they hinder any
coherent discussion of who really owns our industrial corporations.

The easiest way to do so is to turn to the economist Joseph Schumpeter's musings on the subject. As you'll recall from chapter 6,
Schumpeter's views on the link between monopoly and innovation deeply
influenced a whole generation of U.S. economists, judges, and policy
makers. This occurred even though any close study of the *actual* history of innovation reveals Schumpeter's theory to be profoundly flawed.
Much the same is true of Schumpeter's take on capitalism. His theories in his book *Capitalism, Socialism, and Democracy* have profoundly
shaped our thinking about the underlying forces at work in our political economy. And in their own way, these ideas are equally mistaken.
Consider, for instance, the marvelously concise passage from that 1942
work that contains what is today probably the single best-known attempt
to describe American "capitalism":

> The opening up of new markets, foreign or domestic, and the
> organizational development from the craft shop and factory to
> such concerns as U.S. Steel illustrates the same process of indus-
> trial mutation—if I may use the biological term—that incessantly
> revolutionizes the economic structure *from within*, inces-
> santly destroying the old one, incessantly creating a new one.
> This process of creative destruction is the essential fact of capi-
> talism. It is what capitalism consists [of] and what every capitalist
> concern has got to live in. [Emphasis in the original.][12]

Schumpeter is a powerful, evocative writer, and the phrase *creative
destruction* is a brilliant coinage. Yet the problem with this description of
capitalism is obvious as soon as we focus on his central metaphor, which
is that industrial activity is a *biological* process that takes place in a *natural environment* of markets. However innocuous such language seems on

its face, it contains an immensely important political message, which is that whatever we see in our political economy is what must be. Although Schumpeter elsewhere makes clear that he believes people can gain some understanding of how economies work by studying economic phenomena, his language here and elsewhere implies that we cannot alter the workings of the main gears.

This is essentially the same language the so-called Social Darwinists (that is, those who subscribed to Herbert Spencer's theory of the "survival of the fittest") used during the late nineteenth and early twentieth centuries—with devastating, vicious effect—to describe competition among individuals and among nations. The Social Darwinists used this language of evolutionary biology for a conscious political end, which was to justify existing class structures, social relationships, and international orders as natural, necessary, inevitable, and unalterable.

On the surface, it may seem odd that such a framework to describe economic relations within society would ever gain much traction in the United States. In a democratic political system, after all, a fundamental assumption is that human beings enjoy complete free will and that it matters what choices we make using that will. In any serious discussion of political economics, Schumpeter's analysis in the above passage is about as applicable to day-to-day debate as a lyric about a daffodil.

It is by no means clear that Schumpeter personally intended for us to read his work this way. Nevertheless, the fact that it *can* be read this way helps to explain why Schumpeter is so popular with the Chicago School operators, who, as we know, do very much intend for us to understand political economics in just this way. Here, after all, is language that obscures the use by rich people of institutions like Wal-Mart and the so-called market for West Texas Intermediate to shift power from us to them, just as it obscures the fact that U.S. Steel did not grow like a mushroom on the shore of Lake Michigan but was forged by J. P. Morgan, who used two immensely powerful human institutions, the corporation and the bank, to advance his ends. Indeed, here is language that transforms the trading company, the commodity market, the industrial corporation, and the bank from man-made political tools into the most basic and unquestionable elements of life.

So if Schumpeter's biological metaphor is of use only to obscure—through pseudo-scientific mystification—the use of power by people against people, then what is capital-*ism*? To answer that we must first remind ourselves of a few basics.

Capital, we all know, is merely money. And money, in and of itself—be it a chunk of gold, a dollar bill, or some numbers on our bank statement—has no intrinsic value. It is a measure of political power that has been stored for later use, in the form of an enforceable right to exchange these chits for a premeasured amount of real properties and real services. We use money to make life easier. Money means that when we want a pair of shoes, we don't have to go to town lugging a bag of wheat to exchange. Money also means that we don't have to decide right now what we want in exchange for our wheat. If our neighbors want to buy our wheat today, we sell them our wheat today, then decide tomorrow what exactly we want in exchange, be it from them or from another member of society. In and of itself, money is neutral and impersonal, neither creative nor destructive.

In other words, nothing mysterious here.

Now let's look at *concentration* of capital. Individuals combine capital into a common pool in order to use the power thus concentrated to accomplish works beyond the capacity of any one individual, such as building a road or raising an army. Such pools of capital are a basic function and tool of society, and they have been so for millennia. Such pools of capital are also, in and of themselves, politically neutral in nature. In societies in which a few people monopolize political power, those same people also tend to monopolize the ultimate control of the power inherent in such concentrations of capital and use that power to serve their own interests. In societies in which power is more widely distributed, control over these concentrations of capital also tends to be distributed. So, too, are the benefits of using such power.

Private control of capital dates back at least to biblical times. In the modern Atlantic world, however, it was citizens of republics and constitutional monarchies like the Netherlands, Britain, and the United States who in recent centuries have generally enjoyed the most freedom to concentrate and control private pools of capital. Indeed, in these societies, the right to pool and control capital outside the control of the state is generally viewed as a vital check on the power of the state. This is also why citizens in these societies generally developed more complex and powerful private banking enterprises than did their neighbors.

Again, nothing mysterious here.

Karl Marx, in a statement once far more famous than any of Schumpeter's, wrote in *Capital* that "one capitalist always kills many."[13] For a while in the late nineteenth century in the United States, it seemed as if such financiers as J. P. Morgan were in a race to prove Marx right; they used concentrated capital to grab legal hold of corporations, which they then used to concentrate economic activity with shocking swiftness. Yet Americans also proved that for long periods, we were able to effectively use our laws to prevent a few among us from concentrating capital and control over our corporations. The most important such period was before the Civil War. And we proved that we can use our laws to redistribute such powers even once they have been concentrated, as we did during the New Deal era, when we democratized access to, and control over, the power in capital.

Again, nothing mysterious.

Capital-*ism* is, then, at the most basic level, the set of legal arrangements that govern how individual private citizens can combine the vast but neutral power that is contained in a pool of capital with the political power that is inherent in the institutions of the corporation, the bank, and the market. Capitalism's only "nature" is that it reflects the laws in force at any given moment. A people can devise and enforce their laws in ways that enable them to harness the power in concentrated capital to the task of enabling free citizens to build great things. Or a people can allow some group in their midst to devise and enforce laws that enable that group to use the power in concentrated capital to harness free citizens.[14]

The Wall Street Commune

In earlier chapters, we looked at the politics of how the rich use our corporations to enclose our markets and seize our property. We also looked at how the *dynamics* unleashed by their rule lead to the ruin of many of the physical properties held in the corporations they control. What we have not looked at is *why* men like Carl Icahn so blithely destroy the real properties under their control. After all, shouldn't such "capitalists" strive to save and protect the properties they claim to "own"?

Our next task, therefore, is to understand more clearly how capital interlinks with the real world in today's United States. To do so, we must clear away any lingering myths that the business corporation is itself a property rather than a political institution designed to govern people and properties. And we must also clarify our understanding of the relationship between the American business corporation and the various forms of personal private property under its power. To begin, we must remember what personal private property is and what purpose it serves in society as a whole. This should not be hard. Almost all of us have an inborn sense of why personal private property is of value, both to ourselves and to our community.

The basic idea is, of course, that people do not destroy lands or buildings or machines from which they benefit and over which they enjoy control. Instead, they try to improve the properties that they "own," or at least, protect them. There's nothing fancy about this. We see the physical benefits of personal private property in our lives every day, in the difference between how we care for a house or car we own and one we merely rent. We see it, in the inverse, in the degradation of many of the commons over which no one person or nation exercises control, such as the air and oceans.

Ownership means seeing, touching, knowing, caring, protecting.

That is why so many societies choose to divide certain common social activities—such as farming and manufacturing—into portions under the control and care of individuals.

That's also why we can trace personal private property systems back to the first complex agricultural societies thousands of years ago. Common practice then was to disperse land holdings so that every family ended up with a variety of small patches of land of differing fertility and exposures, spread across river bottoms, hillsides, hilltops, and forests.[15] In such a system, the individual benefited from the freedom to decide what is grown or created on his or her parcels, how much work to invest, how to organize the work, and how much profit to take. Society benefits from the wealth created and traded, the generation of new ideas, the competition among the many, and the scattering of political power that might otherwise be concentrated. Society also benefits from the division and clear allocation of responsibility over vital social activities and from the compartmentalization and localization of laziness, incompetence, and loss in the event of hail, fire, flood, or invasion.[16]

Private-property systems, in other words, harmonize the virtues and vices of the individual with the interests of the group as a whole in ways that result in the protection of the properties themselves. Or put another way, private-property systems interlink the political organization of a society with its physical organization through the process of harmonizing personal interest with personal responsibility.

In all societies, the challenge is to strike a political balance between the people who control the institutions authorized to use concentrated capital and the people who control and protect personal private properties. The goal is to enable society to enjoy the benefits of such concentration of power while also protecting itself from the physically and politically destructive nature of such power when wielded by avaricious, absent, or entirely disintegrated governors.

This challenge is not new. The book of Genesis, for instance, instructs us of the need to centralize planning and to socialize certain properties. Joseph convinced Pharaoh to order Egypt's farmers to gather much of their grain during the seven years of plenty into a common pile to ensure that there would be enough grain to feed Egypt during the seven years of famine. And Genesis also instructs us of the *political* dangers that such concentration and socialization can pose to the holders of personal private properties. When the grain was returned to Egypt's farmers, Joseph exacted money, livestock, and land, thereby transforming the farmers from independent property holders into Pharaoh's serfs.

In modern complex societies, the challenge of striking the right balance is no less pressing, yet it is often far more complicated. A society that yields too much control to too many individual holders of private property may lack the common infrastructures necessary to survive. In contrast, a society that centralizes too much control and socializes too many systems may unleash a temporary burst of energy, as the radical socialization of structural risk in industry and finance did in the United States in the late 1980s and the late 1990s. Yet, such a society does so at the risk of locking itself into sclerotic and brittle structures that are potentially subject to cascading collapse and from which all real owners and hence all warning voices have been stripped.

In the early United States, it was relatively easy to strike a balance between concentrated power and individual private property. In that less technologically complex world, there was simply less evident need or ability to concentrate power or centralize control. Another reason is that we had erected and jealously protected a political economic structure that enabled us to guard our own properties from predation by the rich. Indeed, we reserved private corporate governance of economic activities for specific challenges and generally held a tight rein on those governments. As a result, in the early United States, the average industrial enterprise was very small compared to post–Civil War conglomerations. And it was controlled generally by a single true "owner," who combined on-the-ground knowledge of what took place in the operation with a legally reinforced sense of responsibility for the properties within the enterprise.

After the Civil War, however, it became much harder to strike the right balance of power between concentrated power and individual properties. This was due to two main factors. First, as we saw in chapter 4, financiers managed to appropriate the institution of the corporation for their private use by breaking free of control by state legislatures. Second, these financiers managed to "improve" the institution of the corporation by making it much more like a bank; the introduction of limited liability laws for all intents allowed capitalists to deposit money in these enterprises without incurring any responsibility for the actions of the enterprise vis-à-vis real properties either outside or inside the boundaries of the corporation.[17]

One result, as we have seen, was that business corporations swiftly grew vastly bigger. In many cases, financiers used such corporations to monopolize control over entire industrial activities in a process designed to *socialize* their economic risks. The other key result was that the concept of the individual "owner" was, for all intents, *shattered*. The enterprises grew so big that not even the richest of individuals controlled sufficient personal capital to make any traditional claim of control.

To the extent that such an enterprise was "owned," title over the great quantities of real properties held within these industrial estates resided increasingly with ever more distant and ever more amorphous *syndicates* or *unions* of capitalists.[18]

The practical result of this *double socialization* of the U.S. business corporation was that no one within these systems was legally charged anymore with the responsibility of protecting the real properties in the enterprise in the manner we expect from a real owner. Which meant the power concentrated in these systems posed, at least in theory, an immense threat to the skills, technologies, systems, and people within the reach of that power. It was a case of appetite without restraint.

To complete our understanding of the physical danger of ceding all control over the industrial corporation to the absentee financier let's turn to one last remarkable passage in Schumpeter. Here he finally abandons his complex metaphors and focuses on the key flaw in any system that centralizes control over any socialized industrial activity in a commune of capitalists:

> The capitalist process, by substituting a mere parcel of shares for the walls of and machines in a factory, takes the life out of the

idea of property. It loosens the grip that once was so strong—
the grip in the sense of the legal right and the actual ability to
do as one pleases with one's own; the grip also in the sense that
the holder of the title loses the will to fight, economically, physically, politically, for "his" factory and his control over it, to die if
necessary on its steps. . . . Dematerialized, defunctionalized, and
absentee ownership does not impress and call forth moral allegiance as the vital forms of property did. Eventually there will be
nobody left who really cares to stand for it—nobody within and
nobody without the precincts of the big concerns. [Emphasis in
the original.][19]

Let's make sure we understand exactly what Schumpeter is saying
here. Even though he points his finger at the traditional bogeyman of
the elite—the mob—Schumpeter's anger is actually directed not at the
greasy-mitted masses but at the finely manicured money men. What is
preparing the ground for the revolution that Schumpeter fears is imminent is not the subversive teachings of the members of the Socialist
Party, but rather the dynamics of *corporate capitalism* itself. The very
economic destruction we fear resulting from mob worker rule is at bottom
no different from the destruction *already* being wreaked by mob investor
rule. Capitalism is not merely paving the way for socialism, Schumpeter
says. Modern capitalism—due to its inherently socialistic nature—has
already resulted in the greatest danger we fear of socialism, which is the
destruction of the social protections over real property provided by a traditional private-property system.[20]

There's no one home to put out any fire. No one around even to
smell the smoke.

To Have and to Hold

So if the American model of corporate capitalism is doubly socialistic in
nature, and if the capitalist cannot serve as a real owner and hence protec-
tor of the real properties held within the corporation, then why did we not
see a wholesale crushing of real properties long ago? Why did the capitalists not wield their power in ways that collapsed entire production systems
fifty years or a century ago? Why do we see such destruction only now?

The simple answer is that by the time Schumpeter published those lines, in 1942, the American people had already done much to solve the "crisis" of ownership posed by the socialistic nature of corporate capitalism.[21] In this section I want to look at the two-stage, generation-long effort to limit the power of the capitalist over the real properties held within the industrial corporation. The effort centered precisely on establishing *other forms of ownership*, both outside and inside the corporation. James Madison wrote that the system of checks and balances within a political system requires us to recognize and distribute competing "interests" within our government. That is exactly what we did with these industrial governments.

The very first attempt to deflect the power of the capitalist from the properties held within the industrial corporation was undertaken, as we saw earlier, in the late nineteenth century by the industrial engineer. The engineers did so in the very process of weaving "management systems" designed in part to restrict the whims of the man in control, or rather, the appetites of the "commune" in control. In the process, the engineers essentially claimed for themselves a de facto stake in the enterprise as a new and distinct class of owner.[22] Yet although this act helped to protect the properties held within the corporation from concentrated mindless power, the overall tendency during these years in the American political economy as a whole was toward ever greater centralization of power and hence an ever greater threat that the real properties inside our corporations would eventually be crushed.

The first conscious political effort to establish other new forms of ownership within the industrial enterprise was launched by the progressive elites a century ago. Whereas democratic republicans like William Jennings Bryan advocated breaking down Morgan's monopolies into parts that could truly be *owned* by a single entrepreneur—to return, so to speak, to the political economic status quo antebellum—the progressives scorned such ideas as dangerously anachronistic, especially for technologically advanced heavy industry. They agreed that men like J. P. Morgan could not exercise effective ownership over these real properties, but they tended to object to any attempts to break the monopolized industrial enterprises of those years into smaller parts.

Instead, they advocated shifting the power to direct these enterprises from private hands to public hands. Or more bluntly, they advocated formalization of the de facto socialization of these activities already accomplished by the capitalists. As Walter Lippmann put it in 1914, "The cultural basis of property [has been] radically altered, however much the law may lag behind in recognizing the change. So if the stockholders think they are the owners . . . they are colossally mistaken. Whatever the law may be, the people have no such notion. And the men who are connected with these essential properties cannot escape the fact that they are expected to act increasingly as public officials."[23]

The progressives clearly did not imagine themselves as engineering *ownership* over the industrial corporation in any of the usual senses in which we understand the word. Yet the actions of the progressives can in fact be viewed as creating new classes of owners with clear interests in protecting certain properties within these enterprises.

The first such "owner" institutionalized by the progressives was the nation-state itself, or, more specifically, the national defense bureaucracy. Theodore Roosevelt started the process. Roosevelt imagined himself to be a "statesman" who was gifted with sufficient vision to rule over America's industrial enterprises in a way that would ensure that these firms produced the weapons and the wealth necessary to secure the United States in a world marked by ever more dangerous international industrial rivalry.

The problem, of course, is that statesmen come and go. This is why progressives during and immediately after World War I acted to institutionalize this interest within the executive branch as a whole. The result was that bureaucrats began to act much more freely to reorder industrial activity to ensure particular outcomes. One of the more dramatic instances took place in 1919, when Assistant Secretary of the Navy Franklin Roosevelt unified the radio businesses of GE, Westinghouse, and Marconi America into the "private" company RCA.[24]

The second new "owner" created by progressives was the "professional" manager. This was a sort of close cousin of the industrial engineer who applied, as Lippmann put it, the "new science of administration" to the business organization itself, as the engineer did to the assembly line. This was an era, as we saw, when an entire middle management of efficiency engineers, timekeepers, auditors, bookkeepers, inspectors, and production planners was built into these industrial governments to professionalize their operations. Although the main goal of the progressives was to increase the "efficiency" of production and distribution, one of the main practical results was to create another group within the corporation with an interest in protecting the properties and the peoples under the rule of these governments from the evermore ravenous appetites of the evermore abstracted capitalist.[25]

The second stage of the process of creating new classes of owners within the industrial enterprise took place during the early years of the New Deal era. The next owner to be installed in the corporation was the worker. By the early twentieth century, the combination of corporate enclosure, mechanization, and mass importation of foreign labor had reduced the American laborer—celebrated in the age of Andrew Jackson as a prosperous and independent citizen—to an inchoate mass of largely deskilled men and women. Here again, much of the initial effort was undertaken by the progressives, many of whom viewed the labor union as a key counterweight to the power of the industrial lords. As Lippmann put it, the goal of unionization was to make the worker "powerful enough to be respected."[26]

The actual freeing of American workers to form labor unions took place in 1935, in the form of the Wagner Act. The act did not give American labor a literal seat on the company board, as happened in postwar Germany, but it did give workers a very real say in how the work was done, how the profit was distributed, even whether an enterprise might be sold and to whom. In other words, the act transformed the worker from an employee to a true part owner of the industrial enterprise.[27]

The last actor to be transformed into a partial owner of the industrial corporation was the small investor. The story here traces to when Congress passed the Securities and Exchange Act of 1934. This legislation, along with the Securities Act of 1933, was designed to reduce outright fraud in the sale of stocks, and it initially treated the small investor as a consumer of financial products. The goal was to guarantee the basic quality and safety of the equities and other products, in the same way that other laws aimed to guarantee the quality and safety of our food and drugs.

What expanded the rights of the small investor to include an actual stake in the ownership of the industrial enterprise was a patch of vague wording in the 1934 act, which declared that "fair *corporate suffrage* is an important *right* that should attach to every equity security bought on a public exchange." It took a few years for the Securities and Exchange Commission to sketch out exactly what such "corporate suffrage" might entail. The eventual conclusion was that the act gave small investors a right to introduce "shareholder resolutions" at the annual meetings of corporations. It gave small investors, in other words, a right to make their views heard in a routine predictable way, in public.[28]

It might seem that the interest of the small investor and the big capitalist are one and the same: both want a bigger share of the profits. However, there's a big difference between the two. Unlike the grand capitalist and financier, the small investor lacks power, in the form of an ability to bring great concentrations of capital to bear in a strategic fashion, or to manufacture debt.

This means that the interest of the small investor is actually often the exact opposite of that of the big capitalist and financier. Whereas the financier tends to seek opportunities to use artificially magnified power to make a quick killing, the small investor tends to want merely a fair fee for use of his or her real capital and a reasonable assurance that the fee will be paid in a predictable fashion. This in turn means that small investors tend to have a more long-term view of the welfare of a particular enterprise—and the properties held within it—than the big capitalist and financier.[29]

On the surface, granting the small investor a right to speak does not seem especially revolutionary. Yet in the late 1940s, it became clear that this change was, in its own way, as radical as the Wagner Act had been. The first inkling of what had been unleashed took place in 1948 when social activists Bayard Rustin and James Peck each purchased one share of stock in Greyhound Lines, and thereby purchased the right to attend the annual meeting of Greyhound and push for the integration of bus service in the South.

The idea that ownership of a single share of stock entitled a citizen to a say not merely in how a corporation distributes its profits or manages its operations but also in how its operations affect society at large served to confirm the public nature of the American corporation. For all intents, it ratified the status of the publicly traded business corporation as a form of public government, not all that different from a town government. And soon enough, the American people began to use this power to push for all sorts of social change, ranging from divestment from apartheid-era South Africa and Pinochet-era Chile to the improvement of labor standards in sweatshops from Honduras to China to Bangladesh.[30]

Thus, the American people during the New Deal era largely—though certainly not entirely—tamed the immense power of the monopolized industrial corporation that had been unleashed into our political economy by J. P. Morgan and the other neofeudal financiers and then manipulated for a time by the socialistic-minded progressives. We did so by greatly restricting where and how the giant corporation could be used, effectively protecting the properties of the independent farmer and shopkeeper from predation. We did so also by forcing the industrial enterprise to compete with other giant firms, to prevent a corporatist blurring of public and private government.

Finally, we did so by recognizing five classes of actors other than the capitalist as owners of the industrial corporation, with de facto rights to use the corporation to serve their interests. Our conscious goal in doing so was to combine an interest in the properties held in the corporation with a responsibility to protect those properties. The goal was political: to contribute to the rebuilding of a democratic republic of small owners. The goal was also physical: to establish classes of citizens who would serve society as our eyes and ears and hands within the giant industrial enterprises, charged with protecting the machines and skills and technologies on which we all rely.

Louis Brandeis described this last goal especially well at the time of the Pujo Commission hearings in 1913, on the concentration of power on Wall Street:[31]

> While organization has made it possible for the individual man to accomplish infinitely more than he could before, still there is a limit to what that one man can know well; for judgment must be exercised, and in order that judgment may be exercised wisely, it must be exercised on facts and on a comprehension of the significance of the relevant facts. . . . When, therefore, you increase your business to a very great extent, and the multitude of problems increase with its growth, you will find, in the first place, that the man at the head has a diminishing knowledge of the facts and, in the second place, a diminishing opportunity of exercising a careful judgment upon them.[32]

Or as Brandeis put it in a book years later: "Banker-management contravenes the fundamental laws of human limitations: First, that no man can serve two masters, second, that a man cannot at the same time do many things well."[33]

Ownership meant seeing, touching, knowing, caring, protecting. And thinking.[34]

Cerberus Unchained

In 1970, Milton Friedman published a three-thousand-word essay titled "The Social Responsibility of Business Is to Increase Its Profits" in the *New York Times* Sunday magazine. Like most of Friedman's other writings, this was less an argument than a series of assertions, adorned here and there with bloody chunks of meat, such as that his opponents are hawking "pure and unadulterated socialism." Friedman makes his main point in the fourth paragraph, where he declares:

> In a free-enterprise, private-property system, a corporate executive is an employee of the owners of the business. He has direct responsibility to his employers. That responsibility is to conduct the business in accordance with their desires, which generally will be to make as much money as possible.[35]

This is a marvelously economical statement. In three short sentences Friedman transforms the industrial corporation from a doubly socialized destroyer of private property—hence, an institution that must be used sparingly and with great care—into a private property itself. And he alters the ultimate purpose of the industrial corporation from the provision of vital goods and services to the manufacture of cash. And he ignores two centuries of debate about who "owns" the American corporation (and, indeed, how to define ownership itself) and instead substitutes a statement that contradicts both law and custom but which would prove to be of immense political value to his friends among the grand financiers.

In the coming revolution that would sweep all the old individual owners from inside the corporation and return all control over these immensely powerful institutions to the financiers, this was the single most important assertion of right.

Taken in its entirety, however, Friedman's essay on ownership marks one of the few instances when his bubbling fountain of sophistry ran dry. That's because he failed to notice that the activists who were using stock ownership to promote "social responsibility" in businesses—be it to integrate Greyhound buses or to sell off investments in South Africa—had created a language that could be exploited in much the same way that Robert Bork would later employ the word *consumer* to jujitsu Ralph

Nader and the consumer-protection movement. Friedman's confusion is on display when he attacks the "newer phenomenon" of using ownership of stock to pressure managers to "exercise social responsibility" yet fails to harmonize this statement with his basic argument that managers must always serve only the interest of shareholders.

There was one man, however, who did spot the opportunity to co-opt the language of the small investor activist movement unleashed during the New Deal era: Carl Icahn. In late 1979, *Forbes* published a profile of Icahn, who had already developed a reputation as "one of Wall Street's shrewdest risk arbitrageurs." The focus of the piece, however, was on Icahn's profitable use of "a relic of the past—the proxy fight." Icahn, the reporter wrote, was "bringing a new dimension to the old-time" tactic. Rather than seek control of the firms he targeted—in this case, a Chicago real estate investment trust and the electric-appliance maker Tappan—Icahn wanted to "force their sale to outsiders at a big profit." Other investors were experimenting with similar tactics, the reporter noted. But Icahn was the true pioneer, a "one-man trend." It is the quote at the very end of the profile that illustrates just how far in front of the pack Icahn was running. "Management likes to call us raiders," he told the reporter. "But the proxy fight is corporate democracy in action."[36]

The battles that enabled the American financier to retake complete control over the industrial corporation were fought on many fronts. Here I want to look at how the various ownership stakes in the industrial corporation that had been created over the previous century were cancelled out or neutralized. Then I will briefly expand our understanding of how financiers actually function as "owners" of our most vital institutions. Or rather, don't.

The first owner to come under assault by the neofeudalist elite was, to no one's surprise, the unionized worker. The Reagan administration launched a head-on assault on labor as soon as it took power. The result, buttressed by the actions of every president through George W. Bush, was to greatly weaken U.S. unions, especially in our industrial enterprises.

The next target was the national defense bureaucracy, which for a period during the Cold War was the single most powerful "owner" within the industrial enterprise. This coup was accomplished with remarkable swiftness beginning in 1993, when the Clinton administration decided to outsource the management of industrial activity to the trading company, the control of which was promptly captured by foreign mercantilist powers.

(Clinton-era "globalization" also resulted in an important secondary effect; namely, the further weakening of the industrial unions.)

The industrial engineer, meanwhile, who had been the first to carve out an ownership stake in the industrial enterprise, was now taken out of the equation obliquely. The transformation of our industrial corporations into trading companies dedicated to the selling of foreign-made goods simply rendered the industrial engineer superfluous.

Of all the efforts to centralize control of the big industrial corporation in the hands of the financier, perhaps the most brilliant was the Pavlovian rewiring of the CEO to view himself as a "capitalist." This process began in a piecemeal way in the 1980s, as some of the early leveraged buyouts relied on alliances between the financier with managers inside the enterprise. The quantum leap took place under President Clinton. Soon after taking office, his administration placed a $1 million limit on what portion of the CEOs' pay could be deducted from taxes while at the same time making it easier to compensate CEOs with stock "options."

The publicly stated goal of this policy was to clamp down on sky-high salaries. The real goal, as the Chicago School operator Michael Jensen put it in the 1976 essay that served as a battle plan for this front of the revolution, was to establish "incentive compensation systems which serve to identify the manager's interests more closely with those of outside equity holders."[37] Or, in other words, to make sure that the CEO stopped thinking like a "steward" dedicated to the long-term health of the organization under his control and the people in it and more like "financier number one" and run the firm to manufacture cash.[38]

The most cynical act in the capitalists' return to power was the capture of the small shareholder as an ally. This was not hard. After all, the natural corollary of Icahn's co-optation of the language of the small-investor movement was co-optation of the small investors themselves. This was made easier by the *seeming* commonality of interest between the big investor and small investor. It was made easier yet by the fact that for much of the late 1980s and the late 1990s, the financiers did in fact stuff a good deal of cash into the portfolios of the small investors, which is always a good way to win friends. Of all these dispossessions and co-optations, however, this was the one that had the greatest *overall* effect on our society as a whole, which is why it's worth taking a few moments to look at the effects of this alliance in detail. Three especially stand out.

First, this "alliance" between the grand financier and the small investor provided the financiers with a huge public-relations victory. As Icahn appreciated better than any of his contemporaries, to walk arm in arm with the small shareholder enabled the vandal to present himself not as a gore-bespattered despoiler, but as a servant of the little people, even a sort of "democrat" and "reformer." When Icahn shattered TWA, he was vilified for destroying an institution that provided the American people with an important service and with good jobs. By the time he took down Motorola, a far more important institution, two decades later, he was hailed for making us all just a little bit richer.

Second, the "alliance" between the great financier and the small shareholder laid the political and economic foundation of the system that provided the financier with one of his most important sources of working capital over the last generation, at least within our domestic political economy. The central idea here was that Americans should invest their retirement savings in the stock market rather than investing them in bonds or placing them in a savings account in a bank.

Before Reagan, the great majority of Americans relied on Social Security, pensions, and savings for their retirement. Very few ventured into the stock market, because it was a treacherous place. The new model called for the American people to turn their money over to investment "professionals"—especially fund managers. These "professionals" would use their special smarts (for a fee) to invest our money for us, in order to make us a higher return than we could achieve on our own. One way the fund managers would make these higher returns was by exercising power over the corporate managers in ways that no one investor ever could, precisely because the fund managers spoke in the name of thousands or even millions of little investors. Thus, thanks to the alliance, we the American people began to plow more and more of our savings into the stock market or, rather, into the hands of investment bankers and fund runners, who promptly turned the power in *our* capital to grab and smash our *real* properties in order to gather cash and hence power for themselves.

Third, the "alliance" between the great financier and the small investor was formalized at the very moment that the small investor ceased, for all intents, to be able to serve society anymore as an effective "owner." We have already seen how limited liability severed the traditional responsibility of ownership and shattered the person of the owner into tiny pieces. Yet back when small-investor "gadflies" buzzed around the annual meetings of corporations, they often kept their money in the same enterprise for many years and paid minute attention to operations. This class of owner had less of a hands-on understanding than the managers or the workers in the enterprise did, but their place outside the corporation often enabled them to provide a valuable perspective.

What changed this often intimate relationship between the small shareholder and the corporation was the invention of mutual index funds in the mid-1970s. These funds exploded in popularity, and for good reason. For the small investor, the mutual index fund took much of the risk out of investing, both by combining the interest of any one small investor with other small holders, and by enabling the small holder to spread his or her "ownership" across many companies, and in some cases just about all companies. In other words, the mutual index funds socialized the small investors' ownership stake by broadening it to the point of destroying any sense of common interest between the average small investor and any one particular company.

As a result, even as American citizens were urged to view ourselves more and more as a sort of new class of miniature capitalist—or, as President Bush liked to put it, "an ownership society"—the real power shifted away from us to the fund managers and the financiers, who supposedly did our bidding but who instead used our gold to forge the fetters with which to bind us.[39]

So the entire system of distributed and oppositional ownership over the American industrial corporation—developed over the course of a century—was undone in less than a generation. Power was concentrated once more in the capitalist alone, who is the one actor whose interests—once he or she has used a corporation to consolidate control over some market or other—is served not by protecting and improving the properties thereby captured but rather by reducing the number of workers in the system and their skills, by cutting the number of machines in the system and failing to maintain the old, and by stripping out the various forms of wealth built into the system, be it in the form of salaries and pensions, funds for research and development, or safety and redundancy.

And that of course is assuming there's even such a thing as a human capitalist with recognizable interests. In fact, as has been evident for more than a century, the image of the individual capitalist as owner is in most instances a fiction. Control over these properties is shared among

an immensely powerful class that has largely communalized all its holdings and thus escaped all the legal strictures that tie individual owners to
real property. Even when that power is concentrated momentarily in the
body of a real person, like Carl Icahn, the interest remains only to maximize capital and hence power, even if this means tossing another factory
or two full of perfectly necessary machines on the scrap heap.[40]

So let's complete our accounting of what the financiers, armed with
their Chicago School philosophy, achieved with our industrial enterprises. First they killed off three of the key defenders of this citadel:
the worker, the engineer, and the state. Then they corrupted a fourth
defender, the CEO, by rolling a gilded Trojan horse pay package through
the gate. Then they transformed a fifth owner, the small investor, into
a sort of Charley McCarthey doll, mouthing ventriloquated platitudes
about "shareholder" value. Last they anointed a fictional person—in the
form of the "capitalist"—to serve as the human face for their collectiv-
ized and increasingly mechanized predations.

But let's raise one last glass to our financiers. Because they sure did
show us a fine time these last few years, racing through our streets armed
with torches pulled from the great common horde of fire. They even
demonstrated that special American knack for invention, as they turned
the job of arson over to software robots. Homo Farber himself would
surely appreciate the method and skill they displayed in this automation
of conflagration. Or he would have, anyway, if he wasn't strapped to the
pyre. It was a wonderful, hilarious dream, wasn't it? A waltz at the end of
the world, cash raining down on us like cinders.[41]

Control without ownership; power without responsibility; appetite
without mind. Our industrial treasures smashed. Our ability to create
destroyed.

9

To Keep Our Republic

More than two centuries ago, Americans began to cut a broad field out of the wilderness of power that was European feudalism. In the sunlight, out of the reach of all works and webs of man, a new human consciousness flourished. For the first time in the modern world, a people made itself free to govern itself, and to serve one another from positions of strength and not dependency. For the first time, a people made itself free to build, free to create, free to think.

This did not simply happen, nor has it always been true since the beginning of our nation. From the first, Americans were presented with two visions of how to organize our new republic. The first, which we associate with Alexander Hamilton, imagined a society along the lines of the Roman Republic or a constitutional monarchy like England. Maybe one in a 1,000 citizens would be truly independent, of one another as well as of any arbitrary king, made so by the fact that the other 999 labored for them and depended from them. The other vision, which we associate with James Madison and Thomas Jefferson, was of a truly *democratic* republic. All citizens would be independent of one another. All would be secure in their right to hold and work their personal properties, defined most importantly as their skills and labor. All would enjoy the liberty to interact with their fellow citizens in open markets.

We tell ourselves that America was settled by refugees from religious persecution, and political persecution, and economic persecution, and this is true. But our nation was also settled by people who intended to enrich and empower themselves by penning their fellow humans in agricultural and industrial estates. And so even after the Revolution, Americans who wanted to build a democratic republic were forced repeatedly to fight. We fought politically in 1800 against the aristocratic vision of Hamilton, in a process that culminated in the election of Jefferson as president. We fought with arms in the 1860s, in a great war to destroy the slave-owning oligarchy in the South. We fought politically in the decades up to 1920, to win for women the right to vote. We fought with arms again in the twentieth century, to destroy great nation-state incorporations of enslaving power. And we fought politically and in the streets in the 1950s and 1960s, to abolish Jim Crow and other efforts to divide us along racial lines.

The one battle that never ended was at home, against our own would-be economic lords, who repeatedly took advantage of the freedom we won for all to concentrate power sufficient to monopolize that freedom for themselves alone. Often they simply seized what they wanted. Their main tools were two forms of government—the business corporation and the bank. Other times they made us promises. They would deliver us a little more material wealth if we would but cede them a little more political control over our lives.

For most of our history, confident in our ability to provide for ourselves, we resisted their power and resisted their lies. But twice our would-be lords succeeded in capturing the commanding heights. They did so immediately after the Civil War, and they managed to hold that power until the early years of the New Deal. Then a generation ago they did so again. Franklin Roosevelt long ago warned that men flying the banner of "liberty" would seek to "regiment" the majority of Americans "into the service of the privileged few."[1] And so it came to pass.

Under the banners of "free" market and "free" trade and "freedom" from "government regulation" these self-appointed lords seized monopolies, such as our utilities, which we had long regulated for our own good, and transformed them into private taxation systems. And they seized our great industrial enterprises and transformed them into trading companies designed to export our machines and jobs and to import—in place of the products we once made ourselves—shoddy and often dangerous substitutes. And they enclosed with their private corporations the open fields where we farmed and the factory floors where we combined our industrial skills with one another. And they enclosed the open markets where we kept our shops and restaurants and the open streets where we erected our community banks, law offices, doctors' offices, and newspapers.

And so a people who had freely exchanged goods, foods, and ideas with one another were transformed from independent *producers* into captive *consumers*. And we were brought under the direction of great governing systems wherein all decisions about what to sow and grow, what technologies to use and how to use them, and whose property to inflate and whose to crush were made by distant and evermore distracted lords and increasingly by automated and mindless systems geared only toward the manufacture of cash.

And in time the new ways were revealed, which were but the old ways rewrapped in sterilized packaging. Get down, on your knees, and restock that bottom shelf, and I will feed you and yours, they told us. Get down, on your knees, and brush away the crumbs of my meal, and I will feed you and yours. Get down, on your knees, and beg to keep your ad agency job, or insurance agency job, or pilot or truck driver job, or assembly line or "farmer" job, and I will feed you and yours. Get down, on your knees, and snipe that Iraqi bastard, to protect China's oil, so Chinese citizens can make what you used to make, and I will feed you and yours.

But take care. When you are down on your knees, don't dare to sow the wrong seeds, because my friends at Monsanto own that monopoly. And don't dare breed the wrong pigs or chickens, because those monopolies belong to my friends at Smithfield and Tyson. And don't dare to erect a five-and-dime, because Bill Clinton awarded that monopoly to his friends the Waltons in Arkansas. And don't dare to erect a grocery, or garage, or doctor's office, or computer business, or software business, or tool & die shop, or optician shop, because some group of my friends in New York or London or Dubai or Beijing owns that monopoly.

And so we are driven from our communities, and from the security of our properties and skills. Driven to labor and serve not whom we choose but who commands. Driven by massed power wielded by other human beings from our Empire of Light. Reduced to *hoping* the Wall Street–White House Patriciate will deign loan us back a few of those trillions of dollars they vacuumed out of our pockets to make themselves whole.

After in their own besottedness they deranged the one system—finance—we assumed they might know how to operate. After in their own besottedness they deranged even the imperial system that protected their own privilege, and who are themselves now reduced to kowtowing before new lords in those super monopolies headquartered in Moscow and Beijing.

Manufacturing Destruction

For the first time in many years, energetic and well-intentioned public servants work in the antitrust division of the Justice Department, the Commodities Futures Trading Commission, the Securities and Exchange Commission, and the Federal Deposit Insurance Corporation, as well as within various offices of the Federal Reserve and Treasury Department. By the time you read these words, they may have pushed through many seemingly important reforms. Congress may even have established a new consumer financial protection agency. The Obama administration may even have launched a few high-profile antitrust cases. Regulators may even have driven speculators partly out of our markets for oil and wheat.

Yet it is vitally important to be absolutely honest with ourselves. When it comes to the two most fundamental political economic questions in America—whether to allow the few to concentrate power further or to distribute power and opportunity more equitably among the many; and whether to restructure our financial and industrial systems to prevent cascading crashes—nothing has changed.

If there was any hope that the Obama administration or Congress intended to challenge the rule of the financiers, it vanished in July 2009. That was when Goldman Sachs announced a record quarterly profit and a plan to pay its employees a phenomenal $11.4 billion for the year. This was, of course, mere months after taxpayers had to bail out Goldman Sachs and the rest of the banking system.

And if there had been any hope that our "representatives" in Washington would reengineer any of these vital systems to make them more stable, by the summer of 2009 that hope also had been quashed. Reduce the size of our banks and foster more competition? Reimpose walls between the banks and the speculators? Restore complete transparency and stability in our markets for energy and grains? Abolish the credit default swaps and other instruments the financiers use to socialize their risks? Prevent the financiers from wrecking the industrial corporations where we store our most important skills and technologies? Protect the properties of the small entrepreneur and farmer from the predations of distant and absent money men?

Time and again the answer was a resounding no.

Not that the president and Congress did not act tough once in a while. When the financial firm CIT, which provides highly specialized services to nearly a million small and medium-size firms, veered toward bankruptcy in July 2009, the administration at last found the gumption to slam shut the lid to the treasure chest. And when America's workers came to Washington to collect on promises to lower—just ever so slightly—the barriers to unionizing giant corporations like Wal-Mart, the president and Congress somehow found the courage to deny their petition.

Less than a year after the financiers nearly unleashed an economic cataclysm on the world, the only right that *our* government recognized is the right of the financier to use *our* corporations and *our* banks and *our* money to rule *our* political economy and hence *our* communities and *our* families as they alone see fit.

After I completed the first draft of *Cornered*, a few of my early readers urged me to cut the first section of this chapter. The problem was not that they disagreed with my overall analysis. On the contrary, most thought it vital that the people who run our banks, hedge funds, and corporations face up fast to how their actions degrade and destabilize so many of our most important industrial and financial systems. What these readers feared was that any questioning of the motives, let alone privileges, of the American financier would lead these new rulers to turn their back on the fantastic and fast-growing dangers I detail.

I left the passage in for two reasons. First, I believe it now to be an incontrovertible fact that the people who control our financial systems and market systems—and through them the real economy of our nation— have already made absolutely clear they will not abide any fundamental changes in how these systems are regulated, unless compelled to do so. It does not matter whether members of this elite ever come to understand how their actions may be setting the stage for a catastrophic crash of basic industrial systems. They have already demonstrated a stunning ability to disregard the structural flaws and fragilities of the financial system itself. The avarice of these individuals trumps any concern that their actions might endanger their own children, let alone the well being of the nation and the world.

The other reason I left the passage in place is that I no longer believe we can fix the physical flaws in our financial and industrial systems without first resolving the basic flaws in our political economy. It was the overthrow of the political balances that unleashed these vandals. The only way we can stop them from grabbing and smashing our most vital systems is to reverse that revolution and restore the traditional balances. This requires steeling ourselves for a long and brutal fight. This requires that we know the nature of the predators we face.

I have thrown a lot of information at you throughout this book, much of which is profoundly distressing. We have seen how concentrating the power to rule our real economy in the hands of a few absentee lords has resulted in the destruction of one of the most important forms of wealth in our society—the resiliency and flexibility of the industrial and financial systems on which we depend.

We have seen how this concentration of power has resulted in the degradation of the safety and quality of many of our most important products and a decline in variety and real competition in almost every sector of our real economy.

We have seen how this concentration was achieved politically, through the imposition of a feudalistic philosophy of political economics. And we have seen how this concentration was achieved practically, through the imposition of the institution of the trading company and all-directing retailer and the perversion of our open markets.

We have seen how this consolidation of power has resulted in a massive loss of personal liberty, be it to bring the fruits of our farms to open markets, to run a small business safe from predation, to have potential employers actually compete for our work, or to cast a vote that cannot be nullified by an oligarchy that rose to power not through our political system but by seizing control over the fundamental institutions of our political economy.

Yet I hope I also convinced you that we still have the power to retake control of our political economy. The revelation and honest appraisal of the crisis itself, and of the systemic dangers posed by monopolization, was our first step. Knowledge that the Meltdown of the fall of 2008 was a warning of far worse to come should serve, at the very least, as a motivation for us to act.

My more fundamental aim in *Cornered* was to reconnect us to the tools we need for the coming battle. That's why I devoted so much effort to recounting our history as a democratic republican people and to reminding us of the basic principles on which we once based our political economy and the traditional language we used to describe it. It's also why I spent so much time recounting the real nature of the New Deal reforms, especially the ground-up reordering of the institutions of our political economy to once again distribute voice and power among the people.

Not that we actually need any sacred models to follow or special guides to lead the way. As we will discover, once we take our first steps, the wisdom to accomplish all of these tasks lies not in any book or in the mind of any one person or party. The wisdom we want lies in us all.

The American Brain

There is, however, an ultimate question we must consciously answer if we are to reestablish our political economy on firm foundations: to what *end* should we structure the institutions of our political economy? Or, put another way, what should we seek to maximize?

As we have seen, various groups have answered this question in very different ways. J. P. Morgan believed we should maximize production of cash. The progressives of Theodore Roosevelt's day believed we should maximize production of material wealth, and they established a cult of efficiency to help. The Chicago School operators, who devised the neo-feudal intellectual and political regimes we live in today, combined elements of the two; they seek to maximize cash *and* they worship efficiency.

During the last year of World War II, an economist named Friedrich Hayek set out a very different goal. At the time, the incredible achievements of wartime production had led many to believe that industrial activity should be centrally planned and controlled. In a 1945 essay, Hayek assailed the idea that planning in society could ever be centralized, effectively and safely, over the long run, by government, either public or private. "There is something fundamentally wrong," he wrote, "with an approach which habitually disregards an essential part of the phenomena with which we have to deal: the unavoidable imperfection of man's knowledge and the consequent need for a process by which knowledge is constantly communicated and acquired."[2]

The overarching goal in designing a political economy, Hayek believed, is not to produce cash or greater piles of goods. Nor should efficiency be celebrated as means to any end. The "economic problem of society" he wrote, "is mainly one of rapid adaptation to changes in the particular circumstances of time and place." The overarching goal, therefore, was to structure society as a whole *to be able to* change as circumstances change.

In other words, the designers of a political economy should aim to devise institutions that enable people to *gather* and *process* and *transmit* useful information to one another and through society itself, and to keep these institutions small enough and diverse enough to react swiftly to that useful information. Rather than attempt to locate thinking in some central planning authority, public or private, reason and the liberty to use it should be located as much as possible at the bottom, in the individuals who run the local machine shop, the local store, the local farm, the local bank.

"The ultimate decisions," Hayek emphasized, "must be left to the people who are familiar with those circumstances, who know directly of the relevant changes and of the resources immediately available to meet them."[3]

Today, in a time of ever more rapid change in our natural and human environments, Hayek's vision provides us with perhaps the single most eloquent and concise depiction of how to structure a political economy able to process and react to such change.

What I want to emphasize here is that Hayek's vision jibes almost perfectly with our democratic republican tradition. This is of immense importance. It means that in the very act of moving to reverse the concentration of power in our political economy and to distribute ownership and voice once again among the many, we also move toward structuring a political economy that helps us process complex and changing information and to react swiftly to new events in ways that enable us to protect our most vital industrial and financial—and natural—systems.

Democratic republics have long been recognized as less liable to sudden, revolutionary upheaval than societies in which power is concentrated among the few. We must recognize that democratic republics are adept at identifying and manipulating risk in complex systems precisely because they accustom all people to be conservative and empower all people to protect. The parceling out of ownership over real properties enables the individual—and society as a whole—to see and touch what lies in every nook and cranny of our financial, industrial, and physical worlds. And it simultaneously provides the incentive to raise an alarm and to act.

Put these two visions together and we end up with a simple rule: freedom for independent property holders to interact with one another in open markets is freedom to think and freedom to adapt to changing circumstances.

In 1623, the English scientist and philosopher Sir Francis Bacon, the originator of what came to be known as "scientific method," wrote that "all depends on keeping the eye steadily fixed on the facts of nature, and so receiving their images as they are. For God forbid that we should give out a dream of our own imagination for a pattern of the world."[4]

For most of our years in America, we followed Bacon's path. We walked out of our cloisters into the world, through our factories and markets, into the halls of power and along the ramparts of empire, to study not merely what human beings do for one another and with one another, but to one another. We studied the effect of power on our economic actions and relations, and on our ability to master the tools and techniques we need to survive and make and keep ourselves free.

In other words, we gathered and processed information and reacted to it in ways that enabled us to ensure the stability and security of our most vital industrial, financial, and political systems.

The reason we don't do so today is not merely because the financiers have seized control of these institutions. It is also because once in power they erected an intellectual regime designed to hide their use of power against us. In the process of doing so, however, they *also* blinded themselves and us to many of the most basic phenomena and most fantastic risks in our political economy.

This is not the first time this has happened in a modern society. In the Soviet Union under Stalin, Communist Party leaders perverted science in many ways, sometimes to serve consciously constructed political goals, sometimes merely by ceding too much power to some single thug or gang. One of the most destructive instances began in the late 1920s, when an apparatchik masquerading as an agronomist named Tromfin Lysenko captured control of plant-breeding programs at a time when the collectivization of Russian farms had resulted in widespread famine. Lysenko soon rose to a position in charge of all Soviet agricultural science. He then suppressed and eventually outlawed modern genetic research and purged all dissenters from the academy.[5]

In the United States today, our "Lysenkoism" is our "science" of economics. Instead of teaching people how to generate facts and process information, and think for themselves and with one another, our "science" of economics erects over us an icon of a mechanical determining god, and claims a priestly monopoly over interpreting the signs of this god. Instead of leading us to analyze the transcendent questions of political economics today—the monopolization, hence socialization, hence ruination of the *complex* industrial and financial *systems* in which all the peoples of the world depend—contemporary "scientific" economics broadcasts theories derived from theories derived from an intentional political lie.

The "science" of economics today is not merely an institutionalized form of neofeudal philosophy, nor is it merely an ideology of darkness that erects institutions to promote more darkness. It has become a form of madness, a dream of human imagination we mistake for a pattern of the world. It is a path not merely to serfdom but to death.

We do have an alternative, though. We can believe what we see with our own eyes.

To Get Regulation Right

On May 16, 1771, about two thousand small farmers, shopkeepers, and mechanics gathered near Alamance Creek in the Piedmont of North Carolina to meet an organized militia under the direct charge of the colonial governor William Tryon. In the ensuing fight, the people managed to hold their ground for a time. Soon, however, having no leadership or plan, most vanished into the woods. They left behind eighteen dead men (nine from each side), a few score wounded, and fifteen of their own captured. Tryon ordered one man executed on the spot. The colonial government later tried and executed six more.

So ended the "War of the Regulation," as the series of protests up to the showdown at Alamance was known. Although it took place when colonial citizens throughout America were rising against the Stamp Act, this "war" was less a struggle between a coastal merchant class and a distant parliament than a struggle between small property holders and what they viewed as a rapacious elite. Enraged by how tax money was collected and spent—especially galling was Governor Tryon's own new £15,000 mansion—the North Carolinians set out, in their own words, to "regulate abuses of power." The goal was not to take anything from the rich, but to stop the rich from taking so much from them.

A far bigger battle came soon. Although many regulators accepted Tryon's offer of amnesty, hundreds retreated across the Blue Ridge Mountains into the Watauga Valley, in what is now East Tennessee, where they established a democratic government. Some have claimed that the Watauga Association was North America's first independent republic. In the years before the Revolution, however, the settlers recognized the authority of the Cherokee Nation, from whom they leased the land.

The best view of the association's place in the America of those years is through a 1774 letter from the governor of Virginia to Britain's foreign secretary. The settlers, the governor wrote, had "contented themselves with becoming in a manner tributary to the Indians, and have appointed magistrates, and framed laws for their present occasions, and to all intents and purposes, have erected themselves into, though an inconsiderable, yet a separate State; the consequence of which may prove hereafter detrimental to the peace and security of the other colonies; it at least sets a *dangerous example* to the people of America, of forming governments distinct from and independent of his majesty's authority." (Emphasis in the original.)[6]

Watauga very swiftly became much more than this. Within a few years the valley was a base for attacks on British power, including the famous march to Kings Mountain, where a free American militia routed a British army in one of the key turning points in the Revolutionary War. And soon this association of free citizens became a "dangerous example" of independence not merely from British power but from all incorporations of power in the new Republic itself, other than that based directly on the people's own authority.

It was to Watauga that similar "regulator" movements in Massachusetts and Pennsylvania looked at the close of the eighteenth century. It was in East Tennessee that Andrew Jackson first worked as a young lawyer before moving on to battle the British Army and America's homegrown monopolists. It was through the Watauga Valley that the Lincoln family passed on their way to Kentucky and Illinois and Gettysburg.[7] It was Watauga and much of East Tennessee that broke from the South during the Civil War and fought with the Union. It was in Elizabethton, on the banks of Watauga, where American citizens first organized labor unions in the South.

Today we face one of the gravest crises in our history, and I do not mean the recession. Indeed, by the time you read this, our economy may well be perched atop the film of yet another grand and fast inflating bubble. I speak instead of the political and economic effects of monopolization. And I speak of the fragility, due to monopolization, of all the systems on which we rely.

The first thing we must do is to rearm ourselves, with our own language. We must recover our understanding of our institutions and the real intent of our laws. Then we must listen very closely to the words the patricians speak and beware.

They will preach their *free-market fundamentalism* and insist that we dare not interfere in the workings of this magical mechanism. Then they will use their corporations to enclose our *open markets*, and they will use their rigged commodities "markets" to derange and sack our carefully engineered industrial systems.

They will preach their *capitalism* and insist that their corporations and banks are private property. Then they will use these *social* institutions to direct the power in this *communalized* capital in ways that enable them to seize our own real private properties.

They will preach their *libertarianism* and demonstrate through their attacks on our public government that they love freedom as much as we do. Yet the freedom they envision is for themselves alone, to use their private corporate governments—and sometimes our public governments—to rule us and ruin us.

They will preach their *globalism* and insist that we dare not interfere in the "free" flow of inter-nation "trade," lest we unleash war. Then they will use their trading companies to crush American producers in order to chain us to authoritarian regimes abroad, in ways that increase the likelihood of conflict.

They will preach their *intellectualism* and insist that they alone— because they are "the best and the brightest"—understand the mysteries of capital, the mysteries of markets, the mysteries of trade, and the mysterious science of economics. Then they will jet off to mountain mansions and meadows as the systems they deranged collapse at our feet.

And they will, as they have since 1773, preach their *consumerism* and promise us yet more cheap tea for our liberty.

When we finally rise to put an end to their predations, *our regulation* must be simple and sure. Complex bureaucratic regulation is what the rich do to one another and to us. Our regulation must follow the broad-ax tradition, which means that we must use our powers to split and split again the institutions they use to magnify their power.

We have numbers, history, right, and common sense. We have faith and a deep wisdom that derives of experiences that stretch far back beyond when we first began to stitch America together. We remember—every

American remembers—that we have wandered always in our world, across Africa and the Ganges Plain, down the Yangtze and up the Sierra Madre, across the North Atlantic and along the Gulf of Persia and around Sinai. And we know that our lot will always be to wander, that we shall never in this life set foot in Canaan or any other promised land.

Now, more than ever, as our natural and human worlds change so swiftly, we must wander more carefully and consciously. To do so, we merely want freedom to think and to devise what is right for our place, to build and rebuild only what fits. We do not know where we are going. What we do know is how to keep going. And that is to use our power—our common sovereignty—to ensure no one stands in our way.

Notes

Preface
1. George Will, "Socialism? It's Already Here," *Washington Post*, Nov. 16, 2008.
2. Simon Johnson, "The Quiet Coup," *The Atlantic*, May 2009.
3. John Kay, "The Bigger They Come the Harder We Fall," *Financial Times*, Sept. 17, 2008.
4. Phil Longman and T. A. Frank, "Too Small to Fail," *Washington Monthly*, Nov.–Dec. 2008.
5. William Heisel, "Big Pharma Bulks Up with Merck Schering Deal," *Los Angeles Times*, Mar. 10, 2009.
6. Carrie Johnson, "Wall Street, Washington Huddle on U.S. Markets," *Washington Post*, Mar. 14, 2007.
7. Alan R. Mulally, testimony, Senate Banking Committee, Nov. 18, 2008.
8. Milton Friedman, *Capitalism and Freedom* (Chicago: Univ. of Chicago Press), 1962, p. 120.

1. The Hidden Monopolies Everywhere
1. One 615-clinic interstate veterinary chain reported that cases of kidney failure spiked 30 percent during the three months that contaminated food was on the shelves. "Vets Say Kidney Failure Up in Cats," Associated Press, Apr. 10, 2007.
2. Andrew Bridges, "Pet Food Maker Announces Huge Recall Amid Reports of Pet Deaths," Associated Press, Mar. 16, 2007; Charlie Gillis and Anne Kingston, "The Great Pet Food Scandal," *MacLean's*, Apr. 30, 2007.
3. "Mystery Solved?" ABC News transcript, Mar. 23, 2007; Mark Johnson, "Rat Poison in Tainted Pet Food Blamed for Deaths of Dogs and Cats," Associated Press, Mar. 24, 2007.
4. Amanda Gardner, "Researchers Identify Contaminant in Tainted Heparin," *HealthDay News*, Apr. 23, 2008.
5. Colin Campbell, "After Last Spring's Pet Food Scandal, Canada's Menu Foods Fights for Its Life," *MacLean's*, Sept. 3, 2007; Ellen Byron, "101 Brand Names, 1 Manufacturer," *Wall Street Journal*, May 9, 2007.
6. Menu Foods, www.menufoods.com.
7. Just at PetSmart, the recall covered 305 separate products. "PetSmart Still Recovering from Pet Food Recall," Reuters, Sept. 6, 2007.
8. American Veterinary Medical Association (AVMA) recall list, as of Aug. 22, 2007.
9. Before the recall, Menu's share of the total revenues in the pet food market was relatively small, at about $350 million per year out of the total sold of $4.5 billion. One problem is that the complexity of the supply relationships makes it hard to isolate the company's products. Another is that for certain types of food—including wet food in foil pouches—Menu Foods is the only private label manufacturer.
10. Byron, "101 Brand Names, 1 Manufacturer."
11. Chris Burritt, "Campbell Beats Bear Market as Consumers Seek Out Soup," *Bloomberg*, Nov. 21, 2008.
12. Nathan Skid, "Better Made's Better Idea," *Crain's Detroit Business*, Sept. 22, 2008.

13. In the early 1950s, A&P operated some four thousand grocery stores in nearly forty states. Like Wal-Mart, the retailer was famous for its innovations in discount retailing, distribution, and advertising. Unlike Wal-Mart, the firm sold only groceries, and it was merely double the size of its nearest competitor. For our purposes here, what's most important is that its total workforce was, as a percentage of the U.S. population, less than one-fifth as large as Wal-Mart's is now. Barry C. Lynn, "Breaking the Chain: The Antitrust Case against Wal-Mart," *Harper's*, July 2006.

14. Mathieu Robbins, "M&A on Pace for Record Despite Signs of Strain," Reuters, June 29, 2007.

15. Dana Cimilluca, "In Deal Dance BHP and Rio Trip over 'Shared' Partners," *Wall Street Journal*, Feb. 21, 2008.

16. Julia Werdigier, "Chinalco to Invest $19.5 billion in Rio Tinto," *New York Times*, Feb. 12, 2009; Lina Saigol and Kate Burgess, "Chinalco Walks Away from $19.5bn Rio Deal," *Financial Times*, June 5, 2009; Patti Waldmeir and Sundeep Tucker, "China Antitrust Threat Over Plan for BHP-Rio Tinto Joint Venture," *Financial Times*, June 18, 2009; "China May Block BHP-Rio Joint Venture," *Reuters*, Aug. 3, 2009.

17. Ilan Brat, "Turning Managers into Takeover Artists," *Wall Street Journal*, Apr. 6, 2007.

18. Terry Kosdrosky, "Collins & Aikman Creditors Unsure of Automaker's Plans," *Crain's Detroit Business*, Aug. 1, 2005.

19. Dan Roberts, "Our Wild East Ride Will Go Out with a Bang," *Sunday Telegraph*, May 13, 2007.

20. Laura Corb and Timothy Koller, "When to Break Up a Conglomerate: An Interview with Tyco International's CFO," *McKinsey Quarterly*, Oct. 2007.

21. The July 2007 oil rig deal was valued at $18 billion. The new controllers promptly promised their financiers that they would devote future revenue to paying off their debt rather than buying more rigs. In a similar deal, National Oilwell Varco paid $7 billion for Grant Prideco in December 2007, combining two of the top oil industry toolmakers. "Transocean, GlobalSantaFe Settle Patent Lawsuit," *EnergyCurrent*, Feb. 20, 2007; Guy Chazan and Russell Gold, "Transocean Merger Deal May Spur More Tie Ups," *Wall Street Journal*, July 24, 2007.

22. Between 2003 and 2008 the price of uranium shot up by more than 1,000 percent. The Swiss trader Glencore routinely controls 50 to 90 percent of the aluminum that is delivered to warehouses listed in the London Metal Exchange. Its sometimes partner, the Swiss mining giant Xstrata, quintupled the price of vanadium in less than two years by closing two mines. Ann Davis, "Commodity King," *Wall Street Journal*, July 31, 2007.

23. Consider just a few more market share figures:

Appliances. Whirlpool's takeover of Maytag in 2006 gave it control of 50 to 80 percent of U.S. sales of washing machines, dryers, and dishwashers and a very strong position in refrigerators. It also gave the firm control of such brands as Jenn-Air, Amana, Magic Chef, Admiral, and KitchenAid and a dominant position over the Sears Kenmore Brand. Stephen Pearlstein, "Arguments for Whirlpool-Maytag Just Don't Wash," *Washington Post*, Feb. 22, 2006.

Athletic Shoes. Nike imports up to 86 percent of certain shoe types in the United States—for basketball, for instance—and more than half of many others. Worldwide Nike controls almost two-fifths of the sports shoe business, a number that has grown since its two main rivals, Adidas and Reebok, merged in 2005. Thomas Heath, "In Sales Nike Is a Shoe In," *Washington Post*, Nov. 24, 2006.

Internet Search Engines. As of March 2009, Google had captured 64 percent of all online searches in the United States, according to the most conservative of tracking systems, run by comScore (other tracking systems put the figure well above 80 percent). Yahoo! came in second, with 20 percent. In Europe, as of March 2008, comScore put Google's share of the market at 79 percent, with the number two company, eBay, hitting only 3 percent. comScore (Reston, Virginia) press releases, Apr. 15, 2009, and May 7, 2008.

Semiconductors. TSMC and UMC have together captured 60 percent of the world's demand for semiconductor foundry service—in which a company serves as a sort of printing press for chips that are designed and sold by other firms—and have concentrated that business mainly in one industrial city in Taiwan. This understates the total; investment patterns show these firms will soon have far greater control. They also know how to use their power to gain more market share. As one industry publication wrote in late 2007, the "foundries are getting ready to put the squeeze on the semiconductor industry, just as the semiconductor industry decides to depend more and more on the foundries." David Manners, "Foundries Get Ready to Squeeze the Semiconductor Industry," *Electronics Weekly*, Nov. 27, 2007; Kevin Chen, "TSMC Wins Intel Award," *Taipei Times*, Mar. 29, 2007.

LCD Glass. Although Asian firms dominate the manufacture of liquid crystal display (LCD) screens, the American firm Corning has captured a whopping 60 percent share of the business of supplying the glass itself. Peter Marsh, "LCD Televisions Help Turn Corning into a Big Screen Star," June 11, 2007.

Bottles and Bottle Caps. In June 2007, Owens Illinois sold its plastics business to Rexam, giving the British firm a dominant position over the international supply of bottle caps and pharmaceutical bottles. The deal allowed Owens Illinois to concentrate more on grooming its own near monopoly over the supply of glass containers in North and South America, Europe, China, and Australia. In all, OI sells more than one in every two bottles in the world. Nick Hasell, "Plastic Not Fantastic in the Case of Rexam's Owens-Illinois Deal," *The Times of London*, June 12, 2007; "Rexam to Buy Owens Illinois Plastics," Reuters, June 11, 2007.

Electronic Components. The trading firms that dominate our electronics industries have allowed individual firms in Japan, Korea, Taiwan, and China to control more than 50 percent, and often 100 percent, of the production of items ranging from motors for computer disk drives to polarizers for LCDs to capacitors for just about every electronic device you buy. In Japan, for instance, Nidec dominates motors for computer disk drives. *Financial Times*, Apr. 21, 2003.

Credit Cards. Every time you use your credit or debit card, the bank that issued the card collects a fat fee—usually 1 percent of the total charge. Technically, this is paid by the retailer. In reality, this private sales tax is paid by you. The European Commission has moved to limit this fee. If you live in the United States, you continue to pay. "Merchants Must Submit to MasterCard's Power," *Wall Street Journal*, Jan. 10, 2008.

Professional Services. Accounting, business consulting, and law have all been restructured in recent years by waves of consolidation. Emma Schwartz, "Five Questions Law Firms Face in 2006: #1. Will Merger Mania Continue?" *Legal Times*, Jan. 6, 2006; Carrie Johnson, "Accounting for the Future: Too Few to Fail?" *Washington Post*, Mar. 9, 2007; Attila Berry, "Are Two Venerated DC Law Firms Destined for a Slow Fade? In the Era of the Megafirm, Arnold & Porter and Covington & Burling Face a Murky Future," *Legal Times*, Sept. 10, 2007.

Champagne. The French conglomerate LVMH, controlled by the billionaire Bernard Arnault, has captured 19 percent of the world market for champagne, controlling such brands as Veuve Clicquot, Moet & Chandon, and Dom Perignon. Arnault's share of the U.S. market is more than 60 percent. Christina Passariello, "LVMH Bottles Up Champagne Market," *Wall Street Journal*, Jan. 2, 2008.

24. This was the largest initial public offering in New York since 2002. Michael Flaherty and Lilla Zuill, "Blackstone Raises $4.1 Billion," Reuters, June 22, 2007.

25. David Weidner, "Blackstone IPO, Is the Smart Money Cashing Out?" *MarketWatch*, June 15, 2007.

26. Stephanie Rosenbloom, "Seeing Gold in Target's Real Estate," *New York Times*, Oct. 30, 2008.

27. Charles Francis Adams and Henry Adams, *Chapters of Erie and Other Essays* (Boston: James R. Osgood, 1871), p. 12.

28. In 2007, the British Competition Commission reported that four firms control more than 90 percent of the business of retailing food in that country.

29. David Luhnow, "The Secrets of the World's Richest Man," *Wall Street Journal*, Aug. 4, 2007.

30. James Ledbetter, "Bailing Out the Gray Lady," *Newsweek*, Jan. 21, 2009; Eduardo Porter, "Mexico's Plutocracy Thrives on Robber-Baron Concessions," *New York Times*, Aug. 27, 2007.

31. The previous three M&A frenzies took place during the mid- to late 1980s, the early to mid-1990s, and the mid-1990s to 2001.

32. One of the most dramatic examples of how this works is the Simmons Bedding Company. Between 1991 and 2009, the company was sold seven times to what the *New York Times* called a "parade" of different private equity firms. Usually, the deals were structured so that no matter how badly the firm performed, the "owners" not only did not face any risk but were able to walk away with huge piles of cash. During their time in control, these firms raised the Simmons debt from $164 million to $1.3 billion while walking away with some $750 million in "profits" and "fees." Julie Creswell, "Profits for Buyout Firms As Company Debt Soared," *New York Times*, Oct. 5, 2009.

33. Woodrow Wilson, campaign speech delivered in Lincoln, Nebraska, Oct. 5, 1912, available online at www.britannica.com/presidents.

34. Jim Cramer, transcript, CNBC, Feb, 15, 2006.

35. Lowell Bryan and Michele Zanini, "Strategy in an Era of Global Giants," *McKinsey Quarterly*, Nov. 10, 2005.

36. Richard Dobbs, Marc Goedhart, and Hannu Suonio, "Are Companies Getting Better at M&A?" *McKinsey Quarterly*, Dec. 2006.

37. Milind Lele, *Monopoly Rules: How to Find, Capture, and Control the Most Lucrative Markets in Any Business* (New York: Crown Business, 2005), p. 13.

38. Pankaj Ghemawat, "Sustainable Advantage," *Harvard Business Review* vol. 64, no. 5 (Sept.–Oct. 1986), p. 53.

39. Jeremiah McWilliams, "Smithfield's Plan to Buy Rival Spurs Complaints," *Virginian Pilot*, Sept. 23, 2006.

40. Matthew Josephson, *The Robber Barons* (New York: Harcourt, Brace & World, 1934), p. 136. After they captured control of the quarry, Gould and Tweed and company refused to deliver any other stone to builders in New York. Robert Higginson Fuller, *Jubilee Jim: The Life of Colonel James Fisk, Jr.* (New York: Macmillan, 1930), p. 293.

41. In August 2005, Adidas and Reebok used Nike's dominance as an excuse to merge their operations. Mark Landler, "Two Brands Running as a Team to Overtake Nike," *New York Times*, Aug. 4, 2005.

42. Alexei Barrionuevo, "Rising Price of Electricity Sets Off New Debate on Regulation," *New York Times*, Feb. 17, 2007.

43. "Study: Health Insurers Are Near Monopolies," Associated Press, Apr. 19, 2006.

44. Timothy Aeppel, "Seeking Perfect Prices, CEO Tears Up the Rules," *Wall Street Journal*, Mar. 27, 2007.

45. "Cramer's 'Mad Money' Recap: 10 Money-Making Mergers," June 23, 2006, available online at www.thestreet.com.

46. Specter, in an interview, said, "This is a most unusual and extreme situation." America's antitrust law, he said, "is not being enforced and people complaining to me have every right to be furious." David Vise, "Antitrust Chief Sees No Evil; Justice Allows Illegal Pricing," *Washington Post*, Aug. 13, 1982; Howard Metzenbaum and Herman Schwartz, "Merger Madness," *New York Times*, Aug. 5, 1981; Howard Metzenbaum, "Is William Baxter Anti-Antitrust?" *New York Times*, Oct. 18, 1981.

47. Pierre A. Chao, "The Structure and Dynamics of the Defense Industry," CSIS, Mar. 2, 2005; Thomas Leary, FTC commissioner, "The Essential Stability of Merger Policy in the United States," speech delivered to the U.S.-EU Antitrust Conference, Paris, Jan. 17, 2002, available online at www.ftc.gov; Robert Litan and Carl Shapiro, "Antitrust Policy during the Clinton Administration," UC Berkeley, Center for Competition Policy, Working Paper No. CPC01-22, July 2001.

48. "Menu Foods Loses $62 Million in 2007," *Canadian Press*, Feb. 14, 2007 (figures are in Canadian dollars).

49. Marcus Kabel, "Wal-Mart Posts First Profit Fall in a Decade," Associated Press, Aug. 15, 2007; Suzy Jagger, "Profit Warning by Retail Giants as Americans Feel the Squeeze," *Business Times*, Aug. 15, 2007.

50. Keith McArthur, "Total Recall: Can Menu Foods Recover?" *Globe and Mail*, Mar. 24, 2007; Gillis and Kingston, "The Great Pet Food Scandal."

51. In February 2008, a federal grand jury accused two Chinese companies and a Las Vegas firm with manufacturing and importing tainted wheat gluten. Mark Morris, "Firms, Officials Charged in Tainted Pet Food Case," *Kansas City Star*, Feb. 7, 2008.

52. Friedman, *Capitalism and Freedom*, pp. 14–15.

2. Supply and Command

1. "Luxottica Group Net Income Up YOY 22.3 Percent," *P. R. Newswire*, Jan. 30, 2003; "Eyeglass Maker Moving 800-Employee Operation to Cincinnati," *Associated Press*, Oct. 7, 2004; Donald Greenlees, "Fall of Hong Kong Firm a Shock to Investors," *International Herald Tribune*, July 7, 2005; Eric Sylvers, "Eyewear Taking the Long View," *International Herald Tribune*, Sept. 28, 2005; "Supreme Court Refuses to Hear Case on Tennessee Optometrist Law," *Associated Press*, Feb. 21, 2006; John Tagliabue, "An Italian Rivalry Born of Expertise in Glass," *New York Times*, Mar. 24, 2006; Michael Barbaro, "At LensCrafters, Selling Candor and Designer Frames," *New York Times*, Apr. 15, 2006; "Oakley's Second Quarter Earnings Per Share," *PrimeZone Media Network*, July 20, 2006; Amanda Kaiser, "Luxottica Earnings Leap 33%," *Women's Wear Daily*, July 28, 2006; Eric Sylvers, "An Eye for Growth at Luxottica," *International Herald Tribune*, July 29, 2006.

2. Chris Anderson, *The Long Tail: Why the Future of Business Is Selling Less of More* (New York: Hyperion Books, 2006), p. 168.

3. Robert Reich, *Supercapitalism: The Transformation of Business, Democracy, and Everyday Life* (New York: Alfred A. Knopf, 2007), p. 207.

4. Barry Schwartz, *The Paradox of Choice: Why More Is Less* (New York, HarperCollins, 2004).

5. Peter Reid, "An Oligopoly of Beer," *Modern Brewery Age*, Mar. 31, 2003; Nick Passmore, "Micro Beers Brew Up Big Business," *BusinessWeek*, Feb. 5, 2008.

6. South African Breweries (SAB) and Anheuser-Busch InBev often work closely together. If you buy Corona in Canada, for instance, the distribution rights are held by Molson, which was purchased by Coors in 2004, which in turn is now part of SAB. Corona itself is produced in Mexico by a company half owned by Anheuser-Busch InBev.

7. *Costco Wholesale Corporation v. Norm Maleng*, No. 06-35538, D. C. No. CV-04-00360-MJP, U.S. Court of Appeals for the Ninth Circuit.

8. The term *Gilded Age* comes from the title of a novel Mark Twain wrote with Charles Dudley Warner, published in 1873, that looks at the links between lawmakers and financiers. Mark Twain and Charles Dudley Warner, *Gilded Age: A Tale of Today* (New York: Modern Library, 2006).

9. "P&G Second Quarter Earnings," *Fair Disclosure Wire*, Jan. 27, 2006; "P&G First Quarter 07-08 Earnings Results," *Fair Disclosure Wire*, Oct. 30, 2007.

10. P&G also owns Braun, which sells electric razors, electric toothbrushes, and electric coffee makers.

11. The arrangement also results in a trading of control over certain products. In 2005, for instance, Colgate-Palmolive sold off its laundry detergent business, including Ajax and Fab, and in 2006 it sold its bleach business to Clorox. Anjali Cordeiro and Ellen Byron, "Colgate-Palmolive Posts Higher Profits," *Wall Street Journal*, Jan. 31, 2007. The suppliers actually compete for the "privilege" of being a category captain. Claudia Deutsch, "After Buying Rubbermaid, A Deluge of Sorts," *New York Times*, Mar. 20, 2004.

12. Federal Trade Commission Staff, "Report on the Workshop on Slotting Allowances and Other Marketing Practices in the Grocery Industry," Feb. 2001.

13. Lynn, "Breaking the Chain."

14. Charles Fishman, *The Wal-Mart Effect: How the World's Most Powerful Company Really Works* (New York: Penguin, 2006).

15. Rockefeller often represented his predations as acts of philanthropy in which Standard Oil was offering to take on the burdens of the targeted entrepreneurs. As he told his biographer, his message to such men was "we will utilize your ability, we will give you representation, we will unite together and build a substantial structure on the basis of cooperation." Ron Chernow, *Titan: The Life of John D. Rockefeller, Sr.* (New York: Random House, 1998), p. 145.

16. Michael Pollan, *The Omnivore's Dilemma: A Natural History of Four Meals* (New York: Penguin, 2006), p. 145.
17. One of the main reasons it is so hard to get new products into stores is that three giant companies—Coca-Cola, PepsiCo, and Cadbury Schweppes—control almost all the distribution in the United States. Andrew Martin, "Stumping for Shelf Space," *New York Times*, Feb. 20, 2008.
18. Josephson, *The Robber Barons*, p. 381.
19. In 1935, the economist John R. Hicks wrote that "the best of all monopoly profits is a quiet life." John R. Hicks, "Annual Survey of Economic Theory: The Theory of Monopoly," *Econometrica*, vol. 3, no. 1 (1935), p. 8.
20. *Dr. Miles Medical Co. v. John D. Park & Sons Co.*, 220 U.S. 373 (1911); *United States v. Colgate & Co.*, 250 U.S. 300 (1919).
21. We will discuss these laws in more detail in chapter 5. They include the Robinson-Patman Act of 1936, sometimes called the Anti–Price Discrimination or Anti–Chain Store Act, and the Miller-Tydings Fair Trade Act of 1937, which specifically overturned the *Dr. Miles* decision.
22. In 2007, the Supreme Court completed the reversal of the Dr. Miles decision in *Leegin Creative Leather Products, Inc. v. PSKS, Inc.*, 551 U.S. 877 (2007); Joseph Pereira, "Pricing Fixing Makes Comeback after Supreme Court Ruling," *Wall Street Journal*, Aug. 18, 2008.
23. David Boyd, "From 'Mom and Pop' to Wal-Mart: The Impact of the Consumer Goods Pricing Act of 1975 on the Retail Sector in the United States," *Journal of Economic Issues*, Mar. 1, 1997; "Retail Price Maintenance Policies: A Bane for Retailers, but a Boon for Consumers?" *Knowledge@Wharton*, Aug. 8, 2007.
24. Adams and Adams, *Chapters of Erie*, p. 98.
25. Anderson, *The Long Tail*, pp. 17 and 19.
26. Many physical retailers are using the Internet as an excuse to cut back on how much stock they keep on hand. As one article put it, shoppers with "tastes, or sizes, that fall outside the mainstream" are having "more trouble finding what they want in stores as retailers attempt to shift low-volume items to Internet sales." "Can't Find That Dress on the Rack?" *Knowledge@Wharton*, Nov. 1, 2006.
27. President Obama's choice to head the Federal Communications Commission, Julius Genachowski, is a strong supporter of "net neutrality," the term often used to describe common carriage as applied to the Internet. In September 2009, Genachowski proposed guidelines that would prevent the broadband and wireless networks from discriminating against any content or content provider on the Internet.
28. Consider airline seats. In recent years, we've been accustomed to paying more for our seat on the airplane than the person next to us paid, perhaps a lot more. On those occasions when we discover this fact, we have been accustomed to blame it on ourselves; we paid more because we bought our ticket later because we delayed too long deciding, or because we were in too much of a rush to shop around. However, what if we paid more for that ticket because the company from which we purchased the ticket knew we *would* pay more, because that company had gathered enough information from past purchases to know that we are always in a rush or that maybe we aren't so good with numbers? What if that company could sense that we were on a spree and it therefore knew, automatically, that it could safely raise the price it quoted to us by 10 percent or 12 percent? What if this company could—based on its ability to track what sites we visit, what music we listen to, what news we read—design a perfectly personalized advertising campaign to help steer us toward a purchase of an item to which it has attached a perfectly personalized price?

The following three examples illustrate different degrees of such manipulation and coercion of the American citizen:

Define a group. The drugstore chain Duane Reade increased revenue from the sale of baby products like diapers and pacifiers by 27 percent after its studies of buying patterns revealed that parents of newborns don't pay as much attention to price as do the parents of toddlers. Duane Reade may be taking advantage of this group of people, but unless it enjoys a physical monopoly, it is not doing so by actively coercing anyone.

Define the individual. Insurers increasingly use such tools as high-powered disaster modeling software to charge certain people with certain credit scores and certain behavioral patterns, and who live in certain houses constructed in certain years by certain builders, sharply higher rates. Or they cut them off entirely. Such tactics pervert the very concept of insurance.

Manipulate the individual while controlling all supply. A good example here is Ticketmaster. Not only does the firm control more than 90 percent of the original sales of tickets (thanks to its takeover of such one-time rivals as Ticketron), but thanks to its acquisition of the online scalping operation TicketsNow, the company now enjoys the ability to shape the aftermarket as well. The firm also enjoys the power to use its database, which has the capacity to track an individual's tastes and preferences over the last fifteen years, to amplify these powers. One way it does so is by targeting fans of a performer not with special offers but with special "auctions" of tickets, which Ticketmaster uses to ensure that the true fans pay potentially much higher prices than they would if they purchased the tickets along with the rest of the public.

We should also keep in mind what such data-empowered firms can do to a customer who dares to complain too loudly, which is increasingly to lock the customer out of their business entirely. This is true even for companies that have captured de facto monopolies. In recent years, Comcast, Netflix, Sprint, and Best Buy have used information captured in databases to punish customers that they consider too demanding.

Melissa Campanelli, "Should You Use Dynamic Pricing?" *Entrepreneur Magazine*, Oct. 2005; "The Price Is Right, but Maybe It's Not, and How Do You Know?" *Knowledge@Wharton*, Oct. 2, 2007; Peter Gosselin, "The New Deal: Insurers Learn to Pinpoint Risks, and Avoid Them," *Los Angeles Times*, Nov. 28, 2006; Ethan Smith and Sara Silver, "To Protect Its Box-Office Turf, Ticketmaster Plays Rival's Tune," *Wall Street Journal*, Sept. 12, 2006; "Ticketmaster to Buy TicketsNow in Effort to Boost Its Retail Business," Associated Press, Jan. 15, 2008; Gary McWilliams, "Retailer Aims to Outsmart Dogged Bargain Hunters," *Wall Street Journal*, Nov. 8, 2004; Amy Barrett, "When, Why, and How to Fire That Customer," *BusinessWeek Small Business*, Oct.–Nov. 2007; Loren Steffy, "Sound Off," *Houston Chronicle*, July 13, 2007; Chris Nelson, "Ticketmaster Auction Will Let Highest Bidder Set Concert Prices," *New York Times*, Sept. 1, 2003.

29. Alexis de Tocqueville, *Democracy in America*, vol. 1 (New York: Alfred A. Knopf, 1945), p. 86.

3. The Crystal House

1. Nancy Green, "Sweatshop Migrations: The Garment Industry between Home and Shop," in *The Landscape of Modernity: New York City, 1900–1940*, ed. David Ward and Olivier Zunz (Baltimore: Johns Hopkins Univ. Press, 1992), pp. 213–234.
2. Sam Walton, *Made in America: My Story* (New York: Bantam Books, 1992), p. 82.
3. The zoning laws that help to protect the Garment District, and the Diamond District on 47th Street, are also under sustained assault. Gabby Warshawer, "Diamond District: Facets of Change on 47th Street," *The Real Deal*, Jan. 2007.
4. Christopher Gray, "The Macy's Notch: How a Thorn Got in the Lion's Paw," *New York Times*, Nov. 21, 1993.
5. Valerie Seckler, "Designers Engaging in Class Warfare," *Women's Wear Daily*, July 11, 2007.
6. Sally Beatty, "Combined Federated-May Could Stress Apparel Makers," *Wall Street Journal*, Mar. 1, 2005; Michael Barbaro, "A Bold Fashion Statement," *New York Times*, July 31, 2007.
7. To make his decision, Hilfiger only had to look at such companies as Rafaella, where in the first year after the merger revenue fell 14 percent, or Jones Apparel, which over those same twelve months saw revenue fall 9 percent. Michael Barbaro, "Macy's and Hilfiger Strike Exclusive Deal," *New York Times*, Sept. 26, 2007; Whitney Beckett, "Rafaella Rebrands under Cerberus," *Women's Wear Daily*, Nov. 19, 2007; "Jones Aborted Deal Shows Industry Woes," *AFX International*, Aug. 17, 2006.
8. Eventually, there is no support system left for any producer. Timothy Aeppel, "U.S. Shoe Factory Finds Supplies Are Achilles' Heel," *Wall Street Journal*, Mar. 3, 2008.

9. Adam Smith, *The Wealth of Nations* (New York: Modern Library, 1994), p. 84; Edward Hastings Chamberlin, *The Theory of Monopolistic Competition: A Re-orientation of the Theory of Value* (Cambridge, MA: Harvard University Press, 1933), p. 182; Richard Posner, *The Robinson-Patman Act: Federal Regulation of Price Differences* (Washington, DC: American Enterprise Institute, 1976), p. 21.

10. Peter Drucker, *Concept of the Corporation* (New York: John Day, 1946).

11. "Engine Charlie," *Time*, Oct. 6, 1961.

12. Jack Welch, *Jack: Straight from the Gut* (New York: Warner Books, 2001), p. 449.

13. Ibid., p. 105.

14. Barry C. Lynn, *End of the Line: The Rise and Coming Fall of the Global Corporation* (New York: Doubleday, 2005), pp. 73–77.

15. Welch's rule was essentially an updating of a dictum pronounced by the DuPont executive Arthur Moxham in 1903. A big company, Moxham said, should aim not at monopoly but at controlling about 60 percent of the production of any product, always retaining the ability to "price" that production "cheaper than others." In this way, "when slack times come," the dominant firm is able to "keep our capital employed to the full." Alfred Chandler, *The Visible Hand: The Managerial Revolution in American Business* (Cambridge, MA: Harvard Univ. Press, 1977), p. 442.

16. Aliza Pilar Sherman, "The Idol Life," *Entrepreneur*, Jan. 1, 2002.

17. Kozlowski also gained fame for relocating his headquarters to Bermuda and for issuing Tyco debt through a mysterious Luxembourg subsidiary. William Symonds, "The Trouble with Tyco," *BusinessWeek*, Jan. 13, 2006; Vita Reed, "Court Upholds Big Masimo Jury Award against Tyco," *Orange County Business Journal*, Sept. 19, 2005; Emily Lambert, "Battle Scarred," *Forbes*, Mar. 26, 2007.

18. My intent here is not to claim that the vertical integration model is the best model. Since the industrial revolution, we have seen many alternatives to vertical and virtual integration, such as the clusters of small producers in the textile industry in Lancashire in the late nineteenth century, in the metal-bending business in Detroit in the 1920s, or in the hardware and software businesses in the Silicon Valley of the 1970s. In all of these cases, the many small and medium players competed with many rivals and served many traders and retailers. Such cluster systems are, in many senses, the industrial ideal and are characterized by immense creativity, freedom, and rates of innovation. Michael Schwartz and Andrew Fish, "Just-in-Time Inventories in Old Detroit," *Business History*, vol. 40, no. 3 (July 1998), pp. 48–71; Michael Piore and Charles Sabel, *The Second Industrial Divide: Possibilities for Prosperity* (New York: Basic Books, 1984).

19. Deborah Ball, "After Buying Binge, Nestle Goes on a Diet," *Wall Street Journal*, July 23, 2007.

20. Nestlé would have been part of on even bigger conglomerate had its managers accepted an April 2007 merger proposed by PepsiCo.

21. This included nearly half of all Nestlé candy products in the United Kingdom.

22. Brandon Copple, "Shelf-Determination," *Forbes*, Apr. 15, 2002.

23. Suzanne Kapner, "Unlike Its Plastic, Rubbermaid's Glory Can't Last Forever," *TheStreet.com*, Oct. 23, 1998.

24. Jerry Useem, "One Nation under Wal-Mart," *Fortune*, Mar. 3, 2003; Claudia Deutsch, "After Buying Rubbermaid, a Deluge of Sorts," *New York Times*, Mar. 20, 2004; "Rubbermaid to Get Radical," *Home Furnishings News*, May 10, 2004; Jennifer Bayot, "Newell Rubbermaid to Cut 5,000 Jobs," *New York Times*, Sept. 16, 2005; Andrew Ward, "Newell Chief Dishes Up Formula to Revive Fortunes," *Financial Times*, Apr. 28, 2006.

25. Ylan Mui, "Circuit City Calls a Rollout," *Washington Post*, Feb. 7, 2008.

26. For a more detailed account of this dynamic, see Lynn, *Breaking the Chain*.

27. William Greider, "The Education of David Stockman," *The Atlantic*, Dec. 1981.

28. Carrie Johnson, "David Stockman's Reply-Side Strategy," *Washington Post*, Apr. 27, 2007.

29. Collins & Aikman entered business in 1843 as a maker of window shades on the Lower East Side of New York. The company began to supply fabric to automobile manufacturers in the 1920s.

30. Peter Phipps, "R.I. Officials Swallowed Company's Line and Ended up Looking Foolish," *Providence Journal Bulletin*, Mar. 29, 1998.

31. David Snow, "Stockman Spins Out of Blackstone Group," *Buyouts*, Sept. 27, 1999.
32. Danny Hakim, "Selling One (or More) for the Gipper," *New York Times*, Sept. 7, 2003.
33. Jeffrey McCracken, "Chrysler 300 Nearly Idled," *Detroit Free Press*, July 27, 2005.
34. Johnson, "David Stockman's Reply-Side Strategy."
35. Rick Popely, "Rantoul Workers Face Plant Closings," *Chicago Tribune*, Apr. 11, 2006.
36. Similarly, Lear threatened to shut down Chrysler in late 2005. In October 2006, C&A actually did shut down the Ford plant in Hermosillo, Mexico (which assembles the Fusion) for one shift, when it stopped shipping carpet and instrument panels. Jason Roberson, "Lear, DaimlerChrysler in Parts Fight," *Detroit Free Press*, Dec. 3, 2005; Tom Krisher, "Price Dispute with Supplier Forces Ford to Idle Mexican Plant," Associated Press, Oct. 18, 2006.
37. Bruce Urquhart, "The End of Collins & Aikman," *Woodstock Sentinel Review*, Feb. 26, 2008.
38. The Hydra model of monopolization tends almost automatically, over time, to bankrupt both the suppliers and the lead industrial firms. Or at least it does when the heads of the Hydra continue to compete with one another as they do in the wide open market for automobiles. This bankruptcy is a two-step affair, in which the financiers who control the top-tier companies like GM use their power to strip out the suppliers they have spun off, like Delphi, which was the original intent of the restructuring. Josee Valcourt, "Auto Suppliers Face Cash Crisis," *Detroit News*, May 18, 2009. In the case of Delphi, this process ran its course by 2005, when—just like C&A and many other suppliers—the auto parts maker filed for Chapter 11 protection. This in turn, however, results in a sort of rebound bankrupting of the lead firms as the ever more consolidated suppliers send up sudden deranging demands for higher payments for their parts, as we saw in the case of C&A. Which in turn leads the big firms to try to cut the suppliers back to pieces, which simply perpetuates the chaotic back-and-forth stripping out of wealth, at least until the government steps in.
39. Alan R. Mulally, testimony, Senate Banking Committee, Nov. 18, 2008.
40. Chris Isidore, "Auto Parts Makers to Get $5 Billion Bailout," *CNN Money*, March 19, 2009.
41. It is important to make clear that there is no evidence whatsoever that warnings such as those by Mulally actually influenced any of the ultimate decisions about whether and how to keep GM and Chrysler in business. Although members of the Automotive Task Force were clearly concerned about the effect that a GM bankruptcy would have on jobs—and they spoke often of the ripple effects among employees at dealers and repair shops—it is not clear that anyone in the administration had any understanding whatsoever of the degree to which the supplier system had been monopolized, hence communalized.
42. During the Depression, the Detroit automakers experimented with many alternative forms of organization, and one of the most successful was an extremely lean form of organization much like Toyota's, which they called "hand-to-mouth." Schwartz and Fish, "Just-in-Time Inventories in Old Detroit," pp. 48–71.
43. Toshihiro Nishiguchi and Alexandre Beaudet, "Case Study: The Toyota Group and the Aisin Fire," *Sloan Management Review*, vol. 40, no. 1 (1998).
44. Kendra Marr, "Trouble on the Assembly Line: As Auto Suppliers Seek Their Own Bailout, Detroit Three Face Pressure from the Ground Up," *Washington Post*, Feb. 26, 2009; Bill Vlasic, "Auto Parts Suppliers May Get Aid," *New York Times*, Mar. 20, 2009.
45. In any discussion of government regulation, it is useful to look at three of the most dramatic efforts of the last generation to shift the power to regulate price, quality, and variety away from government agencies either to a mix of public and private actors or to private powers alone. Two of these experiments—air transport and telecommunications—at first proved largely successful, before the failure to enforce antitrust law freed financiers to undo these gains. One experiment—the privatization of regulation over electricity—was one of the greatest regulatory disasters in modern U.S. history.

  The history of government regulation in the airline industry dates from 1938, when the Roosevelt administration created the Civil Aeronautics Board to govern all passenger and freight service more or less according to the model used with railroads. The government set most fares at a level that allowed the firms to pay employees a fair wage, to invest in new capital equipment, and to pay modest dividends. The result was an air transport system with a great degree of flexibility and reliability, in which competition tended to take place on the level of service and in which the capital equipment—the airliners—was upgraded on a regular basis.

Most airline managers and employees opposed the change in regulation. So too did the leading conservative politician of the era, Barry Goldwater. Thomas K. McCraw, *Prophets of Regulation: Charles Francis Adams; Louis D. Brandeis; James M. Landis; Alfred E. Kahn* (Cambridge, MA: Belknap Press, 1984), p. 278. Most energy in favor of the changes came from consumer advocates like Ralph Nader and Senator Ted Kennedy, who held that the old system protected the interests of airline managers and employees rather than the flying public. From the consumer's point of view, the initial results in terms of ticket prices were quite promising.

Then two things happened. First, the Reagan administration did not follow through on President Jimmy Carter's plan to use antitrust law to keep the airline companies from consolidating power, which they promptly did through such tactics as establishing "hub and spoke" geographic fortresses. Second, the new competition left a number of companies vulnerable to corporate raiders like Carl Icahn and Frank Lorenzo. By 1998, twenty years after deregulation, the combination of monopolization and assault by predatory financiers had caused service to deteriorate to the point where there was a boom of interest in "reregulating" the industry. Especially damning were studies that showed the price of the average airline ticket fell no faster in the twenty years after deregulation than in the twenty years before. "Deregulation Was Supposed to Cut Prices, Expand Choice, Enhance Service, Improve Your Life. So How Come You're Not Smiling?" *Consumer Reports*, July 2002.

In the case of telecommunications, the story begins in 1982 with the breakup of the American Telephone & Telegraph company. The modern AT&T was another product of J. P. Morgan's monopoly factory. Although elements of AT&T date from Alexander Graham Bell's original company, the move to forge a complete monopoly began only after Morgan installed Theodore Vail as president and gave him sufficient money to buy his competitors. By 1912 Vail had rolled up 65 percent of the telephone business in America, and the following year the Wilson administration decided to short-circuit the process by treating telephony as a natural monopoly. Robert Britt Horwitz, *Irony of Regulatory Reform: The Deregulation of American Telecommunications* (Oxford, UK: Oxford Univ. Press, 1988).

After the breakup, local telephone service was split among seven "Baby Bells," carved out of old Ma Bell's body. AT&T itself was allowed to sell long-distance service, but now it had to compete with MCI and Sprint. Close public regulation of telephony would no longer be necessary, we were told, because competition would keep these firms under control. In long distance the result was indeed a scramble to cut prices and to introduce new services. By 1999, the price per minute of phone service was down by more than half, and Americans were able to boast of having twice as many Internet-linked homes per capita as Japan or Germany. In contrast, the failure to devise effective competition at the local level kept prices high and slowed the roll-out of high-quality mobile phone service.

Then, just as with the airlines, came the mergers. For the company we call Verizon, the process began in 1997, when the Clinton administration allowed Bell Atlantic to buy NYNEX and then, three years later, General Telephone & Electronics (GTE). For the company we call AT&T, the process started in 1998 when the Clinton administration allowed SBC to buy Pacific Telesis and South New England Telephone, and in 1999, Ameritech. When SBC went shopping again in 2005, the Bush administration proved just as amenable, allowing the company to purchase AT&T (whose name it then assumed). Nor were any questions raised in 2006 when the new AT&T grabbed BellSouth, which also solidified SBC's control over the mobile phone company Cingular, and effectively reduced that industry to two big players, Verizon and AT&T. A *Bloomberg* article summed it up well. Twenty-three years after AT&T was broken into eight parts, the article stated, "Ma Bell is back." Amy Thompson and Crayton Harrison, "AT&T, Reminiscent of Ma Bell Days, Increases Dividend," *Bloomberg*, Dec. 11, 2007. A good indication of what this meant came in December 2007, when the new AT&T

announced a record 13 percent dividend and a $15.2 billion stock buyback. This occurred even as it held rates steady and as it slowed its rate of investment in new telecom infrastructure. In a 2007 list of the world's top wireless cities, Seoul, Taipei, Tokyo, Hong Kong, Singapore, and Stockholm all placed above any city in the United States. As for high-speed Internet access by landline, by 2007, the United States had not merely lost its once huge lead but had been surpassed by most of the nations of Western Europe and industrial Asia. Blaine Harden, "Japan's Warp-Speed Ride to Internet Future," *Washington Post*, Aug. 29, 2007; *DailyWireless*, Mar. 6, 2007.

In the case of electricity, Americans could have structured a national electrical system along the same basic lines as our national telephone system. Instead, we ended up with hundreds of local private monopolies woven into a complex and deeply redundant web. This was due mainly to the success of a few entrepreneurs in allying with local governments and thus enabling themselves to keep J. P. Morgan at bay. The power to regulate the different components was held not at the federal level but at the state and local level.

The first coherent proposal to privatize the regulation of the U.S. electricity system was floated by the Reagan administration in 1987, but it wasn't until 1992 that the wholesale trading of power across state lines was finally approved. This did not really alter the underlying structure of control, however. Even after the Clinton administration tried to federalize the process in 1999, most of the actual privatizations took place at the level of the states. The patchwork of rates that resulted ended up providing a remarkably clear answer to whether outright privatization of a monopoly actually lowers the rates that the average person must pay for such services. Between 2002 and 2006, the price of electricity in deregulated states rose an average of 36 percent, whereas in states that retained their old systems of regulation, the prices rose only 21 percent. These numbers were racked up *after* the Federal Energy Regulatory Commission asserted direct control over California's electricity system to restore some sort of order after Enron's market manipulation apparatus in early 2001 triggered thirty-eight blackouts and caused prices there to soar, in some instances by more than a hundred times over pre-deregulation levels. The practical results of "deregulation" in electricity were in fact so damning that even the libertarian Cato Foundation, long one of the most well-funded promoters of private monopoly, in the case of electricity recommended the "total abandonment of restructuring." Paul Davidson, "Shocking Electricity Prices Follow Deregulation," *USA Today*, Aug. 9, 2007; Cato Institute, *Rethinking Electricity Restructuring*, Policy Analysis No. 530, Nov. 30, 2004.

46. Walter Gratzer, *Terrors of the Table: The Curious History of Nutrition* (Oxford, UK: Oxford Univ. Press, 2005), pp. 16, 21.

47. One reason scurvy proved so stubborn was that despite the proofs gathered, the science itself remained confusing and counterintuitive. Scurvy, as we now know, results from a deficiency of a nutrient. Yet in the decades around the turn of the last century, humans were having a hard enough time coming to terms with Louis Pasteur's germ theory of disease: the idea that sickness is caused by an invasion of the body by bad creatures too small to see with the naked eye. This made it tough to accept that disease also sometimes results from the absence of something good and necessary. Only in the early twentieth century did scientists reach a consensus that some diseases—rickets and beriberi are two others—are caused by the lack of a vital element.

48. Jeffrey Rodengen, *The Legend of Pfizer* (Fort Lauderdale, FL: Write Stuff Syndicate, 1999).

49. An excellent account of the cartel and the investigation can be found in John M. Connor, *The Great Global Vitamins Conspiracy: Sanctions and Deterrence*, Working Paper No. 06-02 (Washington, DC: American Antitrust Institute, 2006); see also Jock Ferguson, "Vitamin Giants," *The Nation*, July 2, 2002; and "Firms Pay $255 Million for Vitamin Price Fixing," *Chicago Tribune*, Oct. 11, 2000.

50. Peter Pollak, "Return on Capital: Plant Shutdowns—the New Wave in the Fine Chemicals Industry?" *Chemical Market Reporter*, Jan. 7, 2002.

51. Ron Scherer and Peter Ford, "China's Grip on Key Food Additive," *Christian Science Monitor*, July 20, 2007; John Wilke and Kathy Chen, "Planned Economy: As China's Trade Clout Grows, So Do Price Fixing Accusations," *Wall Street Journal*, Feb. 10, 2006. The *Journal* reporters wrote that "as China becomes ever more dominant in manufacturing, its ability to dictate the prices of industrial and consumer products is steadily rising." In addition to vitamin C, the reporters listed acetaminophen, saccharin, rayon, and magnesite as other products over which the Chinese state has captured control.

52. Fred Aftalion, *A History of the International Chemical Industry: From the "Early Days" to 2000* (Philadelphia: Chemical Heritage Press, 2001), p. 172.

53. David Brown, "How U.S. Got Down to Two Makers of Flu Vaccine," *Washington Post*, Oct. 17, 2004.

54. Bernard Wysocki Jr., "Lack of Vaccines Goes Beyond Flu Inoculations," *Wall Street Journal*, Dec. 8, 2003; David Brown, "Pediatric Vaccine Stockpile at Risk," *Washington Post*, Apr. 17, 2005; Bernard Wysocki, "Margin of Safety: Just-in-Time Inventories Make U.S. Vulnerable in a Pandemic," *Wall Street Journal*, Jan. 12, 2006.

55. David Brown, "$1 Billion Awarded for Flu Vaccine," *Washington Post*, May 5, 2006; Maryn McKenna, "Plant Cancellation Shows Problems in Flu Vaccine Business," *CIDRAP News*, Oct. 3, 2008. Soon after the Bush administration action, the Swiss company AstraZeneca purchased the Maryland-based vaccine maker MedImmune, one of the more advanced pharmaceutical firms left in the United States. Then, in October 2008, members of the European cartel, led by the Belgian company Solvay (which had received the highest U.S. subsidy), began to announce that they did not really want to build vaccine plants in the United States after all.

56. Smith, *The Wealth of Nations*, p. 1.

57. Not only are semiconductor foundries highly concentrated in certain locations, like the industrial city of Hsinchu, Taiwan, they also increasingly specialize among themselves in certain forms of semiconductors. This means that designers are quickly losing their ability to switch from one foundry to the next. Geoffrey James, "Virtual Versus Vertical: How Will DFM Change the Foundries?" *Electronic Business*, Dec. 2005.

58. The most in-depth study of this issue on an international scale is in my previous book, *End of the Line*. An excellent study of such fragility at the level of the individual enterprise is Yossi Sheffi, *The Resilient Enterprise: Overcoming Vulnerability for Competitive Advantage* (Cambridge, MA: MIT Press, 2005).

4. The Market Masters

1. Smith, *The Wealth of Nations*, p. 14.

2. For a society that spends so much time talking about markets, there are remarkably few works that detail how real markets actually work. Good sources include: Peter Temin, *A Market Economy in the Early Roman Empire*, Working Paper No. 01-08 (Cambridge, MA: MIT Department of Economics, 2001); M. I. Finley, *The Ancient Economy* (Berkeley: Univ. of California Press, 1973); Fernand Braudel, *Civilization and Capitalism, 15th–18th Century, vol. 1, The Structure of Everyday Life* (Berkeley: Univ. of California Press, 1992); Christopher Dyer, "Market Towns and the Countryside in Late Medieval England," *Canadian Journal of History*, vol. 31 (1996), pp. 17–35; Theodore Bestor, *Tsukiji: The Fish Market at the Center of the World* (Berkeley: Univ. of California Press, 2004); William Novak, *The People's Welfare: Law and Regulation in Nineteenth-Century America* (Chapel Hill: Univ. of North Carolina Press, 1996).

3. Parliament also hoped to help the politically powerful East India Company offload some of the eighteen million pounds of tea that was stacked up in warehouses in London.

4. Gordon Wood, *The Radicalism of the American Revolution* (New York: Alfred A. Knopf, 1992), pp. 57 and 340.

5. Ibid., pp. 57 and 104.

6. Thomas Carlyle, *Chartism: Past and Present* (Boston: Charles C. Little and James Brown, 1840), p. 58.

7. James Madison, "Property," published originally in the *National Gazette*, Mar. 29, 1792, in *The Selected Writings of James Madison*, ed. Ralph Ketcham (Indianapolis, IN: Hackett, 2006), p. 222.

Madison was largely following in Smith's steps here. "The property which every man has in his own labour, so it is the original foundation of all other property, so it is the most sacred and inviolable. The patrimony of a poor man lies in the strength and dexterity of his hands, and to hinder him from employing this strength and dexterity in what manner he thinks proper, without injury to his neighbor, is a plain violation of this most sacred property. It is a manifest encroachment upon the just liberty both of the workman, and of those who might be disposed to employ him." Smith, *The Wealth of Nations*, p. 140.

Smith in turn followed in the steps of John Locke, who in his *Second Treatise* wrote that "Every man has a property in his own person. This nobody has any right to but himself." *Second Treatise of Government* (Indianapolis, IN: Bobbs-Merrill, 1952), chap. 5, sec. 27, p. 17.

8. Smith, *The Wealth of Nations*, pp. 84, 170, and 700.

9. It would be misleading to credit Hamilton with originating the ideas in the Report on Manufactures, or even with being the first to emphasize the need to use such tools as a protective tariff to foster the growth of industry. James Madison, on the first day of the first Congress of the United States in 1789, after declaring himself a "friend to a very free system of commerce," defended tariffs to develop infant industries, to retaliate against unfair acts by other nations, and to discourage luxury spending. Ralph Ketcham, *James Madison: A Biography* (Newtown, CT: American Political Biography Press, 1971), p. 280.

10. At the time, home distillation was one of the most effective ways to store and transport grain and was therefore a major part of the farm economy.

11. David Hounshell, *From the American System to Mass Production, 1800–1932: The Development of Manufacturing Technology in the United States* (Baltimore: Johns Hopkins Univ. Press, 1984), pp. 24 and 25.

12. John Spencer Bassett, *The Life of Andrew Jackson* (New York: Macmillan, 1925), p. 635.

13. In a letter to William C. Rives in 1819, Jefferson wrote, "Certainly no nation ever before abandoned to the avarice and jugglings of private individuals to regulate, according to their own interests, the quantum of circulating medium for the nation—to inflate, by deluges of paper, the nominal price of property, and then to buy up that property at 1s. [one shilling] in the pound, having first withdrawn the floating medium which might endanger a competition in purchase. Yet this is what has been done, and will be done, unless stayed by the protecting hand of the legislature. The evil has been produced by the error of their sanction of this ruinous machinery of banks: and justice, wisdom, duty, all require that they should interpose and arrest it before the schemes of plunder and spoliation desolate the country." John Foley, ed., *The Jefferson Cyclopedia* (New York: Funk & Wagnalls, 1900), p. 671.

14. During these years, corporate charters were granted largely to convince private citizens to build and run socially useful infrastructure, such as canals, roads, bridges, and ferries. A good example was the New York legislature's grant to Robert Livingstone of a complete monopoly on steamboat service within the state. This enabled Livingstone to secure the investment to enable for his son-in-law, Robert Fulton, to develop the world's first commercially successful steamboat, which ran between Manhattan and Albany. Morton J. Horwitz, *The Transformation of American Law, 1780–1860:* (Cambridge, MA: Harvard Univ. Press, 1977).

15. Tocqueville, *Democracy in America*, vol. 2, pp. 156–157. Tocqueville attributed much of this spectacular achievement to the social environment of democratic life. "Those who live in the midst of democratic fluctuations have always before their eyes the phantom of chance; and they end by liking all undertakings in which chance plays a part. They are therefore all led to engage in commerce, not only for the sake of the profit it holds out to them, but for the love of the constant excitement occasioned by that pursuit" (p. 156). Tocqueville attributed the achievements also to the liberty that Americans enjoyed to choose their own professions. In the United States, any farmer with ambition, he wrote, "sells his plot of ground, leaves his dwelling, and embarks on some hazardous but lucrative calling. Democratic communities abound in men of this kind; and in proportion as the equality of conditions becomes greater, their multitude increases" (p. 154).

The United States, according to Tocqueville, was a producer's utopia that no government could ever have ordered into existence. On the contrary, it was more a product of the liberty to labor free of any control. "Democracy does not give the people the most skillful government," he wrote, "but it produces what the ablest governments are frequently unable to create: namely, an all-pervading and restless activity, a superabundant force, and an energy which is inseparable from it and which may, however unfavorable circumstances may be, produce wonders" (p. 45).

16. In Britain, most of the wealth that was generated by the new industrial machinery and organizations was captured by a compact class of manufacturers, or industrial masters, who fenced the actual men and women who did the productive work within corporate "estates" or even kept them in their homes, where they transformed them into captive pieceworkers. These men then used the wealth thus gathered to push their way into a ruling class that for many centuries had been dominated by the great landlords. Yet with some exceptions, the upstart industrial lords lacked even the rudimentary sense of responsibility toward the people in their domains that characterized the traditional feudal relationship, and so they shared little if any of their new wealth with the people who did the actual work of production. On the contrary, the industrial revolution in Britain resulted in an almost industrial-scale impoverishment of the average mechanic, weaver, seamstress, and loom operator, and these workers did not have much power to do anything about it. The common man in England and Wales did not even get the right to vote until 1867.

17. Adams and Adams, *Chapters of Erie*, pp. 3 and 12.

18. Ron Chernow, *The House of Morgan: An American Banking Dynasty and the Rise of Modern Finance* (New York: Atlantic Monthly Press, 1990), p. 110.

19. Robert Kanigel, *The One Best Way: Frederick Winslow Taylor and the Enigma of Efficiency* (New York: Penguin, 1997).

20. Lippmann said that Woodrow Wilson's vision of "freedom" for the small entrepreneur from the corporations of the rich, was a "freedom for the little profiteer, but no freedom for the nation from the narrowness, the poor incentives, the limited vision of small competitors—no freedom from clamorous advertisement, from wasteful selling, from duplication of plants, from unnecessary enterprise, from the chaos, the welter, the strategy of industrial war." Walter Lippmann, *Drift and Mastery: An Attempt to Diagnose the Current Unrest* (New York: Mitchell Kennerley, 1914), p. 84.

21. In both English and American law, the property of the laborer (work) and the property of the capitalist (land, machines, businesses, and money) were regarded as perfectly analogous. This meant that the courts tended to treat the right of laborers to unionize as analogous to the right of capitalists to join their properties into a single enterprise. This is one reason the elite were able to apply the Sherman Antitrust Act, in the first years after it was enacted, mainly to unions and small cooperatives rather than to the large business monopolies it was intended to target. The landlords and industrial lords simply had more political power, so they were able to appropriate the law for their own purposes.

Adam Smith denounced as hypocritical the tendency to condemn the combinations of the workers and to abide combination by the capitalists. In *The Wealth of Nations*, he wrote that "we rarely hear . . . of the combination of masters, though frequently of those of workmen. But whoever imagines, upon this account, that masters rarely combine is as ignorant of the world as of the subject. Masters are always and everywhere in a sort of tacit, but constant and uniform, combination not to raise the wages of labour above their actual rate. To violate this combination is everywhere a most unpopular action, and a sort of reproach to a master among his neighbors and equals. We seldom, indeed, hear of this combination, because it is the usual, and one may say, the natural state of things which nobody ever hears of" (p. 77). Not that the courts did anything about the combinations of the capitalists, even when they were aware of the fact. "It is not, however, difficult to foresee which of the two parties must, upon all ordinary occasions, have the advantage in the dispute, and force the other into a compliance with their terms," Smith wrote. "The masters, being fewer in number, can combine much more easily; and the law, besides, authorizes, or at least does not prohibit, their combinations, while it prohibits those of the workmen" (pp. 75–76).

The idea that the labor and skill of the worker and the machines and money of the capitalist were all equally "property" was common in the United States until well into the Progressive

Era. Consider the following passage from the legal scholar Frederick H. Cooke, *The Law of Combinations, Monopolies, and Labor Unions* (Chicago: Callaghan, 1909): "It is not apparent why the legality of combinations among employees as such should be subjected to any different test from that applied to combinations among employers as such, or among tradesmen as such."

22. Charles Proteus Steinmetz, *America and the New Epoch* (New York: Harper & Brothers, 1916), pp. viii and 167. Not only did most Americans later entirely forget Steinmetz's radical agitations, they also transformed him into a staple of grade school hagiographies and put his face on a U.S. postage stamp.

23. During World War I, when Hoover served as President Wilson's food czar, a leading American engineer described him as "the engineering method personified." Edward Layton, *The Revolt of the Engineers: Social Responsibility and the American Engineering Profession* (Cleveland, OH: Case Western Reserve Univ. Press, 1971). Hoover was in fact a Stanford University–trained engineer who made a small fortune improving mines in Australia, China, Peru, and many other nations. Hoover was able to refine his vision of cooperation between the public and private sectors as secretary of commerce under both presidents Warren Harding and Calvin Coolidge. After he won the presidency himself in 1928, he intended to develop his experiments in public-private associationalism to a high science, but the stock market crash six months after he took office exploded his laboratory. David Hart, "Herbert Hoover's Last Laugh: The Enduring Significance of the 'Associative State' in the U.S.," *Journal of Policy History*, vol. 10, no. 3 (1998), pp. 419–444; Lawrence Gelfand, *Herbert Hoover: The Great War and Its Aftermath* (Iowa City: Univ. of Iowa Press, 1979).

24. Herbert Croly, *The Promise of American Life* (New York: Macmillan, 1909), p. 29.

25. Wilson, campaign speech, www.britannica.com/presidents.

26. Roosevelt obviously understood from the first that at least some of the political economic crisis was due to the manipulation of the markets. In his first inaugural address, he declared that the problem was not one of production but of how markets had been controlled: "Nature still offers her bounty and human efforts have multiplied it. Plenty is at our doorstep, but a generous use of it languishes in the very sight of the supply. Primarily this is because the rulers of the exchange of mankind's goods have failed, through their own stubbornness and their own incompetence, have admitted their failure, and abdicated. Practices of the unscrupulous money changers stand indicted in the court of public opinion, rejected by the hearts and minds of men."

   One of the premier historians of the New Deal, Ellis Hawley, has noted that the new administration was divided from the start. Roosevelt was under immense pressure to create "organizations and controls that could provide . . . a measure of order and security," on the one hand, and to preserve "democratic values" and something like competition on the other. The president, Hawley concluded, "could hardly be expected to come up with an intellectually coherent and logically consistent set of business policies." Ellis Hawley, *The New Deal and the Problem of Monopoly: A Study in Economic Ambivalence* (Princeton, NJ: Princeton Univ. Press, 1966), p. 14.

27. *Myers v. United States*, 272 U.S. 52, 293, 47 S. Ct. 319, 71 L. Ed. 580 (1927).

28. Wright Patman, *The Robinson-Patman Act: What You Can and Cannot Do Under This Law* (New York: Ronald Press, 1938), p. 3.

29. Ibid., p. 35. The Robinson-Patman Act was one of the most influential pieces of legislation in this country in the mid-twentieth century. At the height of enforcement, in the 1960s, the government brought 518 Robinson-Patman cases. The Reagan administration, in contrast, brought 5 Robinson-Patman cases, and the Clinton administration brought 1. William Kovacic, "The Modern Evolution of U.S. Competition Policy Enforcement Norms," *Antitrust Law Journal*, vol. 71, no. 2 (2003), p. 411.

   Although giant trading firms like Wal-Mart and Home Depot seem to be a new phenomenon, they are merely the latest incarnation of chain stores like Sears and Woolworth's. If the members of the Walton family ever wish to thank anyone in particular for their amazing wealth, they should drink a toast not merely to Ronald Reagan for suspending our antitrust laws but also to Wright Patman for upholding and updating it. If Patman and his allies had not stood up for the rights of Sam Walton to operate his five-and-dime in peace, he would likely have fallen under the power of Woolworth or Kresge decades ago.

30. Richard M. Brunell, "The Social Cost of Mergers: Restoring 'Local Control' as a Factor in Merger Policy," *North Carolina Law Review*, vol. 81, no. 1 (2006), p. 188. Many in Congress believed that, as one representative put it, "the drive for civic improvements of one kind or another generally tends to disappear in towns which have become the victims of outside ownership" (p. 189).

31. *Standard Oil Co. v. United States*, 337 U.S. 293 (1949).

32. An excellent history of this era and process is William Cronon, *Nature's Metropolis: Chicago and the Great West* (New York: W. W. Norton, 1991).

33. Maury Klein, *The Life and Legend of Jay Gould* (Baltimore: Johns Hopkins Univ. Press, 1986), p. 102.

34. The economist Benjamin Graham proposed a modern version of this during the Depression. Benjamin Graham, *Storage and Stability: A Modern Ever-Normal Granary* (New York: McGraw-Hill, 1937).

35. Sinclair Steward and Paul Waldie, "Feeding Frenzy: One Big Culprit in the Global Food Crisis Has Been Overlooked—the Money, Pension, and Index Funds Used a Loophole to Plow Hundreds of Billions of Dollars into Commodities Markets," *Globe and Mail*, May 31, 2008.

36. One of the more honest comments about agricultural markets came from a man who should know. Dwayne Orville Andreas, the former CEO of Archer Daniels Midland, told a reporter that "there isn't one grain of anything in the world that is sold on a free market. Not one! The only place you see a free market is in the speeches of politicians." Dan Carney, "Dwayne's World," *Mother Jones*, July–Aug. 1995.

37. In the case of ocean freight shipping, in late 2007, the traders on the brand-new freight derivatives desks set up by Citigroup, Merrill Lynch, Macquarie Bank, Goldman Sachs, Credit Suisse, Lehman Brothers, Morgan Stanley, and the hedge funds GMI and Akuila Okeanos managed to drive up the daily cost of renting a supertanker from $20,000 to more than $150,000, and they more than tripled the cost of hiring a bulk carrier (from $30,000 per day to more than $100,000) even as shipments of oil and commodities were declining. In all, the amount of money in the market for these futures grew from $50 billion in February 2007 to $125 billion in February 2008. David Oakley, "Freight Derivative Volumes Rise 150% in Year," *Financial Times*, Feb. 24, 2008; Paul Davies, "UBS to Start Freight Future Index," *Financial Times*, Apr. 23, 2008.

Ann Davis, "In Mystery Cotton-Price Spike, Traders Hit by Swirling Forces," *Wall Street Journal*, Aug. 13, 2008; Alexei Barrionuevo and Jenny Anderson, "Wall Street Is Betting on the Farm," *New York Times*, Jan. 19, 2007; David Kesmodel, Lauren Etter, and Aaron Patrick, "Grain Companies' Profits Soar as Global Food Crisis Mounts," *Wall Street Journal*, Apr. 30, 2008; "BP Agrees to Pay a Total of $303 Million in Sanctions to Settle Charges of Manipulation and Attempted Manipulation in the Propane Market," Commodities Futures Trading Commission (CTFC) press release, Oct. 25, 2007; David Cho, "Energy Traders Avoid Scrutiny," *Washington Post*, Oct. 21, 2007; "Statement of Justin Towery, Merchant Member, Parkdale, Arkansas," testimony on behalf of the U.S. Rice Federation and the U.S. Rice Producers Association, CFTC Agricultural Roundtable, Washington, DC, Apr. 22, 2008.

Even auctions for high-end watches and antiques are sometimes rigged. As the *Wall Street Journal* reported, in April 2007 at an auction in the Mandarin Oriental Hotel in Switzerland, a buyer paid $351,000 for a 1950s platinum watch manufactured by Omega. This was a record price, which Omega happily trumpeted. Yet it was also a record that had been artificially manufactured by Omega in alliance with the Swiss auction house Antiquorum. Bidders at such auctions are often anonymous, and in this case Omega simply "bought" the watch from itself. The cofounder of the auction house told the reporter, in defense of the sleight of hand, that "auctions are much stronger than advertising." Stacy Meichtry, "Invisible Hand: How Top Watchmakers Intervene in Auctions," *Wall Street Journal*, Oct. 8, 2007.

5. In the Cockpit

1. *The Man in the Gray Flannel Suit* was a 1955 novel by Sloan Wilson. Gregory Peck starred in the 1956 movie version, in which the main character is a public relations man.

2. Steve Pearlstein, "What Happened to Creative Advertising?" *Washington Post*, Sept. 20, 2006. He writes: "In the search for what went wrong, one path leads to industry consolidation."

3. WPP holds a powerful position even over Washington lobbyists. The company controls three of the firms with the biggest influence-peddling operations—Burson-Marsteller, Ogilvy & Mather, and Hill & Knowlton—as well as three smaller operations. A *Financial Times* reporter wrote that "at a time when the capital's public relations and lobbying organizations are more influential than ever, no single company has concentrated so much Washington influence under one corporate roof as WPP." Stephanie Kirchgaessner, "One Big Country Club," *Financial Times*, Nov. 27, 2007.

4. Robert Reich, *The Work of Nations: Preparing Ourselves for 21st Century Capitalism* (New York: Alfred A. Knopf, 1991), pp. 177, 178, and 179.

5. Perhaps the most stubborn myth of the modern Democratic Party is that the best way to get the United States working is to "educate the next generation of workers," in the words of White House Chief of Staff Rahm Emanuel. "A New Deal for the New Economy," *Wall Street Journal*, Mar. 19, 2008. This was one of the main messages of Reich in *The Work of Nations*, and it was one of the main messages in Thomas Friedman, *The World Is Flat: A Brief History of the Twenty-first Century* (New York: Farrar, Straus and Giroux, 2005), which was essentially an updating of Reich's work. The problem is that an education guarantees nothing in a political environment dominated by corporations designed not to produce goods but cash. As one recent study by the Urban Institute showed, the U.S. education system is already turning out more top-quality science and engineering graduates than there are jobs. Vivek Wadhwa, "The Science Education Myth," *BusinessWeek*, Oct. 26, 2007.

6. In 2006, Wal-Mart took advantage of its new power to impose a de facto labor contract on its 1.3 million employees, especially those in rural and less competitive regions. Steven Greenhouse and Michael Barbaro, "Wal-Mart to Add Wage Caps and Part-Timers," *New York Times*, Oct. 2, 2006. It almost simultaneously launched a get-out-the-vote drive among its dependents. "Wal-Mart Launches Drive to Help Company Associates Register to Vote," PR Newswire, Sept. 19, 2006.

7. Oracle's hostile capture of PeopleSoft in early 2007 was merely one of many recent instances in which a top-tier trading company greatly reduced the freedom of movement of software engineers. Andrew Ross Sorkin, "Hostility Has Its Rewards," *New York Times*, Mar. 11, 2008. Much of this activity never catches the eye of the national media, however. Consider the effort by LensCrafters and Cole Managed Vision to overturn a Tennessee law designed to protect independent optometrists like John Cottam; this is just one of the many such state-by-state campaigns run by large corporations against independent entrepreneurs. "Supreme Court Refuses to Hear Case on Tennessee Optometrist Law," Associated Press, Feb. 21, 2006.

8. In 166 of 294 metropolitan areas, a single insurer controls more than half of the business in preferred provider networks and health maintenance organizations. Such power, the study said, gives these firms the ability to dictate prices and coverage terms to both the patient and the doctor. "Study: Health Insurers Are Near Monopolies," Associated Press, Apr. 19, 2006. Concern over such power led even the usually Pollyannish Clinton Antitrust Division to challenge a 1999 consolidation of the HMO businesses of Aetna and Prudential. Marius Schwartz, "Buyer Power Concerns and the Aetna-Prudential Merger," Fifth Annual Health Care Antitrust Forum, Northwestern University School of Law, Chicago, Oct. 20, 1999.

9. Americans as a whole prefer small business by a very large margin. In one 2007 survey, nearly five times as many expressed "substantial confidence" in small businesses (54 percent) than in large corporations (11 percent). John Harwood, "America's Economic Mood: Gloomy," *Wall Street Journal*, Aug. 2, 2007.

10. John Schmitt and Nathan Lane, "An International Comparison of Small Business Employment." Study for the Center for Economic and Policy Research (CEPR), August 2009. The underlying mythos of American entrepreneurship is so strong that few writers or academics

seem to have noticed this decline or found much success in publicizing the fact. Instead, the task of speaking this truth has been left largely to foreigners, like the Canadian academics who were astounded to discover that entrepreneurship is much healthier in cranky old Canada. Marilyn Manser and Garnett Picot, "Self-Employment in Canada and the United States," *Canadian Economic Observer*, vol. 12, no. 3 (Mar. 1999), pp. 37–44. Then there was the Australian political scientist who, after looking at the numbers, concluded that the idea that the United States is a nation composed of independent entrepreneurs is a "myth." Rachel Parker, "The Myth of the Entrepreneurial Economy: Employment and Innovation in Small Firms," *Work, Employment & Society*, vol. 15, no. 2 (2001), pp. 239–253.

One exception was the conservative columnist David Brooks, who urged his fellow Republicans to recognize that "the entrepreneur is no longer king. The wage-earner is king." David Brooks, "Middle-Class Capitalists," *New York Times*, Jan. 11, 2008.

11. Although many of us associate franchising with the 1950s, when Ray Kroc, the founder of McDonald's, and his brothers began to partner with other families, franchising dates back at least 150 years, to when the sewing machine manufacturer Singer affiliated with local entrepreneurs to open branded stores. Car manufacturers and Coca-Cola also pursued the same basic model with their dealers and their bottlers in the early twentieth century. In all, there are at least 650,000 individual units in the United States, representing more than 2,000 companies in at least 70 industries, including coffee shops, gyms, hardware stores, motels and hotels, muffler shops, convenience stores, and pet kennels. A recent PricewaterhouseCoopers study estimated that as of 2005, franchises (including corporate owned units) account for eleven million jobs, or 8.1 percent of the private-sector total, and about $880 billion in annual revenue, or 4.4 percent of all private-sector output. PricewaterhouseCoopers, *The Economic Impact of Franchised Businesses*, vol. 2, *Results for 2005: National Economic Consulting*, Jan. 31, 2008.

12. In 1979, the Federal Trade Commission (FTC) began to require franchisors to make standard detailed disclosures about their businesses to potential franchisees. The FTC further standardized the disclosure document in 1993. At least thirteen states, including New York, California, Illinois, and Virginia, have some form of additional regulation. Nevertheless, in recent years, the people who control these corporations have managed to greatly weaken the protections for franchisees.

13. Cheryl Kane, "Quiznos Enters South Florida Market," *South Florida Business Journal*, July 23, 1993; Alex Goff, "Customers Get Taste for Quiznos," *The Olympian*, June 20, 2001.

14. The Small Business Administration (SBA) tracks failure rates among different franchising operations. The SBA is supposed to keep the list secret, but an online franchising news service named Blue Mau Mau used a Freedom of Information Act request to get a copy for 2001–2005. During this time, the worst performer in the United States was a company named Obee's Soup, Salad, and Subs. Other bad bets, from the point of view of a would-be franchisee, include Godfather's Pizza, Lee Myles Transmission, Blimpie, and Executive Tans.

15. Jessica Centers, "You're Toast," *Westword*, May 3, 2007.

16. Julie Creswell, "When Disillusion Sets In," *New York Times*, Feb. 24, 2007; Jonathan Maze, "Quiznos Conflict: Chain Faces National Lawsuits," *Franchise Times*, Oct. 2007.

17. This included filing "disparagement lawsuits" against franchisees who posted comments on an online forum. Centers, "You're Toast."

18. Per person, the top 1 percent of the population "received 440 times as much as the average person in the bottom half" of the population, according to a 2007 study of tax receipts. This nearly doubled the gap that existed in 1980 and returned the disparity to a level last seen in 1928. David Cay Johnston, "Income Gap Is Widening, Data Shows," *New York Times*, Mar. 29, 2007.

19. Centers, "You're Toast."

20. Leonard Silk, "Antitrust Issues Facing Reagan," *New York Times*, Feb. 13, 1981.

21. John McGee, "Predatory Price Cutting: The Standard Oil (N.J.) Case," *Journal of Law and Economics*, vol. 1 (Oct. 1958), pp. 137-169.

22. Alan Greenspan, "Antitrust," in *Capitalism: The Unknown Ideal*, ed. Ayn Rand, Nathaniel Branden, Alan Greenspan, and Robert Hessen (New York: New American Library, 1966), p. 63.

23. Robert H. Bork, *The Antitrust Paradox* (New York: Basic Books, 1978), p. 7.
24. Ibid., p. 51.
25. "Washington News," *United Press International*, Jan. 12, 1984.
26. David Hackett Fischer, *Albion's Seed: Four British Folkways in America* (New York: Oxford Univ. Press, 1989), pp. 411 and 412.
27. Harvey Cox, "The Market as God," *The Atlantic*, Mar. 1999.
28. Karl Marx, "A Contribution to the Critique of Hegel's Philosophy of Right," in *Marx: Early Political Writings*, ed. Joseph O'Malley (Cambridge, UK: Cambridge Univ. Press, 1994), p. 57.
29. Smith, *The Wealth of Nations*, p. 705.
30. Alfred Marshall, *Principles of Economics* (London: Macmillan, 1898), p. 477.
31. F. A. Hayek, *The Road to Serfdom* (Chicago: Univ. of Chicago Press, 1994), p. 116.
32. One of the more fascinating iterations of the idea that the market exists outside and around society is in Karl Polanyi, *The Great Transformation* (New York: Holt, Rinehart and Winston, 1944).
33. Friedman, *Capitalism and Freedom*. Two other extremely important terms in the neofeudal dictionary are *technology* and *globalization*. Both of these have proven extremely useful in buttressing the idea that the forces we see at work in our political economy—especially those that result in the shift of power from the great many of us to the few of them—are due to natural forces outside society and hence are impossible to manipulate through political means. The basic idea behind both *technology* and *globalization* is that we have seen such a revolutionary breaking down of borders—between economic activities and between nations—that all previous human institutional relationships have been rendered null and void, along with our ability to use the old structures and old laws to affect the world around us. The most influential recent iteration of this argument was in Thomas Friedman's *The World Is Flat*.
34. Friedman, *Capitalism and Freedom*. No human economic activity can ever truly be *deregulated*. Today, anytime we choose not to use our public government to regulate an activity, we are merely shifting the power to regulate that activity to private actors. *Deregulation* is merely a euphemism, either for privatization or for a shift to an alternative form of public regulation.
    The first use of the term *deregulation* I could find in a search of news articles on Nexis was in a 1970 story about a group of Texas and Wyoming politicians—including the young congressman George H. W. Bush—who introduced a bill to stop the government from "regulating prices that owners of gas wells can charge." (Article Synopsis) *New York Times*, Aug. 13, 1970. It was a group of liberals and neoprogressives, however, who really brought the term into vogue. This included Ralph Nader, Edward Kennedy, and Jimmy Carter, and their initial target was the airline industry.
    When Carter and Nader spoke of *deregulation*, what they actually meant is that they planned to shift the task of regulating the airline industry away from a micromanaging government agency—the Civil Aeronautics Board—to the Antitrust Division of the Justice Department. In doing so, they expected the result to be a more efficient form of regulation, in which most of the mundane details of business would pass from the desk of the public bureaucrat to the private manager. When the Texas oil men, in contrast, spoke of *deregulation*, what they imagined was the shifting of complete control over prefabricated monopolies directly into their hands.
35. Hayek, *Road to Serfdom*, pp. 22 and 41.
36. Friedman, *Capitalism and Freedom*, pp. 116 and 155.
37. Robert Jackson, "Financial Monopoly: The Road to Socialism," *The Forum*, vol. 100 (1938), available at www. roberthjackson. org.
38. Lester Thurow, "Let's Abolish the Antitrust Laws," *New York Times*, Oct. 19, 1980; Steve Lohr, "Antitrust: Big Business Breathes Easier," *New York Times*, Feb. 15, 1981; Lester Thurow, "The New Era of Competition," *Newsweek*, Jan. 18, 1982.
39. Lippmann's vision of a consumer movement was highly developed for 1914, as is clear from the following: "Many radical socialists pretend to regard the consumer's interest as a rather mythical one. 'All the people' sounds so sentimental, so far removed from the clash of actual events. But we are finding, I think, that the real power emerging today in democratic politics

is just the mass of people who are crying out against the 'high cost of living.' That is a consumer's cry. Far from being an impotent one, it is, I believe, destined to be stronger than the interests of either labor or capital. With the consumer awake, neither the worker nor the employer can use politics for his special interest. The public, which is more numerous than either side, is coming to be the determining force in government." Lippmann, *Drift and Mastery*, p. 54.

40. Galbraith's arguments were almost as sophisticated as those of the Chicago School operators. Consider the conflict he sets up in the following: "The market system"—meaning independent farmers and shopkeepers—"buys at prices which are extensively subject to the power of the planning system"—meaning the giant industrial corporations like IBM and GE. "And an important part of its products and services are sold at prices which it does not control but which may be subject to the market power of the planning system. Given this distribution of power, there is a prima facie case that things will work better for the planning system than for the market system. The terms of trade between the two systems will have an insouciant tendency to favor the system that controls its prices and costs and therewith the prices and costs of the other system as well." There are many problems with this passage, especially the fact that Galbraith mixes different forms of human enterprise into a single blurred mass. However, the main problem is his conclusion. Rather than say that the socialized systems are powerful and enjoy certain advantages and therefore must be controlled with great care, he says that because they are powerful and enjoy certain advantages, we should therefore centralize top-down control over all human activities. John Kenneth Galbraith, *Economics and the Public Purpose* (Boston: Houghton Mifflin, 1973), p. 55.

41. Robert Bork, *The Antitrust Paradox*, with updated introduction and epilogue (New York: Free Press, 1993), p. xiii.

42. As Robert Reich explains, "consumer power" is "aggregated and enlarged by mass retailers like Wal-Mart that use the collective bargaining clout of millions of consumers to get great deals from suppliers." Reich, *Supercapitalism*, p. 7.

43. Insurers have even become adept at pitting U.S. doctors against doctors in countries like Mexico, India, and Thailand, such as by flying patients abroad for treatment. Sarah Skidmore, "The Mexico Option," *San Diego Union Tribune*, Oct. 16, 2005.

44. Vanessa O'Connell, "Retailers Reprogram Workers in Efficiency Push," *Wall Street Journal*, Sept. 10, 2008; Vanessa O'Connell, "Stores Count Seconds to Trim Labor Costs," *Wall Street Journal*, Nov. 13, 2008; Michele Conlin, "Shirking Working: The War on Hooky," *BusinessWeek*, Nov. 12, 2007.

45. Eric Palmer, "Bankruptcy Judge Approves Sell-Off of Farmland Industries' Refinery, Plant," Knight Ridder, Nov. 5, 2003; Caroline Daniel, "Chapter 11 Could Be End of Story for U.S. Farm Co-Ops," *Financial Times*, June 5, 2002.

46. Andrew Martin, "Yes, It's a Cooperative. But for Whom?" *New York Times*, May 18, 2008; John Wilke, "Dairy Co-Op Faces Price-Manipulation Probe," *Wall Street Journal*, May 19, 2008; "The Big Get Bigger: An Unalterable Trend in U.S. Agriculture," *Kiplinger Agriculture Letter*, July 17, 1998.

47. In 1979, there were 650,000 hog farms in the United States. By 2004, the number was down to 70,000. Yet the total output of pork had exploded by six billion pounds per year. Nathanael Johnson, "Swine of the Times," *Harper's*, May 2006. Nowadays, the industry increasingly operates like franchising; the "farmer" puts up the cash, and a company like Smithfield puts up the "content." It provides the "farmer" with the pigs, the feed, the drugs, and detailed instructions on how to assemble this into hogs ready to go on the hook.

Even if a hog farmer or any other farmer manages to escape dependence on such a monopolized system, he or she faces monopolies in almost all other directions. The meat "brokerage" business—which puts meat into the Safeways and Krogers of the United States—is dominated by three big concerns. Supply of fertilizer is dominated by Cargill and Yara. Grain elevators and grain transport are dominated by Cargill and ADM, both often with regional monopolies. Seeds, as we will see in the next chapter, are dominated increasingly by Monsanto.

If the farmer still manages to escape, he or she often faces an assault by government "regulators" who in recent years have often applied health and safety laws in ways that favor only the monopolist, such as by using government to close local slaughterhouses. Heather Ramsay, "Can't Slaughter Like You Used To," *The Tyee*, Feb. 8, 2006; Michelle Locke, "Raw Milk Fans Oppose New California Rules," Associated Press, Dec. 28, 2007.

48. Amish families have become far more active in growing produce for the Kansas City Market since the "local" dairy "cooperatives" began to refuse to pick up the milk they produce.

49. "Is Dickel in a Pickel?" available online at www.straightbourbon.com; Joe Edwards, "George Dickel No. 8 Runs Short Just in Time for Holiday Parties," Associated Press, Dec. 17, 2007.

6. Lightning Escapes the Bottle

1. Pablo Lastra, "Hijacking at the Hospital," *Ft. Worth Weekly*, Nov. 23, 2005; Allnurses: A Nursing Community for Nurses, www. allnurses. com/forums/f8/hiv-needlestick-304018. html.

2. Much of the background information in this section comes from two sets of excellent articles in 1998 by Reynolds Holding and William Carlsen of the *San Francisco Chronicle*. The first three articles ran Apr. 13, 14, 15 and were titled "Epidemic Ravages Caregivers," "High Profits—At What Cost?," and "Watchdogs Fail Health Workers." The second set of three articles ran Oct. 27, 28, and 29 and were entitled "Fast Track to Global Disaster," "Lost Chance to Avert Crisis," and "Epidemic's Devastating Toll." The Las Vegas clinic information is from Kathleen Hennessey, "Vegas Clinic May Have Sickened Thousands," Associated Press (in *USA Today*), Mar. 6, 2008.

3. The invention of the hollow needle revolutionized medicine in the mid-1800s. By the 1920s, however, doctors knew that needlestick injuries and needle reuse could spread disease. In 1967, the American Medical Association first called on needle manufacturers to "adopt designs to prevent reuse." The FDA first began to promote the idea in 1983, and the Service Employees International Union followed in 1986. The first functional one-time-use syringe was introduced in the late 1980s, and the first safety syringe dates to roughly the same time. The first congressional hearing on the subject took place in 1992.

4. Barry Meier, "Questioning $1 Million Fee in a Needle Deal," *New York Times*, July 19, 2002.

5. Curt Werner, "Senate Asks for Quicker GPO Reform," *Healthcare Purchasing News*, Sept. 1, 2003; John Lawn, "The GPOs: Where Do They Go from Here?" *Food Management*, Jan. 2005; Walt Bogdanich, "Hospital Chiefs Get Pay and Perks for Advice on Selling to Hospitals," *New York Times*, July 17, 2006.

6. Many GPO-purchased products are more costly and less patient-friendly, as well as more dangerous. "Locked Out of the Hospital," *BusinessWeek*, Mar. 16, 1998. The GPOs also trade in carpeting, ballpoint pens, and even food service. Lawn, "The GPOs: Where Do They Go from Here?"

7. GPO executives have sometimes used their power of governance to establish lucrative new businesses in their own hands. At Premier, executives steered millions of dollars in drug import contracts to a brand-new company they established in their own name. Walt Bogdanich, Barry Meier, and Mary Williams Walsh, "When a Buyer for Hospitals Has a Stake in the Drugs It Buys," *New York Times*, Mar. 26, 2002. In at least one such case, the newly created company imported tainted antibiotics from China. Edward Pound and Steve Sternberg, "Antibiotic Imports May Have Killed 17," *USA Today*, May 9, 2000; Regina Herzlinger, "Why Innovation in Health Care Is So Hard," *Harvard Business Review*, May 2006.

8. As one Becton, Dickinson spokesman said in court, the job of making the company's safety syringes safe is not up to the company but rather "the people who are using our products."*San Francisco Chronicle*, Apr. 15, 1998.

9. Einer Elhauge, "Antitrust Analysis of GPO Exclusionary Agreements," Department of Justice–Federal Trade Commission Hearing on GPOs, Sept. 26, 2003; Einer Elhauge, "Tying, Bundled Discounts, and the Death of the Single Monopoly Profit Theory," to be published in the *Harvard Law Review*, Dec. 2009. Elhauge is a Harvard Law School professor.

10. In one independent test, the Becton, Dickinson SafetyLok product was rated "unacceptable." Meier, "Questioning $1 Million Fee in a Needle Deal"; Roy Appleton, "The Short End of the Stick," *Dallas Morning News*, Nov. 21, 2004.

11. Shaw's case was also buttressed by the Government Accountability Office, which found in a study that hospitals that buy through GPOs pay far more than those that don't. Mary Williams

Walsh and Barry Meier, "Hospitals Find Big Buying Groups May Not Come Up with Savings," *New York Times*, Apr. 30, 2003. Shaw was also supported by congressional hearings that showed that firms like Johnson & Johnson use GPOs to push their products onto hospitals. Mary Williams Walsh, "New Scrutiny Directed at Bundled Sale of Hospital Supplies," *New York Times*, July 17, 2003. Shaw was also supported by a whistle-blower who used to work for Novation. Mary Williams Walsh, "Blowing the Whistle, Many Times," *New York Times*, Nov. 18, 2007.

12. Angela Laramie, Letitia Davis, Natalia Firsova, James Laing, Alfred DeMaria, and Laurie Robert, "Sharps Injuries among Hospital Workers in Massachusetts 2004: Findings from the Massachusetts Sharps Injury Surveillance System," Apr. 2007.

13. Shawn Rhea, "The Top Exchange Rate," *Modern Healthcare*, July 23, 2007.

14. Lastra, "Hijacking at the Hospital"; Patricia Gray, "Stick It to 'Em," *Fortune Small Business*, Mar. 1, 2005.

15. *Becton, Dickinson and Company et al. v. Retractable Technologies*, Texas Eastern District Court, Sept. 6, 2007.

16. Benjamin Franklin, "Letter to Peter Collinson," in *The Works of Benjamin Franklin*, ed. John Bigelow (New York: G. P. Putnam's Sons, 1904), p. 8; H. W. Brands, *The First American: The Life and Times of Benjamin Franklin* (New York: Doubleday, 2000); I. Bernard Cohen, *Benjamin Franklin's Science* (Cambridge, MA: Harvard Univ. Press, 1990); Philip Dray, *Stealing God's Thunder:Benjamin Franklin's Lightning Rod* (New York, Random House, 2005).

17. One historian notes that "the difference was in how this technical knowledge and skill was used. The European manufacturer used it to make a product. The American used it to make a process for making a product." Joseph Litterer, "Systematic Management," *Business History Review*, 1961, quoted in Yehouda Shenhav, *Manufacturing Rationality: The Engineering Foundations of the Managerial Revolution* (Oxford, UK: Oxford Univ. Press, 1999), p. 49.

18. Hounshell, *From the American System to Mass Production, 1800–1932*, pp. 61–65.

19. Article I, Section 8. The United States rejected the notion that ideas were property even though many in Britain had already begun to promote the idea. B. Zorina Kahn, *The Democratization of Invention: Patents and Copyrights in American Economic Development, 1790–1920* (Cambridge, UK: Cambridge Univ. Press, 2005); Adam Mossoff, "Rethinking the Development of Patents," *Hastings Law Journal*, vol. 52, p. 1255 2001.

20. Benjamin Franklin, *Autobiography* (London: J. M. Dent, 1905), p. 140.

21. Thomas Jefferson, Letter to Isaac MacPherson, August 13, 1813, in *Jefferson: Political Writings*, eds. Joyce Appleby and Terence Ball (Cambridge, UK: Cambridge Univ. Press, 1999), p. 581.

22. Thomas Malthus, *An Essay on the Principle of Population* (Cambridge, UK: Cambridge Univ. Press), 1992.

23. E. P. Hutchinson, *The Population Debate: The Development of Conflicting Theories Up to 1900* (Boston: Houghton Mifflin, 1967).

24. Ralph Waldo Emerson, "Fortune of the Republic," in *Selected Lectures*, ed. Ronald Bosco (Athens: Univ. of Georgia Press, 2005), p. 318.

25. Matthew Josephson, *Edison* (New York: McGraw-Hill, 1959); Jill Jonnes, *Empires of Light: Edison, Tesla, Westinghouse, and the Race to Electrify the World* (New York: Random House, 2003); Margaret Cheny, *Tesla: Man Out of Time* (New York: Touchstone, 1981).

26. John Wasik, *The Merchant of Power: Sam Insull, Thomas Edison, and the Creation of the Modern Metropolis* (New York: Palgrave Macmillan, 2006), p. 35.

27. Jonnes, *Empires of Light*, p. 361.

28. As David F. Noble explained the process, in reference to the electrical equipment and chemical industries in the United States, "Through consolidation, patent monopoly, and merger, the science-based electrical and chemical industries came, by the turn of the century, to be dominated by a handful of giant firms. Through control over the educational process and licensing, the professional engineers gradually gained a monopoly over the practice of scientific technology. And through the massive employment of technically trained people, the industrial corporations secured a monopoly over the professional engineers." David F. Noble, *America by Design: Science, Technology, and the Rise of Corporate Capitalism* (New York: Alfred A. Knopf, 1977), p xxiv.

29. Alex Berenson, "Market Forces Cited in Lymphoma Drugs' Disuse," *New York Times*, July 14, 2007.

30. The economist Jagdish Bhagwati, a very strong supporter of liberal trade, is also a harsh critic of one of the main components of the WTO legal regime put into place by the Clinton administration. This was something called Trade-Related Aspects of Intellectual Property Rights (TRIPS), and it was designed to force poor nations to fortify the protections they give to foreign-"owned" ideas through their patent and copyright regimes. "This subject," Bhagwati wrote, "does not really belong to the WTO, whose organizing principle must be [that] trade liberalization is a mutual-gain policy. We cannot even claim that the agreement advances the world good: nearly all economists agree, for instance, that the 20-year patent length . . . is almost certainly inefficient and *exploitative* of the vast majority of the developing-country nations." Bhagwati concludes that the agreement is part of a "crusade" by rich countries against poor countries that reverses many of the most important gains the latter were promised from more liberal trade. Jagdish Bhagwati, *The Wind of the Hundred Days: How Washington Mismanaged Globalization* (Cambridge, MA: MIT Press, 2000), p. 279.

   One thing Bhagwati leaves unexplored is *who* within the rich countries this new intellectual-property regime was designed to serve. For most citizens of the United States, this is the central question. On the surface, the argument that people in countries like China and India are out to "steal" the ideas of U.S. inventors and innovators certainly seems to justify forcing poor countries to ratchet up their patent protections. Yet the argument starts to fall apart when we look at the fact that the Clinton administration oversaw the fortification of patent and copyright laws right here in the United States at the very same time, even though the existing legal regime had proven itself more than adequate. The first big change came in 1995, when—to bring U.S. law into alignment with the newly signed agreement that established the WTO—the basic term of a patent was extended from seventeen years, what it had been since 1861, to twenty years. The next big change came in 1998, in the form of an extension of copyright protection, from a twenty-eight-year term that could be extended by another twenty-eight years to the life of the author plus another seventy years.

31. Angela Riley, "St. Louis–based Zoltek Wins Right to Sue U.S. Contractor," *Daily Record and the Kansas City Daily News Press*, Feb. 9, 2009; William Fitzpatrick and Samuel Dilullo, "Eminent Domain or Imminent Threat," *Competition Forum*, vol. 5, no. 1, p. 137, 2007.

32. The California Lighting Technology Center reported in early 2009 that Wal-Mart's green decree led only to great reductions in the quality of the bulbs and a highly damaging reaction against them by consumers. Leora Broydo Vestel, "Green Inc.," *New York Times*, Jan. 27, 2009.

33. Andrew Ross Sorkin, "Hostility Has Its Rewards," *New York Times*, Mar. 11, 2008; Jeanne Whalen, "Drug Maker Cuts Risk by Buying Others' Pills," *Wall Street Journal*, Apr. 2, 2008; Catherine Holahan, "Ravenous for Small Tech: Cash-Rich Titans Like eBay and Microsoft Are Finding Conditions Ripe for Buying Sprees," *BusinessWeek*, Apr. 7, 2008; Ashlee Vance, "Rivals Say IBM Stifles Competition," *New York Times*, Mar. 23, 2009; David Hamilton, "Biotech Start-ups Increasingly Opt for a Sale to Drug Firms over an IPO," *Wall Street Journal*, July 13, 2006. One venture capitalist told the *Journal* that the new model of organization "is a sea change in our industry that's really radically important."

34. Jennifer Washburn, "Big Oil Buys Berkeley," *Los Angeles Times*, Mar. 24, 2007; "Climate Change II: Stanford and Energy Companies Announce Partnership," *Greenwire*, Nov. 21, 2002.

35. Barry C. Lynn, "Today's Promises, Tomorrow's Cars? Lessons for Freedomcar from the Ghosts of Supercars Past" (New York: Environmental Defense, 2004).

36. Shenhav, *Manufacturing Rationality*, p. 61.

37. Significant small independent businesses still survive in this country because the American people—through Congress—require that 23 percent of federal contracts go to small businesses. Given that the federal government spends more than $300 billion per year on procurement, this adds up to big money. Nor is it surprising that the people who operate big corporations would like to get their hands on these funds. The result has been a variety of efforts to roll back these procurement rules, including the successful exemption of procurement operations at both the

Pentagon and NASA. One of the more aggressive efforts now under way targets government research contracts. Under the old rules, government funds could go only to firms where the founding entrepreneur retained at least 51 percent of control. Under the new rules, these subsidies would also be made available to "small companies" that are actually controlled, through venture capital infusions, by big corporations, big funds, and big universities. Joseph Fried, "A Map for the Maze of Federal Contracts," *New York Times*, Apr. 1, 2007; Elizabeth Olson, "A Battle over Venture Capital for Small Businesses," *New York Times*, Oct. 25, 2007.

38. Slashing research and development (R&D) spending did not come naturally to Welch. An engineer himself, he came to power with plans to invest big in new ideas, and in October 1982 he opened a $130 million laboratory. He learned fast, however. Once he started to scrimp on R&D, he knew where to direct the savings. In November 1989 he plowed $10 billion into buying back stock, which was by far the biggest such gesture up to that time. Thomas F. O'Boyle, *At Any Cost: Jack Welch, General Electric, and the Pursuit of Profit* (New York: Alfred A. Knopf, 1998), pp. 36, 123, and 128.

39. "At 3M: A Struggle between Efficiency and Creativity," *BusinessWeek*, June 11, 2007.

40. Weathermen testified that between 1994 and 2001, the share of all companies financed by venture capital funds dropped from 22 percent to around 5 percent. "One of the reasons for this relative decline in new investment is a lack of market access brought about by the business practices and the increasing power of GPOs," she said. "GPO practices such as contract exclusivity, substantial fee structures, and product bundling, if allowed to continue, will so constrict potential markets that product segments where these practices are widely adopted will simply not be considered for venture capital backing." Bess Weathermen, testimony, Antitrust, Business Rights, and Competition Subcommittee of the U.S. Senate Judiciary Committee, Apr. 30, 2002.

41. Another way that monopolization hobbles innovation is that it destroys the culture, or environment, in which innovation can occur. When Ben Franklin was working on his Leyden jar, he only had to walk down the street to find workmen who could shape the implements and tools he needed to his exact specifications. Not so long ago, a dress designer or a Broadway costumer was able to find the materials and skills necessary to concoct almost any vision right within the few blocks of the Garment District. Consider, in contrast, this recent report from Britain. After local governments there launched an effort to develop a fashion and design industry to compete with that of Italy and France, the governments soon ran into a big problem. Almost no one manufactures clothing in Britain anymore, which means that the new designers have no access to either the materials or the skilled labor they need to realize their visions. In the United States, the same thing is happening in dozens if not hundreds of industries as monopolization and outsourcing result in the collapse of the support systems necessary for any rival to enter the market. "British Designers Crimped by Lack of Factories," Reuters, Feb. 21, 2008.

42. Schumpeter, *Capitalism, Socialism, and Democracy*, pp. 91 and 101.

43. It would be a mistake to view Thurmond Arnold as operating in the tradition of Jefferson, Madison, and Brandeis. Arnold was more of a classical progressive who believed that the prime goal of government regulation in the political economy was to ensure the efficient production and distribution of goods, not liberties. In his often brilliant 1937 critique of the American political economy, *The Folklore of Capitalism*, Arnold derided the idea of private property as an anachronism and assailed the antitrust laws of the day—not incorrectly—as serving mainly in buttressing the plutocracy's myth of market. Arnold also shared the classical progressive conviction that the political economy should be governed by a highly educated, technocratic elite, although he differed from many other classical progressives in his willingness to use the "myths" of Jeffersonian America to disguise this rule. Once installed by President Roosevelt atop the Antitrust Division, however, Arnold put into place a highly pragmatic—and effective—regime designed both to force corporate powers to compete, whenever possible, and to force them to share their intellectual treasures with the public.

44. D. A. Mindel, "Automation's Finest Hour: Bell Labs and Automatic Control in World War II," *IEEE Control Systems Magazine*, Dec. 1995; M. D. Fagen, *A History of Engineering and Science in the Bell System: National Service in War and Peace (1925 to 1975)*, (New York: Bell Telephone Laboratories, 1975).

45. F. M. Scherer, "Technological Innovation and Monopolization," Antitrust Division of the Justice Department, Mar. 2006, p. 24.

46. Alfred Chandler, *Inventing the Electronic Century* (New York: Free Press, 1991), p. 123.

47. David Serafino, "Survey of Patent Pools Demonstrates Variety of Purposes and Management Structures," Knowledge Ecology International Research Note 2007, June 4, 2007, available online at www. keionline. org/content/view/69.

48. "RCA Takes on Ford," *Time*, Apr. 27, 1962.

49. "As You Were," *Forbes*, Mar. 15, 1975; Scherer, "Technological Innovation and Monopolization," p. 17.

50. Study by the Senate Judiciary Committee. In David Hart, *Forged Consensus: Science, Technology, and Economic Policy in the United States, 1921–1953* (Princeton, NJ: Princeton University Press, 1996).

51. David Hounshell, *Science and Corporate Strategy: DuPont R&D, 1902–1980* (New York: Cambridge Univ. Press, 1988), pp. 597 and 600.

52. Chandler, *Inventing the Electronic Century*, p. 249.

53. Barry Jaruzelski and W. Frank Jones, "Manufacturing Analysts Survey—the 2007 Industrial Landscape: Six Issues Will Separate Winners from Losers," *The Manufacturer's Edge*, published by the Mid-America Manufacturing Technology Center.

54. Much of the information in this story comes from Douglas Brinkley, *Wheels for the World: Henry Ford, His Company, and a Century of Progress* (New York: Viking Press, 2003).

55. The dangers of this were illustrated in Germany during World War II. Even though aeronautical engineers perfected the world's first operational jet fighter in 1943, the Me 262, at the end of the war, in 1945, efforts to build great numbers of the aircraft were thwarted by the fact that the Luftwaffe's industrial engineers had embraced Fordist ideas even before the war. One result was that the main aircraft assembly lines were still tooled to crank out the Me 109, which had been an excellent plane in 1936. Adam Tooze, *The Wages of Destruction: The Making and Breaking of the Nazi Economy* (New York: Viking Press, 2006).

56. Ellen Byron, "Merger Challenge: United Toothbrush, Toothpaste," *Wall Street Journal*, Apr. 24, 2007.

57. Brian Hindo, "Winning the Ground War," *Business Week*, Dec. 17, 2007; U.S. Department of Agriculture, Economic Research Service, www.ers.usda.gov/StateFacts/US.htm; Elisabeth Rosenthal, "Backyard Gardens Shelter Europe's Orphan Seeds," *New York Times*, Nov. 27, 2007.

58. William Finnegan, "Blank Monday: Could Grubby Clark Destroy Surfing?" *New Yorker*, Aug. 21, 2006; Shawn Price, "Making a Comeback," *Orange County Register*, Dec. 22, 2006; "Wipe Out on Surf Pipeline," *Orange County Register*, Dec. 7, 2005.

59. Emerson, "Fortune of the Republic."

7. The American Piece

1. When BP Amoco took control of Atlantic Ritchfield Company (ARCO) in 2000, the Clinton administration required it to sell off ARCO's Cushing tank farms and pipelines as part of the deal; otherwise, the concentration of control would have been nearly complete.

2. Ruth Sheldon Knowles, *The Greatest Gamblers: The Epic of American Oil Exploration* (Norman: Univ. of Oklahoma, 1978), pp. 111–112.

3. Natural gas pipelines, by contrast, are regulated under the Natural Gas Act of 1938 and are treated as utilities. Natural Gas Supply Association, "The History of Regulation," available online at www.naturalgas.org/regulation/history.asp#earlydays.

4. Others were France's Compagnie Francaise de Petroles (CFP) and Royal Dutch/Shell of the Netherlands. Daniel Yergin, *The Prize: The Epic Quest for Oil, Money, and Power* (New York: Simon & Schuster, 1991).

5. The legislation was called the Petroleum Industry Competition Act of 1976. Janice Rubin, "Price Gouging: The Antitrust Laws and Vertical Integration in the Petroleum Industry," Congressional Research Service Report, Order Code RS22262, Mar. 15, 2007.

6. Reagan named a dentist, James B. Edwards, as his first energy secretary. Even before he took office, Edwards presented himself as a free-market man. "Good Answers on Energy," *Washington*

Post, Jan. 13, 1981. On the day that Reagan abolished federal controls on pricing, Edwards admitted to a reporter he was "a little confused" about the details of the legislation. Terence Hunt, Associated Press, Jan. 28, 1981.

7. Yergin, *The Prize*, p. 688.

8. Bassam Fattouh, "The Origins and Evolution of the Current International Oil Pricing System," in *Oil in the 21st Century: Issues, Challenges, and Opportunites*, ed. Robert Mabro (Oxford, UK: Oxford Univ. Press, 2006), p. 57; Francisco Parra, *Oil Politics: A Modern History of Petroleum* (London: I. B. Tauris, 2004), p. 320.

9. In one of the more perverse incentives in recent economic history, our gasoline refiners are rewarded for failures to maintain their plants. Jad Mouawad, "Record Failures at Oil Refineries Raise Gas Prices," *New York Times*, July 22, 2007.

10. Donald Spence, *Futures and Options* (Chicago: Glenlake, 1999), p. 18.

11. In December 2000, as the Clinton administration was drawing to a close and the Supreme Court was deciding *Bush v. Gore*, Senator Phil Gramm quietly attached the Commodity Futures Modernization Act to an eleven-thousand-page appropriations bill, which was then signed by President Clinton. James Ridgeway, "Phil Gramm's Enron Favor," *Village Voice*, Jan. 15, 2002. The bill allowed trading to move from regulated exchanges like NYMEX to unregulated online exchanges. As a result, most trading now takes place on the Intercontinental Exchange, which has an office in Atlanta but is regulated under Britain's looser market regulation laws and increasingly outside any regulated exchange whatsoever.

12. Chris Cook, "Oil Market Collapse Waiting to Happen," *Asia Times*, Sept. 24, 2008; Ed Wallace, "Oil Prices Are All Speculation," *BusinessWeek*, June 27, 2008. In June 2008, OPEC secretary general Abdullah al-Badri said that the total world demand for oil was 87 million barrels per day but that traders were exchanging 1.36 billion barrels per day on the "paper" market. "Saudis to Host Oil Producers, Consumers to Talk Prices," Reuters, June 10, 2008.

13. David Cho, "A Few Speculators Dominate Vast Market for Oil Trading," *Washington Post*, Aug. 21, 2008.

14. By mid-2007, some U.S. regulators had all but concluded that the market for oil was being heavily manipulated. Bart Chilton, "Dark Markets," Commodities Futures Trading Commission hearing, Sept. 18, 2007; Bart Stupak, testimony, House Subcommittee on Oversight and Investigations hearing on "Energy Speculation: Is Greater Regulation Necessary to Stop Price Manipulation?" Dec. 12, 2007; Ann Davis, "West Texas Oil Falters in Its Role as a Benchmark," *Wall Street Journal*, Apr. 23, 2007; Neil King Jr. and Spencer Swartz, "Oil Prices Detach from Demand in West," *Wall Street Journal*, Jan. 15, 2008; Steve Mufson, "Oil's Recent Rise Not as Familiar as It Looks," *Washington Post*, Nov. 7, 2007.

15. One of the main reasons Americans have had such a hard time recognizing the power that speculators can exert over the prices we pay for energy is that so few of our economists have ever bothered to study how these markets are actually structured. In one of the more embarrassing instances, Paul Krugman, in a series of columns and blog posts on the soaring price of oil during the spring of 2008, lectured his readers on the basic rules of supply and demand in physical markets without any apparent understanding of the fact that the price of oil is, in fact, made in the futures markets. To understand how such futures markets can be manipulated, Krugman and the other preachers of supply and demand need only have studied two recent instances in which energy markets were, in fact, cornered, and the corners were made public. The first instance took place in the winter of 2004 when energy traders working for BP cornered much of the U.S. market for propane in such a sloppy fashion that they were caught even by the Bush administration's Commodities Futures Trading Commission (CFTC). The traders cornered 90 percent of deliveries on the pipeline that runs from Mont Belvieu, Texas, to New York, enabling themselves to raise the price by at least 40 percent for this fuel, which is used mainly by rural and poor Americans to cook their food and heat their homes. "BP Agrees to Pay a Total of $303 Million in Sanctions to Settle Charges of Manipulation and Attempted Manipulation in the Propane Market," CFTC Press Release, Oct. 25, 2007. The second instance took place in the summer of 2006 when a trader for a hedge fund named Amaranth Advisors rolled up control of 70 percent

of natural gas futures contracts that were set for delivery in November of that year and 40 percent of contracts for the whole winter. After NYMEX forced the trader to release his holdings, he replicated his power on an unregulated exchange, where his corner was eventually broken by another trader. It is hard to add up the full cost of the Amaranth predation, but one utility estimated that the Amaranth manipulation cost its 243,000 customers $18 million, or $74 per family. David Cho, "Energy Traders Avoid Scrutiny," *Washington Post*, Oct. 21, 2007. In the summer of 2009, Krugman did finally admit that speculators were now able to move the oil markets.

16. In contrast, Southern planters remained strong advocates of direct seizure of territory in the Caribbean and in Central America until the Civil War.

17. The Irish political philosopher Edmund Burke was one of the leaders of the attacks on the East India Company, and he spoke in Parliament in support of a bill to reduce the company's power. Edmund Burke, "Speech on Fox's East India Bill, December 1, 1783," in *The Speeches of the Right Hon. Edmund Burke* (Dublin, Ireland: James Duffy, 1862).

18. Stanley Karnow, *In Our Image: America's Empire in the Philippines* (New York, Ballantine Books, 1989).

19. Robert Skidelsky, *John Maynard Keynes: Fighting for Freedom, 1937–1946* (New York: Penguin, 2000); Daniel Drache, *The Short but Significant Life of the International Trade Organization: Lessons for Our Time*, Working Paper No. 62/00 (Coventry, UK: University of Warwick Centre for the Study of Globalisation and Regionalisation, 2000).

20. Robert Gilpin, *U.S. Power and the Multinational Corporation: The Political Economy of Foreign Direct Investment* (New York, Basic Books, 1975); Lynn, *End of the Line*, chapters 1–3; Barry C. Lynn, "War Trade and Utopia," *National Interest*, no. 82, p. 31, Winter 2005–2006.

21. John Gillingham, *Coal, Steel, and the Rebirth of Europe, 1945–1955: The Germans and French from Ruhr Conflict to Economic Community* (New York: Cambridge Univ. Press, 1991).

22. After Japan set up the puppet state of Manchukuo in northern China in the 1930s, the Japanese military established a major industrial center there, with factories capable of producing airplanes, trucks, automobiles, locomotives, heavy weapons, and machine tools. The Soviets seized most of the machinery after the war.

23. The big boost in Japan took place during the Korean War, which began in 1950, as the United States began to enlist Japanese manufacturers to build trucks and other equipment for the war effort (in order not to disrupt civilian production at home). The Americans never really turned back. The desire to turn Japanese industrial capacity and know-how against the Soviet bloc, combined with the desire to tie Japan so intimately to the U.S. economy that the nation could never break free, led to a series of decisions to transfer both technology and market share to Japanese manufacturers that continues today (if, for instance, we consider the recent Boeing technology transfer and production policy for the 787 Dreamliner). The experiment in Japan proved so successful that beginning in the mid-1950s we extended the same basic model to both South Korea and Taiwan (then known as Nationalist China). A decade later, as the Vietnam War heated up, we extended our industrial web to Thailand, Malaysia, and Singapore.

24. One of the most subtle efforts was engineered by President George H. W. Bush, when the government used supposed safety issues to threaten Chile's lucrative exports of fruit and wine and thereby helped to push General Augusto Pinochet from power.

25. Geir Lundestad, *"Empire" by Integration: The United States and European Integration, 1945–1997* (New York: Oxford Univ. Press, 1998).

26. Kenichi Ohmae, *The Borderless World: Power and Strategy in the Interlinked Economy* (New York: HarperCollins, 1990), p. 216.

27. Milton Friedman's utopian approach to trade is captured in his 1980 essay "The Tyranny of Controls," in which he states, "We should move unilaterally to free trade, not instantaneously but over a period of, say, five years, at a pace announced in advance. Few measures that we could take would do more to promote the cause of freedom at home and abroad than complete free trade. Instead of making grants to foreign governments in the name of economic aid—thereby promoting socialism—while at the same time imposing restrictions on the products they produce—thereby hindering free enterprise—we could assume a consistent and principled stance.

We could say to the rest of the world: We believe in freedom and intend to practice it. We cannot force you to be free. But we can offer full cooperation on equal terms to all. Our market is open to you without tariffs or any restrictions. Sell here what you can and wish to. Buy whatever you can and wish to. In that way cooperation among individual can be worldwide and free." The essay can be found in Milton Friedman and Rose Friedman, *Free to Choose: A Personal Statement* (New York: Harcourt Brace Jovanovich, 1980).

28. E. J. Dionne, "Inventing Clintonomics," *Washington Post*, Oct. 15, 1992.
29. Reich, *The Work of Nations*, p. 3.
30. Bill Clinton, foreign policy statement, Federal News Service, Oct. 24, 1997.
31. The same year, in contrast, the Clinton administration offered then democratic Russia membership not in the WTO but in the Group of Seven.
32. "Energising Europe: A Real Market with Secure Energy," European Commission press release, IP/07/1361, Sept. 19, 2007.
33. Oxford Analytica, "EU Considers Energy Market Competition," *Forbes*, Sept. 20, 2007.
34. Russia forged strategic alliances with Algeria, Egypt, and Libya, as well as with Nigeria in western Africa. It also declared itself in de facto control, in December 2007, of a pipeline that was planned to carry oil from Turkmenistan and Kazakhstan to western Europe through the international waters of the Caspian Sea and into the border of Russia. In early 2008, Russia also secured tighter control over Serbia's state energy company and won permission to control the pipelines that cross Bulgaria to western Europe.
35. The United States and the European Union have long feared that Russia would cobble together a natural gas cartel. The reality is worse. In early 2008, Europe imported nearly 60 percent of its gas, and by that time Russia had captured some control over the delivery and pricing of about 60 percent of that. Both percentages are growing fast. For many individual European nations and allies—Hungary, Poland, the Czech Republic, and Turkey—direct dependence on Russia for gas ranges from 65 to nearly 100 percent.
36. Italy also signed a bilateral pipeline deal with Russia.
37. Chernow, *Titan*, p. 208.
38. This strategy was first attempted in 1956 by one of Putin's predecessors in the Kremlin, Nikita Khrushchev. Not only did Khrushchev support the Egyptian president Gamal Abdel Nasser's seizure of the Suez Canal, through which most of Europe's oil imports then passed, which lured Britain and France into their politically disastrous war in Egypt; the Soviet premier followed this up with an intentional effort to destabilize Western oil prices and to forge direct dependencies.
39. Ernesto Londoño, "Iraq Rejects No-Bid Contracts," *Washington Post*, Sept. 12, 2008; Erica Goode and Riyadh Mohammed, "Iraq Signs Oil Deal with China Worth up to $3 Billion," *New York Times*, Aug. 28, 2008.
40. China also apparently benefits from Russia's stranglehold on Europe. Michael Ritchie, "China Pumps Cash into Turkmen Gas Pipe," *International Oil Daily*, Dec. 31, 2007.
41. Japan also took a harder line after BHP Billiton announced plans to acquire Rio Tinto. Norie Hata, "Japan to Probe Rio Tinto–BHP Billiton Nexus," *Financial Times*, Mar. 24, 2008.
42. Julia Werdigier, "Chinalco to Invest $19.5 billion in Rio Tinto," *New York Times*, Feb. 12, 2009; Lina Saigol and Kate Burgess, "Chinalco Walks Away from $19.5bn Rio Deal," *Financial Times*, June 5, 2009; Patti Waldmeir and Sundeep Tucker, "China Antitrust Threat Over Plan for BHP-Rio Tinto Joint Venture," *Financial Times*, June 18, 2009; "China May Block BHP-Rio Joint Venture," Reuters, Aug. 3, 2009.

    The United States provided China with the model. In 1928, the Canadian mining company Inco rolled up control over the nickel mines near Sudbury, Ontario, giving it pricing power over 90 percent of all nickel sold in the United States. Throughout the next eighteen years, through the Depression and the war, Inco kept the price of a pound of nickel at 35 cents. In 1946, the U.S. government filed an antitrust suit against the firm and three of its U.S. officers. As a result, the government of Quebec soon leased out new nickel-filled lands to about three dozen mining companies. "War against Nickel," *Time*, May 27, 1946; "Competition in Nickel," *Time*, July 22, 1957.

43. Ariana Eunjung Cha, "China Gains Key Assets in Spate of Purchases," *Washington Post*, Mar. 17, 2009.

44. The editor of *Foreign Policy* magazine has called this "rogue aid." Moises Naim, "Help Not Wanted," *New York Times*, Feb. 15, 2007. One of China's most effective ploys is to pretend to be far less wealthy than it actually is; in late 2008 it convinced the World Bank to revise its numbers to make China look poorer, at the very time that its power was swelling most swiftly. Keith Bradsher, "A Revisionist Tale: Why a Poor China Seems Richer," *New York Times*, Dec. 21, 2007. Indeed, China managed this trick even as it was using some of its $2 trillion in foreign reserves in highly sophisticated ways to project power against countries like Taiwan. Jamil Anderlini, "Beijing Uses Forex Reserves to Target Taiwan," *Financial Times*, Sept. 11. 2008.

45. China has been a less aggressive user of the sovereign wealth fund, in which a state invests surplus funds in overseas businesses and projects. Perhaps the main reason is that China prefers to have its hands much more firmly on the levers of power. Larry Summers, the director of President Obama's National Economic Council, once stated that sovereign wealth funds challenge the "nature of global capitalism." Larry Summers, "Sovereign Funds Shake the Logic of Capitalism," *Financial Times*, July 30, 2007. It's not clear, however, that such funds differ from any other form of direct or indirect control over corporations, other than that the funds are actually much less effective in projecting power than an industrial corporation or a trading company.

46. Like the East India Company, Wal-Mart enjoys the power to suppress production in the target market, the right to interfere blatantly in politics at all levels, and a de facto form of police power. Michael Barbaro, "Wal-Mart Chief Offers a Social Manifesto" and "Wal-Mart: The New Washington," *New York Times*, Jan. 24 and Feb. 3, 2008; Joyce Smith, "Motto of the Future: In Wal-Mart We Trust," *Kansas City Star*, Jan. 24, 2008; Marcus Kabel, "Wal-Mart Recruits Intelligence Officers," Associated Press, Apr. 24, 2007.

47. The head of the Peterson Institute for International Economics advocates rewarding China for its refusal to cooperate within the existing international system, however imperfect, by ditching that system and establishing a special coregency over the world. C. Fred Bergsten, "A Partnership of Equals," *Foreign Affairs*, July–Aug. 2008.

48. "Pumping Cash, Not Oil," *BusinessWeek*, May 28, 2007. Every year from 1976 to 1997, ExxonMobil invested more than it made. Now it devotes less than half of its profits to investment. Floyd Norris, "High Profits, Sluggish Investments," *New York Times*, Feb. 3, 2006.

49. "Shell Settles Final Claim on Misreporting of Reserves," *Financial Times*, Mar. 7, 2008; "Shell Urges SEC to Ease Rules," *Financial Times*, Feb. 23, 2008.

50. The U.S. government is one of the most aggressive mercantilists in the world. What makes our mercantilism different from that of China, France, Germany, or Japan is that there is no strategic content to ours whatsoever. It is more a mercantilism for hire. One of the corporations that has made the best use of this power is Monsanto. "Spain's Customs Seizes Argentine Soymeal Shipments at U.S.-Based Monsanto's Request," *Daily Report for Executives*, Jan. 30, 2006; John Miller, "U.S. Threatens Sanctions on EU," *Wall Street Journal*, Jan. 18, 2008.

51. Many other countries have also proved adept at such resource raids. One of the more sophisticated was run by India in the seemingly mundane chemical known as soda ash, which is used in a variety of activities, including the manufacture of glass and detergents, and which is found in natural deposits or can be synthesized chemically. For many years, India maintained the highest soda ash tariff in the world, to protect Tata Chemicals, Gujarat Heavy Chemicals, and Birla VXL India, a stance that led to trade tensions with the Clinton administration in 2000. There was, to be honest, good reason for India to protect itself: during those same years, the members of the European chemical cartel, led by ICI and Solvay, were overseeing both a massive elimination of soda ash capacity around the world and the maintenance of a high fixed price. By 2005, these companies had managed to trim down the domestic supply of soda ash in the United States to the point that U.S. producers were sold out and prices began to rise. In November 2007, the Indian soap and detergent maker Nirma purchased Searles Valley Minerals of California in order to begin shipping U.S. mined soda ash to India, with profits going to the Indian company. Nancy Dunne, "Clinton Team Acts on Soda Ash Dispute," *Financial Times*, Feb. 15, 2000;

"Commission Adopts New Decisions Fining Solvay and ICI over Soda Ash Cartel," *European Report*, Dec. 16, 2000; "Soda Ash Plant Closures: 1990–2004," slide presentation by Owens Illinois to investors, Nov. 15, 2005; Michael Wilson, "Soda Ash and Hydrogen Peroxide Update," FMC Corporation, Mar. 11, 2005, available at www.fmc.com; "Nirma to Acquire U.S. Firm," *Times of India*, Nov. 28, 2007.

8. Wreckonomics 101

1. Scottsdale Residential Single-Family Neighborhood Development Themes, 1947–1960, available online at www.scottsdaleaz.gov/assets/documents/historiczoning/postwarthemes.pdf.
2. Dylan McGrath, "'Silicon Desert' Blooms in Arizona," *Electronic News*, Mar. 30, 1998; Edyth Jensen, "Motorola to Move Employees to Tempe," *Arizona Republic*, June 14, 2007; Jane Larsen, "High-Tech Leaders Unveil Arizona Economic Development Plan," *Arizona Republic*, Dec. 19, 2003.
3. Lynn, *End of the Line*.
4. Before Ed Zander was ousted as head of Motorola, he was fond of declaring, "I love my job. I hate my customers," by which he meant not the American consumer but Verizon and AT&T. Christopher Rhoads and Li Yuan, "How Motorola Fell a Giant Step Behind," *Wall Street Journal*, Apr. 27, 2007. Nor was Zander alone in this sentiment. Nokia CEO Olli-Pekka Kallasvuo told investors, "In China, we do have about 1.3 billion customers—or potential customers—meaning the consumers in that market. In the U.S., we have four—and I'm not talking about billions here. Four customers . . . Verizon Wireless, Sprint Nextel, AT&T, and T-Mobile, the four customers that really are very, very important in the totality." Nokia Q1 2007 Earnings Call transcript, Apr. 19, 2007.
5. Julie Johnsson, "Zander's Motorola: How a Brash New CEO Tore Down Walls," *Crain's Chicago Business*, July 10, 2006.
6. O'Boyle, *At Any Cost*, p. 36.
7. Rob Kaiser, "Motorola CEO Galvin Resigns," *Chicago Tribune*, Sept. 20, 2003; Roger O. Crockett, "How Motorola Got Its Groove Back," *BusinessWeek*, Aug. 8, 2005.
8. Li Yuan and Christopher Rhoads, "Icahn Bid Adds to Woes Dogging Motorola CEO," *Wall Street Journal*, Jan. 31, 2007; Sara Silver, "Motorola Hung Up by Handsets," *Wall Street Journal*, Feb. 22, 2008; Sara Silver and Roger Cheng, "Motorola Handset Sales Fall 39%," *Wall Street Journal*, Apr. 25, 2008; Emily Thornton, "When a Buyout Goes Bad," *BusinessWeek*, Apr. 14, 2008.
9. Bryan Burrough, and John Helyar, *Barbarians at the Gate: The Fall of RJR Nabisco* (New York: Harper & Row, 1990).
10. Germany may err somewhat in the other direction. Historian Adam Tooze recently searched for all of the industrial companies listed in Nazi armaments minister Albert Speer's address book, and he found every one still alive and well. Tooze, *The Wages of Destruction*.
11. Anthony Faiola, "The End of American Capitalism?" *Washington Post*, Oct. 10, 2008.
12. Schumpeter, *Capitalism, Socialism, and Democracy*, p. 83.
13. Karl Marx, *Capital* (Chicago: Charles H. Kerr, 1906), p. 836.
14. A modern truism holds that capitalism, as one former editor of the *Economist* put it, is "inherently unstable." This is nonsense. The only thing that is unstable is the political system we use to govern the naturally volatile element that is the human being. Bill Emmott, *20:21 Vision: Twentieth-Century Lessons for the Twenty-first Century* (London: Allen Lane, 2003) p. 228.
15. "If the plots were dispersed . . . everyone had some hope of avoiding the full impact of natural or human disasters." Marc Bloch, *French Rural History: An Essay on Its Basic Characteristics* (Berkeley: Univ. of California Press, 1966), p. 55. Anthropologists have documented such scattering in Britain, France, Greece, and Japan and among Native American nations. Donald N. McCloskey, "The Open Fields of England: Rent, Risk, and Rate of Interest, 1300–1850," in *Markets in History: Economic Studies of the Past*, ed. David Galenson (Cambridge, UK: Cambridge Univ. Press, 1989), pp. 5–51.
16. The link between property concentration and power was well illustrated after the Norman invasion of England, when William the Conqueror rewarded his followers not with whole fiefs but rather with properties scattered across the countryside, so as to make it hard if not impossible

for the new lords to raise a force that would be able to topple him from power. Emile Boutmy, *The English Constitution*, trans. Isabel Eaden (London: Macmillan, 1891).

17. Limited liability law was first introduced in New York in 1848. It was rarely used, however, and most larger enterprises tended to be small partnerships. It was only after the Civil War that New York financiers, and financiers elsewhere, really began to experiment with the "immensely greater opportunities" afforded by this alternative form of bank. Charles R. Van Hise, *Big Business: Economic Power in a Free Society* (New York: Macmillan, 1912), p. 21.

18. Adolf Berle and Gardiner Means in 1932 wrote that the American system was one of "*collective capitalism.*" Adolf Berle and Gardiner Means, *The Modern Corporation and Private Property* (New York: Harcourt, Brace & World, 1968).

19. Schumpeter, *Capitalism, Socialism, and Democracy*, p. 142.

20. Adam Smith attacked the dangers of such ownership in 1776. "Joint stock" companies, he wrote, are bastions of "negligence and profusion," not least because investors "seldom pretend to understand anything of the business." Smith, *The Wealth of Nations*, p. 800. A century later, the speculator Jay Gould was popularly known as the "destroying angel of Wall Street." Joseph-son, *Edison*, p. 96. See also Henry Hansmann, Reinier Kraakman, and Richard Squire, "Law and the Rise of the Firm," *Harvard Law Review*, vol. 119:1333 (Mar. 2006), pp. 1333–1403.

21. The most complete work on this subject—Berle and Means, *The Modern Corporation and Private Property*—was originally published in 1932, ten years before Schumpeter's own com-plaint. The most eloquent view can be found in chapter 3 of Lippmann, *Drift and Mastery*, where he wrote, "When a man buys stock in some large corporate he becomes in theory one of its owners. He is supposed to be exercising his instinct of private property. But how in fact does he exercise that instinct which we are told is the only real force in civilization? He may never *see* his property. He may not know where his property is situated. He is not consulted as to its management. He would be utterly incapable of advice if he were consulted. Contact with his property is limited to reading in the newspapers what it is worth each day, and hoping that dividends will be paid. The processes which make him rich in the morning and poor in the evening, increase his income or decrease it, are inscrutable mysteries. . . . No one has ever had a more abstract relation to the thing he owned. The absentee landlord is one of the sin-ister figures of history. But the modern shareholder is not only an absentee, he is a transient too." Lippmann concluded that "the modern shareholder is a person of no account whatever" (pp. 45–46 and 47).

22. Yehouda Shenhav, *Manufacturing Rationality*, posits that the modern industrial firm was largely imagined in the first place by scientists and engineers as a way to organize the world to serve themselves. Engineers were the "main actors in this drama," he writes. They "sought ascendancy for their systems and themselves in a context where capital and labor were much more powerful. Engineers triumphed." The result was a "relocation of power from the tradi-tional capitalist order into the hands of technocrats" (pp. 3, 45.)

    As David F. Noble, *America by Design*, put it, "These engineers held some important advan-tages which their opposition lacked. First, they enjoyed great social power and prestige, based upon their exalted positions within the new corporations and a web of political, economic, social, and family ties among the country's propertied elite. Second, and of equal importance, they marched under a banner which confounded their opposition: the banner of science" (p. xxv).

23. Lippmann, *Drift and Mastery*, p. 32.

24. Kenneth Bilby, *The General: David Sarnoff and the Rise of the Communications Industry* (New York: Harper & Row, 1986), pp. 46–47.

25. By 1932, many had come to see these professional managers as "economic autocrat[s]." Berle and Means, *The Modern Corporation and Private Property*, p. 116.

26. Lippmann, *Drift and Mastery*, p. 59.

27. We see unionized labor functioning as one of the owners of an enterprise most obviously when mergers and acquisitions are proposed, such as the Delta Airlines takeover of Northwest Air-lines, or when Cerberus considered a bid for the auto parts maker Delphi. Jeffrey McCracken, "Talks to Buy Delphi Hit Snag with Union," *Wall Street Journal*, Apr. 17, 2007.

28. Much of the thinking on this issue was shaped by Berle and Means, *The Modern Corporation and Private Property*.

29. As one of the main "gadfly" activists who helped to win this change in the law put it, "More corporate democracy means more corporate dividends." Lewis Gilbert, *Dividends and Democracy* (Larchmont, NY: American Research Council, 1956), p. 3.

30. In 1976, activists submitted at least 336 resolutions at the meetings of 217 companies pushing for the corporations to show greater "social responsibility" on such issues as investments in Rhodesia, the Arab boycott of Israel, and nuclear power. By 1980, the idea had become central to a push by Ralph Nader and John Kenneth Galbraith for a piece of legislation called the Corporate Democracy Act. Richard Marens, "Inventing Corporate Governance: The Mid-Century Emergence of Shareholder Activism," *Journal of Business and Management*, vol. 8 no. 4 (Fall 2002), pp. 365–389.

31. The phenomenal degree of concentration in the U.S. economy under Morgan and the progressives was made evident to the American people only in 1912, when members of the House Banking Committee ordered J. P. Morgan to Capitol Hill to explain the working of what at the time was called the Money Trust. This was a banking cartel—solidified by interlocking investments and directorates—that Morgan had used to all but formally unify the operations of the nation's top three banks, J. P. Morgan & Co., First National, and National City. Morgan used the trust, which also included three other large banks, to govern the market for bonds and other securities in a way that largely enabled him to govern the entire industrial system in the United States. Despite Theodore Roosevelt's claim to be a trustbuster, the Pujo hearings made clear that he had in fact left the great trust maker largely free to continue his acts of *morganization*, with the apparent intent of then using the state to take direct control over the resulting apparatus. (Chernow, *The House of Morgan*, p. 156.)

32. Louis Brandeis, testimony before the Senate Committee on Interstate Commerce, Dec. 14, 1911. In "Control of Corporations, Persons, and Firms Engaged in Interstate Commerce," Report of the Committee on Interstate Commerce: United States Senate (Washington, D.C.: Government Printing Office, 1913) p. 1147.

33. Louis Brandeis, *Other People's Money and How the Bankers Use It* (New York: F. A. Stokes, 1914), p. 139.

34. Where the New Deal–era democratic republicans came up short was in formalizing their constitutionalist approach to reordering the U.S. political economy. In 1959, Harvard economist Edward Mason assembled a remarkable set of essays by some of our premier legal scholars and political economists on the institutional interlinkages between the Constitution and the limited liability business corporation. In his introduction, Mason summed up this failure with a personal prayer for a "twentieth-century [philosopher like Thomas] Hobbes or [John] Locke to bring some order into our thinking about the corporation and its role in society." Edward Mason, ed., *The Corporation in Modern Society* (Cambridge, MA: Harvard Univ. Press, 1959), p. 19. Unfortunately, this never happened.

35. Milton Friedman, "The Social Responsibility of Business Is to Increase Its Profits," *New York Times*, Sept. 13, 1970.

36. Richard Phalom, "The Return of the Proxy Fighter," *Forbes*, Nov. 12, 1979.

37. During the 1992 campaign, the Clintonites assailed CEOs as greedy, because in the twelve years after the election of Ronald Reagan their salaries jumped from about fifty times that of the lowest-paid janitor on their staff to about a hundred times, or nearly $4 million per year. The new rules meant that some CEOs began to walk away at the end of the year with hundreds of millions of dollars in their pockets. Michael Jensen and William Meckling, "Theory of the Firm: Management Behavior, Agency Costs and Ownership Structure," *Journal of Financial Economics*, vol. 3, no. 4 (Oct. 1976), pp. 122–126.

38. It is not surprising that much of that cash ends up in the hands of the CEO, who has his hands on the levers of power. Between 1999 and 2001, the CEOs of the twenty-five biggest corporate wrecks—including Enron, WorldCom, and Global Crossing—sailed off with $33 billion in their pockets. It is important to be clear that these men had very little in common with the CEO of

the stakeholder era. The problem is not the office of the CEO per se. The problem is to combine the CEO and the capitalist. In large industrial firms, we want the CEO to stand up against the capitalist. Ian Cheng, "Barons of Bankruptcy," *Financial Times*, Aug. 1, 2002.

39. This is a rephrasing of the famous statement in Brandeis, *Other People's Money and How the Bankers Use It*, "The fetters which bind the people are forged from the people's own gold" (p. 57).

40. Bankers today are, of course, just as able to concentrate power in a conscious manner and to distribute market share as was Morgan with his Money Trust. Dennis Berman and Russell Gold, "Believe It: A Goldman, Morgan Stanley Tango," *Wall Street Journal*, Jan. 24, 2007.

41. Even Jack Welch finally stepped up to denounce the assaults, admitting in the process that the shareholder-value movement was a "dumb idea." Francisco Guerrera, "Welch Denounces Corporate Obsessions," *Financial Times*, Mar. 13, 2009.

9. To Keep Our Republic

1. Franklin Roosevelt, "Government and Modern Capitalism," September 30, 1934, fireside chat, in *FDR's Fireside Chats*, ed. Russell D. Buhite and David W. Levy (Norman: Univ. of Oklahoma, 1992), p. 62.

2. Friedrich Hayek, "The Use of Knowledge in Society," *American Economic Review*, vol. 35, no. 4, pp. 519–530.

3. Ibid.

4. Francis Bacon, "The Great Instauration," in *Collected Works*, ed. James Spedding, (London: Routledge, 1996), p. 32.

5. Loren R. Graham, *Science, Philosophy, and Human Behavior in the Soviet Union* (New York: Columbia Univ. Press, 1987).

6. Mary French Caldwell, *Tennessee: The Dangerous Example* (Nashville: Aurora, 1974), p. 29.

7. John Nicolay, *A Short Life of Abraham Lincoln* (New York: Century, 1917), p. 5.

Select Bibliography

Acheson, Dean. *Power and Diplomacy.* Cambridge, MA: Harvard Univ. Press, 1958.

Adams, Charles F., and Henry Adams. *Chapters of Erie and Other Essays.* Boston: James R. Osgood, 1871.

Adelman, M. A., *A&P: A Study in Price-Cost Behavior and Public Policy.* Cambridge, MA: Harvard Univ. Press, 1966.

Aftalion, Fred. *A History of the International Chemical Industry.* Philadelphia: Chemical Heritage Press, 2001.

Anderson, Chris. *The Long Tail: Why the Future of Business Is Selling Less of More.* New York: Hyperion Books, 2006.

Appleby, Joyce. *Capitalism and a New Social Order: The Republican Vision of the 1790s.* New York: New York Univ. Press, 1984.

Arnold, Thurman. *The Bottlenecks of Business.* New York: Reynal & Hitchcock, 1940.

———. *The Folklore of Capitalism.* New Haven, CT: Yale Univ. Press, 1937.

Ayres, C. E. *Toward a Reasonable Society.* Austin: Univ. of Texas Press, 1961.

Bacon, Francis. "The Great Instauration." In *Collected Works,* ed. James Spedding. London: Routledge, 1996.

Bagehot, Walter. *The English Constitution and Other Political Essays.* New York: D. Appleton, 1904.

Bassett, John Spencer. *The Life of Andrew Jackson.* New York: Macmillan, 1925.

Bean, Jonathan. *Beyond the Broker State: Federal Policies toward Small Business, 1936–1961.* Chapel Hill: Univ. of North Carolina Press, 1996.

Berle, Adolf, and Gardiner Means. *The Modern Corporation and Private Property.* New York: Harcourt, Brace, & World, 1968.

Bestor, Theodore. *Tsukiji: The Fish Market at the Center of the World.* Berkeley: Univ. of California Press, 2004.

Bhagwati, Jagdish. *The Wind of the Hundred Days: How Washington Mismanaged Globalization.* Cambridge, MA: MIT Press, 2000.

Bilby, Kenneth. *The General: David Sarnoff and the Rise of the Communications Industry.* New York: Harper & Row, 1986.

Blair, Margaret. *Ownership and Control: Rethinking Corporate Governance for the Twenty-First Century.* Washington, DC: Brookings Institution Press, 1995.

Bloch, Marc. *French Rural History: An Essay on Its Basic Characteristics.* Berkeley: Univ. of California Press, 1966.

Bork, Robert H. *The Antitrust Paradox.* New York: Basic Books, 1978.

Boutmy, Emile. *The English Constitution,* trans. Isabel Eaden. London: Macmillan, 1891.

Brandeis, Louis. *Other People's Money and How the Bankers Use It.* New York: F. A. Stokes, 1914.

Brands, H. W. *The First American: The Life and Times of Benjamin Franklin.* New York: Doubleday, 2000.

Braudel, Fernand. *Civilization and Capitalism, 15th–18th Century.* vol. 2, *The Wheels of Capitalism.* Berkeley: Univ. of California Press, 1992.

Brinkley, Douglas. *Wheels for the World: Henry Ford, His Company, and a Century of Progress.* New York: Viking Press, 2003.

Brownlee, Shannon. *Overtreated: Why Too Much Medicine Is Making Us Sicker and Poorer.* New York: Bloomsbury, 2007.

Brunell, Richard M. "The Social Cost of Mergers: Restoring 'Local Control' as a Factor in Merger Policy." *North Carolina Law Review,* vol. 81, no. 1 (2006).

Burke, Edmund. "Speech on Fox's East India Bill, December 1, 1783." In *The Speeches of the Right Hon. Edmund Burke.* Dublin, Ireland: James Duffy, 1862.

Burnham, James. *The Managerial Revolution.* New York: John Day, 1941.

Burrough, Bryan, and John Helyar. *Barbarians at the Gate: The Fall of RJR Nabisco.* New York: Harper & Row, 1990.

Butler, Michael. *Cautious Visionary: Cordell Hull and Trade Reform, 1933–1937.* Kent, OH: Kent State Univ. Press, 1998.

Caldwell, Mary French. *Tennessee: The Dangerous Example.* Nashville: Aurora, 1974.

Carlyle, Thomas. *Chartism: Past and Present.* Boston: Charles C. Little and James Brown, 1840.

Chamberlin, Edward Hastings. *The Theory of Monopolistic Competition: A Reorientation of the Theory of Value.* Cambridge, MA: Harvard Univ. Press, 1933.

Chandler, Alfred. *Inventing the Electronic Century.* New York: Free Press, 1991.

———. *Scale and Scope: The Dynamics of Industrial Capitalism.* Cambridge, MA: Harvard Univ. Press, 1990.

———. *The Visible Hand: The Managerial Revolution in American Business.* Cambridge, MA: Harvard Univ. Press, 1977.

Cheny, Margaret. *Tesla: Man Out of Time.* New York: Touchstone, 1981.

Chernow, Ron. *Alexander Hamilton,* New York, Penguin, 2004.

———. *The House of Morgan: An American Banking Dynasty and the Rise of Modern Finance.* New York: Atlantic Monthly Press, 1990.

———. *Titan: The Life of John D. Rockefeller, Sr.* New York: Random House, 1998.

Coase, Ronald. "The Nature of the Firm." In *The Firm, the Market, and the Law.* Chicago: Univ. of Chicago Press, 1990.

Cohen, I. Bernard. *Benjamin Franklin's Science.* Cambridge, MA: Harvard Univ. Press, 1990.

Coletta, Paolo. *William Jennings Bryan: Political Evangelist.* Lincoln: Univ. of Nebraska Press, 1964.

Coll, Steve. *The Deal of the Century: The Breakup of AT&T.* New York: Touchstone, 1986.

Commons, John R. *Legal Foundations of Capitalism.* New York: Macmillan, 1924.

Connor, John M. "The Great Global Vitamins Conspiracy: Sanctions and Deterrence." Working Paper No. 06–02. Washington, DC: American Antitrust Institute, 2006.

Cooke, Frederick H. *The Law of Combinations, Monopolies, and Labor Unions.* Chicago: Callaghan, 1909.

Cox, Harvey. "The Market as God." *The Atlantic,* Mar. 1999.

Croly, Herbert. *The Promise of American Life.* New York: Macmillan, 1909.

Cronon, William. *Nature's Metropolis: Chicago and the Great West.* New York: W. W. Norton, 1991.

Davidow, William, and Michael Malone. *The Virtual Corporation: Structuring and Revitalizing the Corporation for the 21st Century.* New York: HarperBusiness, 1992.

Drache, Daniel. "The Short but Significant Life of the International Trade Organization: Lessons for Our Time." Working Paper No. 62/00. Coventry, UK: University of Warwick Centre for the Study of Globalisation and Regionalisation, 2000.

Dray, Philip. *Stealing God's Thunder: Benjamin Franklin's Lightning Rod.* New York: Random House, 2005.

Drucker, Peter. *Concept of the Corporation.* New York: John Day, 1946.

———. *The Unseen Revolution: How Pension Fund Socialism Came to America.* New York: Harper & Row, 1976.

Dyer, Christopher. "Market Towns and the Countryside in Late Medieval England." *Canadian Journal of History,* vol. 31 (1996), pp. 17–35.

Emerson, Ralph Waldo. "Fortune of the Republic." In *Selected Lectures,* ed. Ronald Bosco, pp. 319–335. Athens: Univ. of Georgia Press, 2005.

Emmott, Bill. *20:21 Vision: Twentieth-Century Lessons for the Twenty-first Century.* London: Allen Lane, 2003.

Ewen, Stuart. *Captains of Consciousness: Advertising and the Social Roots of the Consumer Culture.* New York: McGraw-Hill, 1976.

Fagen, M. D. "A History of Engineering and Science in the Bell System: National Service in War and Peace (1925 to 1975)." New York: Bell Telephone Laboratories, 1975.

Fattouh, Bassam. "The Origins and Evolution of the Current International Oil Pricing System." In *Oil in the 21st Century: Issues, Challenges, and Opportunities,* ed. Robert Mabro, pp. 41–100. Oxford, UK: Oxford Univ. Press, 2006.

Finley, M. I. *The Ancient Economy.* Berkeley: Univ. of California Press, 1973.

Fischer, David Hackett. *Albion's Seed: Four British Folkways in America.* New York: Oxford Univ. Press, 1989.

Fishman, Charles. *The Wal-Mart Effect: How the World's Most Powerful Company Really Works.* New York: Penguin, 2006.

Foley, John, ed. *The Jefferson Cyclopedia.* New York: Funk & Wagnalls, 1900.

Foner, Eric. *Free Soil, Free Labor, Free Men: The Ideology of the Republican Party before the Civil War.* New York: Oxford Univ. Press, 1970.

Fox, J. Ronald. *Arming America: How the U.S. Buys Weapons.* Cambridge, MA: Harvard Univ. Press, 1974.

Franklin, Benjamin. *Autobiography.* London: J. M. Dent, 1905.

———. "Letter to Peter Collinson." In *The Works of Benjamin Franklin,* ed. John Bigelow. New York: G. P. Putnam's Sons, 1904.

Freeland, Robert. "Creating Holdup through Vertical Integration: Fisher Body Revisited," *Journal of Law and Economics,* vol. 43, no. 1 (2000), pp. 33–66.

Friedman, Milton. *Capitalism and Freedom.* Chicago: Univ. of Chicago Press, 1962.

———. "The Social Responsibility of Business Is to Increase Its Profits." *New York Times,* Sept. 13, 1970.

Friedman, Milton, and Rose Friedman. *Free to Choose: A Personal Statement.* New York: Harcourt Brace Jovanovich, 1980.

Friedman, Thomas. *The World Is Flat: A Brief History of the Twenty-first Century.* New York: Farrar, Straus and Giroux, 2005.

Fuller, Robert Higginson. *Jubilee Jim: The Life of Colonel James Fisk, Jr.* New York: Macmillan, 1930.

Galbraith, James K. *The Predator State: How Conservatives Abandoned the Free Market and Why Liberals Should Too.* New York: Free Press, 2008.

Galbraith, John Kenneth. *Economics and the Public Purpose.* Boston: Houghton Mifflin, 1973.

———. *The New Industrial State.* Boston: Houghton Mifflin, 1967.

Gardner, Joseph L. *Departing Glory: Theodore Roosevelt as Ex-President.* New York: Charles Scribner's Sons, 1973.

Gelfand, Lawrence. *Herbert Hoover: The Great War and Its Aftermath.* Iowa City: Univ. of Iowa Press, 1979.

George, Henry. *Progress and Poverty: An Inquiry into the Cause of Industrial Depressions, and of Increase of Want with Increase of Wealth.* New York: Robert Schalkenbach Foundation, 1966.

Ghemawat, Pankaj. "Sustainable Advantage." *Harvard Business Review,* vol. 64, no. 5 (Sept.–Oct. 1986), p. 53.

Gilbert, Lewis. *Dividends and Democracy.* Larchmont, NY: American Research Council, 1956.

Gillingham, John. *Coal, Steel, and the Rebirth of Europe, 1945–1955: The Germans and French from Ruhr Conflict to Economic Community.* New York: Cambridge Univ. Press, 1991.

Gilpin, Robert. *U.S. Power and the Multinational Corporation: The Political Economy of Foreign Direct Investment.* New York: Basic Books, 1975.

Gordon, Colin. *New Deals: Business, Labor, and Politics in America, 1920–1935.* Cambridge, UK: Cambridge Univ. Press, 1994.

Graham, Benjamin. *Storage and Stability: A Modern Ever-Normal Granary.* New York: McGraw-Hill, 1937.

Graham, Loren R. *Science, Philosophy, and Human Behavior in the Soviet Union.* New York: Columbia Univ. Press, 1987.

Gratzer, Walter. *Terrors of the Table: The Curious History of Nutrition.* Oxford, UK: Oxford Univ. Press, 2005.

Green, Nancy. "Sweatshop Migrations: The Garment Industry between Home and Shop." In *The Landscape of Modernity: New York City 1900–1940,* ed. David Ward and Oliver Zunz, pp. 213–234. Baltimore: Johns Hopkins Univ. Press, 1992.

Greenspan, Alan. "Antitrust." In *Capitalism: The Unknown Ideal,* ed. Ayn Rand, Nathaniel Branden, Alan Greenspan, and Robert Hessen. New York: New American Library, 1966.

Hammer, Michael, and James Champy. *Reengineering the Corporation: A Manifesto for Business Revolution.* New York: Harper Business, 1993.

Handlin, Oscar, and Mary Flug Handlin. *Commonwealth: A Study of the Role of Government in the American Economy: Massachusetts, 1774–1861.* New York: New York Univ. Press, 1947.

Hansmann, Henry, Reinier Kraakman, and Richard Squire. "Law and the Rise of the Firm."*Harvard Law Review,* vol. 119 (Mar. 2006), pp. 1333–1403.

Harrison, Bennett. *Lean and Mean: The Changing Landscape of Corporate Power in the Age of Flexibility.* New York: Basic Books, 1994.

Hart, David M. "Antitrust and Technological Innovation in the U.S." *Issues in Science and Technology,* vol. 15, no. 2 (Winter 1998), pp. 75–82.

———. *Forged Consensus: Science, Technology, and Economic Policy in the United States, 1921–1953.* Princeton, NJ: Princeton Univ. Press, 1998.

———. "Herbert Hoover's Last Laugh: The Enduring Significance of the 'Associative State' in the U. S."*Journal of Policy History,* vol. 10, no. 3 (1998), pp. 419–444.

Hartz, Louis. *Economic Policy and Democratic Thought: Pennsylvania, 1776–1860.* Cambridge, MA: Harvard Univ. Press, 1948.

———. *The Liberal Tradition in America.* New York: Harcourt Brace, 1955.

Hawley, Ellis. *The New Deal and the Problem of Monopoly: A Study in Economic Ambivalence.* Princeton, NJ: Princeton Univ. Press, 1966.

Hayek, Friedrich A. *The Road to Serfdom.* Chicago: Univ. of Chicago Press, 1994.

———. "The Use of Knowledge in Society."*American Economic Review,* vol. 35, no. 4 (1945), pp. 519–530.

Hays, Samuel P. *Conservation and the Gospel of Efficiency: The Progressive Conservation Movement, 1890–1920.* Cambridge, MA: Harvard Univ. Press, 1959.

Heller, Francis, and John Gillingham. *The United States and the Integration of Europe.* New York: St. Martin's Press, 1996.

Hicks, John R. "Annual Survey of Economic Theory: The Theory of Monopoly," *Econometrica,* vol. 3, no. 1. (1935), pp. 1–20.

Hirschman, Albert O. *National Power and the Structure of Foreign Trade.* Berkeley: Univ. of California Press, 1945.

———. *The Rhetoric of Reaction: Perversity, Futility, Jeopardy.* Cambridge, MA: Belknap Press, 1991.

Hobbes, Thomas. *Leviathan.* New York: W. W. Norton, 1997.

Hofstadter, Richard. *Social Darwinism in American Thought.* Philadelphia: Univ. of Pennsylvania Press, 1944.

Horwitz, Morton J. *The Transformation of American Law, 1780–1860.* Cambridge, MA: Harvard Univ. Press, 1977.

Horwitz, Robert Britt. *Irony of Regulatory Reform: The Deregulation of American Telecommunications.* Oxford, UK: Oxford Univ. Press, 1988.

Hounshell, David. *From the American System to Mass Production, 1800–1932: The Development of Manufacturing Technology in the United States.* Baltimore: Johns Hopkins Univ. Press, 1984.

———. *Science and Corporate Strategy: DuPont R&D, 1902–1980.* New York: Cambridge Univ. Press, 1988.

Hoyt, Edwin. *That Wonderful A&P.* New York: Hawthorn Press, 1969.

Hutchinson, E. P. *The Population Debate: The Development of Conflicting Theories up to 1900*. Boston: Houghton Mifflin, 1967.

Jackson, Robert. "Financial Monopoly: The Road to Socialism." *The Forum*, vol. 100 (1938), available at www. roberthjackson. org.

Jensen, Michael, and William Meckling. "Theory of the Firm: Management Behavior, Agency Costs and Ownership Structure." *Journal of Financial Economics*, vol. 3, no. 4 (Oct. 1976).

Jonnes, Jill. *Empires of Light: Edison, Tesla, Westinghouse, and the Race to Electrify the World*. New York: Random House, 2003.

Joo, Thomas, ed. *Corporate Governance: Law, Theory and Policy*. Durham, NC: Carolina Academy Press, 2004.

Jorde, Thomas, and David Teece, eds. *Antitrust, Innovation, and Competitiveness*. New York: Oxford Univ. Press, 1992.

Josephson, Matthew. *Edison: A Biography*. New York: McGraw-Hill, 1959.

———. *The Robber Barons*. New York: Harcourt, Brace & World, 1934.

Kahn, B. Zorina. *The Democratization of Invention: Patents and Copyrights in American Economic Development, 1790–1920*. Cambridge, UK: Cambridge Univ. Press, 2005.

Kanigel, Robert. *The One Best Way: Frederick Winslow Taylor and the Enigma of Efficiency*. New York: Penguin, 1997.

Karnow, Stanley. *In Our Image: America's Empire in the Philippines*. New York: Ballantine Books, 1989.

Kars, Marjoleine. *Breaking Loose Together: The Regulator Rebellion in Pre-Revolutionary North Carolina*. Chapel Hill: Univ. of North Carolina, 2002.

Kaysen, Carl, ed. *The American Corporation Today*. New York: Oxford Univ. Press, 1996.

Kazin, Michael. *A Godly Hero: The Life of William Jennings Bryan*. New York: Alfred A. Knopf, 2006.

Keay, John. *The Honourable Company: A History of the English East India Company*. New York: Macmillan, 1991.

Keillor, Steven. *Cooperative Commonwealth: Co-Ops in Rural Minnesota, 1859–1939*. St. Paul: Minnesota Historical Society, 2000.

Keohane, Robert O., and Joseph S. Nye. *Power and Interdependence*. New York: Longman, 2001.

Ketcham, Ralph. *James Madison: A Biography*. Newton, CT: American Political Biography Press, 1971.

Keynes, John Maynard. *The General Theory of Employment, Interest, and Money*. New York: Harcourt, Brace, 1936.

Klein, Maury. *The Life and Legend of Jay Gould*. Baltimore: Johns Hopkins Univ. Press, 1986.

Kloppenburg, Jack Ralph Jr. *First the Seed: The Political Economy of Plant Biotechnology*. Cambridge, UK: Cambridge Univ. 1988.

Knowles, Ruth Sheldon. *The Greatest Gamblers: The Epic of American Oil Exploration*. Norman: Univ. of Oklahoma Press, 1978.

Kolko, Gabriel. *The Triumph of Conservatism*. New York: Free Press, 1963.

Kovacic, William. "The Modern Evolution of U.S. Competition Policy Enforcement Norms." *Antitrust Law Journal*, vol. 71, no. 2 (2003), pp. 377–477.

Kuhn, Thomas. *The Structure of Scientific Revolutions*. Chicago: Univ. of Chicago Press, 1962.

Langlois, Richard, and Paul Robertson. "Explaining Vertical Integration: Lessons from the American Automobile Industry." *Journal of Economic History*, vol. 49, no. 2 (June 1989), pp. 377–478.

———. *Firms, Markets, and Economic Change: A Dynamic Theory of Business Institutions*. London: Routledge, 1995.

Lasch, Christopher. *The Revolt of the Elites and the Betrayal of Democracy*. New York: W. W. Norton, 1995.

———. *The True and Only Heaven: Progress and Its Critics*. New York: W. W. Norton, 1991.

Layton, Edward. *The Revolt of the Engineers: Social Responsibility and the American Engineering Profession*. Cleveland, OH: Case Western Reserve Univ. Press, 1971.

Lazonick, William. *Business Organization and the Myth of the Market Economy*. Cambridge, UK: Cambridge Univ. Press, 1991.

Lee, Gerald Stanley. *Inspired Millionaires*. Northampton, MA: Mount Tom Press, 1908.

Lele, Milind. *Monopoly Rules: How to Find, Capture, and Control the Most Lucrative Markets in Any Business*. New York: Crown Business, 2005.

Lewalski, Barbara. *The Life of John Milton: A Critical Biography*. Oxford, UK: Blackwell, 2000.

Lind, Michael, *The American Way of Strategy: U.S. Foreign Policy and the American Way of Life*, Oxford, UK: Oxford Univ., 2006.

Lippmann, Walter. *Drift and Mastery: An Attempt to Diagnose the Current Unrest*. New York: Mitchell Kennerley, 1914.

———. *The Good Society*. New York: Little, Brown, 1937.

Litan, Robert, and Carl Shapiro. "Antitrust Policy During the Clinton Administration." Working Paper No. CPC01–22. Berkeley: Univ. of California Center for Competition Policy, 2001.

Locke, John. *Second Treatise*. Indianapolis, IN: Bobbs-Merrill, 1952.

Lundestad, Geir. *The American "Empire."* Oxford, UK: Oxford Univ. Press, 1990.

———. *"Empire" by Integration: The United States and European Integration, 1945–1997*. New York: Oxford Univ. Press, 1998.

Lynn, Barry C. "Breaking the Chain: The Antitrust Case against Wal-Mart." *Harper's*, July 2006.

———. *End of the Line: The Rise and Coming Fall of the Global Corporation*. New York: Doubleday, 2005.

———. "War Trade and Utopia." *National Interest*, no. 82 (Winter 2005–2006), pp. 31–38.

MacPherson, Alan, and David Pritchard. "International Decentralization of U.S. Commercial Aircraft Production." Occasional Paper No. 26. Buffalo, NY: Canada–United States Trade Center, 2002.

Madison, James, "Federalist 51," in Alexander Hamilton, John Jay, and James Hamilton, *The Federalist: A Commentary on the Constitution of the United States*, ed. Robert Scigliano, p. 332. New York: Modern Library, 2001.

———. "Property," originally published in the *National Gazette*, Mar. 29, 1792. In *The Selected Writings of James Madison*, ed. Ralph Ketcham, pp. 222–225. Indianapolis, IN: Hackett, 2006.

Malthus, Thomas. *An Essay on the Principle of Population*. Cambridge, UK: Cambridge Univ. Press, 1992.

Manser, Marilyn, and Garnett Picot. "Self-Employment in Canada and the United States." *Canadian Economic Observer*, vol. 12, no. 3 (Mar. 1999), pp. 10–25.

Marens, Richard. "Inventing Corporate Governance: The Mid-Century Emergence of Shareholder Activism." *Journal of Business and Management*, vol. 8 no. 4 (Fall 2002), pp. 365–389.

Marshall, Alfred. *Principles of Economics*. London: Macmillan, 1898.

Marx, Karl. *Capital*. Chicago: Charles H. Kerr, 1906.

———. "A Contribution to the Critique of Hegel's Philosophy of Right." In *Marx: Early Political Writings*, ed. Joseph O'Malley, p. 129. Cambridge, UK: Cambridge Univ. Press, 1994.

Mason, Edward, ed. *The Corporation in Modern Society*. Cambridge, MA: Harvard Univ. Press, 1959.

McCloskey, Donald. "The Open Fields of England: Rent, Risk, and Rate of Interest, 1300–1850." In *Markets in History: Economic Studies of the Past*, ed. David Galenson, pp. 5–51. Cambridge, UK: Cambridge Univ. Press, 1989.

McConnell, Grant. *The Decline of Agrarian Democracy*. Berkeley: Univ. of California Press, 1953.

McCoy, Drew. *The Elusive Republic: Political Economy in Jeffersonian America*. Chapel Hill: Univ. of North Carolina Press, 1980.

McCraw, Thomas K. *Prophets of Regulation: Charles Francis Adams; Louis D. Brandeis; James M. Landis; Alfred E. Kahn*. Cambridge, MA: Belknap Press, 1984.

McDonald, Forrest. *Alexander Hamilton: A Biography*. New York: W. W. Norton, 1979.

McGee, John. "Predatory Price Cutting: The Standard Oil (N.J.) Case." *Journal of Law and Economics*, vol. 1 (Oct. 1958), pp. 137–169.

McMillan, John. *Reinventing the Bazaar: A Natural History of Markets*. New York: W. W. Norton, 2002.

Mindel, D. A. "Automation's Finest Hour: Bell Labs and Automatic Control in World War II," *IEEE Control Systems Magazine*, Dec. 1995.

Mitchell, Stacy. *Big-Box Swindle: The True Cost of Mega-Retailers and the Fight for America's Independent Businesses*. Boston: Beacon Press, 2006.

Monks, Robert. *Corpocracy: How CEOs and the Business Roundtable Hijacked the World's Greatest Wealth Machine*. Hoboken, NJ: John Wiley & Sons, 2007.

Monks, Robert, and Nell Minow. *Corporate Governance*. Cambridge, MA: Blackwell, 1995.

Morris, Edmund. *The Rise of Theodore Roosevelt*. New York: Coward, McGann & Geoghegan, 1979.

———. *Theodore Rex*. New York: Random House, 2001.

Mossoff, Adam. "Rethinking the Development of Patents." *Hastings Law Journal*, vol. 52, (2001), p. 1255.

Nader, Ralph, Mark Green, and Joel Seligman. *Taming the Giant Corporation*. New York: W. W. Norton, 1976.

Nishiguchi, Toshihiro, and Alexandre Beaudet. "Case Study: The Toyota Group and the Aisin Fire." *Sloan Management Review*, vol. 40, no. 1 (1998), pp. 49–59.

Noble, David F. *America by Design: Science, Technology, and the Rise of Corporate Capitalism*. New York: Alfred A. Knopf, 1977.

Noble, David W. *The Progressive Mind, 1890–1970*. Chicago: Rand McNally, 1970.

Novak, William. *The People's Welfare: Law and Regulation in Nineteenth-Century America*. Chapel Hill: Univ. of North Carolina Press, 1996.

O'Boyle, Thomas F. *At Any Cost: Jack Welch, General Electric, and the Pursuit of Profit*. New York: Alfred A. Knopf, 1998.

Ohmae, Kenichi. *The Borderless World: Power and Strategy in the Interlinked Economy*. New York: HarperCollins, 1990.

Ohno, Taiichi. *Toyota Production System: Beyond Large-Scale Production*. Cambridge, MA: Productivity Press, 1988.

Pakenham, Thomas. *The Scramble for Africa: White Man's Conquest of the Dark Continent*. New York: Random House, 1991.

Papazian, Charlie, *The New Complete Joy of Home Brewing*. New York: Avon Books, 1991.

Parker, Rachel. "The Myth of the Entrepreneurial Economy: Employment and Innovation in Small Firms." *Work, Employment & Society*, vol. 15, no. 2 (2001), pp. 239–253.

Parker, Richard. *John Kenneth Galbraith: His Life, His Politics, His Economics*. New York: Farrar, Straus and Giroux, 2005.

Parra, Francisco. *Oil Politics: A Modern History of Petroleum*. London: I. B. Tauris, 2004.

Parrington, Vernon Louis. *The Beginnings of Critical Realism in America, 1860–1920*, New York: Harcourt, Brace, 1930.

———. *The Colonial Mind, 1620–1800*. New York: Harcourt, Brace, 1927.

Patman, Wright. *The Robinson-Patman Act: What You Can and Cannot Do under this Law*. New York: Ronald Press, 1938.

Peritz, Rudolf. *Competition Policy in America: History, Rhetoric, Law*. New York: Oxford Univ. Press, 1996.

Perret, Geoffrey. *A Country Made by War*. New York: Random House, 1989.

Perrow, Charles. *Normal Accidents: Living with High-Risk Technologies*. New York: Basic Books, 1984.

———. *Organizing America: Wealth, Power, and the Origins of Corporate Capitalism*. Princeton, NJ: Princeton Univ. Press, 2002.

Piore, Michael, and Charles Sabel. *The Second Industrial Divide: Possibilities for Prosperity*. New York: Basic Books, 1984.

Polanyi, Karl. *The Great Transformation*. New York: Holt, Rinehart and Winston, 1944.

Pollan, Michael. *The Omnivore's Dilemma: A Natural History of Four Meals*. New York: Penguin, 2006.

Posner, Richard. *Antitrust Law*. Chicago: Univ. of Chicago Press, 1976.

Peterson, Merrill D. *Thomas Jefferson and the New Nation: A Biography*. New York: Oxford Univ. Press, 1970.

Powell, William S. *The War of the Regulation and the Battle of Alamance*. Raleigh: North Carolina Dept. of Cultural Resources, 1976.

Reich, Robert. *Supercapitalism: The Transformation of Business, Democracy, and Everyday Life.* New York: Alfred A. Knopf, 2007.

———. *The Work of Nations: Preparing Ourselves for 21st Century Capitalism.* New York: Alfred A. Knopf, 1991.

Remini, Robert. *Henry Clay: Statesman for the Union.* New York: W. W. Norton, 1991.

———. *The Life of Andrew Jackson.* New York: Harper & Row, 1988.

Ricardo, David. *On the Principles of Political Economy and Taxation.* London: J. M. Dent, 1992.

Robins, Nick. *The Corporation That Changed the World: How the East India Company Shaped the Modern Multinational.* London: Pluto Books, 2006.

Robinson, Joan. *The Economics of Imperfect Competition.* London: Macmillan, 1933.

Rodengen, Jeffrey. *The Legend of Pfizer.* Fort Lauderdale, FL: Write Stuff Syndicate, 1999.

Roosevelt, Franklin. "Government and Modern Capitalism." Sept. 30, 1934, fireside chat. In *FDR's Fireside Chats*, ed. Russell D. Buhite and David W. Levy, pp. 53–62. Norman: Univ. of Oklahoma, 1992.

Roth, Aleda, Andy Tsay, Madeleine Pullman, and John Gray. "Unraveling the Food Supply Chain: Strategic Insights from China and the 2007 Recalls." *Journal of Supply Chain Management*, Winter 2008, pp. 22–39.

Sanders, Elizabeth. *Roots of Reform: Farmers, Workers, and the American State, 1877–1917.* Chicago: Univ. of Chicago Press, 1999.

Schaede, Ulrike. *Cooperative Capitalism: Self-Regulation, Trade Associations, and the Antimonopoly Law in Japan.* Oxford, UK: Oxford Univ. Press, 2000.

Scherer, F. M. *Competition Policies for an Integrated World Economy.* Washington, DC: Brookings Institution Press, 1994.

———. *The Economics of Multi-Plant Operation: An International Comparisons Study.* Cambridge, MA: Harvard Univ. Press, 1975.

———. *Industrial Market Structure and Economic Performance.* Chicago: Rand McNally, 1970.

———. "Technological Innovation and Monopolization." KSG Working Paper No. RWPO7–043, October 2007.

Schumpeter, Joseph. *Capitalism, Socialism, and Democracy.* New York: Harper & Brothers, 1942.

Schwartz, Barry. *The Paradox of Choice: Why More Is Less.* New York: HarperCollins, 2004.

Schwartz, Michael, and Andrew Fish. "Just-in-Time Inventories in Old Detroit." *Business History*, vol. 40, no. 3 (July 1998), pp. 48–71.

Schwarz, Jordan. *The New Dealers: Power Politics in the Age of Roosevelt.* New York: Alfred A. Knopf, 1993.

Serafino, David. "Survey of Patent Pools Demonstrates Variety of Purposes and Management Structures." Knowledge Ecology International Research Note, June 4, 2007. Available online at www .keionline.org/content/view/69.

Sheffi, Yossi. *The Resilient Enterprise: Overcoming Vulnerability for Competitive Advantage.* Cambridge, MA: MIT Press, 2005.

Shenhav, Yehouda. *Manufacturing Rationality: The Engineering Foundations of the Managerial Revolution.* Oxford, UK: Oxford Univ. Press, 1999.

Simms, Andrew. *Tescopoly: How One Shop Came Out on Top and Why It Matters.* London: Constable, 2007.

Skidelsky, Robert. *John Maynard Keynes: The Economist as Savior, 1920–1936.* London: Penguin, 1994.

———. *John Maynard Keynes: Fighting for Freedom, 1937–1946.* New York: Penguin, 2000.

Sklar, Martin. *The Corporate Reconstruction of American Capitalism: The Market, the Law, and Politics.* New York: Cambridge Univ. Press, 1988.

Sloan, Alfred P. *My Years with General Motors.* Garden City, NY: Doubleday, 1964.

Smith, Adam. *The Wealth of Nations.* New York: Random House, 1994.

Spence, Donald. *Futures and Options.* Chicago: Glenlake, 1999.

Steinmetz, Charles Proteus. *America and the New Epoch.* New York: Harper & Brothers, 1916.

Strum, Philippa. *Louis D. Brandeis: Justice for the People.* Cambridge, MA: Harvard Univ. Press, 1984.

Tainter, Joseph A. *The Collapse of Complex Societies*. New York: Cambridge Univ. Press, 1988.

Taussig, Frank. *Tariff History of the United States*. New York: G. P. Putnam's Sons, 1910.

Taylor, Alan. *William Cooper's Town: Power and Persuasion on the Frontier of the Early American Republic*. New York: Alfred A. Knopf, 1996.

Temin, Peter. *The Jacksonian Economy*. New York: W. W. Norton, 1969.

———. "A Market Economy in the Early Roman Empire." Working Paper No. 01–08. Cambridge, MA: MIT Dept. of Economics, (2001).

Thorelli, Hans Birger. *Federal Antitrust Policy: Origination of an American Tradition*. Baltimore: Johns Hopkins Univ. Press, 1954.

Tocqueville, Alexis de. *Democracy in America*. 2 vols. New York: Alfred A. Knopf, 1994.

Tooze, Adam. *The Wages of Destruction: The Making and Breaking of the Nazi Economy*. New York: Viking Press, 2006.

Trollope, Frances. *Domestic Manners of the Americans*. New York: Alfred A. Knopf, 1949.

Twain, Mark, and Charles Dudley Warner. *Gilded Age: A Tale of Today*. New York: Modern Library, 2006.

Van Hise, Charles R. *Big Business: Economic Power in a Free Society*. New York: Macmillan, 1912.

Veblen, Thorstein. *Absentee Ownership: Business Enterprise in Recent Times: The Case of America*. New Brunswick, NJ: Transaction Books, 2004.

———. *The Engineers and the Price System*. New York: Harcourt, Brace & World, 1921.

Vernon, Raymond. *Sovereignty at Bay: The Multinational Spread of U.S. Enterprises*. New York: Basic Books, 1971.

Viner, Jacob. "Political Aspects of International Finance," *Journal of Business of the University of Chicago*, vol. 1 (Apr. 1928), pp. 141–173.

———. *Studies in the Theory of International Trade*. Cambridge, MA: Harvard Univ. Press, 1965.

Vlasic, Bill, and Bradley Stertz. *Taken for a Ride: How Daimler-Benz Drove Off with Chrysler*. New York: HarperCollins, 2000.

Walsh, William. *The Rise and Decline of the Great Atlantic & Pacific Tea Company*. Secaucus, NJ: Lyle Stuart, 1986.

Walton, Sam, with John Huey. *Sam Walton: Made in America*. New York: Doubleday, 1992.

Washburn, Jennifer. *University Inc.: The Corporate Corruption of Higher Education*. New York: Basic Books, 2005.

Wasik, John. *The Merchant of Power: Sam Insull, Thomas Edison, and the Creation of the Modern Metropolis*. New York: Palgrave Macmillan, 2006.

Welch, Jack. *Jack: Straight from the Gut*. New York: Warner Books, 2001.

Wells, Wyatt. *Antitrust and the Formation of the Postwar World*. New York: Columbia Univ. Press, 2002.

White, Albert Beebe. *The Making of the English Constitution, 449–1485*. New York: G. P. Putnam's Sons, 1925.

Wiebe, Robert. *The Search for Order, 1877–1920*. New York: Hill and Wang, 1967.

Wilkins, Mira. *The Emergence of Multinational Enterprise: American Business Abroad from the Colonial Era to 1914*. Cambridge, MA: Harvard Univ. Press, 1970.

———. *The Maturing of Multinational Enterprise: American Business Abroad from 1914–1970*. Cambridge, MA: Harvard Univ. Press, 1974.

Winner, Langdon. "Complexity and the Limits of Human Understanding." In *Organized Social Complexity: Challenge to Politics and Policy*, ed. Todd R. La Porte. Princeton, NJ: Princeton Univ. Press, 1975, pp. 40–76.

Womack, James P., Daniel T. Jones, and Daniel Roos. *The Machine That Changed the World: The Story of Lean Production*. New York: Rawson Associates, 1990.

Wood, Gordon. *The Creation of the American Republic*. Chapel Hill: Univ. of North Carolina Press, 1969.

———. *The Radicalism of the American Revolution*. New York: Alfred A. Knopf, 1992.

Yergin, Daniel. *The Prize: The Epic Quest for Oil, Money, and Power*. New York: Simon & Schuster, 1991.

Index

ABN AMRO, 11
Acer, 8
Ackman, William, 13
acquisitions. *See* mergers and acquisitions
(M&A)
Adams, Charles Francis, 13, 105
Advanced Micro Devices (AMD), 13, 166
advertising, 10, 124, 125
Aftalion, Fred, 86
agricultural commodities, 118–23
agriculture, 21, 45, 147–51, 177–78
Akzo Nobel, 11
Alcan, 9
Alcoa, 9, 171
Alliance Boots, 11
alliances, technology, 167–68
aluminum, 171
Aluminum Corporation of China
(Chinalco), 9–10
AMD (Advanced Micro Devices), 13, 166
American Revolution, 23, 98–99, 252–55
Anderson, Chris, 36, 53, 54
Anheuser-Busch InBev, 6, 38, 39–42
antimonopoly laws. *See* antitrust laws
antitrust laws
  AT&T case (1950s), 171
  Clayton Antitrust Act, 112, 137
  and Clinton administration, 25, 26, 144
  and Democratic Party, 143–45
  efficiency argument, 135–38
  enforcement of, 6, 25–26
  and innovation, 170–73
  Friedman's views, 142
  Microsoft case, 168
  New Deal era suspension, 113

and Obama administration, 246
RCA case (1950s), 171
and Reagan administration, 25, 137, 143
Sherman Antitrust Act, 106–7, 137
Antitrust Paradox (Bork), 137–38, 145–46
AOL, 10
A&P, 6
appliances, 22
Aprica, 73
aQuantive, 10
Archer Daniels Midland (ADM), 86, 177
Arnold, Thurmond, 170
assembly line, 174
AstraZeneca, 8
athletic shoes, 19
AT&T (American Telephone and
  Telegraph), 9, 19, 26, 170–71, 218
Australia, grocery industry, 14
authoritarianism, 56
automobile industry
  crisis and bailout (2008), xii–xiv, 81–82
  Ford Model T, 173–75
  outsourcing of parts-making, 75–78
  production model, 173–75
  structure of, xiii, 79–83
  technology alliances, 167–68
  vertical integration history, 62–63, 69–70
automotive parts, 10, 75–78

Bacon, Francis, 251
banking
  central bank origins, 102–3
  mergers and acquisitions, viii–ix, 9, 11, 12
  Progressive Era, 116
Bank of America, viii–ix

sugar, 47, 48
Sunglass Hut, 32, 33
supermarkets, 5–7, 14
Supreme Court, 50, 114, 136, 186
surfboards, 178–82
survival of the fittest, 139, 225
Swift & Company, 8
SXR Uranium One, 11
syringes, 152–57

Tacoda, 10
Taleb, Nassim Nicholas, 79
Target, 12–13
tariffs, 202
TARP (Troubled Asset Relief Program),
    viii–ix
tax, price as, 56
Taylor, Frederick Winslow, 109
Tea Act (1773), 98
Technical Concepts, 73
technology alliances, 167–68
telecommunications, 9, 19, 54, 218
Telegraph, 10–11
television, 171
Tesco, 14
Tesla, Nikola, 162, 163
Thermo Electron, 11
Thompson Electronics, 67
Thomson, 11
Thurow, Lester, 144
Tocqueville, Alexis de, 56, 103–4
Tommy Hilfiger, 61
Tom's of Maine, 44
toothpaste, 3–4, 5, 44
Toyota, 75–76, 81, 82–83
trade. *See* international trade
trade unions, 234, 238, 253
trading companies, 66–71
trading monopolies, 19
Treasury Department, 12
Troubled Asset Relief Program
    (TARP), viii–ix
Truman administration, 199–200
Tryon, William, 252
TWA, 240
Twenty-First Amendment, 41
Tyco International, 11, 70
Tyson, 21, 26, 177

Ukraine, Russia's natural gas shut off,
    209–10
Unifi, 78
Unilever, 45
unions and unionization, 106–7, 234,
    238, 253
United Biscuit, 72
United Fruit Company, 196
United Kingdom. *See* Great Britain
United Nations, 212
United Shoe Machinery, 172
universities, research agenda of Energy
    Biosciences Institute, 167
University of California, Berkeley, 167
uranium, 11
UrAsia Energy, 11

venture capital, 169
Verizon, 218
vertical integration, 63, 76, 193, 218–19
vitamin C, 84–86

Wachovia, viii, 9
Wagner Act (1935), 234
Wall Street Journal, 5, 8, 14, 22, 71, 176
Wal-Mart
    and Chinese production, 213
    control over producers, 44, 165–66
    as modern East India Company, 213
    as home-base monopoly, 18
    and Newell, 72–73
    pet food recall, 2, 4, 27–30
    power and dominance of, 6, 29–30, 52
    in Prescott, Ariz., 1–2, 8
    and Target, 12
Walton, Sam, 58
War of the Regulation, 252
Washington Mutual, viii
Washington Post, 223
Watauga Association, 253
Watauga Valley, 148, 150
water, bottled, 6
Wealth of Nations (Smith), 46, 89,
    100, 141
Weathermen, Bess, 169
Welch, Jack, 66–68, 168–69, 219–20
Wells Fargo, viii
Westinghouse, 162, 172

www.ingramcontent.com/pod-product-compliance
Lightning Source LLC
Jackson TN
JSHW080102141224
75386JS00028B/828